أ , نون ‎ ‎ ‎ (אַרְנוֹן)

ﮔﻞ א, ﮔﻞ ... ‎ ‎ ‎ $10

All right, then. Enjoy your
angels & demons.

פמין מאנוﮞ אוﭏﭏﭏﭏﭏﭏﭏﭏﭏﭏﭏﭏﭏﭏﭏﭏﭏ , אוﭏﭏﭏﭏﭏﭏﭏﭏﭏﭏﭏﭏﭏﭏ

אוﭏﭏﭏﭏﭏﭏ ‎ ‎ ‎ ﭏﭏﭏﭏﭏﭏﭏ

(مونيك)

] גﭏ מﭏﭏﭏ מﭏﭏﭏﭏﭏﭏ ?
[whatever ‎ ‎ ‎ ‎ ‎ ‎ ‎ ‎ .

6-25-07
(25/06/2007)

Antonio's Devils

STANFORD STUDIES IN JEWISH HISTORY AND CULTURE

EDITED BY *Aron Rodrigue and Steven J. Zipperstein*

Antonio's Devils

*Writers of the Jewish Enlightenment
and the Birth of Modern Hebrew
and Yiddish Literature*

Jeremy Dauber

STANFORD UNIVERSITY PRESS

STANFORD, CALIFORNIA

2004

Stanford University Press
Stanford, California

© 2004 by the Board of Trustees of the
Leland Stanford Junior University. All rights reserved.

Publication of this book was made possible by generous support
from the Koret Foundation.

Printed in the United States of America
on acid-free, archival-quality paper

Library of Congress Cataloging-in-Publication Data
Dauber, Jeremy Asher.
  Antonio's devils : writers of the Jewish enlightenment and the
birth of modern Hebrew and Yiddish literature / Jeremy Dauber.
      p. cm.
  Includes bibliographical references and index.
  ISBN 0-8047-4901-9 (cloth)
  1. Jewish literature—History and criticism. 2. Haskalah.
3. Jewish authors—Biography. 4. Mendelssohn, Moses.
5. Halle-Wolfssohn, A. 6. Perl, Joseph. I. Title.
PN6067 .D38 2004
892.4'09—dc22

                                                    2003023990

Original Printing 2004

Last figure below indicates year of this printing:
13   12   11   10   09   08   07   06   05   04

Typeset by Classic Typography in 10.5/14 Galliard

For my parents

Contents

Acknowledgments

This book began as a doctoral dissertation at the University of Oxford. I thank the Rhodes Trust and its then Warden, Sir Anthony Kenny, for their generosity, both for the scholarship that allowed me to attend the university in the first place and for the travel funding that allowed me to undertake other research. The Oxford Center for Hebrew and Jewish Studies' Segal Fund was also helpful in this regard.

Thanks are also due to the Institute for Advanced Study at Hebrew University and particularly to the late Isidore Twersky, Isaiah Gafni, and David Ruderman for their financial support in allowing me to attend several helpful summer institutes.

Dov-Ber Kerler advised the dissertation from beginning to end; his extensive comments and bibliographic suggestions were invaluable. Thanks are also due to Dafna Clifford for her advisory role and to Joel Berkowitz and Leon Yudkin for their suggestions and advice.

The dissertation might have been written, but would never have been printed and submitted were it not for the indefatigable efforts of Joshua Civin, Jonathan Levine, Ben Novick, and Rebecca Wright.

Since my arrival at Columbia, I have benefited greatly from the advice and comments of colleagues, particularly Michael Stanislawski, Dorothea von Mücke, Mark Anderson, Michael Eskin, and Eileen Gillooly. Peggy Quisenberry and Bill Dellinger have also been vital resources. David Roskies and Seth Wolitz have been very helpful in my efforts to get my feet on the ground, academically speaking.

At Stanford University Press I am deeply grateful for the support, guidance, and experience of Steve Zipperstein, Norris Pope, and Judith

Hibbard. I would also like to thank the Koret Foundation for their generous subsidy supporting this book's publication.

I cannot thank Ruth Wisse enough for her generosity and her support. She is the very definition of a teacher and a scholar, and all of us who have been lucky enough to be taught by her or learn from her know what that means.

Finally, though a simple line is not even vaguely sufficient to acknowledge my parents' and siblings' support, I suppose it will have to do.

Note on Orthography

In a work dealing with Hebrew, Yiddish, and Hebrew quotations appearing in Yiddish works, questions of orthography are necessarily difficult. Distinctions could potentially have been made between Eastern and Western Yiddish, Ashkenazic and Sephardic Hebrew; for the sake of simplicity and clarity, however, I have adopted the following guidelines:

1. All quotations from Hebrew follow the system set forth in the *Encyclopaedia Judaica*, with the following modifications: *khet* is transcribed *kh*; *tsadek* is transcribed *ts*; and words with a final "ah" at the end conclude with *a*, not *ah*.

2. All quotations from Yiddish follow standard YIVO transcription.

3. Quotations from within a work follow the main language of a work; for example, the phrase "sin begets sin," appearing in the (partially) Yiddish *Laykhtzin un fremelay*, is transcribed as *aveyre goyreres aveyre*, and not *aveira goreret aveira*.

4. Names of individuals or books follow Hebrew transliteration (e.g., *Toldot Yaakov Yosef*) unless specifically referring to a work in Yiddish (e.g., the Yiddish version of *Shivkhei HaBesht* is the *Shivkhey HaBesht*).

5. Words that have become standard in English follow generally accepted English spellings, unless they are direct quotes or transliterated (e.g., "Hasidism").

List of Abbreviations

BT	*Babylonian Talmud*
GJH	*German-Jewish History in Modern Times* (ed. Michael A. Meyer)
HUCA	*Hebrew Union College Annual*
JJS	*Journal of Jewish Studies*
JubA	Moses Mendelssohn, *Gesammelte Schriften: Jubiläumsausgabe*
JQR	*Jewish Quarterly Review*
JSS	*Jewish Social Studies*
KOMI	*Kongres olami lemakhshevet yisrael*
LBIYB	*Leo Baeck Institute Year Book*
MMBS	Alexander Altmann, *Moses Mendelssohn: A Biographical Study*
MME	Allan Arkush, *Moses Mendelssohn and the Enlightenment*
MMRE	David Sorkin, *Moses Mendelssohn and the Religious Enlightenment*
PAAJR	*Proceedings of the American Academy for Jewish Research*
PAJHS	*Proceedings of the American Jewish Historical Society*
PW	Moses Mendelssohn, *Philosophical Writings*
SB	*Shivkhey HaBesht*
S/W	Joseph Perl, *Maasiyot veigrot mitsadikim umeanshei shlomeinu* (eds. Khone Shmeruk and Shmuel Werses)

SHYLOCK   *Well, then, your bond. And let me see—but hear you:*
Methoughts you said you neither lend nor borrow
Upon advantage.

ANTONIO   *I do never use it.*

SHYLOCK   *When Jacob grazed his uncle Laban's sheep—*
This Jacob from our holy Abram was,
As his wise mother wrought in his behalf,
The third possessor; ay, he was the third—

ANTONIO   *And what of him? Did he take interest?*

SHYLOCK   *No, not take interest, not as you would say*
Directly interest. Mark what Jacob did.
When Laban and himself were compromised
That all the eanlings which were streaked and pied
Should fall as Jacob's hire, the ewes, being rank,
In end of autumn turned to the rams,
And when the work of generation was
Between these wooly breeders in the act,
The skillful shepherd peeled me certain wands,
And in the doing of the deed of kind
He stuck them up before the fulsome ewes,
Who then conceiving did in eaning time
Fall parti-colored lambs, and those were Jacob's.
This was a way to thrive, and he was blest;
And thrift is blessing, if men steal it not.

ANTONIO   *This was a venture, sir, that Jacob served for,*
A thing not in his power to bring to pass,
But swayed and fashioned by the hand of heaven.
Was this inserted to make interest good?
Or is your gold and silver ewes and rams?

SHYLOCK   *I cannot tell. I make it breed as fast.*
But note me, signor—

ANTONIO   *Mark you this, Bassanio.*
The devil can cite Scripture for his purpose.

—THE MERCHANT OF VENICE, I:3:69–96

Part One   Setting the Stage

Shylock, Allusion, and the Birth
of Modern Jewish Literature

Genesis: Original Scenes and Biblical Allusions

Beginning a book on the origins of modern Jewish literature by quoting Shakespeare at length may seem surprising; after all, well over a century and a half passes between the first performance of *The Merchant of Venice* and the first works by the writers of the Jewish Enlightenment.[1] The truly surprising discovery, however, is how apt Shakespeare's words are—on so many levels—for a discussion of the early stages of modern Jewish literature. The process of determining how precisely that might be can set the stage for this book as a whole.

While this analysis of a scene from *The Merchant of Venice* is used primarily to elucidate the methodological approach employed throughout the book—to show how careful examination of a work's textual allusions may have significant repercussions for studying the text as a whole—this book hopes to go further and suggest a role for textual allusion, properly understood, as a lens through which to explore historical questions of the emergence of modern Jewish literature and identity. As we will see, Shakespeare's text may have surprisingly relevant insight in this regard as well.

The Merchant of Venice is well known for "its unusually explicit and pervasive scriptural allusiveness,"[2] and noted critics have viewed the

1. According to the title page of the First Quarto (1600), the play had already been performed "divers times" by the Lord Chamberlain's Servants. See John Gross, *Shylock: Four Hundred Years in the Life of a Legend* (London: Chatto & Windus, 1992), 89.

2. Lawrence Danson, *The Harmonies of The Merchant of Venice* (New Haven: Yale University Press, 1978), 8.

play's Biblical allusivity as key to its thematic structure.[3] The scene cited as the book's epigraph, in which Antonio and Shylock first meet on stage, is arguably the most Biblically allusive, not merely in the play, but perhaps in the entire Shakespearean corpus.[4] Given that, it seems reasonable to assume its centrality in any interpretive scheme based on an understanding of the play's Biblical allusions, and, perhaps, in any understanding of the play as a whole. However, perhaps due to the allusion's puzzling features, most critics have either remained silent or offered largely unconvincing explanations for the scene.[5]

And the scene, and its allusion, is indeed puzzling. A quick review of the allusion's context may be in order. Antonio agrees to take on the obligation of borrowing three thousand ducats from Shylock in order to help out his close friend, Bassanio, despite his known abhorrence of lending or borrowing money "upon advantage," that is, with interest. Shylock, hearing this, asks him if it is indeed true that he neither borrows nor lends at interest. Antonio responds, curtly, that he does not, implying that in certain cases like this one, when the need is great, he is willing to bend his principles.

It is immediately following Antonio's brief response that Shylock tells the story of Jacob and Laban from Genesis 30:25–43. The story is fairly straightforward, and Shylock relates it fairly accurately: Laban

3. For example, Barbara Lewalski finds in *The Merchant of Venice* "patterns of Biblical allusion and imagery so precise and pervasive as to be patently deliberate" and "that such language clearly reveals an important theological dimension in the play and points toward consistent and unmistakable allegorical meanings." Barbara K. Lewalski, "Biblical Allusion and Allegory in *The Merchant of Venice*," in Sylvan Barnet, ed., *Twentieth Century Interpretations of The Merchant of Venice* (Prentice Hall: Englewood Cliffs, NJ: 1970), 33–54, 34.

4. Gross (31) refers to this as "the most obviously biblical speech in the whole of Shakespeare." Though Naseeb Shaheen, in his *Biblical References in Shakespeare's Comedies* (Newark: University of Delaware Press, 1993), cautions that Shakespeare may often have borrowed not directly from the Bible, but from his original literary source, which itself borrowed from the Bible (7–9), in his discussion of this particular passage Shaheen cites the Biblical source as paramount (109–113).

5. Lewalski's seminal article, to take just one example, barely addresses the scene.

and Jacob agree that Jacob, pasturing Laban's flock, will receive all the striped, speckled, and spotted lambs that result from the next lambing. Jacob uses (hitherto unreported) skills in animal husbandry to peel sticks in a certain way, which he then places in front of the breeding sheep. In some Lamarckian fashion, the peeled sticks' presence causes the sheep to give birth to a vastly disproportionate number of striped and spotted lambs, lambs that now belong to Jacob.

Readers of this scene can emulate Antonio in two ways in understanding Shylock's allusive behavior. The first focuses on the last lines of Shylock's speech and Antonio's apparently triumphant response. In this traditional view, when Shylock says, speaking of Jacob's actions, "This was a way to thrive, and he was blest;/And thrift is blessing, if men steal it not," he makes what is sometimes referred to as the "thrift" argument: that "if Jacob 'was blest' despite the artificial manner in which he had influenced the ostensibly 'natural' process of breeding, the moneylender may similarly thrive though *his* artificial means of breeding."[6] In other words, Shylock is using the passage to legitimate the taking of interest. Antonio's response, say the critics, polemically rebuts Shylock's argument: when he says that "This was a venture, sir, that Jacob served for,/A thing not in his power to bring to pass,/But swayed and fashioned by the hand of heaven" and finishes with the question "Or is your gold and silver ewes and rams?," critics suggest he refers both to the "commonplace Christian argument (based upon Aristotle) that to take interest is to 'breed' barren metal, which is unnatural"[7] and that Divine intervention on Jacob's behalf should not serve as a paradigm for everyday Venetian economic behavior.

In other words, critical consensus suggests that this allusion serves as the locus for a debate over the status of usury between Jews and Christians in Venice; indeed, the only such locus within the play. However, granted that this is so, the careful reader must focus not on Antonio's definitive rejection of Shylock's argument, a reading which, on a superficial level, recapitulates the Christological defeat of the Jew

6. Danson 149.

7. Lewalski 39–40. See also Jacob Lopes Cardozo, *The Contemporary Jew in the Elizabethan Drama* (Amsterdam: 1925), 315–321.

seen in the play, and instead follow the confusions and uncertainties that both Antonio and his later readers sense in the scene. For in this scene, Antonio does not seem entirely certain of himself; even on the heels of his supposedly triumphant rebuttal, he poses a question, and his question, as well as his subsequent comment, indicate his dissatisfaction with his own answer. And if he is dissatisfied, then so should we be; there is more to this allusion than a simple debate over usury.

Extensive research on the role of usury in Elizabethan England and its connection to *The Merchant of Venice* has been done and need not be repeated here. Suffice it to say that a general sentiment prevailed against the Christian practice of usury, both borrowing and lending. In practice, though, many of the moneylenders in Shakespeare's England were in fact non-Jewish, and, from a theological perspective, the usury question was in fact a question of Biblical interpretation dependent on the definition of the words "brother" and "stranger" in Deuteronomy 23:19–20: "Thou shalt not giue to usurie to thy brother: *as* usurie of money, usurie of meat, usurie of anie thing that is put to usurie. Unto a stranger thou maiest lend upon usurie, but thou shalt not led upon usurie unto thy brother, that the Lord thy God may blesse thee in all that thou settest thine hand to, in the land whether thou goest to possesse it."[8] Jews considered the word "brother" to refer only to fellow Jews; non-Jews, for whom the Hebrew Bible was of course also a holy text, were less certain.[9]

If Shylock's citative behavior is indeed entirely legitimative, as most critics suggest—that is, if this scene should be considered the latest broadside in a Jewish/Christian polemic about usury—then Shylock

8. All Biblical quotations in this chapter, unless otherwise noted, are from the *Geneva Bible*, facsimile of 1560 edition (Madison, WI: University of Wisconsin Press, 1969).

9. See, for example, Danson 141–148 and W.H. Auden, "Brothers & Others," in Thomas Wheeler, ed., *The Merchant of Venice: Critical Essays* (New York: Garland Publishing, 1991), 59–78, 64–68. On the complexity of the system of money lending in Shakespeare's England, and the fact that "by the end of the sixteenth century . . . Jews were increasingly identified not with usury per se, but with outrageous and exploitative lending for profit," see James Shapiro, *Shakespeare and the Jews* (New York: Columbia University Press, 1996), 98–100, citation from 99.

hardly succeeds in holding up his end. Were Shylock to summon the best possible texts to support his argument, he could and should have chosen others, like the Deuteronomic passages cited above.[10] Why cite a story whose connection to the taking of interest is, at best, oblique?

None other than Antonio himself raises this question: the man who remarks that "the Devil can cite Scripture for his purpose" understands the ways in which citative behavior and legitimate text quotation work. As soon as Shylock mentions Jacob, Antonio asks: "And what of him? Did he take interest?" and, after Shylock's retelling of the Genesis story ends, "Was this inserted to make interest good?" As we discuss in more detail later, Antonio's critique of the relevancy of Shylock's text crucially illuminates a changing dynamic in Jewish/Christian textual relations; for now, though, we will limit ourselves to explicating the scene, and the play.

Recent critics have begun to follow Antonio's lead in questioning the allusion's relevancy; however, their approaches seem to be minimalist, choosing to downplay Shylock's intelligence, rather than maximizing the scene's resonance and potential. One critic writes that "Shylock justifies his practice of interest taking by way of a rather loose and self-serving reading of a biblical text" and suggests that "Shylock's appeal to the Bible may also either be uninformed or naïve," part of an effort to create a space for Shylock as an unobservant, unrepresentative Jew, rather than the archetypal Jewish figure many previous readings of the play have suggested.[11] However, this

10. There may be a sly reference on Shylock's part to these passages, though, in his somewhat incongruous addition of the phrase "and he was blest," a phrase resembling the language in Deut. 23:20.

11. Martin D. Yaffe, *Shylock and the Jewish Question* (Baltimore: Johns Hopkins University Press, 1997), 62–63. While it may be partially true that "Shakespeare identifies Shylock's Jewishness here with his law-abidingness, that is, with his pious deference to the legal demands of Jewish orthodoxy"(4), there is also clear textual evidence that Shylock's claims of piety occasionally arise from less religious motives, like helping to waste his enemies' money. In this sense, Yaffe is correct (24) that "Shylock's turning to criminal behavior is . . . tantamount to his stepping outside the bounds of recognized Jewish teaching." See also Yaffe 61. Shylock also clearly misrepresents classic Jewish positions, purposefully or not, during the play. For example, in his famous "Hath Not a Jew" speech, he elucidates an "eye

suggestion seems unlikely, given the evidence of the passage itself: Shylock's excellent recall of a somewhat marginal episode of Biblical history seems to indicate fairly good awareness of the Bible, and presumably a professional moneylender would be particularly well aware of the Biblical passages relevant to usury.[12] And given Antonio's dismissal of the story as irrelevant, this citation hardly seems self-serving. So again, why this passage?

In his construction of this encounter, Shakespeare portrays Shylock as, perhaps, cleverer than Antonio understands. "Shylock uses language as he uses money: carefully, and as a weapon."[13] Looking carefully at Shylock's words, what he does and does not say, may help us understand his present behavior. Shylock expresses two different motivations in his aside before his encounter with Antonio. Firstly, and more broadly, Shylock explicitly reframes his conflict with Antonio not as a personal encounter, but as a national, religious, and allegorical one, saying that Antonio "hates our sacred nation," and "Cursed be my tribe/if I forgive him!" (1.3.44, 47–48).

This allegorical dimension of the *Merchant of Venice*, the awareness that the play and particularly the encounter between Antonio and Shylock can be seen as a literary inscription of the Christian/Jewish polemic, has been well documented by critics.[14] And indeed, this confrontation is and remains a religious one, ending with Shylock's forced conversion to Christianity, an understandable turn of events when the play is viewed through this allegorical religious lens but difficult to accept otherwise in terms of the play's sources or in terms of

---

for an eye" approach clearly different from traditional Jewish understanding; see Danson 108–110. However, this error (if error it is—Shylock may be purposefully blurring the logical grounds of the argument) as well as his other "non-observant" actions, are linked directly to his anger and passion for revenge. Though this makes him human, and thus prone to error, it should not obfuscate our ability to focus on Shakespeare's presentation of Shylock as representative of a larger error—the error common to all Jews by virtue of their religion.

12. Indeed, Yaffe later states that "[p]resumably Shylock is as aware as Antonio is of the Bible's obvious legal prohibition of interest taking among 'brothers,' though neither mentions it directly." Yaffe 129.

13. Danson 140.

14. See, for example, Lewalski 39.

contemporary Venetian legal norms.[15] Even the play's title page, in the Second Quarto, casts the play in these terms, titling it "The Excellent History of the Merchant of Venice. With the extreme cruelty of Shylock the Iew towards the saide Merchant, in cutting a iust pound of his flesh . . ."[16]

Furthermore, some of the play's most perceptive critics have reminded us that given the paucity of contemporary plays concerned with Jews, it should be remembered that "Shakespeare *chose* to write the play, because it was in fact an extraordinary choice to make . . . Even when all the nondramatic sources that have been claimed for *The Merchant of Venice* are taken into account, Shakespeare's decision to write about Jews remains remarkable."[17] In writing this play about Jews and Christians, though Shakespeare was clearly not, as E. E. Stoll put it, "like any other easy-going churchman,"[18] given his ability to reexamine and to reframe old ideas and conflicts in stunningly new and fresh ways, it also seems, as Robert Alter suggests, that "[i]t was clearly not part of Shakespeare's conscious design to question the received wisdom of Christian hostility towards the Jews."[19] Further analysis of this scene will, I hope, make this position even more compelling.

Shylock's motivations are not merely national or allegorical, however; they're personal. Perhaps more precisely stated, his national and religious grievances are refracted to him (and to us) through a personal lens:[20] Shylock is personally affronted by Antonio's hypocrisy on

15. On the increased interest in converting Jews in Shakespeare's time, see Shapiro 140–144.

16. Cited in Nevill Coghill, "The Theme of *The Merchant of Venice*," in Barnet 108–113, 108.

17. Danson 58–59, italics author's. For a more detailed look at the sources for *The Merchant of Venice*, see Gross chap. 1 and Cardozo *passim*.

18. Cited in Danson 133.

19. Cited in Yaffe 16.

20. Admittedly, it is an open question whether Shylock is merely using national and religious claims to cover up personal grievances, just as he at least partially uses religious complaints to mask personal desires. Shakespeare's subtle writing allows us to consider the play as an examination of these national, religious, and allegorical struggles as we simultaneously question Shylock's motivations in claiming them.

the matter of interest.[21] This personal pique goes beyond Shylock's normal representation as *homo economicus*: though at first we may suspect that Shylock's anger at Antonio is that of a business competitor ("He lends out money gratis and brings down/The rate of usance here with us in Venice," 1.3.40–41), in reading the full exchange, we see that it is Antonio's perceived hypocrisy, his high-minded rejection of the taking of interest coupled with his immediate willingness to do so for Bassanio's sake, that truly irks Shylock. It is Antonio's response—"I do never use it"—curtly, unabashedly, and unashamedly hypocritical,[22] that provokes Shylock to tell the story of Laban and Jacob, a story which, as we will see, well expresses his anger at hypocrisy and his sense of moral, not merely economic, superiority.

Antonio's critique is thus partially correct: this Biblical citation does not work nearly so well as others would were its goal merely to legitimate the taking of interest. (Indeed, Shylock, responding to Antonio's challenge of relevancy, admits this, saying: "No, not take interest, not as you would say/directly interest.") Once we broaden the allusion's scope, however, to address moral, national, thematic, allegorical, and personal concerns, Shylock's purposes become much clearer: given his earlier recasting of this encounter as national, almost allegorical, one can safely assume that Shylock is referring to himself as Jacob and Antonio, by inference, as Laban.

21. Danson writes (5) that "there are many instances of Christian hypocrisy on the play, and . . . Shakespeare expects us to recognize them. (Shakespeare is always keen in his exposure of hypocrisy, regardless of the hypocrite's race, creed, color, or place of national origin.)" Bill Overton specifically points out this example of Antonio's hypocrisy in his "The Problem of Shylock," in Wheeler 293–313, 301, though fails to connect it to the Biblical allusion. Ironically, Yaffe refers to *Shylock's* appeal to the Bible in this case as possibly being "hypocritical" (63).

22. This is the most extreme example of a larger instance of Antonio's hypocrisy within the act. In his dealings with Bassanio he is portrayed as "a merchant who is (apparently) so far from being guilty of a lack of charity that he comes perilously close to completing literally an *imitatio Christi*"; his "self-righteously unrepentant answer to Shylock" in this scene is shockingly uncharitable: "I am as like to call thee [dog] again/To spet on thee again, to spurn thee too" (1.3.125–126). For a discussion, see Danson 31–32; quotes from 31.

Critics have previously noted Shylock's identification with Jacob throughout the play, both by himself and by Shakespeare; for example, he swears "by Jacob's staff" (2.5.36) and his wife's name, like Jacob's, is Leah.[23] These references become more significant when one realizes, at least according to Richmond Noble's indices, that Shakespeare makes no other references to Jacob (or, for that matter, Laban) in any of his other plays.[24] With that in mind, Shylock's allusion to Jacob's encounter with Laban, the character considered the paradigmatic hypocrite in the Hebrew Bible, immediately following this overt display of hypocrisy can hardly be coincidental.[25] Shylock's identification of Antonio with Laban must be seen as a subtle dig at the improprieties of Antonio's own behavior.

Shylock may begin telling the Genesis story as a dig at Antonio, but continues it as a warning, if Antonio has but the cleverness to heed it. In telling him to "Mark what Jacob did," he implies that if indeed the two of them are positioned similarly to Laban and Jacob, he should remember that the bargain made between the two Biblical characters redounded to Jacob's benefit and Laban's ruin. Though Antonio may believe he has the upper hand, as Laban certainly does as the Biblical

23. See Danson 73–74 and Gross 56. John Russell Brown also argues that Shylock's phrase "if I can catch him once upon the hip" "is both an everyday idiom and a possible allusion to Jacob's wrestling with the angel (Gen. 32 *passim*); certainly it is no casual thought, for it awakens, in 'I will feed fat the ancient grudge I bear him,' the physical idea of devouring as a beast, linked with the solemn connotations of 'ancient.'" John Russell Brown, "The Realization of Shylock: A Theatrical Criticism," in Wheeler 263–291, 279. This latter case provides a classic example of what I will refer to as "retextualization," a phrase not inherently allusive to a particular reading community whose context calls attention to its allusive capacities. "Retextualization" will be further discussed in Chapter Two.

24. Richmond Noble, *Shakespeare's Biblical Knowledge* (New York: Octagon Books, 1970), 268–270, 273.

25. Critics also seem to have failed to note that Antonio's response to Shylock, "This was a venture, sir, that Jacob served for,/A thing not in his power to bring to pass,/But swayed and fashioned by the hand of heaven," echoes an earlier statement of Laban's. Speaking to Eliezer about Rebecca, Laban, in his first Biblical appearance, says: "*This thing is proceded of the Lord*: we can not therefore saie unto thee, nether euil nor good." (Gen. 24:50, emphasis mine).

story opens, sudden changes in state may deliver him into his opponent's hands.[26] If so, Shylock is not, as Antonio suggests, an ineffec-
tual or incorrect user of text: he is merely making a subtle point that
Antonio fails to grasp—a threat veiled in an apparent appeal to a
shared Biblical text.

In the process, Shylock seems to amuse himself at Antonio's expense,
delivering oracular speeches with hidden meanings Antonio is clever
enough to sense but not quite clever enough to comprehend. Shylock,
normally spare of words, famously has a weakness for the pun; in both
the pun and the allusion, one gets two meanings for the price of one, a
bargain that well appeals to his nature.[27] Read this way, Antonio's
adoption of harsher language, his shift from "sir" to "the devil," makes
more sense: though whether he understands Shylock's hidden meaning is at best an open question, he certainly seems to sense the threat
in Shylock's tone, and his aside to Bassanio that "the devil can cite
Scripture for his purpose" may indicate some inchoate awareness of
Shylock's darker designs. After all, if Antonio has triumphed over Shylock in polemical debate, why such rancor?

Indeed, Shakespeare may have subtly indicated Antonio's shift
from inchoate sense to clear comprehension of Shylock's rhetorical
strategies; this indication, though, only takes place much later, once
Shylock's homicidal designs become clear to all concerned. During the
trial scene, when Shylock refuses to accept any amount of money to
redeem his bond, insisting instead on his pound of flesh, Antonio
somewhat incongruously uses an ovine metaphor to refer to himself:
"I am a tainted wether of the flock/meetest for death" (4.117–118). This
famous statement can be understood more clearly if viewed as Antonio's acknowledgment of his being tricked by Shylock precisely as

26. Sudden changes of state are not uncommon in the universe of *The Merchant of Venice*. Take, for example, the sudden destruction of Antonio's ships, or
the dismissal of the suitors who choose the wrong casket, or, for that matter, the
outcome of the trial scene.

27. See Danson 140, 150. Additionally, as Danson suggests, Shylock's seeming
non sequitur (though, as we have shown, it only *seems* a non sequitur) has the
strategic advantage of throwing Antonio off guard, possibly rendering him less
wary of Shylock's later suggestion of the bond's conditions. See Danson 152–153.

Laban was by Jacob, that Shylock warned him, and he failed to comprehend that warning. It is here, at this moment in the trial scene, that Jewish power is at its height, that it stands triumphant.

Shylock's victory in the trial scene is, of course, temporary, and in fact the seeds of Shylock's later failure are alluded to in our own scene. Antonio's remark, that the devil cites Scripture for his own purpose, gains an ironic force that Antonio never intended but that his creator did: for Shakespeare, the Jews in general, and Shylock in particular do indeed cite Scripture for their own purposes—mistaken purposes and ones doomed to failure, however, as we will see through further investigation of this allusion.

Shakespeare's Biblical knowledge, generally acknowledged to be fairly substantial,[28] necessitates an even broader reading of the allusion, a reading that may lead to a deeper understanding of this scene's importance to the play as a whole. Given the fairly clear identification of Shylock/Jacob and Antonio/Laban, a further look at the history of the two Biblical characters may illuminate the fates of the two Shakespearean characters.[29] And in looking, we can observe a remarkable correlation: the final encounter between Laban and Jacob prefigures the tragic end of Shylock's story.

In Genesis 31, particularly verses 17–45, Jacob escapes from the house of Laban with his family and all his possessions.[30] Though Jacob

28. In fact, Richmond Noble cites this very episode out of the entire Shakespearean corpus (42–43) to prove Shakespeare had clearly read the book of Genesis. For more general discussion of Shakespeare's Biblical knowledge, including critical discussion as to the varying editions he used, see Noble 18–21, 45–49, 59–61.

29. Gross also fruitfully takes this approach with respect to this scene (31–33), even ending his discussion with the sentence: "We are meant to think of Shylock as misusing his biblical heritage—misappropriating it, even, since it now belongs to Christianity." He fails to discuss Jacob's later dealings with Laban at all, however. He significantly notes, though, that the identification of Shylock with Jacob is by no means simple, given Jacob's deceptive nature, exemplified by his "theft" of his brother's blessing and (arguably) his behavior in the deal with Laban discussed here.

30. Earlier critics, such as Noble (96–98), have commented on the parallelism between this episode and Jessica's theft of her father's belongings as she flees his

attempts to take nothing that is not his,[31] Rachel steals Laban's *ter-afim*, his household gods. Laban overtakes Jacob and confronts him.[32] Jacob angrily swears that he has not taken the *terafim,* and that whoever has the gods, "let him not liue" (Gen. 31:32). Jacob's rash words, the oath that he has taken without fully considering the consequences, will come back to haunt him when Rachel dies in childbirth a few short chapters later.[33] While the Biblical author, unsurprisingly, displaces much of the punishment for Jacob's false testimony onto the thieving Rachel, the final emotional punishment still belongs to Jacob, who spends the rest of his days longing for the beloved wife of his youth.[34] Like Shylock's insistence on a pound of Antonio's flesh,

---

house. They have not, however, developed this into a full-fledged parallel reading, perhaps stymied by the fact that the aspect of the Biblical story upon which they have chosen to focus is reversed by Shakespeare: in *The Merchant of Venice,* Jessica flees *from* the symbol of Jacob rather than *with* him.

31. The Biblical author insistently repeats the phrase "which he had gotten" (*asher rakhash*) in Gen. 31:18, seeming to accentuate Jacob's legal ownership of his possessions, contrasting with the use of the word "stolen" (*vatignov*) in referring to Rachel's behavior in the next verse.

32. Careful reading of Laban's speeches in this episode accentuates interpretations stressing his hypocritical nature: though he intends his first statement to Jacob to provide an avuncular impression ("Wherefore diddest thou flee so secretly & steale away from me & diddest not tel me, that I might haue sent thee forthe with mirth & with songs, with timbrel & with harpe? But thou hast not suffered me to kisse my sonnes and my daughters: now thou hast done foolishly in doing so." (Gen. 31:27–28)), in the very next breath he unsubtly threatens him. ("I am able to do you euil: but the God of your father spake unto me yester night, saying, Take hede that thou speake not to Iaakob oght faue good." Gen 31:29). A comparison with Antonio's rapidly shifting mode of address toward Shylock might well prove instructive.

33. Cf. Gen. 35:16–19. Though the Biblical author does not explicitly connect the two events, not only does common exegetical understanding link them, but given that only Rachel's death, of any of Jacob's wives, is mentioned in the Bible, to say nothing of the fact that it is the only death of a patriarch or matriarch from circumstances other than old age, such a connection is not unreasonable.

34. The evidence of this longing is oblique but undeniably present; Jacob's sons, for example, credit this as the explanation for his apparent favoritism toward Rachel's sons Joseph and Benjamin. See, for example, Gen. 37:3, 42:4, 43:6, and especially 42:38, 43:14, and 44:20–22, 26–31.

words that bind him to conditions he later lives to rue, Jacob's rash oath convicts him and his Rachel.

The Jacob and Laban story, then, can be seen not merely as illustrative of Shylock's present cleverness, but also of his ultimate ignorance: while Shylock has learned the lessons of the Biblical text to a certain degree, he has tragically (for him) failed to follow those lessons to their natural end.[35] Able to dig deeply into the meaning of a text in its particular moment, he is blind to the full consequences and contexts of those texts.[36] This scene, then, far from being marginal, is central to the themes and the narrative of the play as a whole, not merely foreshadowing the play's end, but recapitulating its underlying allegorical structures, and strengthening opposition to any sustained anti-Christian reading.[37]

This reading of Shylock's and Antonio's encounter is intended to demonstrate the type of analysis at the methodological heart of this book, illustrating that—and how—the deep analysis of Biblical and rabbinic allusions in literature helps to illuminate understandings of individual works of literature as a whole. In the readings of the German,

35. Shakespeare's strategy here can thus be instructively compared to Marlowe's presentation of Shylock's literary predecessor, Barabas, who also cites Biblical passages selectively and misleadingly. On Barabas, see Yaffe, chap. 2, *passim*, esp. 35–36. Barabas' mis-citations seem to be conscious, an outgrowth of his evil essence. Shylock's misunderstanding seems to be unconscious and thus tragic.

36. The metaphor of blindness to reflect the Jew's theological condition in medieval and early modern Christian eyes is well known; see Shapiro 34 for examples. Compare John Lyon's statement that "Shylock knows more truths about himself than the others know about their own natures, and he is prepared to tell them and to use them." "Beginning in the Middle," in Wheeler 217–240, 230. Shakespeare's genius is that this is both true and false: Shylock, unlike (apparently) Antonio, is aware that this is indeed an encounter not between mere individuals, but types; what he does not realize is that in Shakespeare's universe, such an encounter can have but one ending.

37. For some reasons that such a reading has become problematic in recent decades, see Danson 14–16, 126–129. Compare, however, one of the stronger and more nuanced readings calling into the question the "scapegoating" of the play: René Girard, "'To Entrap the Wisest': A Reading of *The Merchant of Venice*," in Edward Said, ed., *Literature and Society* (Baltimore: Johns Hopkins University Press, 1980), 100–119, esp. 108–109.

Hebrew, and Yiddish texts chosen—works by Moses Mendelssohn, Aaron Halle-Wolfssohn, and Joseph Perl—I will follow Shakespeare's approach and not Shylock's, looking at the allusions both horizontally and vertically, that is, investigating the way the allusions function in the borrowed text more broadly. This will facilitate a more profound understanding of the work that uses these allusions in its totality, not merely in the particular moment of the allusion's occurrence. Though in subsequent textual analyses I will spend less time on each individual allusion than I have done here, I hope to build up sustained readings of how allusions within a given text support arguments illuminating thematic aspects of the works in which they appear.

Methodologically, the idea that understanding textual allusion leads to a better understanding of the text is hardly new. In the next chapter, I address some theoretical questions related to allusion and suggest how the work of the *Haskala*, or the Jewish Enlightenment, may have something to say to all students of the technique. For now, however, a return to Shakespeare and to Shylock will show us how further study of this and a related scene can help hone our methodological approach, in addition to illuminating Shakespeare's Jewish history and its links to the period under discussion in this book.

A Jew in the Text:
History and the Art of Textual Interpretation

What kind of a Jew is Shylock? In the previous section, we have argued for his role in the play as an archetype—an allegory of the Jewish nation—who will be ultimately defeated by the Christian church. This does not imply one-dimensionality: Shakespeare's complex construction simultaneously casts Shylock as a marginal figure in the Jewish community. His brief references to Jewish practice and his friendship with another Jew, Tubal,[38] can hardly disguise his seeming separation from the community in which Antonio and the other Venetian merchants so blithely place him. In fact, portraying Shylock, Shakespeare

38. See, for example, 1.3.30–34 and 3.1.70–115.

takes great pains to stress precisely the anxiety of his failed efforts to integrate within the community of Venetian businessmen.[39] Shylock is caught in a bind; tainted by the non-Jewish economic community he spends his time with, that community's denial of social equality in turn results in homicidal frustration.

This tension between shared heritage and differentiated heritage is well expressed in Shylock's usage of Biblical text. Harley Granville-Barker's words on the subject are evocative: "With this [the quotation of the Jacob story] the larger issue opens up between Gentile and Jew, united and divided by the scripture they revere, and held from their business by this tale of it—of flocks and herds and the ancient East."[40] On the one hand, Shylock seems to claim this story as his own particularly Jewish tale: the figure of the Old Testament, a Jacob, using his own texts to defeat the hostile Christian. But such an attack, of course, *can only be based on the supposition of shared fundamental assumptions about the validity of not only text, but also textual interpretation.*

That is, critics who assume as Antonio does that Shylock cites this passage for purposes of legitimation must assume that Shylock and Antonio share certain assumptions concerning the sacral nature of the Bible, the claim its words have on contemporary behavior, and the way those words may be interpreted in order to understand precisely the nature of that claim. As we will see, Shylock and Antonio share the first two assumptions, but differ on the third—and it is this difference,

---

39. Gross notes (25) that "there is nothing in the play to suggest that Shylock does not speak the same flawless English as the other characters—and Shakespeare would certainly have been capable of fitting him out with a distinctive accent if he had wanted to." Additionally, Portia, entering the courtroom in the trial scene dressed as Balthazar, seems unable to distinguish between Shylock and Antonio on the basis of physical appearance, asking, "Which is the merchant here? And which the Jew?" (4.1.176). Even assuming Portia is taking additional steps to preserve her disguise by pretending not to recognize Antonio, such a question would seem simple-minded and incongruous were Jews dressed markedly differently from Christians. Both proofs seem to offer strong evidence of a far less marginal Shylock than often assumed.

40. Even the perceptive Granville-Barker, though, while recognizing the importance of textual quotation here, essentially regards the episode as a distraction. Harley Granville-Barker, "The Merchant of Venice," Barnet 55–80, 72.

hinted at in this scene, that lays the groundwork for Portia's victory in the later trial. It is also this difference that illuminates and exemplifies the contemporary place of textual interpretation in the Jewish/Christian polemic, a highly relevant concept to the earliest figures of the Haskala and their strategies of textual citation and allusion.

As previously noted, Antonio presumes that Shylock tells the Genesis story to legitimate the taking of interest: his interjection at the beginning of the story ("And what of him? Did he take interest?"), his subsequent reaction to the story ("Was this inserted to make interest good? Or is your gold and silver rams and ewes?"), and his interruption of Shylock after the latter's witty attempt to duck the question ("I cannot tell. I make it breed as fast. But note me, signior—") all seem to indicate such an approach.

Antonio's first comment already suggests his familiarity with the Biblical passage in question and, equally, his agreement to the basic principle that Scriptural citation is indeed, at least theoretically, a valid means of legitimating one's polemic stance. However, simultaneously, and in his subsequent responses, Antonio dismisses Shylock's particular legitimating efforts by dismissing his proof on grounds of relevance. In his reading, the passage is unrelated to the topic under discussion and therefore its lessons (including, perhaps, the more subtle lessons we discussed in the first section) can be ignored.[41] It is these aspects of the scene—the foregrounding of the role of *relevance* as key to a text's legitimating power, and the constitution of that relevance through a *literalist*[42] reading of the passages in question—that allows us to analyze this scene not merely literarily but historically; not merely as a clever means to elucidate character development or as a

41. It is perhaps conscious irony on Shakespeare's part that Antonio's final dismissive aside here, that the devil can cite Scripture for his purpose, is itself a scriptural allusion, as Noble points out (164); see Matthew 4:5 and Luke 4:10.

42. The distinction here between "literal" and "literalist" is crucial, as we will see; to define "literalist," an idea that also echoes in Mendelssohn's expanded definition of *peshat*, I use David Weiss Halivni's definition of "the plain meaning of a text," that is, "the meaning that scrupulously follows the tenor of the words and the thrust of the context." *Peshat and Derash: Plain and Applied Meaning in Rabbinic Exegesis* (New York: Oxford University Press, 1991), 5.

thematic recapitulation of the play as a whole (though, as argued earlier, I believe that it does both those things), but also as a characterization of the state of Jewish/non-Jewish relations at the time.[43]

Shakespeare's era was a changing age for European Jewry, who were experiencing "a new political and historical self-consciousness."[44] One notable change, though, was external: a transformation in the Christian attitude toward Hebrew texts and interpretations. Christian England had already recognized "the importance of the Hebrew tradition for the correct comprehension of Holy Writ" in the case of Henry VIII's divorce,[45] where the Biblical law was unclear. Indeed, Shakespeare lived in "a post-Reformation Europe where increasing numbers of ordinary men, women . . . and even children . . . could read and sometimes even speak the language of the Jews."[46] And Christians were writing works that acknowledged the importance of "knowledge of Hebrew and rabbinical scholarship," like Edward Lively's study of the end of the ninth book of Daniel[47] and the works of the Puritan writer and preacher Hugh Broughton.[48] These and other Biblical readings by Protestant reformers began to show an "interest in the historical rather than the symbolic interpretation" of Biblical texts, "traced back to Luther's decision in the 1540s to reject the allegorical readings Augustine had successfully imposed on these works."[49]

43. This is hardly to suggest that *The Merchant of Venice* is a historical play. In fact, the strong strain of criticism viewing the play as a form of dark fairy tale is highly persuasive. See, for example, John Middleton Murray, "Shakespeare's Method: *The Merchant of Venice*" in Wheeler 37–57, esp. 42, and Gross's description of the atmosphere of the play as "half-romantic, half-naturalistic" (17). This said, the parameters that dictate the shape and flow and the type of fairy tale told are themselves historically conditioned.

44. Shapiro 6.

45. Cecil Roth, *History of the Jews in England* 145; cited in Danson 58.

46. Shapiro 41.

47. See Shapiro 137.

48. On Broughton, a fascinating figure who refused "to dismiss Talmudic and other rabbinic authorities out of hand," but did so in order to "facilitate the conversion of the Jews," see Shapiro 147–149. For other examples of non-Jews drawing on "Jewish precedents" and the Talmud for legal purposes, see Shapiro 174.

49. Shapiro 136. See also 151.

One might suppose that such movement by Christian Hebraists away from classic Christological Biblical interpretations, to say nothing of the increasing adoption of Jewish and rabbinical scholarship, could only lead to positive rapprochement between Jew and non-Jew. A simple look at our scene from *The Merchant of Venice* shows how wrong such a supposition would be. First, proximity brings anxiety as well as comfort: Antonio's remark that the devil cites Scripture for his own purpose implies not only an understanding of the purpose in question, but a violent disagreement with it.[50] The anxieties Shapiro locates in contemporary Christians—that "a Christian is the antithesis of a Jew and yet, in certain circumstances, is potentially indistinguishable from one"[51]—are adumbrated in this exchange over Biblical texts: can agreement over principles of textual debate lead to an undesired, even heretical, rapprochement?

Second, such closeness may not lead merely to anxiety, but rather to Jewish sublimation or even religious annihilation: for example, Hugh Broughton used Talmudic and rabbinic sources for purposes of proselytization,[52] and given the end of the *Merchant of Venice*, we may well feel that Shakespeare is doing the same: illustrating Jews engaging in strategies of textual citation and interpretation, which may symbolize their temporary advantage, but doing so precisely to reveal their ultimate defeat at the hands of a refined and reformed (that is, Christian) interpretive strategy.

Indeed, the war between Shylock and Antonio, and, more broadly, Jews and Christians of the early modern era, is not about the Biblical text but its interpretation. Christians attacked Jews not for the Bible itself—how could they?—but for their "corruption" of it through what they perceived to be the excesses of Jewish interpretation, and particularly their inability to hew to a literalist understanding of the text.[53] Much of this "corruption" was identified with Talmudic readings and the Talmud in general and, as we will see, Christian attacks

---

50. Though, as we have said, it may be that Antonio is mistaken about what he believes to be Shylock's purpose.

51. Shapiro 8.

52. See n.48 *supra*.

53. This will be discussed more fully in Chapters Three and Four.

on the Talmud persist from Shakespeare's day well into the eighteenth century.[54]

To return to our scene, Antonio challenges Shylock's use of this allusion on the grounds of relevance, or, we may say, literalism: though perhaps a "corrupt" Jewish interpretation may twist this passage to refer to interest—and indeed Shylock does coyly seem to link this story to the topic under discussion ("No, not take interest; not as you would say, *directly* interest"),[55] an honest Christian literalist reading can find no such support here. A similar understanding may underlie E. E. Stoll's reading of the passage, when he writes that "very evidently . . . Shylock is discomfited by Antonio's question 'Did he take interest?' for he falters and stumbles in his reply—'No, not take interest, not, as you would say,/Directly, interest,—' and is worsted, in the eyes of the audience if not in his own . . . in the second question, 'Or is your gold and silver ewes and rams?'"[56] Though Stoll explains Shylock's defeat in terms of the Aristotelian argument mentioned above, we can see his discomfiture, faltering, and stumbling in another way: what truly staggers Shylock is the literalist challenge to relevance, in an almost Spinozistic fashion *avant la lettre*.[57] For it is the challenge of literalism that will be the ultimate source of Shylock's downfall, a downfall foreshadowed here.

Shylock's downfall, of course, takes place in the famous trial scene, which bears brief study for our purposes. It is in this scene that allegorical interpretations of the play receive their strongest support. As one of the play's most important critics has written: "Allegorically, the scene develops the sharpest opposition of Old Law and New in terms

54. For an example of an anti-Talmudic statement in Elizabethan times, see Shapiro 30.

55. 1.3.75–76, my emphasis; Shylock does seem to be trying to have it both ways, paying lip service to Antonio's objection while simultaneously trying to maintain some sort of legitimating stance. Of course, this chapter's general argument—that Shylock's purpose in bringing this story has other motivations equally or more important than legitimating usury—helps explain the allusion's weakness as a legitimating text.

56. E.E. Stoll, "Shylock," in Wheeler 247–262, 251.

57. Yaffe (22, 129–130) has importantly suggested a Spinozist approach to the play, though one very different from the analysis here.

of their respective theological principles, Justice and Mercy, Right-eousness and Faith; it culminates in the final defeat of the Old Law and the symbolic conversion of the Jew."[58] Though numerous binary oppositions are apparent in the scene, critics often frame it as "an ar-gument between Old Testament legalism and New Testament reliance on grace."[59]

As some critics have noted, however, such a dichotomy is an over-simplification: while Portia may deliver a lovely speech about the quality of mercy, she does so in the robes of the legal scholar Balt-hazar, and thus stands for Law as well: as such, one perceptive critic has instead spoken of two competing "legalisms."[60] A slight modifi-cation of this analysis may even further illuminate the scene and our discussion. Indeed, "modification" seems to be the watchword for Portia; Christian victory is achieved not by destroying the bond or eliminating it, but rather by modifying the communal reading and in-terpretation of the bond's terms in order to render them deadly to pre-cisely the opposite party than originally intended. Lawrence Danson's characterization of Portia as "feigning surprise but totally in control of the situation—a situation, it now appears, *she has engineered to show that she too can be a master of literalism*" is particularly apt.[61] In fact, Portia cannot and does not wish to abandon the law completely: her behavior in the trial marks a return to the law, though admittedly to a

58. Lewalski 47. For a seminal account of this approach, see Lewalski 35, 38–43. See also Danson 56–57. On the important aspect of salvation history within the play, see Danson 165–166.

59. C.L. Barber, "The Merchants and the Jew of Venice: Wealth's Communion and an Intruder," in Barnet 11–32, 27. See also Alice N. Benston, "Portia, the Law, and the Tripartite Structure of *The Merchant of Venice*," in Wheeler 163–194, esp. 165, 175–179.

60. Barber 26. Though Yaffe's claim (61) that "Portia turns to the law, to Venetian law, because Shylock has already done so" may have some merit, her ringing affirmation of the law in light of Bassanio's plea to "Wrest once the law to your authority/To do a great right, do a little wrong": "It *must* not be, there is no power in Venice can alter a decree established" (4.1.220–224, emphasis mine), may indicate a respect for the law over and above the merely instrumental.

61. Danson 62, emphasis mine.

"proper" understanding of the law that, to her mind, "satisfies both justice and mercy."[62]

In other words, the two models are not competing legalisms, but competing *literalisms*—different ways of interpreting the text of the bond, ways that are coded Jewish and Christian. Portia disguises herself not merely as a man and as a scholar, but also, interpretively speaking, as a Jew, in order to demonstrate the failure of Jewish interpretation *on its own terms*. To clarify, we must illuminate the definitional slippage that occurs in the trial scene, a fairly simple linguistic sleight of hand on Portia's part that seems to outfox Shylock, who until now has been so clever with text and language.

In the court scene, two different interpretations of the essential term of the bond are employed:

1. A pound of flesh—that is, an exact pound of flesh and nothing else.
2. A pound of flesh—an approximate amount, including the blood that would flow in the process of acquisition.

Definition 2 is clearly the "working definition" of the term subscribed to by *everyone* in the court, Jew and Christian alike, until Portia reinterprets the term in 4.1.316–317 and expands it in 4.1.337–343, and presents definition 1 as the "correct" definition.

Definition 2 is clearly the "literalist" definition, as I have previously defined the term: presumably, if one contracts to cut a pound of flesh out of a living human body, there is a reasonable expectation of blood flow. Additionally, given late sixteenth century medical technology, measuring a pound of flesh still on the body must be a relatively approximate endeavor.[63] Given the Christian universe of reformed, "literalist"

---

62. Danson 63. Danson also compares (64) Portia's speech and the Sermon on the Mount, significantly noting of the latter, "its lesson is charity and mercy . . . much of its context is severely legalistic . . . it is such a law, with its equal regard for the letter and the spirit, that Christ comes not to overthrow but to fulfill."

63. Naturally, all this assumes that such a contract is *prima facie* valid, an assumption seemingly shared at first by all parties involved, though how such a contract would be valid in light of the Venetian law Portia cites forbidding an alien to "by direct or indirect attempts . . . seek the life of any citizen" (4.1.362–364) is at best unclear.

textual understanding, we can understand why Antonio and his friends are stymied for so long: employing the "literalist" approach, as Shakespeare suggests Christians should and must do, Shylock seems to have the insuperable advantage.

Portia's genius, like that of the Christian Hebraists who learned Jewish texts and interpretations to turn them against their original users,[64] is her ability to confront Shylock on his own terms. She switches from a literalist understanding of the bond to a literal one, moving from definition 2 to definition 1, twisting and corrupting the "plain meaning" of the bond to make her point, just as Jews supposedly twisted and corrupted the plain meanings of texts. Portia's behavior then begs the question: if she can switch, why cannot Shylock do the same? Why does he not object to Portia's semantic shift, and militate for definition 2, the clear and (until now) universally understood "plain meaning" of the bond?[65]

Employing this interpretation of the scene's competing forces, the reasons become clear, and speak volumes about Shakespeare's construction of Shylock and the Jews he represents. Shylock, a Jew and a creature of Jewish interpretation, has become so inextricably connected with the literal meaning of texts, *regardless and sometimes even in spite of their "plain meanings,"* that when presented with a situation that does violence to a text's plain meaning, he is powerless to object to

64. These scenes can thus also be seen as metaphors for the transformation of Christian Hebraism from a potential means of rapprochement to a weapon against Jewish teachings and of Christian Hebraists from students and potential ecumenical mediators to polemical proselytizers. Critical discussion of the transformation of Portia from learner to teacher, and Shylock the reverse (see, for example, Danson 46–47) seems highly resonant here.

65. Many critics have remarked on Shylock's surprising silence in the second half of the trial scene; in marked contrast to his garrulousness at the beginning of the scene (see 4.1.36–63, 66, 68, 70, 86–87, 91–105, 140–145, 179, 188, 211–212, 228–229, 231, 233–235, 241–250, 253, 257–258, 260–262, 265, 271, 304–308, 311, 314), once Portia has begun to switch definitions, he speaks only seven times, almost always briefly (325, 329–330, 348, 354, 357–358, 387–390, 407), and, aside from a brief "Is that the law?" (4.1.325) makes essentially no objection to Portia's legal maneuvers, attempting only to escape the situation as a whole.

it.[66] His silence is not personal, nor contextual, but, for lack of a better phrase, hermeneutical: the Jew, always insistent on a literal reading in which words mean not their "plain meaning," but some narrow, twisted analogue, must accept that such a reading allows him to be bound by Portia's literal construction of the bond's terms. And so Shylock's error causes him, in the words of the casket in Belmont, "to get what he deserves."[67]

Thus understood, much of the Christian fear of Shylock can be seen to be, in Danson's marvelous phrase, "the fear of a diabolical literalism," the "arch-literalist" being the Scripture-citing devil himself,[68] but not a fear of a general, reformed approach to literalism.[69] Jewish recognition of this Christian fear, and the recognition of a possible means to alleviate it by reforming and rehabilitating Jewish Biblical interpretation, will play a major role in early Haskala writing, as we will see.

Though this book deals with neither the history of the Jews of Shakespeare's England nor the Jewish presence in British literature—both topics well treated elsewhere[70]—the historical considerations illustrated here usefully illuminate a certain methodological approach, one that uses the tension between Shylock's textual expertise and textual clumsiness to refer not to the struggle of one particular Jew and Christian, but of Jews and Christians themselves. Shakespeare, in

66. In this light, Shylock's response to Gratiano's "Can no prayers pierce thee?" is notable: "No, *none that thou hast wit enough to make*" (4.1.129–130, emphasis mine). Shylock does in fact acknowledge that Antonio's dilemma has a possible solution. However, since such a solution would, in Shylock's mind, necessitate a "Jewish" interpretive approach to the text of the bond, an approach he believes the Christians too textually simple-minded to make, he feels secure in his position. Of course, Portia proves him wrong, as we have said, with her display of "wit." See also 4.1.145, where Shylock reproves Gratiano to "repair thy wit."

67. A connection between the play's two plots is developed by John Russell Brown in his "Love's Wealth and the Judgment of *The Merchant of Venice*," in Barnet 81–90, 82.

68. Danson 86.

69. Danson memorably remarks (89): "the power of literalism can be either diabolical or divine, and it may at times be difficult to tell the one from the other."

70. See Shapiro *passim*.

hinting at the national dimensions of Shylock's struggle with Antonio and presenting Shylock's ultimate failure as a textual failure, also adumbrates much of the tension between Jews and Christians in the early modern period—a tension at the heart of the development of the writing of Haskala, and thus, eventually, modern Jewish literature. And it is using this approach, referring both to the literary contexts of the allusive material and the historical and social factors that shaped the ways in which that material was employed, that this book hopes to illuminate the beginnings of modern Jewish literature, both in analysis of specific works and more generally.

From Venice to Berlin: Shylock and the Haskala

Not coincidentally, at the beginning of the Jewish Enlightenment in Prussia—the true beginning of this book—Shakespeare in general and *The Merchant of Venice* in particular had special appeal to audiences. The play was notably staged in Hamburg in 1777 by Friedrich Ludwig Schröder, and Lessing's play *Nathan the Wise*, which featured one of the first positive Jewish characters on the European stage, was "composed in blank verse inspired by Shakespeare's example."[71] August Wilhelm Schlegel, who began translating Shakespeare's plays in 1797 and whose brother Friedrich married Moses Mendelssohn's daughter, was taken with the character of Shylock, and notably viewed him as a symbol of extreme literalism. In his *Lectures on Dramatic Art and Literalism* (1809–1811), he wrote: "The letter of the law is Shylock's idol. . . . He insists on severe and inflexible justice, and it at last recoils on his own head. Here he becomes a symbol of the general history of his unfortunate nation."[72]

We have argued for Shylock as archetype and allegory, and indeed in the early modern period, much of modern Jewish history, and certainly modern Jewish literature, reflects precisely the factors adumbrated in this brief scene. Both broadly and in greater detail, this book

71. Gross 211.
72. Cited in Gross 213.

traces the origins of modern Jewish literature by following the progress of a few remarkable individuals who did, for various reasons and in various ways, cite Scripture for their own purpose. These *maskilim*, as they were known, were Antonio's devils.

The word *maskilim* (pl., sing. *maskil*) refers to individuals who subscribed to the tenets of a movement called the *Haskala*, often translated as "the Jewish Enlightenment." The English term is problematic for several reasons. It lends itself to a too-rigorous identification with the tenets of the Enlightenment, and also implies a group cohesiveness that certainly did not exist; as we will see, this book hopes to illustrate that the Haskala, often viewed monolithically, substantially differed in varied times and places.

An overly intensive focus on real discontinuities, though, tends to obscure the connections between the maskilim of different places and times, ranging from Prussia in the 1780s to the Russian Pale of Settlement a century later. Regardless of geography or chronology, these figures all saw themselves as trying to bridge two worlds: the world of external, non-Jewish culture and the world of Jewish tradition. Contrary to contemporary and current popular belief, many of these figures, particularly in the Haskala's first generation, did not wish to abandon Jewish tradition. Many were themselves traditionally observant. This did not stop their traditionalist opponents from harassing them, haranguing them, and even (in some cases) dancing on their graves: the maskilim were not merely Antonio's devils, but demonic figures for much of the traditional Jewish community as well.

It is this group of people, these outsiders who fought to reform and to modernize the Jewish people, who are at this book's heart. They saw themselves as engaged in a holy mission, at war. It was a war fought on two fronts: they needed to change their community and, in the process, to legitimate it in the eyes of the non-Jews. In medieval Venice, Shylock may have hoped for simple tolerance; these Jews, living under enlightened despots and the age of the French Revolution, craved equality and respect.

To fight a war, one needs weapons, and the maskilim used the same weapons Jews had used for centuries: words and texts. They tried to

convince traditional Jews to reform their thoughts and actions to accord as much as possible with those of cultured Europeans, particularly Prussians. (Thus, hundreds of miles from Berlin, a local Eastern
European Jew subscribing to maskilic beliefs could be disparagingly
referred to as a *daytsh*, a "German.") They could hardly do so, of
course, by citing the cherished European thinkers of their enlightened
age; they had to speak their audience's language. So the maskilim, like
Shylock, turned to Jewish canonical texts for their proofs, particularly
to the Bible, Talmud, and Midrash. The maskilic actual or implied audience, however, was not always composed entirely of Jews: in certain
times and places, they also had to address non-Jewish audiences, conceptions, and prejudices. The delicate balancing act that resulted led
to a very specific approach to Jewish texts and Jewish languages, an
approach that laid the groundwork for modern Jewish literature.

The first generation of maskilim found themselves, like Shylock on
the Rialto, in an uncomfortable and marginal position. Drawn to
non-traditional (and occasionally anti-traditional) ideas, they craved
acceptance by the non-Jewish world, but were well aware of the obstacle their religion posed. By the middle of the eighteenth century,
though, changing social and economic factors created, perhaps for the
first time, the glimmer of a possibility that social and political equality could be attainable.

The maskilim felt they could prove themselves worthy of inclusion
into a general, semi-neutral society by creating philosophical and literary works indicating their modern, cultured nature. Still, the maskilim were well aware that though currently in rare cases an individual
Jew like Moses Mendelssohn might be tolerated, widespread social acceptance would be contingent on widespread social and cultural reform. Given that the traditionalist Jewish audience viewed social and
cultural developments through the prism of religious practice, this
meant religious reform.

The contours of this reform and the means by which the maskilim
militated for it were significantly shaped by local historical circumstances. The Haskala is not monolithic, as this book will argue, but
rather is shaped by the particular nature of the time and place in which
the maskilim found themselves. As conditions changed for the Jews,

so too did the way in which the maskilim wrote. However, maskilic literary efforts cannot only be viewed locally: each new generation of maskilim was influenced by the one preceding it, even at times when local factors rendered earlier struggles and positions less relevant. The case of Yiddish shows how a maskilic bias against using the language, more understandable in a Prussian context, was maintained for almost a century in Eastern Europe, where different conditions might have suggested a very different approach.

Generally, though, much of this reformist battle, in all its various forms, can and should be viewed in textual terms. The first group of Prussian maskilim needed to legitimate themselves to a non-Jewish audience. As illustrated by our paradigmatic scene from *The Merchant of Venice*, Jewish efforts for ecumenical understanding and cooperation were often framed textually, particularly by appealing to shared texts like the Hebrew Bible. Implicit in this appeal was the suggestion that the Jews, with their centuries of textual study, understood the Bible and its lessons far better than the Christians did.

However, Antonio's challenge still thrived among the Christians: Christian Biblical scholarship had created a situation in which Jewish textual interpretation was mocked as rabbinically "corrupted" and quite simply false to the text. Jews therefore needed both to salvage their claims of textual superiority while simultaneously defending their interpretive approaches and the lessons those approaches generated. In studying several works by Moses Mendelssohn, the leading light of eighteenth century Prussian Jewry and the Haskala's spiritual father, we will see his efforts to present an image of a rehabilitated Jewish society through a rehabilitation and re-presentation of the Jewish canon. These efforts, fundamentally conservative in approach, generated a correspondingly conservative tone that marked the Prussian Haskala's first stage.

Conditions changed markedly in Prussia in a few short years. Mendelssohn's death, radicalization in the French Revolution's wake, and political and demographic shifts created a sense of greater freedom, which yielded a new type of maskilic work. It is at this point, as we will see, that maskilim begin to engage not merely in acts of conservative legitimation and defensive re-creation, but of internal satirical critique. They did so not merely to persuade Jewish audiences to necessary social, cultural, and educational reforms—indeed, Prussian Jews had changed so rapidly that some maskilim were equally worried about the consequences of false Enlightenment as they were anxious for the rewards of true Enlightenment—but also to convince non-Jewish audiences that not all Jews were alike. An examination and textual analysis of works by Aaron Halle-Wolfssohn, a talented and prolific maskil who flourished at the end of the eighteenth century, shows the beginnings of these trends, so vital to the history of the Haskala as a whole.

As the eighteenth century waned, the front lines of the Haskala moved eastward, and the story of modern Hebrew and Yiddish literature moves with it to Galicia. In his writings, Wolfssohn decries the growth of the new Hasidic movement; Hasidism, however, had made scarce inroads into Prussia or any of the German principalities. Galicia's Jewry differed greatly from Prussia's, though: far more traditional and with much less contact between Jews and Gentiles, Hasidism had spread there like wildfire. It is thus in Galicia where the Haskala, which viewed the Hasidic movement as a superstitious stumbling block to emancipation's progress, moved into a fervent anti-Hasidic phase. Examining the work of Joseph Perl, the Galician Haskala's most vitriolic anti-Hasidic writer, reveals that much of the maskilic attack is expressed as a struggle over the Jewish canon and its interpretation: which books and interpretations will be accepted by the Jewish community? Perl presses his points by attacking not merely Hasidic interpretative methodology but also Hasidic text: his most notable works, analyzed here in detail, parody two of the major Hasidic writings of the early nineteenth century.

Ironically, in the shaping of these maskilic attacks, the traditionalists win a major victory. For in this battle, conducted almost entirely internally (in Galicia, the non-Jewish authorities cared little about internal Jewish struggles), the maskilim determine that to win the propaganda war, they must reach and win over the mass audiences so enamored with Hasidism. To do that, they had to compose entertaining and persuasive material in a language accessible to the general Jewish population, a language, notably, in which the Hasidim had few compunctions writing. This turn to Yiddish leads ineluctably to Mendele Moykher Seforim and the explosion of modern Yiddish and Hebrew literature.

In sum, by looking at these three authors' work, and their historical and social contexts, I hope to focus attention on the magnificent and highly complex allusive games the maskilim play, and to show not only how Jewish literature can deepen our understanding of allusion, but also how understanding allusion can deepen our knowledge of Jewish literature. To achieve the second goal, different maskilic strategies of allusion will be shown to illuminate the Haskala's chronological development as it moves toward Eastern Europe, and much of the book is dedicated to individual readings of foundational texts by some of the early Haskala's most interesting and important authors. Though some of these authors may be unfamiliar to a general audience, the works they created are lively, funny, and fascinating, providing sufficient merit for their inclusion here.

The book's structure follows this general approach: after a brief chapter suggesting how the study of literary theory sheds light on the study of the Haskala, and vice versa (Chapter Two), the first, introductory section of the book ends with a chapter that provides the overall historical context so vital to a nuanced understanding of the literary texts under discussion (Chapter Three). The book's second section focuses on Prussia in the age of Moses Mendelssohn (Chapter Four) and Aaron Halle-Wolfssohn (Chapter Five). The third and final section discusses Joseph Perl, the giant of the Galician Haskala, and his relationship to Hasidic literature and the new Yiddish literature (Chapters Six and Seven). A brief coda offers suggestions for further study and research.

For many years, it was taken as a commonplace in the study of Jewish literature that modern Hebrew and Yiddish literature boasted the same founding figure, Sholem Yankev Abramovitch (better known as Mendele Moykher Seforim), who began writing almost half a century after this book's period ends. This book is dedicated to the notion, now beginning to gain wider currency, that the literature of the Haskala is every bit as important and deserving of study as its later descendants. This work is thus also an attempt to reclaim material that, until recently, has languished in the dusty pages of antiquated histories of Jewish literature, and, quite frankly, should be seen not merely as historically momentous, but literarily meritorious on its own terms.

Two   Allusion in a Jewish Key

Literary Theory and the
Study of Haskala Literature

Introduction

In recent years, much scholarly effort has been dedicated to the study of the Haskala.[1] The period's history has been studied in great detail,[2] and recently its literature, earlier often ridiculed and marginalized, has become the object of greater scrutiny.[3]

Maskilic literature fascinates in its usage of classical Jewish texts, quotations or references from the Bible, the Talmud, and other works of rabbinic Judaism. When a maskilic decision was made to write in the

1. For bibliographic surveys of recent research, see Shmuel Werses, "Mekhkarim khadashim vegam yeshenim besifrut hahaskala utekufata," *Madaei hayahadut* 36 (1996), 43–72, an update of his "Al mekhkar sifrut hahaskala beyameinu" in Werses, *Megamot vetsurot besifrut hahaskala* (Jerusalem: Magnes Press, 1990), 356–412. See also Shulamit S. Magnus, "German Jewish History," *Modern Judaism* 11 (1991), 125–146.

2. On the dating and definition of the Haskala, see Uzi Shavit, "Hahaskala mahi—leveirur musag hahaskala besifrut haivrit," in *Baalot hashakhar: shirat ha-haskala: mifgash im hamoderniut* (Tel Aviv: Hakibbutz Hameukhad, 1996), 12–36.

3. For two admirable overviews of the scholarly literature on the origins of Haskala literature, see Arnold J. Band, "The Beginnings of Modern Hebrew Literature: Perspectives on 'Modernity,'" *AJSReview* 13:1–2 (1988), 1–26, and Moshe Pelli's "Likviat reshita shel sifrut hahaskala haivrit uvkhinat hamodernism," in Shlomo Nash, ed., *Bein historia lesifrut* (Keren Yitchak Kiyov: Jerusalem, 1997), 235–269, as well as the works cited there. Compare Baruch Kurzweil, *Sifruteinu hakhadasha: hemshekh o mahapekha?* (Jerusalem: Schocken, 1960), 19–26. On methodological approaches for the study of maskilic literature, see Shmuel Werses, "Orkhot veshvilim bekheker sifrut hahaskala," *Mekhkerei yerushalayim besifrut ivrit* 13 (1992), 7–28. Importantly, Werses, in an approach adopted by this work, suggests treating all maskilic work, regardless of language, as an integrated whole (11), and focusing on the texts themselves (12–13).

Hebrew language, some type of usage of these canonical texts was unavoidable; the language itself, after all, is largely composed of words appearing in these classical texts. Maskilic ideologies of and approaches to language have allowed scholars to discuss maskilic style by focusing on the use of differing strata of the Hebrew language, and, by extension, classical Hebrew texts.

The consensus on the composition of those strata has changed over time. While early scholars like Joseph Klausner claimed German maskilim used the "predominantly poetical and rhapsodic" Biblical Hebrew, and that later strata of Mishnaic, Talmudic, aggadic, and medieval Hebrew were resolutely eliminated from their work, to say nothing of Aramaic, or loan words from other languages,[4] current research has shown that the "language of enlightenment was not as homogeneously Biblical as it was previously assumed. Rabbinic and Tibonite elements were freely used from Mendelssohn till Bialik."[5]

Despite these revisions, the vast majority of scholarly work on maskilic literature has remained focused on analyzing these and similar questions of maskilic style;[6] some scholars claim the maskilic literary revolution to be a stylistic revolution above all else, a claim that, for a long time, allowed other maskilic usages of these classical texts to go unanalyzed.[7] Though these works' stylistic usage will be briefly

4. *A History of Modern Hebrew Literature (1785–1930)* (London: M.L. Cailingold, 1932), 2.

5. Eisig Silberschlag, *From Renaissance to Renaissance: Hebrew Literature from 1492–1970* (New York: Ktav Publishing House, Inc., 1973), 82. See also Yosef Yitzchaki, "Deoteihem shel sofrei hahaskala al lashon haivrit vedarkheihem beharkhavata vekhidusha," *Leshonenu* 34:4 (1963), 287–305; 35:1 (1964), 39–59, 35:2, 140–159.

6. See, for example, Uzi Shavit, "Shira vehaskala: kesher simbiotit," in Shavit *Baalot hashakhar*; "Lemaamada shel hashira bitnuat hahaskala haivrit," in *Shira veidiologia* (Tel Aviv: Hakibbutz Hameukhad, 1987), 99–113; Yair Mazor, "The Poetics of Composition of the Hebrew Short Story in the Haskalah Period," *AJSReview* 10:1 (1985), 89–110; Yehudit Bar-El, "Hapoema haivrit mereshita: hapoetika shel hazhanr," *KOMI* 10C2 (1990), 129–136; and Noah Rosenbloom, *Haeifus hamikrai meieidan hahaskala vehaparshanut* (Rubin Mass: Jerusalem, 1983), 7–16.

7. For example, Robert Alter's reference to maskilic writers' "cult of the biblical phrase" and characterization of the resulting style as "a lifeless pastiche of

addressed, this book focuses on two other aspects of maskilic textual usage: their allusiveness and their thematic and polemic effects, both literarily and historically contextualized.

As mentioned previously, the Haskala was an ideological movement and maskilic literature was, in the main, an ideological literature, written and disseminated to convince others of its tenets.[8] The maskilim thus needed to employ legitimative strategies resonant to their audiences, and traditionalist Jews, arguably their largest and most important audience, would accept as legitimate only proofs drawn from classical Jewish texts.[9] This strategy was hardly new: similar usages of Biblical and Talmudic "prooftexts" occurred throughout Jewish history, not merely justifying conservative norms of behavior, but also allowing traditional communities to develop contemporary responses to changing social situations.[10] Indeed, Max Weinreich coined the

---

biblical fragments" risks throwing out the thematic baby with the stylistic bathwater. Robert Alter, ed., *Modern Hebrew Literature* (West Orange, NJ: Behrman House, Inc., 1975), 23–24.

8. As Simon Halkin notes, "Throughout the period of haskalah, no hard and fast line can be drawn between the purely literary character of Hebrew letters and their social or publicistic character." Simon Halkin, *Modern Hebrew Literature: Trends and Values* (New York: Schocken Books, 1950), 74. An excellent overview of Enlightenment ideals and their adoption and adaptation by the Haskala is given in Lois C. Dubin, "The Social and Cultural Context: Eighteenth-Century Enlightenment," in Daniel H. Frank and Oliver Leaman, eds., *History of Jewish Philosophy* (London: Routledge Press, 1997), 636–659. Dubin stresses the Enlightenment premise that nature could be rationally comprehended through a combination of reason and experience. This rationalism was combined with, at least in Germany, a turn toward a conception of a "universal, rational, commonsensical, and moral" natural religion (645). As we will see, this combination offered new possibilities for the maskilim. See also Isaac Eisenstein-Barzilay, "The Ideology of the Berlin Haskalah," *PAAJR* 25 (1956), 1–37; Uzi Shavit, *Bepetakh hashira haivrit hakhadasha: masat mavo* (Tel Aviv: Tel Aviv University, 1986); and Ernst Cassirer, *The Philosophy of the Enlightenment* (Princeton: Princeton University Press, 1951), vii, 5–7, 29–35, 136–138, 167–75, 182–196.

9. See Michael S. Berger, *Rabbinic Authority* (New York: Oxford University Press, 1998), esp. 12–13, 114–131.

10. A classic early example is the rabbinic institution of the *prozbul* to allow debts to remain valid during the sabbatical year, despite the Biblical injunction to forgive all debts at the beginning of the year (Deuteronomy 15:2). The rabbis

phrase "vertical legitimation" to illustrate precisely this tendency of traditional Ashkenazic society to mask innovation as tradition.[11] David
Roskies expresses this approach well: "The new was always reinter-
preted in the light of classical sources. Present and past were fused
into a type of panchronism as Ashkenazic Jews accommodated all
change into a midrashic system."[12]

Though the continuities between many early maskilim and traditional society are fairly evident,[13] maskilic Enlightenment-inspired
goals were certainly more subversive and externally originated than
those of most previous innovators. Nonetheless, these maskilim were
forced to walk a careful line: on the one hand, their textual usage had
to be sufficiently subversive to suggest new interpretations in line with
their new thinking, but also sufficiently subtle so as not to be quickly
dismissed as heresy by traditional audiences, to whom even slight de-
viations occasioned great suspicion.[14]

---

legitimate the *prozbul* by citing and interpreting the passage in question to mean
its essential opposite. See the discussion in *BT Gitin* 36a-b and the other Biblical
passages cited *ad loc* regarding rabbinic power.

11. For a detailed discussion, see Max Weinreich, *Geshikhte fun der yidisher
shprakh* (New York: Bibliotek fun YIVO, 1973), 1:214–218, 231–233. See also Jacob
Katz, *Out of the Ghetto: The Social Background of Jewish Emancipation 1770–1870*
(New York: Schocken Books, 1978), 5–6, and *Tradition and Crisis: Jewish Society at
the End of the Middle Ages* (New York: Schocken Books, 1993), 9, 19, 33, 58 on the
traditional Ashkenazic community's methods of legitimating change.

12. David G. Roskies, "The Emancipation of Yiddish," *Prooftexts* 1 (1981),
28–42, 31. Compare Ithamar Gruenwald's comments in "Midrash & The 'Midrashic Condition': Preliminary Considerations," in Michael Fishbane, ed., *The
Midrashic Imagination: Jewish Exegesis, Thought, and History* (Albany, NY: State
University of New York Press, 1993), 6–22, 11–12.

13. See Eliezer Schweid, "The Impact of Enlightenment on Religion," *Judaism*
38:4 (1989), 389–98, esp. 392.

14. Indeed, Roskies characterizes maskilic technique as "creative betrayal," describing the maskilim as "wolves in shepherds' clothing . . . predators feeding off
the seemingly unusable past." David G. Roskies, *A Bridge of Longing: The Lost Art
of Yiddish Storytelling* (Cambridge, MA: Harvard University Press, 1995), 6, 17. For
a formulation of the same dilemma in a slightly different context, see Edward
Breuer, "(Re)Creating Traditions of Language and Texts: The Haskalah and Cultural Continuity," *Modern Judaism* 16:2 (1996), 161–183, 162. See also Dubin 654
and Berger 122–124.

The resulting careful balance they struck deserves accordingly careful analysis; to do so both in literary and historically contextual terms, the limited work done so far on maskilic allusion must be first surveyed and analyzed. Subsequently, a broader theoretical approach to understanding maskilic allusion can be suggested, one drawing on different strands of contemporary literary theory and possibly suggesting some larger lessons for scholars of allusion and for scholars of Jewish literature.

Maskilic Allusion: The State of the Field

Two scholars in particular have addressed the subject of the maskilic usage of classical Jewish texts. Moshe Pelli has produced a stream of articles on the early Haskala and has contributed significantly to the reexamination of the maskilic approach to the classical Jewish canon.[15] Pelli's work has revised the traditional scholarly dismissal of maskilic usage of classical texts as mere slavish Biblicism, or *melitsa*, changing that strategy from an object of scorn to a subject of pure analysis.[16] Many of his articles briefly discuss the usage of classical texts as one satirical strategy among many,[17] or as one strategy for understanding

15. Much of his work has been collected in *Bemaavakei tmura: iyunim behaskala haivrit begermania beshilhei hamea hayud khet* (Tel Aviv: Mifalim Universitiyim, 1988), *The Age of Haskalah: Studies in Hebrew Literature of the Enlightenment in Germany* (Leiden: E.J. Brill, 1979); and *Sugot vesugyot basifrut hahaskala* (Tel Aviv: Hakibbutz Hameukhad, 1999); the last fruitfully applies genre theory to taxonomize maskilic literature (see esp. pp. 11–27).

16. For an overview of the various definitions of the word *melitsa* during the Haskala, ranging from "rhetoric" to "use of fragments of Biblical verses for their own sake," see Pelli, "Tfisat hamelitsa bereshit sifrut hahaskala haivrit," *Lashon veivrit* 8 (1991), 31–48, as well as his "Leshimusha shel hamelitsa besifrut hahaskala—piknik leshoni im Romaneli, Aykhl veakherim," *Bikoret ufarshanut* 31 (1995), 53–65, 53–55, where Bialik's influence on the debate is discussed. The subjects of these papers are combined, in an abbreviated form, in Pelli's "On the Role of *Melitzah* in the Literature of the Hebrew Enlightenment," in Lewis Glinert, ed., *Hebrew in Ashkenaz: A Language in Exile* (Oxford: Oxford University Press, 1993), 99–110.

17. See, for example, *Bemaavakei tmura* 35–43; *Age* 48–72; and "'Ktav Yosher' leShaul Berlin: lereshita shel hasatira behaskala haivrit begermania," *HUCA* 64 (1994), 1–25, 19–25.

particular maskilic works, such as Romanelli's *Masa Bearav*.[18] Pelli has notably illuminated the stylistic debt of the maskilim to the Andalusian *shibuts* and the expansion of the range of maskilic citation to Talmudic and later sources.[19] However, Pelli generally seems more interested in these citations for their stylistic aspects than for their use as vehicles for expressing ideological positions.[20]

The most interesting theoretical work on the subject thus far appears in a series of articles by Tova Cohen. Cohen posits the centrality of intertextuality, particularly from classical Jewish texts, in maskilic literature.[21] She also posits the essentially polemic nature of the maskilic effort, and argues that commonalities in the social, educational, developmental, and, above all, textual milieu of both maskilic writer and traditionalist reader would lead to a shared community of discourse: "The maskilic writer knew well how his reader would absorb a text, for he read the same way, and as a result it can be imagined that he directed his writing in such a way that it would appeal to this type of absorption."[22]

Cohen pays particular attention to the education of the maskilim as children,[23] arguing that as a result of their intensive training, the

18. Moshe Pelli, "The Literary Genre of the Travelogue in Hebrew Haskalah Literature: Shmuel Romanelli's Masa Ba'arav," *Modern Judaism* 11:2 (1991), 241–260, and "Leshimusha" 58, 65, where his conclusion, that textual citations are not mere verse fragments but carefully selected citations that illuminate and comment on the narrative, is vital to any understanding of maskilic literature.

19. Pelli "Ktav Yosher" 23 and "Leshimusha" 55–56.

20. Pelli "Literary Genre" 249. Compare, however, Pelli's remarks on citing classical texts as educational tools (251–255).

21. Tova Cohen, "Hatekhnika halamdanit—tsofen shel sifrut hahaskala," *Mekhkerei yerushalayim besifrut ivrit* 13 (1992), 137–169. Cohen writes: "My premise is that a full understanding of the literature of the Haskala will only become possible through a reconstruction of the ways of reading and writing of the maskilic 'interpretive community'" (138), a premise shared by this book. An abridged English version appears as "The Maskil as Lamdan: The Influence of Jewish Education on Haskalah Writing Techniques," in Glenda Abramson and Tudor Parfitt, eds., *Jewish Education and Learning* (Reading, Berkshire: Harwood Academic Publishers, 1994), 61–74.

22. Cohen "Hatekhnika" 139–140, quote from 139.

23. Cohen "Hatekhnika" 143. Compare Berger's discussion of the childhood roots of rabbinic authority (3–5).

classical texts are alive, familiar, and flexible entities for them.[24] Cohen's strength as a critic, though, stems from her insistence that maskilic literature, due to its ideological nature, must be viewed in terms of both its writers' and its readers' perspectives. She posits the development of a reading technique, gleaned from years of studying texts together with commentaries and supercommentaries, which allowed readers to keep two texts, one commenting on the other, constantly in mind as they read.[25] Cohen writes that "the premise within the maskilic interpretive community was of the vitality of the canonical text and the close recognition of it by the reader . . . an image from the world of the *sefer* was not, in the eyes of the maskilic reader and writer, 'dry,' 'conventional,' or 'distant from the reader,' but just the opposite . . . ."[26] Cohen also observes that these intertexts must be interpreted not merely based on their appearance in the classical Jewish canon, but also on their appearance in contemporary Jewish *life*, most notably the liturgy.[27]

The approach toward maskilic textual usage exemplified in Pelli and Cohen's work is vital to any understanding of Haskala literature, and

24. Alter (*Modern* 8) wonderfully characterizes their ability as "an aptitude that the Germans call Sprachgefühl—an innate sense, like perfect pitch in music, for how language should properly sound, joined with a relish for the sonorities and the semantic colorations of Hebrew words in their classical idiomatic combinations." Traditional Jewish education has been discussed at length elsewhere; a good overview is given in Iris Parush, "Mabat akher al 'khayei haivrit hameta,'" *Alpayim* 13 (1987), 65–106. For a nuanced reexamination of many assumptions about Jewish knowledge, see Shaul Stampfer's important article, "What Did 'Knowing Hebrew' Mean in Eastern Europe?" in Glinert 1995:129–140. See also Philip Friedman, "Yoysef Perl vi a bildungs-tuer un zayn shul in Tarnopol," *YIVO-Bleter*, 21–22 (1948), 131–190, 133–138, for a detailed but somewhat uncritical overview, tinged with the critical fire of the Haskala.

25. Cohen refers to the technique as "simultaneous reading." See her discussion of the Pentateuch and Rashi, and the Talmudic folio, where this multivocality is expressed visually, in "Hatekhnika" 148, 165–166.

26. Cohen "Hatekhnika" 155–156.

27. Tova Cohen, "Bein-tekstualiut besifrut hahaskala: mekomo shel hatekst habilti katuv," *Bikoret ufarshanut* 31 (1995), 37–52. See also Cohen "Hatekhnika" 145–150, particularly her comments on the reading of the weekly Torah portion (146). See also Katz *Tradition* 57, 158 and Alter *Modern* 6–7.

their work should and must serve as a starting point for any critical endeavor attempting to study this literature. Indeed, much of the analysis in this book's later chapters follows these works' critical assumptions: a strong authorial hand using the vital and familiar canonical text in the (partial) expectation of a learned reader,[28] accompanied by the authorial assumption that said reader would have greater familiarity with, and stronger affect toward, canonical material with strong resonances in Jewish life and liturgy. The author knows what material that might be by virtue of belonging to an identical or nearly identical interpretive community with that learned reader. However, significant work remains to be done on their model of maskilic usage: these scholars may have provided the broad strokes, but much detail remains to be filled in.

Most importantly, Pelli and Cohen's work implicitly seems to treat the Haskala as monolithic. They seem to posit an interpretive community that, based on the traditional Jewish community of *Ashkenaz*, reads and writes in a similar fashion from Germany to Russia and from the mid-eighteenth century to the beginning of the twentieth century. For example, Cohen refers to N. H. Wessely, who wrote in late eighteenth century Prussia, and S. Y. Abramovitch, who wrote in late nineteenth-century Tsarist Russia, in the same article without distinguishing between their strategies of usage. Though Pelli's work is significantly more temporally circumscribed, he never calls attention to this issue in his analyses. While overlapping continuities unquestionably exist between these various times and regions, it is reasonable to assume that particular social and cultural circumstances in Prussia gave rise to a somewhat different set of textual strategies than in Galicia.[29] This book argues that the Haskala should not be viewed

28. As we will see, our model takes into account authorial expectations of different educational levels on the part of the readers, particularly, though not only, when questions of language choice apply.

29. Despite the promising title of Uzi Shavit's "Intertekstualiut keevenbokhan lemaavar bein tkufa letkufa: Yalag ke'historiyon khadash'" in Shavit *Baalot* 85–96, he only uses Gordon's changing usage of classical texts to demarcate the revolutionary change between the Haskala and the "modern" period of Hebrew literature, not within the Haskala itself. Nonetheless, a modification of the methodological assumptions Shavit employs is at work here as well.

monolithically; in analyzing the maskilic works that follow, historical and biographical information is provided to locate the three authors of the works in particular and yet related maskilic milieus.[30]

Secondly, both Cohen and Pelli intentionally limit their work to a discussion of intertextuality in *Hebrew* literature, perhaps because of a greater interest in the development of Hebrew literary style than in examining the polemical or legitimating function of these prooftexts. However, maskilim also wrote for audiences in other languages, most notably Yiddish.[31] These works also employ textual citations and references to classical Jewish literature, often for similar legitimative purposes. This leads to another refinement of the Pelli/Cohen position: we can attempt to analyze the usage of classical texts not merely to indicate differences in time and place, the "flavor" of the local Haskala, but also to identify differing audiences being addressed and these ideologues' understanding of those different audiences' textual capabilities, even in the same place.

The audiences for which these maskilim wrote can be differentiated in various ways. One obvious (and vital) division is between Jews and non-Jews: at times, maskilim wrote to gain the appeal and social approval of non-Jewish audiences, not (or not merely) to convince Jewish audiences of their positions, even if they were writing in Jewish languages.[32] Audiences can also be divided along linguistic and sexual axes, but, as recent research on the gendering of Hebrew and Yiddish literature has shown, this approach is not always fruitful:[33] rather, ed-

---

30. On the differing character of various maskilic centers, see Menukha Gilboa, "Merkazei hasifrut haivrit hekhadasha ad mea haesrim," in Ziva Shamir and Avner Holzman, eds. *Nekudot mifne besifrut haivrit vezikatan lemagaim im sifruyot akherim* (Tel Aviv University: Tel Aviv, 1993), 113–123.

31. For a limited bibliography, see Anita Norich, "Yiddish Literary Studies," *Modern Judaism* 10:3 (1990), 297–309.

32. See Alan Mintz, *"Banished from Their Father's Table": Loss of Faith and Hebrew Autobiography* (Bloomington: Indiana University Press, 1989), 9, where this issue appears in a slightly different context.

33. A recent treatment of this question appears in Naomi Seidman, *A Marriage Made in Heaven: The Sexual Politics of Hebrew and Yiddish* (Berkeley: University of California Press, 1997), 1–10; for a more classic formulation, see Shmuel Niger, "Di yidishe literatur un di lezerin," in his *Bleter-geshikhte fun der yidisher lit-*

ucation and textual familiarity, perhaps unsurprisingly, provide the best method of audience differentiation.[34] The maskilim wrote works full of in-jokes and sly allusions aimed at their elite colleagues, true; but they also wrote works whose polemical message was clear to those still needing persuasion. And sometimes, the two works could be identical.

In analyzing one Mendelssohnian work written for Jews in Hebrew and one for non-Jews in German, we see the author's use of classical Jewish texts remain static—a testament to the integrity of his public positions on Enlightenment issues. Aaron Halle-Wolfssohn's half-German, half-Yiddish play, written as a programmatic replacement for older Purim plays, provides an early example of a trend of using texts to ground characters in a specific social context for an audience and to provide sympathetic and less sympathetic resonances; and finally, comparing Hebrew and Yiddish versions of Joseph Perl's particular writings will enable us to see how a master polemicist changes his

---

eratur (New York: Alveltlekhn yidishn kultur-kongres, 1959), 37–107, esp. 43–54. See also Iris Parush, "The Politics of Literacy: Women and Foreign Languages in Jewish Society of 19th Century Eastern Europe," *Modern Judaism* 15:2 (1995), 183–206; Chava Weissler, "The Religion of Traditional Ashkenazic Women: Some Methodological Issues," *AJSReview* 12:1 (1987), 73–94; and Shaul Stampfer's important article, "Gender Differentiation and Education of the Jewish Woman in Nineteenth-Century Eastern Europe," *Polin 7* (1992), 63–87, 68–70. On female knowledge in the Haskala, see Anne Sheffer, "Beyond Heder, Haskalah, and Honeybees: Genius and Gender in the Education of Seventeenth and Eighteenth Century Judeo German Women," in Peter J. Haas, ed., *Recovering the Role of Women: Power and Authority in Rabbinic Jewish Society* (Atlanta, GA: Scholars Press, 1992), 85–112, 88. See also Kathryn Hellerstein's annotated bibliography "Gender Studies and Yiddish Literature," 249–255, and Naomi Sokoloff's annotated bibliography "Gender Studies and Modern Hebrew Literature," 257–263 in Naomi B. Sokoloff, Anne Lapidus Lerner, and Anita Norich, eds., *Gender and Text in Modern Hebrew and Yiddish Literature* (New York: Jewish Theological Seminary, 1992).

34. See Iris Parush, "Readers in Cameo: Women Readers in Jewish Society of Nineteenth Century Eastern Europe," *Prooftexts* 14 (1994), 1–23, which notes, "Jewish readers constituted a stratified reading public that was exposed to a multifaceted and multilingual literary system" (6). See also the Stampfer article cited in note 24 *supra*, and Katz *Tradition* 162–163.

examples (though not his ideas) to take into account the needs of two different audiences.

In short, the aim of this book is to achieve a theoretical goal through an intensely practical method, that is, to illustrate the methodological developments discussed above through a close reading of these three authors' work. Hopefully, the chapters that follow will, taken separately, contribute to the understanding of the work of these three important maskilim. Taken together, the chapters are intended to provide a first step to a more detailed use of that most crucial component of Jewish literature, the textual citation, in understanding maskilic literature, and to serve as guideposts to a contextualized historical development of the early Haskala.

Before engaging in the practical work of reading these authors, however, we must first see how our refinements of Pelli and Cohen's position might function within a broader theoretical model of textual citation in a multilingual, historically dynamic system.

The Four Questions:
A Theoretical Approach to Maskilic Allusions

In studying maskilic literature in a less monolithic fashion, the following theoretical questions are being addressed, harnessed together by virtue of their juxtaposition in the historical practice of maskilic writing and reading:

1. What is the nature and function of an allusion?
2. What is the nature of an interpretive community, and how does it change or stay the same under changing historical conditions?
3. How can an interpretive community be constituted given systemic differentiation in interpretive capacities on the part of the audience (both in terms of differing textual or interpretive capabilities, and how are those differing capabilities expressed through language choice)?
4. How do conceptions of power and ideology relate to allusive practice, and how do contemporary literary theories (particularly new historicism, cultural materialism, and the concept of "minor

literatures") help explicate the relationship of reader, writer, and community as developed in the answers to the first three questions?

The proposed answers to these questions blend theoretical approaches with a practical awareness of the conditions of a concrete case study—this book's subject—maskilic allusion.

In his important recent study of allusion, Joseph Pucci has both admirably summarized the essential critical literature on the subject and taken issue with much of it.[35] His summation and argument have much to offer, both in what they say and leave unsaid.

First, Pucci's history of critical approaches to allusion recognizes theorists who argue that alluding authors are circumscribed by social and historical contexts.[36] Pucci's history continues, though, to reveal that historically such authorial circumscription was taken to imply increased authorial impotence at the expense of correspondingly readerly power. This transition is exemplified by Ziva Ben-Porat, who, in the 1970s, attempted to "deploy a formal notion of allusive signification (what she called 'definition') to frame specific readings of literary works."[37] Ben-Porat's careful reasoning features the "actualization" of the allusion on the reader's part by the "recognition" of a marker that points to the "referent" text, subsequent identification of that referent text, and the modification of the allusion in the reader's understanding in light of the interaction between these two texts.[38] Since perception of the textual interaction is dependent on the reader's perspective, which in turn is shaped by his or her position "within the 'intertextual' system," the resulting implication is a limitation of authorial power and the empowerment of both the reader and the system of signification itself.[39]

---

35. For Pucci's summation of current definitions of allusion and his critical analysis, see Joseph Pucci, *The Full-Knowing Reader: Allusion and the Power of the Reader in the Western Literary Tradition* (New Haven: Yale University Press, 1998), 3–7.

36. See Pucci 13–14.

37. Pucci 16. See Ziva Ben-Porat, "The Poetics of Literary Allusion," *PTL: A Journal for Descriptive Poetics and Theory of Literature* 1 (1976), 105–128.

38. See discussion in Ben-Porat 107–112 and Pucci 17.

39. Pucci 16–17.

Carmela Perri, modifying and extending this approach, argues that an allusion suggests not only itself, but its interpretation:

> it is a manner of signifying in which some kind of marker (simple or complex, overt or covert) not only signifies un-allusively, within the imagined possible world of the alluding text, but through echo also denotes a source text and specifies some discrete, recoverable property(ies) belonging to the intention of this source text . . . the property(ies) evoked modifies the alluding text, and possibly activates further, larger, inter- and intra-textual patterns of properties with the consequent further modification of the alluding text.[40]

This approach, post-Structuralist critiques notwithstanding,[41] seems to accord well with our model of the Haskala: while a "strong author" who uses particular source texts may exist, if his[42] "strength" is defined by the way in which he may use those texts, then he is indeed limited, given that the texts he cites do, given their classic interpretations enshrined in Jewish canonical tradition, have certain "discrete, recoverable properties" within the system of signification. However, this certainly does not imply that the author, with myriad texts from which

40. Cited in Pucci 18. See, however, Perri's full treatment of the issue in "On Alluding," *Poetics* 7 (1978), 289–307. Perri has notably formulated a ten-step process for how the allusion "works" (299–303).

41. For example, the theorist Pietro Pucci argues for a strong reader, seeing the text as, in Joseph Pucci's words, "a ludic landscape that privileged the continual movement of literary language in a series of 'noddings, winks, gestures,' and which disavowed the power of the author to control that movement, whose intentions, in any case, were unknown 'fully or in part' to the author himself. In place of system and of author, however, Pucci offered a special sort of reader, possessed of certain key competencies that enabled him to 'decode' the allusion, to play with it, in order for interpretation to occur." Pucci 22. Despite this work's valuation of a strong authorial approach, a modified "strong reader" approach also figures importantly in our theoretical model.

42. This discussion uses the male pronoun, given that the authors discussed in this work are all male. Though a number of female writers surfaced in the later Haskala, they were the exception that proved the rule: Haskala authorship was an almost entirely male enterprise. Readership, of course, is a more complicated issue, which is not discussed at length here; see notes 33–34 *supra* and the sources cited there.

to choose, does not play a strong role in choosing *which* texts to use, when to use them, how to juxtapose them with non-citative narrative or stylistic elements, and so forth.

It is in this sense, and perhaps only in this sense, that the recent return to strong authorial approaches to allusion is well taken. Pucci's discussion of Allan Pasco's work, which combines Structuralist systemic approaches with the statement that "the author is everywhere the controlling principle,"[43] his mention of the work of Gian Conte, who saw "a balance between reader and author within the system in which the allusion functioned,"[44] and his citation of the *Princeton Encyclopedia of Poetry*'s definition of allusion, with its characterization of allusion as "a poet's deliberate incorporation of identifiable elements from other sources" and the author as "a figure who intends the allusion in order to control tradition, demonstrate learning, or embellish meaning in his use of older literary material and whose intentions presuppose a model reader who is up to the literary, cultural, and aesthetic demands of the author,"[45] all seem to suggest the relevance of recent trends in allusion study to Haskala literature.

Ironically, Pucci's critique of these trends itself provides the best means of understanding how modifying contemporary approaches to allusion helps us build our own model. Briefly, though Pucci does argue for the allusion as a complicated interaction between text, reader, and the reading that the reader does, he essentially supports the "strong reader" approach, assigning "the power of allusive meaning to the work being read, not to the author who wrote it" and "privileg[ing] the reader in the process of unraveling allusive meaning and in the

43. Pucci 25. See Allan H. Pasco, *Allusion: A Literary Graft* (Toronto: University of Toronto Press, 1994), esp. 5, where Pasco differentiates between citative strategies of "imitation," "opposition," and "allusion," and 12–14, 17–18, where he discusses the varying roles of the author, reader, and text.

44. Pucci 23. See Gian Biagio Conte, *The Rhetoric of Imitation: Genre and Poetic Memory in Virgil and Other Latin Poets* (Ithaca: Cornell University Press, 1986), esp. 24–30, 48–50. Conte memorably writes (30) that "the author *establishes* the competence of the Model Reader, that is, the author constructs the addressee and motivates the text in order to do so."

45. Cited in Pucci 5–6.

function of that meaning."[46] His most significant contribution to the debate is his positing of an "allusive space" in which "the reading constructed by the full-knowing reader is . . . formulated" which is "not entirely textual, not entirely mental, but curiously both."[47]

Pucci characterizes the author as someone who "makes possible the allusion by the placement of words on a page, but . . . does not direct or control how the allusion is created or what sort of interpretations arise from it." In contrast to the New Critics, who locate intent within the author himself, or Structuralist critics, some of whom suggest the author's words activate a special sign that refers to the earlier text and possibly certain properties of interpretation, for Pucci, that author's "intentionality is solely causative and unmotivated. It is not, in other words, consciously and willfully directed at a specific interpretation. Specific interpretations are only implicit in the author's intent."[48]

Though Pucci's awareness that *in potentio* a practically infinite set of readerly interpretations exist may provide a useful reminder to those who completely discount the reader's active role, the abstract joys of this theoretical infinitude, with its links to postmodern playfulness,[49] may lead to insufficient consideration of the notion that those outcomes are generally shaped and drastically limited by historical and cultural circumstances. These circumstances may constitute the set of ways in which the interpretive outcomes available to both writer and reader are configured, thus allowing the author to display his virtuosity and "strength" in the *ways* he draws on a set of consensual, communal meanings of a particular text.

However, this begs a question generally unaddressed by most allusion theorists: is it possible to speak more practically about the system that configures these interpretive outcomes, which provides the "discrete, recoverable properties" spoken of by Carmela Perri? Is there

46. Pucci xi.
47. Ibid.
48. Pucci 41.
49. For example, see Pucci's characterization of the assumption of this readerly power (43) as "represent[ing] the purity of the moment in which allusive meaning is constructed, its limitlessness, the momentary burgeoning of potential meanings, all playing for attention and vying for consideration."

room for more concrete consideration than, say, Pucci's abstract "allusive space" or Ben-Porat's "intertextual system"?

Our answer necessitates a return to Tova Cohen's work on intertextuality in Haskala literature and the interpretive community of maskilic writers and readers she posits. Though Cohen has not framed it in these terms, it seems clear that a conceptual relationship exists between the maskilic interpretive community and the intertextual system it commonly employs. The expansion of that conceptual relationship— *the idea that any given interpretive community should, by definition, hew to a common intertextual system* —can naturally be expanded to systems and communities beyond the Haskala.

Expanding this conception requires a deeper look at Tova Cohen's sources, notably reading reception theory, exemplified by the work of Stanley Fish.[50] Though the term "reading reception theory" incorporates numerous approaches, many phenomenological in nature,[51] Fish

> pursues an argument which places meaning within the reader rather than in the text or in the literary or linguistic system. . . . [He] concerns himself with "descriptions of a succession of decisions made by readers about an author's intention; decisions that are not limited to the specifying of purpose but include the specifying of every aspect of successively intended worlds; decisions that are precisely the shape, because they are the content, of the reader's activities."[52]

50. See Stanley Fish, *Is There a Text in This Class?* (Cambridge, MA: Harvard University Press, 1980), esp. 161–173. Berger (132–152), in a very different context, also uses Fish's theory of "interpretive communities" in his discussion of Jewish law and authority. For other efforts in Jewish literary criticism to link similar materials to literary-theoretical constructs, see Band "Beginnings" 15–16; Susan Handelman, "'Everything Is in It': Rabbinic Interpretation and Modern Literary Theory," *Judaism* 35:4 (1986), 429–40; and Ziva Ben-Porat, "Hakore, hatekst, veharemiza hasifrutit," *Hasifrut* 26 (1978), 1–25.

51. For a survey of various approaches, such as those of George Poulet and Roman Ingarden, see the discussion in James Knowles, "Reader-Response Criticism," in Richard Bradford, ed., *Introducing Literary Studies* (London: Prentice-Hall, 1996), 559–567, esp. 560.

52. Knowles 562; citation from Fish "Interpreting the *Variorum*." For a full development and explanation of this process, see Fish's important essay, "Literature and the Reader," in *Self-Consuming Artifacts: The Experience of Seventeenth Century*

While such a statement once more summons the vision of an all-powerful reader, Fish's conception of "interpretive communities" dispels any such notion. Fish "argues that 'all meaning is communal and conventional' and that it is the 'interpretive communities' . . . who generate the protocols by which we read."[53] One way to understand this is to characterize a given interpretive community as establishing a certain set of ways, a certain system, for understanding and interpreting a given set of canonical texts.[54] Obviously, the same system can provide a number of different meanings to any given text—simply think of, for example, the fourfold exegetical model of Jewish textual interpretation, with its insistence on the equivalent validity of literal, homiletic, typological, and esoteric approaches to understanding an identical passage—but there is a bounded set of interpretations, comprising those that are canonically accepted and, to a lesser extent, those that are acceptable.

This is a vital point. In the Jewish tradition, a real distinction exists between three types of interpretation of a classical text: citation of an already canonically established interpretation (quotation, comparable to *traditio*), development of a new interpretation following traditional methodological approaches and established within communal ideological norms (a *khidesh,* comparable to *innovatio*), and the suggestion of a new interpretation that violates communal norms, either ideologically or methodologically (for example, within traditional Jewish communities, an interpretation based on emendation of the Biblical text, or, taking an ideologically fraught example, based on the assumption that the Exodus account had no historical basis).[55] Clear bound-

---

Literature (Berkeley, CA: University of California Press, 1972), 383–427, esp. 401–410, and Fish *Text* 2–4, 93–95.

53. Knowles 565; for more detail, see Fish *Text* 4–5, 7, 12–14, 171–173, 342–343.

54. Compare, *mutatis mutandis*, Fish's comments (*Self-Consuming* 402): where he suggests, borrowing from modern linguistic theory, that one can "'characterize a linguistic system that every speaker shares.'" Developing responses of the reader then "take place within the regulating and organizing mechanism" of the system (404). Fish's conception of these system-sharing communities is, in his words, "radically historical" (*Self-Consuming* 407). This model attempts to further concretize the historical approach Fish employs.

55. For a similar account, see Moshe Halbertal, *People of the Book: Canon, Meaning, and Authority* (Cambridge, MA: Harvard University Press, 1997), 8–9.

aries exist within an interpretive community beyond which interpretation simply cannot go.

The maskilim provide such an important illustration of this model because they were forced within the limits of their interpretive community, and to those limits. Reformers, they could not use the texts cherished by their interpretive community too subversively; if they did, first the *writers* would lose any coercive power, and second, the *texts* themselves might do so. That their subversive tactics nonetheless led to polemic success within the interpretive community in the short run, and at times a transvaluation or abandonment of that community in the long run, suggests that Fish's definition of the reader as "self-consuming"[56] can apply to the maskilim, too.

Seeing the maskilim as paradigmatic readers and writers using a given intertextual system belonging to a particular interpretive community illuminates both the strengths and weaknesses of Brian Stock's concept of "textual communities." In these textual communities, "the interpretation and knowledge of particular texts shape the behavior of religious groups and societies, inculcating group consciousness and solidarity."[57] Though Stock's work tends to focus on the role of this textual and interpretive knowledge in forming ritual and behavior, nothing in his work would deny expanding his ideas to the ritual of creating and decoding literary meaning, or writerly or readerly behavior. Given Stock's emphasis on creation of group consciousness and behavioral norms, though,[58] it is perhaps unsurprising that he focuses less on the potential subversion of those norms: using that group interpretation and knowledge of texts as a basis to call itself into question.[59] Haskala literature, by its very nature polemically subversive,

56. Fish *Self-Consuming* 3.

57. Knowles 566. See Brian Stock, *Listening for the Text: On the Uses of the Past* (Baltimore: Johns Hopkins University Press, 1990), esp. 12–13, 22–24, 37, 146–158.

58. See particularly Stock 152–153.

59. Intriguingly, Stock's original paradigm of the textual community was based on groups who themselves were "small, isolated, heretical, and reformist." Stock 151. Even in those cases, though, his model suggests that textual solidarity exists within the group itself *qua* group. Compare, however, Halbertal (5–6), who provides a sophisticated account of subversive activity within a "text-centered community."

illustrates that textual interpretation and knowledge can be used not only to ensure group solidarity, but to polemically sow dissent as well.

Viewed in light of reader-response criticism, we see the allusion theorists' arguments over the strength of an authorial or readerly presence are somewhat beside the point. Because all the authors are readers first: readers of classical Jewish texts and their midrashic and aggadic interpretations, in the case of the Haskala, or the alluding texts and their communally agreed-upon interpretations, more generally speaking. And in their joint readership, they share essentially similar systemic positioning. What distinguishes the writers is how they recontextualize those meanings and interpretations in new, sometimes revolutionary, polemic ways. Put another way, the first-order interpretations employed by maskilim aren't new, within certain limits; they're all agreed upon by both writers and readers.[60] They must be, or they would have no polemic function. It's the second-order interpretations, the ones resulting from the careful placing and ordering of those texts with their agreed upon interpretations, which provide authorial strength, that allow the writers to be of the interpretive community and simultaneously call it into question.

Before closing this discussion of the interpretive community, another of its features needs amplification. The somewhat blithe assertion that any given interpretive community should, definitionally, hew to a common intertextual system begs the question: how do actual, historical individuals participate in such a system? Can we differentiate between the system itself and actual participation within it?

Theorists of the interpretive community have tended to elide these issues, generally relying upon an ahistorical ideal reader; Fish himself remarks that "my reader is a construct, an ideal or idealized reader."[61]

---

60. Compare Fish's comment (*Text* 14) that while "the thoughts an individual can think and the mental operations he can perform have their source in some or other interpretive community, he is as much a product of that community (acting as an extension of it) as the meanings it enables him to produce. At a stroke the dilemma that gave rise to the debate between the champions of the text and the champions of the reader . . . is dissolved because the competing entities are no longer perceived as independent."

61. Fish *Self-Consuming* 406.

Though Fish seems aware of the possibilities of expanding his work into a historical mode,[62] he largely chooses not to do so, perhaps because he generally focuses on currently compelling textual interpretations, perhaps because of genuine doubt about the possibility of ever stepping outside his own interpretive community.[63] We may be able to suggest some possibilities, however, after looking at our particular case study, the Haskala.

Given the polemic nature of maskilic literature, and the centrality of allusion—particularly classical textual citation—to their polemic strategy, we may make two further assumptions. First, for these allusions to achieve their polemic effect, they must be understood and internalized by their audience.[64] Second, the corollary assumption, that the maskilic authors, if good polemicists, are aware of their audience's general levels of understanding of allusion.

Returning momentarily to the theoretical frame, one can characterize the distinction between the intertextual system of allusion shared by a given interpretive community and individual participation in that system as metaphorically similar to the distinction between *langue* and

62. This awareness is particularly evident in his discussion of differing historical responses to the same classic works of English literature. He writes, for example (*Text* 109–110), that "all aesthetics, then, are local and conventional rather than universal, reflecting a collective decision as to what will count as literature. . . . The history of aesthetics becomes an empirical rather than a theoretical study, one that is isomorphic with the history of tastes." He also notes (*Text* 171–172) that "interpretive communities grow larger and decline, and individuals move from one to another," clearly a historical process. This approach can be expanded to refer to collective decisions concerning, for example, interpretation of certain allusive texts within a given historical community, as we attempt to do here. This may in turn lead to efforts to constitute the ways in which meaning and interpretation worked within that community.

63. See Fish *Text* 356–371, esp. 361–362.

64. Fish (*Text* 325–326) suggests that an individual may recognize certain texts as *demanding* a certain type of interpretation, and that recognition is itself conditioned by the individual's membership in a given interpretive community. In other words, a given interpretive community will create ways understood by both readers and writers for readers to recognize and interpret texts, especially (as in our case) preexistent texts. Such activity is a necessary precondition for polemic works using allusion as a polemical strategy.

parole: the system consists of all of the textual interpretations, the conceptions, and accrued knowledge possibly "recoverable" (to use Perri's term) by the ideal scholarly reader and potentially drawn upon by the bookish author. The reader, however, draws upon said system only to the extent of his or her knowledge, training, and experience. For an author or a scholar to precisely identify any individual's level of knowledge, training, and experience is of course impossible; to speculate intelligently on the levels of an "interpretive sub-community," a targeted audience segment, is done constantly, whenever authors and scholars create work to be understood and accepted by a particular sub-community.

In very different contexts, Fish employs this terminology and hints at this idea, referring to "sub-communities" within "the literary community" that continually cause "the boundaries of the acceptable [modes of interpretation] to be redrawn."[65] Though his examples are all schools of literary criticism,[66] there seems no reason why this conception should not be expanded to historical textual interpretive approaches lived and practiced within other historical communities whose "literary criticism" might have been institutionally perceived as theology, political activism, or simply reading. Fish also refers to these groups' constitution as determined by "a structure of assumptions, of practices understood to be relevant in relation to purposes and goals that are already in place,"[67] and it can be argued that such a structure is historically constituted and thus recoverable and apprehensible to a certain extent.

A case in point? In this book's final chapter, by comparing Hebrew and Yiddish versions of Joseph Perl's *Megale Temirin*, we will see Perl make choices about maintaining, omitting, or altering certain allusions within his text. These choices are seemingly predicated on Perl's sophisticated sense of his Hebrew- and Yiddish-reading audiences' varying levels of textual knowledge.

Perl's strategies of differentiation suggest certain clues we should use to delineate these various "interpretive sub-communities": lan-

---

65. Fish *Text* 343.
66. Fish *Text* 343–344.
67. Fish *Text* 318.

guage choice in bi- and multi-lingual systems, and, crucially, the markers surrounding the allusions themselves. To what extent does the author feel it necessary to announce the presence and allusivity of these allusions? To what extent does the author feel the allusion needs explanation or expansion? If the degree to which a given allusion is extrusive or primary within a system is determinable (for example, as "Jesus" is extrusive within the contemporary American system, "Picasso" slightly less so, and "Aaron Halle-Wolfssohn," sadly, not at all), does internal evidence within the work indicate the allusion's importance to the work's central points?

Our comparative case, as well as the other works discussed, shows that a work can and often does contain allusions that indicate the author's overt awareness of differentiated knowledge levels; in such cases, we may choose to study these allusive texts as historical and practical operations within a particular intertextual system, the attempt of representatives of two sub-interpretive communities to meet in a specific manner. Alternatively, we may choose to view the author's relationship with the reader as with either a generically constituted "ideal reader" or with a historical, actual reader whose competencies approximate those of the "ideal reader." Again, the maskilim provide a useful paradigm, as they wrote for one another (or for their "ideal maskil") as frequently as for the traditionalists they attempted to convince. As such, current academic efforts to recover in-jokes and subtle allusions may well be historically replicating contemporary maskilic readerly activity in which substantial knowledge of canonical text and interpretation was brought to bear on the texts at hand.

Before concluding, one final point should be raised: a twin issue stemming from the individual cases of Yiddish and Hebrew literature, one that will not only prove important in our subsequent analyses, but can also serve to exemplify the methodological care that must be taken in dealing with the individual features of any given intertextual system. I will refer to the issue as "the potentiality of hyperallusivity."

Any analysis of classical texts in Yiddish belletristic work must acknowledge the difficulty that a recognized Hebraic (or "Semitic") component exists within Yiddish. Such Semitic words and phrases could be seen simply as usages of "standard Yiddish," and thus bear no additional ideological or thematic resonances. A similar difficulty exists in the case of Hebrew literature, where almost every word is a potential calque from a canonical source and thus a potential prooftext; with Yiddish, the danger is to consider every Semitic word as a potential prooftext.[68] Some attempt must be made to distinguish between potential and actual prooftexts.

Max Weinreich's approach to the question of Semitic components of Yiddish, foundational as it is, reveals the dangers of going too far in this regard. Weinreich brings numerous examples to show that the original sources of even the most common words of the Semitic component are from texts, notably the Bible, the Talmud, and the liturgy, though some come from the language of scholars, Hasidic groups, and the Kabbala, tightly linking Semitic components and classical texts.[69]

Clearly, as Dovid Katz suggests, any "text theory" that accounts for the entire Semitic component in Yiddish is flawed,[70] and Weinreich himself describes certain of these words as "neutralized" from their textual origins; that is, when a Yiddish writer uses these words and phrases, he is not necessarily calling on the textual sources from which those words and phrases may have originated.[71] However, an important distinction must be made between Semitic components of Yid-

---

68. It is also significant that, graphologically speaking, the different appearance between Semitic components/phrases and non-Semitic components *itself* calls attention to the foreignness of these components. Though the reader must, of course, subsequently compare the particular word or phrase in question to his or her own sense of the group of Semitic components in the Yiddish language, it is unquestionably true that, phenomenologically speaking, this difference is significant, and both readers and writers have treated it as such.

69. See Weinreich 1:222–231; 3:232–234. In fact, the search for textual sources of Semitic Yiddish phrases is even more difficult and demands even further scholarship, as Yehuda Elzet shows: see his "Shmuesn vegn hebreyish-yidish un yidish-hebreyish," in Yudl Mark, ed., *Yuda A. Yofe-bukh* (New York: Bibliotek fun YIVO, 1958), 236–256.

70. See Dovid Katz, "Hebrew, Aramaic, and the Rise of Yiddish," in Joshua A. Fishman, ed., *Readings in the Sociology of Jewish Languages* (Leiden: E.J. Brill, 1985), 85–103, 88–89, 92–95, 98–100, esp. 89.

71. Weinreich 1:248–249.

dish and a quote from the classical textual tradition, used by a Yiddish writer in a Yiddish work, of a "Semitic" phrase not part of standard Yiddish. In the latter case, it is clear that the citation is intended to be just that. Even Yudl Mark, whose maximalist approach theorizes that every word used in Yiddish by Yiddish speakers when speaking Yiddish is a Yiddish word, distinguishes between a word and a citation.[72] Similarly, if a Hebrew writer uses a citation self-consciously as a citation, the words employed are clearly more than linguistic building blocks.

By and large, this analysis focuses on citations of this second sort; attempts have been made, through consultation of dictionaries of Hebraisms in Yiddish, to identify those phrases and words under analysis that are and are not part of Yiddish's "standard Semitic component."[73] However, literarily speaking, it is eminently possible that even certain standard Semitic phrases within Yiddish, and any phrase from the Hebrew, can be "retextualized" when juxtaposed with a theme or topic that calls attention to its original textual source, thus allowing their textual origins to resonate anew with the reader.

For example, Weinreich notes that the phrase *shiker vi lot* ("as drunk as Lot") is a phrase that has passed into common usage among Yiddish speakers.[74] Arguably, the phrase has been neutralized; it could be used without any intent to refer to the Biblical circumstances that gave rise to the phrase, where Lot's daughters, after witnessing the destruction of Sodom and Gomorrah, inebriate him in order to have sexual relations to repopulate the earth (Gen. 19:30–38). Nonetheless, if an author were, for example, writing about incest, usage of the particular phrase might well bring its original meanings to the fore for either writer or reader.

72. Yudl Mark, "Vos iz a vort fun der yidisher shprakh?," in Mark *Yofe-bukh* 287–298, 294–295.

73. Dictionaries consulted include: Tsvi Nison Golomb, *Milim bilshoyni: hebreyish-yidishes verter-bukh* (Vilna: Yavorski, 1910); N. Perferkovitsh, *Hebreyismen in yidish* (Riga: 1931); Yisroel Shteynberg, *Hebreyismen in der yidisher shprakh* (Warsaw: "Nidershleyze," 1949); and Khaim Spivak and Yehoyesh [Shloyme Blumgarten], *Yidish veterbukh.* (New York: Yehoyesh, 1911). Phrases that are part of the standard Yiddish lexicon are identified as such in the footnotes.

74. Weinreich 1:227.

This approach can be employed in analysis of both Hebrew and Yiddish maskilic works. Obviously, any prooftext explicitly cited as such is not problematic, but even linguistically necessary or stylistically desirable phrases or words will be the subject of similar analysis if a thematic link can be established between the word or phrase and the subject. To relate this concept to our earlier points, retextualization, an act performed by the writer and recognized by the reader, takes advantage of mutual recognition that these particular words or phrases, used in this particular context, extrude from their surroundings and become semantically meaningful parts of an intertextual system constituted by a particular interpretive community, though they might not so extrude in other contexts. Our recognition of such retextualization is predicated on our abilities to understand the nature and constitution of that particular system, which in turn demands a certain degree of analytic and historical work. Though obviously impossible to position ourselves as a member of that system, we can at least try to understand the perspectives and positions of that system's members.

How we might do so, accompanied by some other final considerations, is the subject of this chapter's final section.

Contemporary Theory and Maskilic Allusion

Our discussion of allusion, augmented by reading reception theory, particularly the notion of interpretive communities, has so far reached the following conclusions. Though allusions partake of, and indeed serve as the paradigmatic examples of, an intertextual system participated in by both readers and writers, the writers in question are also readers positioned similarly to their audience. Their authorial strength stems from their organization and contextualization of these texts, themselves linked with certain interpretations communally understood by virtue of both parties' common membership in a given interpretive community. In some cases, writers can and do employ this system not merely to establish group solidarity (as Stock's model of "textual communities" might suggest), but to subvert and to manipulate the system, simultaneously weakening and undermining communal bonds. Such employment may lead to one of two possible conclusions: either these liminal writers become "self-consuming," to use Fish's term, or they create a "minor literature," differently understood, within the interpretive community. This second possibility will be discussed presently.

I have also suggested the system to be a maximalist institution, containing the set of interpretations available to the most learned and canonically experienced authors and readers. Those authors and readers are simultaneously aware of interpretive sub-communities with limited systemic access, those limitations dependent on differing levels of textual acquisition, language ability, educational status, and so on, as well as other factors characteristic of the given sub-community.[75] Writers may or may not choose to structure their works on levels consciously acknowledging recognized sub-communities; such information may be recoverable based on certain textual elements and markers. In practice, of course, individual writers themselves may have also been unable to take advantage of all the systemic elements; given the extensive scholarship of most maskilic writers, however, it seems reasonable to assume that a tremendous amount of the systemic information was available to them for their use. Biographical research can assist in determining these particular authorial levels of knowledge.

The final question is: to what extent can this system be reconstructed through historical and textual knowledge? And in the process of reconstruction, to what extent can we (a) determine the relative weight or extrusion of given elements within the system and (b) account for changes in those relative weights or extrusions in response to historical or geographical changes?

This chapter's second section discussed Cohen and Pelli's work on intertextuality within Haskala literature. This chapter's third section did not generally take issue with many of those two scholars' basic premises; rather, it attempted to explicate more precisely the theoretical structure

75. Obviously individual variation within the system also exists; however, writers since the start of the age of printing have been addressing the group, not the individual. The question simply is which group they are addressing, and how that group is defined and constituted.

that implicitly underlay those premises, a structure that in turn would suggest differences, modifications, and expansions of the Cohen/Pelli model.

Cohen and Pelli's implicit assumptions of "what the maskilim knew" are thus certainly acceptable as the bases for the material forming this intertextual system's backbone: the canonical Biblical, Talmudic, and midrashic texts, as well as their accumulated commentaries and super-commentaries, the corpus I have designated more generally as "classical Jewish texts." Cohen's reasonable and important reminder that mask-ilim and their readers would have been more strongly drawn to mate-rials also appearing in liturgy and daily life activities can be taken as one essential criterion for the "weighting" of certain systemic elements. Much of this book's work follows these assumptions, as mentioned earlier.

The Cohen/Pelli model requires certain modifications, though, modifications now clear in light of our refined theoretical model. While the broad intertextual system itself may remain essentially static throughout *Ashkenaz* during the entire Haskala period, and thus, in the broadest possible sense, constitute just one interpretive commu-nity, the unquestionable variation in concerns, traditions, ways of reading and of understanding in the period under discussion requires subtler distinctions—distinctions explicated more clearly by using our new concept of interpretive sub-communities.

Another framing statement may be useful: *just as an interpretive community is linked with and analogous to a given intertextual system, var-ious interpretive sub-communities are linked with and analogous to differ-ent weightings of the elements within that intertextual system.* Such differ-ent weightings, as mentioned, can be and are based on numerous conditions linked to the constitutive factors of that community: for example, the given sub-community's particular textual skills, if it is structured around education or knowledge, or the sub-community's particular historical development or contemporary political and cul-tural conditions, if it is structured around a geographical and tempo-ral locus. Such different constitutive methodologies naturally yield different types of sub-communities that must in turn be analyzed in different fashions.

Particular weightings are not static, naturally, since the sub-communities creating the weightings change over time in response to various internal and external factors, including, of course, the presence and effect of the literary texts produced by the sub-communities' authors themselves; though this book tends to present "snapshots" of given authors and sub-communities at a particular moment, the later snapshots include authorial reaction and response to their previous counterparts, and the previous systems within which they participated. Wolfgang Iser's notion of recursivity, in which "the recursive interactions between levels, components, and processes of the system result in a network of mutual interconnectedness, which keeps specifying their function by making them reciprocally select from and impinge on one another"[76] may be relevant here to describe the system's behavior itself as it moves through history. To describe the behavior of these interpretive sub-communities, their respective weightings of elements within the intertextual system, as unrelated to or uninfluenced by one another would quite simply be wrong, and describing these sub-communities' relation to one another is almost as important to our project as the operation of the system itself.

This work, then, attempts to focus on how these different weightings, these concerns about which texts to use and how to use them, about what is acceptable and polemically necessary usage and interpretation and what is not, play themselves out in these three writers' works. In doing so, these writers are presented both as strong authors and as significantly influenced in their textual choices by numerous factors related to their navigation (and subversive negotiation) of the various, overlapping interpretive sub-communities that they recognized and in which they lived.

Any discussion of the relationship of literature and history, especially one featuring writers' subversive use of texts, particularly canonical ones, to struggle against the general communal position must consider some of the current extant critical literature on new historicism and cultural materialism. While categorical efforts to characterize

---

76. Wolfgang Iser, *The Range of Interpretation* (New York: Columbia University Press, 2000), xii. See also 65, 85.

this work as new historicist, cultural materialist, or firmly located within any other particular theoretical schema are somewhat reductive—hopefully, this work's own methodological approach has been clearly spelled out somewhat clearly in these first chapters—certain insights gleaned from these movements allow us to make some final points about the subversive nature of maskilic activity and to focus on its essential paradox: that what started as a subversive, at best marginal endeavor ended up creating the foundational texts of modern Jewish literature.

New historicism, in the words of one of its most important explicators, claims "that every act of unmasking, critique, and opposition uses the tools it condemns and risks falling prey to the practice it exposes."[77] The conception of the apparently counter-hegemonic as, in some sense, conservative is useful for the analysis of maskilic works, both in light of current research stressing the Haskala's continuity with earlier movements and periods[78] and the notion that textual citation—one of the most important maskilic strategies—is, as has been noted, a classically Jewish strategy. Indeed, maskilic textual citation's subversive nature is matched—perhaps overmatched—by the essential conservatism of the dynamics of citation itself. Indeed, Stephen Greenblatt, one of new historicism's most important proponents, has written that "a gesture of dissent may be an element in a larger legitimation process, while an attempt to stabilize the order of things may turn out to subvert it."[79]

New historicist conceptions relating an individual's circumscription within a given system and his or her efforts to stretch that sys-

77. H. Aram Veeser, "The New Historicism," in H. Aram Veeser, ed., *The New Historicism Reader* (New York: Routledge, 1994), 1–32, 2.

78. See Chapter Three *infra* for bibliographical references.

79. Stephen Greenblatt, "Resonance and Wonder," reprinted in Kiernan Ryan, ed., *New Historicism and Cultural Materialism: A Reader* (London: Arnold, 1996), (excerpt) 55–60, 55–56. On new historicism's attraction to this "entrapment model" of ideology and power, "whereby even, or especially, manoeuvres that seem designed to challenge the system help to maintain it," see Alan Sinfield, "Cultural Materialism, *Othello*, and the Politics of Plausibility," in Ryan *New Historicism* 61–82, 70.

tem's boundaries are clearly illuminated in the allusive work of the maskilim, as seen above. However, this agreement on some basic principles does not make this book a work of new historicism. For example, the way in which "new historicists cold-shoulder approaches that claim to ground their accounts of literature in a factual historical reality that can be recovered and related to the poems, plays and novels that reflect it," while perhaps a strong statement of the new historicist position, is also a stronger claim than this work wishes to make.[80] That said, the Haskala is certainly an engaged literature, and the compelling arguments of the related approach of cultural materialism, which views "culture less as a self-determined system of representations to be appraised in subsequent detachment, and more as an arena in which the battle for the meaning of those representations continued to be fought,"[81] have important resonances for our study of the Haskala.

Raymond Williams's conceptions of hegemonic and counter-hegemonic culture, of base and superstructure, are well known and need no review here. However, we may fruitfully identify our intertextual system, and our interpretive community's readings and understandings, with the "central system of practices, meanings, and values" Williams refers to as the organized and lived "dominant effective culture." Indeed, Williams's characterization of hegemonic culture, which "constitutes . . . a sense of absolute because experienced reality beyond which it is very difficult for most members of the society to move, in most areas of their lives" and which depends on processes and modes of incorporation "of great social significance," especially, "[t]he educational institutions[, which] are usually the main agencies of the effective dominant culture," serving as "a major economic as well as a cultural activity"[82] is well reflected in any description and discussion of

---

80. Kiernan Ryan, "Introduction," in Ryan *New Historicism* viii–xviii, xiii. For an incisive defense of the position Ryan critiques, see Lee Patterson, "Historical Criticism and the Claims of Humanism," in Ryan *New Historicism* 92–102, esp. 92. Patterson also argues against "the New Historicist refusal to specify authorial intention"; for his eloquent and compelling defense of this position, see 101.

81. Ryan "Introduction" xv.

82. Raymond Williams, "Base and Superstructure in Marxist Cultural Theory," in Ryan *New Historicism* 22–28. Quote from 22–23.

the *lebenswelt* of Jewish textual practice, with its cherished educational institutions and the commodification of its scholars as marriage prospects.[83] Hardly coincidentally, the latter two concepts are also central topoi in Haskala literature.

Maskilic writing is by definition non-hegemonic; though Williams writes that "most writing in any period . . . is a form of contribution to the dominant effective culture,"[84] there is space in Williams's approach for non-hegemonic writing as well. Williams's conceptions of alternative and oppositional cultures, of "residual" and "emergent" forms, which encounter varying degrees of acceptance and hostility within the dominant effective culture,[85] can provide a neat theoretical lens through which to view the maskilic struggle for communal acceptance while simultaneously advocating change in hegemonic cultural norms.

Alan Sinfield's development of Williams's schema allows further definition and delineation of the sphere of maskilic marginality. Beginning with the assumption that "the same structure informs individuals and the society,"[86] Sinfield questions the possibility and nature of dissidence in a hegemonic culture:

> If we come to consciousness within a language that is continuous with the power structures that sustain the social order, how can we conceive, let alone organize, resistance? . . . The reason why textual analysis can so readily demonstrate dissidence[87] being incorporated is that dissidence operates, necessarily, with reference to dominant structures. It has to invoke those structures to oppose them, and

83. Compare also Stock 157 for a discussion of the role of "textually organized education of the members in the groups, which effectively transcended their backgrounds, professional allegiances, and antecedent beliefs" in his model of the textual community.

84. Williams 27.

85. Williams 23–25.

86. Sinfield 64.

87. Sinfield prefers the term "dissidence" to "subversion," explaining (80), "since the latter may seem to apply achievement—that something *was subverted* . . . 'dissidence' I take to imply refusal of an aspect of dominant, without prejudging an outcome." Emphasis author's. While Sinfield's distinction is useful, given this work's primarily authorial view of literary production, it will continue to employ the term "subversion."

therefore can always, ipso facto, be discovered reinscribing that which it proposes to critique.[88]

Sinfield also notes the obvious corollary: "in fact, a dissident text may derive its leverage, its purchase, precisely from its partial implication with the dominant."[89]

Sinfield's referents are entirely unrelated to the Haskala, but his words are highly resonant: naturally this group of marginal or oppositional writers is implicated in dominant cultural practices. The very legitimative strategies they employ, the very words they use, assure it. This is a subtler and more far reaching point than simply noting that early maskilim were often significantly more traditional in dogma and praxis than later critics (and contemporary opponents) perceived them to be: it locates their traditionalism in the very choices they made to express their reformist positions.

The maskilic position as thus walking the line in the most essential and deep-rooted sense between tradition and reform may suggest one last metaphorical paradigm: maskilic writers and similar groups may be seen as exempla of a new type of "minor literature" along the lines suggested by Deleuze and Guattari in their seminal essay on Kafka.[90] According to the two theorists' definition, of course, maskilic writing is hardly a minor literature: for them, a minor literature "doesn't come from a minor language; it is that which a minority constructs within a major language."[91]

However, reading their other definitions of the term, we cannot fail to be struck by their applicability to maskilic literature. The literature of the Haskala can certainly be described as one where "language is affected by a high coefficient of deterritorialization" and that

> everything in them is political . . . its cramped space forces each individual intrigue to connect immediately to politics. The individual concern thus becomes all the more necessary, indispensable, individual, because a whole other story is vibrating within it . . . [I]n it

88. Sinfield 67, 78.
89. Sinfield 78–79.
90. Gilles Deleuze and Félix Guattari, *Kafka: Toward a Minor Literature*, trans. Dana Polan (Minneapolis: University of Minnesota, 1986).
91. Deleuze and Guattari 16.

everything takes on a collective value . . . what each author says individually already constitutes a common action, and what he or she
says or does is necessarily political, even if others aren't in agreement.
The political domain has contaminated every statement. . . . It is literature that produces an active solidarity in spite of skepticism; and if
the writer is in the margins or completely outside his or her fragile
community, this situation allows the writer all the more the possibility to express another possible community and to forge the means for
another consciousness and another sensibility . . . the literary machine
thus becomes the relay for a revolutionary machine-to-come . . .[92]

Perhaps, then, Haskala literature, both in Hebrew and Yiddish, may
be viewed as a "minor literature" vis-à-vis the structure of Jewish language hegemony as a whole.

In doing so, we can build upon two previous attempts to critique
Deleuze and Guattari in a Jewish key. Chana Kronfeld writes that Deleuze and Guattari's narrative denies "not only [Kafka's] links to the
textual practices of Hebrew and Yiddish literature but also the very
possibility of producing such oppositional literatures in the major languages"[93] and refers to the impossibility of Hebrew as a language of a
minor literature for Deleuze and Guattari "because it is associated with
Zionism, mysticism, and a reterritorialization of language in the service
of a nation-building process—all ways in which a minority literature
replicates the formations of a hegemonic, major culture."[94] If we agree
with Kronfeld's assessment, and then subsequently decide to treat the
Jewish linguistic polysystem as its own system—as it is here—with its
own hegemonic major cultures and counter-hegemonic oppositional
cultures, it may be possible to suggest that a minor literature can be
created *within* rather than *of* these languages, a literature whose minority is based on stylistic strategies and strategies of textual usage.

92. Deleuze and Guattari 16–18, emphasis author's.
93. Chana Kronfeld, in "Beyond Deleuze and Guattari: Hebrew and Yiddish
Modernism in the Age of Privileged Difference," in Jonathan Boyarin and Daniel
Boyarin, eds., *Jews and Other Differences: The New Jewish Cultural Studies* (Minneapolis: University of Minnesota Press, 1997), 257–278, 261–264, 266–269; quote
from 268.
94. Kronfeld 268.

In this sense, we may also follow Ruth Wisse's thoughtful critique of Deleuze and Guattari, when she notes that "they themselves substitute imaginary political categories for those that Kafka knew to be actual and real."[95] Wisse's insistence on grounding Jewish writers within real historical and political contexts accompanied by her refusal to call Jewish literature a "minor" literature may in turn suggest the possibility of viewing Haskala literature as itself "minor" within a larger Jewish literary system.

There are other aspects of the theory of minor literatures that prove useful in understanding maskilic literature. Deleuze and Guattari's conception that aspects of Kafka's writing, such as sound, present both themselves and their own abolition,[96] can then be linked to ideas discussed earlier concerning subversive materials simultaneously implicated in the dominant effective culture's perpetuation, or the characterization of maskilim as self-consuming, constructing a transitional identity bearing within it the seeds of its own destruction. Doubters may look at Moses Mendelssohn's delicate balancing act, to take one example, and judge its success.

Other elements of Deleuze and Guattari's schema are also useful in understanding maskilic stylistic elements in general and allusion in particular. For example, the two theorists suggest that a minor literature contains "linguistic elements, however varied they may be, which express the 'internal tensions of a language' [called] *intensives* or *tensors* . . . the language of a minor literature particularly develops these tensors or these intensives."[97] Many types of linguistic elements could potentially act as such; Deleuze and Guattari do use extra-grammatical elements as examples, such as "terms that connote pain,"[98] and so elements like allusive texts, Semitic connotative terms in Yiddish, could presumably also serve as such indicators. That is, if the creators of a minority literature use language highly specifically to express their minority status or sensibility, by looking at how the maskilim use language, we can

95. Ruth Wisse, *The Modern Jewish Canon: A Journey Through Language and Culture* (New York: The Free Press, 2000), 85–86; quote from 86.

96. Deleuze and Guattari 6.

97. Deleuze and Guattari 22–23. Compare Kronfeld 269.

98. Deleuze and Guattari 22.

expand our sense of what a minor literature is to include groups whose identities are predicated not merely on race, ethnicity, or nationality, but also ideological or even aesthetic principles.

This discussion of the Haskala and literary theory has firmly followed the model of the hermeneutic circle first suggested by Friedrich Schleiermacher: the part has been used to understand the whole and vice versa.[99] The Haskala, as a particular case, has helped us examine the various literary subfields of allusion theory, reading reception theory, the theory of minor literatures, and, to a lesser extent, new historicist and cultural materialist approaches. As such, these case studies may be instructive as ways of reading texts that allow these various subfields to speak to one another in a practical manner.

Conversely, the lessons these various fields teach help us analyze the Haskala in a more refined and nuanced manner, ensuring that we focus both on the movement's significant continuities with traditional culture, not just its marginal status, and that we see it as a movement with both global continuity and local expression. These models may also provide sobering perspective when it comes to judgment, in an admittedly more subjective fashion, of the Haskala's goals and methods: to what extent were these methods more or less promising in light of the considerations these literary theoretical considerations provide on the methods themselves? Though the success or failure of the project of Jewish *modernity* had less to do with maskilic writing than its proponents hoped and many of its earlier critics asserted, as we will see in future chapters, the Haskala had an unquestioned effect on the production of modern Jewish *literature*. Though this book focuses on the movement itself, its goals, and its expression in its literature, not that literature's success or impact within a broader historical context, these questions remain vital for anyone interested in Jewish literature.

99. On the development of Schleiermacher's hermeneutic circle, see Iser 45–52.

Three   Historical Background

As the previous two chapters suggested, understanding maskilic usage of classical Jewish texts requires knowledge of the social, cultural, and textual circumstances in which these authors lived. To give the full and properly contextualized background of these circumstances would be to recreate their lives, a task impossible here. However, a certain amount of historical and social information, culled from many scholars' extensive research and appropriately organized for these purposes, will greatly aid our understanding of their work. This final introductory chapter is dedicated to illuminating the milieus in which these writers lived; more detailed biographical information on the individual writers themselves is provided in the chapters dedicated to their work. Before beginning, however, the cautionary words of Benjamin Harshav should be noted and remembered in an introduction to an analysis of a group of figures that stems, ultimately, from their maskilic affiliation:

> [T]he individual cannot be seen simply as an embodiment of an ideology. . . . To be sure, individuals often embrace ideologies or various beliefs, and some hold to them for a long time. Yet, in principle, it would be more appropriate to see the individual as an open semantic field through which various tendencies crisscross: some of them are involuntary and some he himself embraced and helped formulate, some become dominant and others merely hover in the field of consciousness.[1]

1. Benjamin Harshav, *Language in Time of Revolution* (Stanford: Stanford University Press, 1999), 53–54.

The Early Prussian Haskala (to the Mid-1780s): Moses Mendelssohn

For proponents of the Haskala in cities like Berlin and Königsberg in the early 1780s, the events of the past decades seemed to indicate that the dawning of a new age was at hand.[2] Politically, doctrines of individualism and notions of religious toleration, stemming from the Religious Peace of Augsburg (1555) and the Peace of Westphalia (1648)[3] and further developed by the English political philosophers Locke and Toland, began to gain currency in intellectual circles.[4] In some cases, this actually led to limited social toleration, at least in "semineutral societies" like freemasonry and certain intellectuals' social clubs.[5]

The eighteenth century was marked in general by a tremendous population growth, and the Jewish community was no exception; by century's end, 175,000 Jews lived in Germany and 70,000 in the Austrian empire.[6] While this still meant that Jews were less than one per-

2. Azriel Shohat has shown that the Haskala should not be viewed as a revolution; changes in the German Jewish community, such as adoption of non-Jewish customs and mores, an early interest in secular sciences and new methods of pedagogy, and a decline of traditional communal standards had been taking place decades before Mendelssohn's arrival in Berlin. See his *Im khilufei tekufot: reishit hahaskala beyahadut germania* (Jerusalem: Mossad Bialik, 1960), esp. 52–58, 72–122, 139–161, 174–241. See, however, Steven Lowenstein's remarks in "Two Silent Minorities: Orthodox Jews and Poor Jews in Berlin 1770–1823," *LBIYB* 36 (1991), 3–25, 4ff.

3. See Michael A. Meyer, ed., *German Jewish History in Modern Times: Volume I* (New York: Columbia University Press, 1996, hereafter *GJH* I), 69, 81–82.

4. See Michael A. Meyer, *The Origins of the Modern Jew: Jewish Identity and European Culture in Germany, 1749–1824* (Detroit: Wayne State University Press, 1967), 14–16 and Katz *Ghetto* 38–41, who also notes the important influence of the French Encyclopedists. See also Jacob Katz, "The Term 'Jewish Emancipation': Its Origin and Historical Impact," in *Emancipation and Assimilation: Studies in Modern Jewish History* (Westmead: Gregg International Publishers, 1972), 21–45, 22–29, 32–36.

5. For more on these clubs, some of which claimed Moses Mendelssohn as a member, see David Sorkin's excellent book *Moses Mendelssohn and the Religious Enlightenment* (London: Peter Halban, 1996, hereafter *MMRE*), 108–109 and Katz *Ghetto* 43–46, as well as his seminal article "Freemasons and Jews," in Katz *Emancipation* 147–158.

6. For a detailed demographic study of the growth and comparative slowdown of the Jewish community during the century, tied to an analysis of changing

cent of the population, their presence could be greatly disproportionate in various communities and principalities due to present and historical residency limitations.[7] The cities were growing, and residency requirements, while still onerous, were occasionally relaxed. This resulted in a steady "brain drain" of Jews from the country to the cities.[8] Additionally, for the first time, Jews were allowed to matriculate at university faculties of medicine: between 1724 and 1800, an estimated 150 to 180 Jews matriculated at university; 59 completed their studies with a doctorate in medicine.[9]

These phenomena reached their apogee in the "boom town" of Berlin, whose population doubled over the first half of the century, reaching 100,000 in 1755.[10] Berlin's Jewish community was recently reestablished (1671), and its numbers grew along with the city. New members came from many different regions, leading to a less entrenched sense of local tradition.[11] As Steven Lowenstein points out, "the peculiar social setting of the pioneering city made room for 'new men' in a way not possible in cities with a long standing urban patrician class like Frankfurt."[12]

Economically, the rise of the absolutist state,[13] particularly under the reign of the "enlightened philosopher" and absolutist ruler Frederick II (1740–1786), and the necessity for a bureaucracy to manage it,

residency restrictions, see Jonathan I. Israel, *European Jewry in the Age of Mercantilism, 1550–1750* (Oxford: Clarendon Press, 1989), 237–250.

7. Katz *Ghetto* 9–19 and Israel 149–163.

8. On urbanization, see Lionel E. Kochan, "La fin de la kehila: Forces sociales dans la société juive d'Europe centrale et orientale aux xviie et xviiie siècles," *Le société juive a travers l'histoire* I (1992), 531–563.

9. *GJH* 1:240–241.

10. The most important examination of contemporary Berlin Jewish life is Steven M. Lowenstein's *The Berlin Jewish Community: Enlightenment, Family, and Crisis, 1770–1830* (Oxford: Oxford University Press, 1994). Citation from 4.

11. See Lowenstein *Berlin* 13–16.

12. Lowenstein "Social Dynamics" 334; *Berlin* 19–20. See also Tsemach Tsamriyon, *Moshe Mendelson vehaidiologia shel hahaskala* (Tel Aviv: University Publishing Press, 1984), 20–23.

13. The standard work on the subject remains Selma Stern's monumental *Di preussiche Staat und die Juden* (Tübingen: J.C.B. Mohr, 1962–1975). See 2:3–105, 123–149; 3:1–27, 134–226, 364–422.

led to the development of a class of intelligentsia to which both Jews and Christians could belong, however unequally.[14] Simultaneously, traditional Jewish social structures were weakening due to state interference in communal autonomy;[15] one of many possible examples of this phenomenon was the increasing tendency for Jews to favor non-Jewish courts over Jewish ones.[16] A rising Jewish middle class shifted from usury to commerce, and a new elite of parvenu property-owning bourgeois Jewish entrepreneurs emerged, who, in accordance with mercantilist policy, were often given privileges and monopolies and exempted from many of the traditional legal restrictions levied on Jews.[17] These were not the "Court Jews" of the past, but a new class inextricably woven into everyday German economic life.[18]

14. See *GJH* 1:300 on the unequal prospects for Jews and non-Jews who entered the intellectual elite.

15. The absolutist attitude toward Jewish autonomy was complex: "[o]n the one hand, such autonomy contradicted the conception of the centralist state and its opposition to corporate bodies of any kind. On the other hand, the ruler did not wish to abandon this tried and tested machinery of taxation, which relieved him of the necessity to collect the taxes of each protected Jew individually." *GJH* 1:251. See also *GJH* 1:3–4, 264–265 for the inconsistent approach symbolized by Frederick II's legislation: for example, the "political testament" of 1752 contrasting with the "Jewry reglement" or Revised General Code of 1750. See Katz *Tradition* 84–106; David Sorkin, *The Transformation of German Jewry, 1780–1840* (Oxford: Oxford University Press, 1987), 42–44; Jacob Katz, "Rabbinical Authority and Authorization in the Middle Ages," in Isidore Twersky, ed., *Studies in Medieval Jewish History and Literature* (Cambridge, MA: Harvard University Press, 1979), 41–56.

16. See *GJH* 1:101, 253, 256.

17. See Shohat Chapter 2. See also *GJH* 1:269–270. For a detailed study of one such family, see the excellent article by Steven M. Lowenstein, "Jewish Upper Crust and Berlin Jewish Enlightenment: The Family of Daniel Itzig," in Frances Malino and David Sorkin, eds., *From East and West: Jews in a Changing Europe, 1750–1870* (London: Basil Blackwell, 1990), 182–201.

18. The main work on the development of Jewish economic life in the early modern period is Israel, *European Jewry*. See also *GJH* 1:128–134, 266–267, and Steven M. Lowenstein, "The Social Dynamics of Jewish Responses to Moses Mendelssohn (with Special Emphasis on the Mendelssohn Bible Translation and on the Berlin Jewish Community)," in Michael Albrecht, Eva J. Engel, and Norbert Hinske, eds., *Moses Mendelssohn und die Kreise seiner Wirksamkeit* (Tübingen:

Most of the social and cultural changes of the Haskala took place disproportionately among this Jewish upper middle class. "This was the group that tended to be most articulate, that first turned to new lifestyles, supported the Enlightenment and was most likely to convert to Christianity."[19] Though the Berlin community remained largely traditional through most of the eighteenth century, the pace of assimilation began to increase in the 1760s and 1770s among the elite, at least as far as "matters of cultural style" went.[20] As Steven Aschheim notes, "German Jewry never had a wide social base. Jews did not integrate into some abstract *Volk* but into the middle class, and they spent much of the nineteenth century internalizing the economic, ethical, and aesthetic standards of that class."[21]

These standards were set by contemporary non-Jewish Enlightenment figures like Lessing and von Dohm who, aside from preaching the possibilities of toleration and social coexistence that Jewish listeners found so appealing, articulated a social ideal of *Bildung*. This Enlightenment ideal "centered on the theme of self-improvement and referred to an integrated conception of 'rationality' and 'refinement' . . . most simply, *Bildung* implied the cultivation of a 'cultured' personality."[22] Many of these Jews engaged in the acquisition of material items and affected mannerisms in order to imitate their non-Jewish economic counterparts in the upper middle classes; examples include speaking French and playing the piano. We will see these mannerisms

---

Max Niemayer Verlag, 1994), 333–348, 334–337. On the political and financial power of the "Court Jews" as well as their relaxed religious observance, see Selma Stern, *The Court Jew* (Philadelphia: Jewish Publication Society, 1950), 177–207, 227–246; Israel 133–144; Katz *Ghetto* 29–30; and *GJH* 1:104–126.

19. Lowenstein "Orthodox" 3.

20. Lowenstein "Orthodox" 5, 9.

21. Steven E. Aschheim, *Brothers and Strangers: The East European Jew in German and German Jewish Consciousness, 1800–1923* (Madison: University of Wisconsin Press, 1982), 7.

22. Aschheim 7–8. See also Sorkin *Transformation* 13–33, 41–62, and Shulamit Volkov, "Juden und Judentum im Zeitalter der Emanzipation: Einheit und Vielfalt," in Wolfgang Beck, ed., *Die Juden in der europäischen Geschichte* (Munich: Verlag C.H. Beck, 1992), 86–108, 89–91.

satirized by Aaron Halle-Wolfssohn in his play, discussed in Chapter Five.[23]

Bildung can also be translated as "education," and it is thus hardly surprising to find the maskilim highly emphasizing the Enlightenment-inspired ideal of modern education: "The assumption [was] taken for granted, that in order to achieve the social integration that the enlightened community—Jews as well as non-Jews—had yearned for, it would be up to the Jews to undergo a process of education, in order to bridge the cultural gap that they believed had been created between them and their neighbors in the last few generations."[24] However, balancing was required between this "modern" education—ethics, philosophy, German and other non-Jewish languages—and traditional Jewish educational demands. The difficult position that these elites were thus placed in is exemplified in their choices of instructors. One of the main motifs of Wolfssohn's play, as we will see, is the question of which instructor—which educational tradition—is trustworthy.

On the one hand, the drive for social integration through educational refashioning meant that this nouveau riche class served as the patrons for the scholars and intellectuals of the Haskala. "A material socioeconomic basis was necessary before their intellectual circle could launch a movement to transform culture and society . . . such a basis existed in the Jewish community—in the homes of affluent merchants,"[25] which also led to at least some conservatism on the part of the maskilim.[26] Conversely, these Jews still wished to provide their children with, at the very least, the rudiments of a traditional education. The awkward result often meant the children of these parvenu elites received instruction in French and German by maskilim[27] and non-Jews side by side with Tal-

23. See Lowenstein *Berlin* 44–50 on issues of dress, language, and theater attendance. Speaking foreign languages was not merely a sign of culture, of course, but was a prerequisite for the bourgeoisie to participate in international business; see *GJH* 1:240.

24. Reuven Michael, "Hahaskala bitkufat hamahapekha hatsarfatit—hakets le'haskalat berlin'?," *Zion* 56:3 (1991), 275–298, 281.

25. *GJH* 1:298.

26. See Lowenstein "Itzig" 190; "Social Dynamic" 338–339; and *Berlin* 34–42.

27. In Meyer's wonderful phrase, the private tutorial "provided the laboratory for the implementation of enlightened ideas in practice." *GJH* 1:302.

mud tutoring by Polish rabbis.[28] Not all of the latter were roundly accepted: Azriel Shohat cites a contemporary source, Yaakov b. R. Meir, to the effect that many of the tutors were "youths who were trash and there was no essence to them . . . they know the meanings of the words in the Bible with difficulty . . . and they certainly do not know how the verses fit together, and there is no need even to mention the fact that they are asleep with regard to the Mishna and their eyes are closed as far as the Gemara is concerned." Not a ringing endorsement, certainly, though the obvious polemical bent of the piece generates a certain skepticism.[29]

Polish and other Eastern European Jews (known as *Ostjuden* to the Germans) were an actual and not uncommon presence in late eighteenth-century German urban centers: after the devastation wreaked on Eastern European Jewish communities after the Thirty Years War, to say nothing of numerous pogroms and massacres, a deluge of scholars from the area, particularly Poland, Lithuania, and Bohemia, tried to settle in Germany.[30] Since their residential rights in cities like Berlin were tenuous at best, dependent on employment status and the support of local citizens, they tried to make more permanent connections with the local Jewish families, including through marriage.

One prominent *Ostjude* who came to Berlin, Solomon Maimon, complained bitterly about his cool reception at the hands of German Jews, not because his intellect was disparaged (he was then considered to be one of the foremost expositors of Kant's philosophy), but because of his clothes, his manners, and, most damningly, his accent and language.[31] Though the German community established philanthropic institutions for the *Ostjuden*'s benefit, their attitude toward the Eastern Jews was hardly charitable. As far as the German Jews were concerned:

a generalized negative thinking prevailed . . . East European
Jews were held to be dirty, loud, and coarse. They were regarded

28. For examples, see Lowenstein "Orthodox" 8 and *Berlin* 50–53. See also *GJH* 1:184, 209–211, 256, 300–303 and Shohat 90, 94–95.

29. Shohat 134.

30. See *GJH* 1:98 on the immigration and the subsequent non-Jewish reaction.

31. For two excellent treatments of Maimon and the impression he made on Berlin Jewry, see Alexander Altmann, *Moses Mendelssohn: A Biographical Study*

as immoral, culturally backward creatures of ugly and anachronistic ghettoes. In large part this was a view formulated and propagated by West European and especially German Jews, serving as a symbolic construct by which they could distinguish themselves from their less fortunate, unemancipated East European brethren.[32]

Anti-*Ostjude* sentiment was often concretized in the form of anti-Hasidic sentiment. Though maskilic anti-Hasidic efforts were to reach their height only in the Galician and Russian Haskala, where maskilim and Hasidim actually lived side by side, the cultural dynamics of German Jewish emancipation still allowed a fair amount of hostility toward the movement. Accounts of Hasidic dogmas and practices had made their way into Germany by means of individuals such as Maimon,[33] and the resulting image of the unredeemed and unredeemable *Ostjude* and Hasid, common among non-Jews as well as Jews, may well have been part of the reason that despite efforts on the part of the richer Jews and the speeches of certain non-Jews, social equality was hardly forthcoming in any real sense:

> Between 1750 and 1800 legislation relating to the status of Jewry in Prussia and other German states stagnated. . . . Guided by reason and respect for science, the scholars exercised tolerance—while the Prussian king disregarded it in practice. This gaping discrepancy between

(Philadelphia: Jewish Publication Society, 1973, hereafter *MMBS*), 360–364, and Sander L. Gilman, *Jewish Self-Hatred* (Baltimore: Johns Hopkins University Press, 1986), 124–132. For a more general overview of Maimon, see Menakhem Gilboa, "Shlomo Maimon: sefer khaiei Shlomo Maimon—katuv bidei atsmo," in Nash 75–99.

32. Aschheim 3. The most detailed treatment of the *Ostjuden* is Aschheim's *Brothers and Strangers*, esp. 3–12. See also David E. Fishman, "A Polish Rabbi Meets the Berlin Haskalah: The Case of R. Barukh Schick," *AJSReview* 12:1 (1987), 95–121, 97, 108–112, for one account of how Mendelssohn's circle first grew interested in the "problem" of Polish Jewry.

33. See the section of Maimon's autobiography, written for a German-reading audience, which digresses into an anthropological account of Hasidic theory and practice: "On a Secret Society, and Therefore a Long Chapter," in Gershon David Hundert, ed., *Essential Papers on Hasidism* (New York University Press: New York, 1991), 11–24.

his attitude and the views of the "republic of intellectuals" was pivotal for the genesis phase of the Jewish Enlightenment.[34]

Indeed, despite the rise of a new Jewish elite, mercantilist export prohibitions and tariffs deprived many Jewish entrepreneurs of their living and led to widening economic stratification: most German Jews belonged to the lower economic classes, with about twenty-five percent in the middle classes and twenty percent well off. Of the total Jewish population in Germany, ten percent were vagrants and beggars (*Betteljuden*) with no fixed residence.[35] Occupational choices still required approval by Christian authorities.[36] But these realities in the Jewish and non-Jewish world were often explained away by newly emergent elites and their intellectuals. Jews tended to internalize this failure, feeling they were insufficiently *gebildetet*, that they had yet to acquire the proper education and mores—and even if they had done so, their Eastern European counterparts had not. Only once that took place would they fully be accepted into German society.[37]

Contemporary intellectual life also provided a combination of encouraging and discouraging features.[38] The flourishing of Christian Hebraism in Europe, a movement that had begun in Shakespeare's day but had reached its zenith in the eighteenth century, yielded greater familiarity with, and respect for, the Hebrew Bible and the people with whom that Bible was identified.[39] With the movement's

34. *GJH* 1:270. See also Michael A. Meyer, ed., *German Jewish History in Modern Times: Volume 2: Emancipation and Acculturation 1780–1871* (New York: Columbia University Press, 1997, hereafter "*GJH 2*"), 21.

35. See *GJH* 1:244–247; Sorkin *Transformation* 43; Lowenstein "Social Dynamics" 338; Israel 250–252.

36. See *GJH* 2:60.

37. For Mendelssohn's own negative reactions toward Eastern Jewry, see Isaac E. Barzilay, "Smolenskin's Polemic Against Mendelssohn in Historical Perspective," *PAAJR* 53 (1986) 11–48, 29–30.

38. The general sense of the age, with the philosopher-king Frederick II at its head, is wonderfully summed up by Eva Engel Holland in "The World of Moses Mendelssohn," *LBIYB* 36 (1991), 27–43, 28.

39. On Christian Hebraism, see Chapter One, as well as Israel 14–21, 54–56; Frank E. Manuel, *The Broken Staff: Judaism Through Christian Eyes* (Cambridge,

broader acceptance, "Jews and Christians were seen as participating in a common culture that reaffirmed, with all its attendant political implications, a shared humanity. The return to Hebrew language and scripture also offered a sense of universal relevance and an opportunity to develop literary-aesthetic sensibilities."[40]

The Jews were thus in a (relatively) privileged position: with the non-Jewish acceptance of the value of the Hebrew Bible, Jews could, at least theoretically, claim a superior hermeneutical position in Biblically based polemics, particularly since so many Christian interpretations did violence to the Biblical text's plain meaning—often for overtly or covertly polemical reasons.[41] Indeed, for a thinker and writer like Moses Mendelssohn, an essential problem in Jewish/non-Jewish relations was, as Edward Breuer puts it, "the fundamentally different way in which Jews and Christians read the Bible."[42] Mendelssohn's optimism lay in his belief that new conditions might allow those differences to be eradicated. Perhaps the changing political situation and

---

MA: Harvard University Press, 1992); and Robert Bonfil, *The Jews of Renaissance Italy* (Berkeley: University of California Press, 1994), 158–159, 162–167. See also Arthur M. Lesley, "Proverbs, Figures, and Riddles: The *Dialogues of Love* as a Hebrew Humanist Composition," in Fishbane 204–225, 211–213. On similarities between the Berlin Haskala and this earlier period in Italian Jewish history, see Isaac Eisenstein-Barzilay, "The Italian and Berlin Haskalah," *PAAJR* 29 (1960), 17–54. On the Christian Hebraists' attitude to Yiddish, see Dovid Katz, "On Yiddish, in Yiddish, and for Yiddish: 500 Years of Yiddish Scholarship," in Mark H. Gelber, ed., *Identity and Ethos* (New York: Peter Lang, 1986), 23–36, 23–28, and the annotated bibliography in Ber Borokhov, "Di bibliotek funem yidishn filolog," in his *Shprakh-forshung un literatur-geshikhte* (Tel Aviv: Y.L. Peretz Farlag, 1966), 76–136.

40. Edward Breuer, *The Limits of Enlightenment: Jews, Germans, and the Eighteenth-Century Study of Scripture* (Cambridge, MA: Harvard University Press, 1996), 20.

41. See Breuer *Limits* 21, 149. On the continuation of such polemical interpretations in the modern period, see Israel 81–84; Jeremy Cohen, "Medieval Jews on Christianity: Polemical Strategies and Theological Defense," in Eugene J. Fisher, ed., *Interwoven Destinies: Jews and Christians Through the Ages* (New York: Paulist Press, 1993), 77–89, 78–80; and Jacob Katz, "Judaism and Christianity Against the Background of Modern Secularism," in Katz *Emancipation* 111–127, 112–114.

42. *Limits* 159. See also Altmann *MMBS* 287.

the adoption of the principle of religious toleration would render polemics unnecessary. For the first time, the vision of a carefully balanced social and economic integration seemed attainable. "In their enthusiasm, some Jews saw it not merely as the dawning of a new age, but greeted it with something approaching messianic enthusiasm."[43]

However, even enlightened non-Jews admired not the contemporary Jews, but rather the Jews of Biblical times, and viewed the Talmud and rabbinic Judaism with scorn, believing Judaism too primitive and irrational to become a modern religion.[44] Jonathan Israel phrases it well, writing that "[I]dealizing the ancient Israelites, which now suddenly came into fashion, proved to be perfectly compatible with perpetuating anti-Semitic attitudes toward their descendants," and cites the Abbé Fleury's *Les Moeurs des Israelites* (1681), which argued that "ancient Israelite society had been the most admirable and excellent on earth, but the Jews had subsequently suffered an 'entire reprobation' and were now the most 'sordid, despicable people' known to man."[45]

Certain anti-Semitic Orientalists would cull rabbinic literature for damaging quotations to be decontextualized and leveled against contemporary Jews. The most notorious works of the genre were Johann Eisenmenger's *Entdecktes Judentum* (1700) and Johann Christoph Wagenseil's *Tela ignea Satanae* (1681).[46] Simultaneously, developments in Biblical critical scholarship threatened the Jew's picture of his own Bible. Numerous complaints were leveled against the rabbis both for

43. Michael A. Meyer, "Modernity as a Crisis for the Jews," *Modern Judaism* 9:2 (1989), 151–164, 151. See also Barbara Fischer, "Residues of Otherness: On Jewish Emancipation during the Age of German Enlightenment," in Dagmar C.G. Lorenz and Gabriele Weinberger, eds., *Insiders and Outsiders: Jewish and Gentile Culture in Germany and Austria* (Detroit: Wayne State University Press, 1994), 30–38, 30–31, and Jacob Katz, "The German-Jewish Utopia of Social Emancipation," in Katz *Emancipation* 90–110.

44. Israel 218.

45. Ibid. See also Sorkin *Transformation* 23 and Meyer *Origins* 50.

46. On these and other similar books, see Gilman 71–72; *GJH* 1:157; Altmann *MMBS* 216; Meyer "Modernity" 156; and Edward Breuer, "Rabbinic Law and Spirituality in Mendelssohn's *Jerusalem*," *JQR* 86:3–4 (1996), 299–321, 302.

adding accretions to a pristine and pure Biblical Judaism and for using hermeneutical methods that seemed to do violence to the Biblical text's plain meaning. The contemporary German view of rabbinic Jewish interpretation may have been best expressed by Reimarus in his *Wolfenbuttel Fragments* (of which Mendelssohn was well aware): "'they invented a kind of allegorical, mystical, symbolic, indeed kabbalistic interpretation of scripture.' This constituted an art of turning anything at all into anything at all, 'of proving from Scripture whatever one wished.'"[47] As we have seen in the first chapter, these developments had begun some time ago, but were reaching critical mass at the time of the beginning of the Haskala.[48]

These negative trends did not permanently discourage the Jews: rather, they were seen merely as an obstacle to be overcome on the way to a universal society. The maskilim firmly believed in the Enlightenment principles of the efficacy and cardinal importance of reason. In Mendelssohn's words, "Reason's house of worship has no need of locked doors. It does not have to guard anything inside nor does it have to prevent anyone from entering."[49] If Jews could prove their tradition and their texts—including the parts rejected by non-Jews—to be reasonable, that should be sufficient for non-Jews to recognize the rightness of their claim. The intellectuals, led by Mendelssohn, thus naturally attempt to present the entire classical Jewish canon in a manner where it can be perceived as reasonable.[50]

47. Quoted in Allan Arkush, *Moses Mendelssohn and the Enlightenment* (Albany: State University of New York Press, 1994, hereafter *MME*), 155.

48. For more on the literalist trends in German Biblical scholarship in and leading up to the eighteenth century, see Hans W. Frei, *The Eclipse of Biblical Narrative: A Study in Eighteenth and Nineteenth Century Hermeneutics* (New Haven: Yale University Press, 1974), esp. 7–9, 18–19, 37–39, 55, 107–110, 165–166.

49. Cited in Alexander Altmann, "Introduction," in Moses Mendelssohn, *Jerusalem*, trans. and ed. Allan Arkush (Hanover, NH: University Press of New England, 1983, hereafter *Introduction*), 5. Similarly, in a letter to Elkan Herz on July 22, 1771, Mendelssohn also wrote: "[B]lessed be the Lord, who gave us the Torah of truth. We have no principles [*ikarim*] that are contrary to, or above, reason." *JubA* 16:150; translation from Altmann *MMBS* 249.

50. For one account of Mendelssohn's "reasonable understanding of Judaism," see Sorkin *MMRE* 13ff. See also Breuer *Limits* 116.

This strategy, as we will see, consists of reinterpretation, selective citation, and rehabilitation, the last strategy particularly of the rabbinic canon.[51] This does not mean Mendelssohn felt the current state of rabbinic Judaism was optimal, as we will see; to a certain extent, he viewed certain perceived irrationalities of rabbinism as an "accretion" on a "pure" or "ideal" Judaism. This being said, the traditionalist Mendelssohn was a strong defender of rabbinic Judaism and certainly spared no effort to polemically rehabilitate the rabbis into a state where they would no longer be perceived as a corruption of pure Judaism, but rather its organic continuation. Mendelssohn's ideological and rationalist usage of texts sets the tone for similar maskilic strategies throughout the Haskala.

It is no coincidence, then, that Mendelssohn was the avatar of rationalism—the leading exponent of the rationalist Leibnizian/Wolffian philosophy.[52] It is also hardly coincidental that Mendelssohn's views overlapped with those of the Religious Enlightenment, a contemporary non-Jewish movement whose proponents agreed that certain limits to rational explanation existed, but all else was subordinated to reason.[53] Sorkin writes that the movement sought "a way to reconcile

51. Compare Pelli *Age* 54–59, which discusses the positive maskilic attitude toward the Talmud, and his suggestion of their motivations on 70–72.

52. For an excellent and detailed discussion of the similarities between late eighteenth-century Leibnizian/Wolffian rationalist philosophy and Mendelssohn's own work, see Arkush *MME*, particularly chapters 1–4; Daniel O. Dahlstrom, "Introduction," in *Moses Mendelssohn: Philosophical Writings* (Cambridge: Cambridge University Press, 1997, hereafter *PW*), ix–xxxix, xxv–xxx, and Altmann *MMBS* 28–32.

53. This is the thesis of Sorkin's excellent *Moses Mendelssohn and the Religious Enlightenment*. See also David Sorkin, "The Case for Comparison: Moses Mendelssohn and the Religious Enlightenment," *Modern Judaism* 14:2 (1994), 121–138; Michael Brenner's review in *JJS* 48:1 (1997), 178–180; and Allan Arkush's review in *Modern Judaism* 17 (1997), 179–185. Arkush's critique, that "[t]o claim, as Sorkin does, that Mendelssohn conceived of philosophy primarily as an instrument for articulating the contents of Jewish faith is greatly to underestimate the role he assigned to philosophy in matters pertaining to revealed religion" (185) is well taken, but the picture Arkush then creates of a Mendelssohnian deist sacrificing revelation on the altar of reason seems to me to be overstated. See the discussion on Mendelssohn as traditionalist in Chapter Four, esp. n.10.

faith and reason by enlisting substantial portions of Enlightenment thought to support, renew, and reinvigorate belief";[54] this seems to be as precise a description of the Mendelssohnian project as any. And it is thus hardly surprising that Mendelssohn professed himself unable to understand the reason-crushing work of Kant,[55] and that the religious emotionalism of a Schleiermacher or a Schlegel, the latter of whom would marry his converted daughter, was beyond him.[56] Mendelssohn as an individual—and the maskilim as a group—refused to understand this. They passionately clung to rationalism as their best and only hope; their ideological assumptions, and the resulting literature, was thus rationalist. We can thus also assert that their usage of classical texts is rationalistic, ideological, and purposeful.

Continuities certainly exist between Mendelssohnian textual interpretation and traditional Jewish interpretive schemas.[57] Sorkin describes the transition to the Haskala by noting that "when the Haskala emerged as a public movement in the last third of the eighteenth century (1770s) it borrowed many forms and categories from the Enlightenment, but its contents were largely derived from medieval Jewish philosophy and biblical exegesis."[58] These schemas, however, assumed varying relationships to textual practices and models in vogue within contemporary Ashkenazic Jewry.

54. Sorkin MMRE xxi.

55. On Mendelssohn's meeting with Kant, which evocatively illustrates the dynamics of the Enlightenment, see Paul Mendes-Flohr and Jehuda Reinharz, eds., *The Jew in the Modern World* (New York: Oxford University Press, 1995), 61. Before Kant enters the classroom, his students jeer Mendelssohn; they behave respectfully only when Kant treats Mendelssohn as a friend.

56. Mendelssohn, toward the end of his life, did express doubt that all metaphysical questions could be answered through reason. This shift was partially influenced by Kant and Jacobi (see Arkush *MME* 69–77) but it also, I believe, resulted from the pressure of political realities. See Arkush *MME* 87–88.

57. See Breuer *Limits* 131 and Pelli *Age* 33–38, as well as the discussion of Mendelssohn's Bible translation in Chapter Four.

58. Sorkin *MMRE* xxi–xxii. See also Halivni 28–29 and David Sorkin, "Jews, the Enlightenment, and Religious Toleration—Some Reflections," *LBIYB* 37 (1992) 3–16, 10–11, as well as the German version: "Juden und Aufklärung: Religiöse Quellen der Toleranz," in Beck 50–66, 59.

For example, many of the maskilic Jewish influences came not from Ashkenaz, but rather from Spanish Jews and their descendants. The Sephardic model, corporealized for German Jewry by Portuguese communities in Amsterdam and Hamburg, provided the maskilim with a seductive example of a community that never separated science, philosophy, art, and traditional values,[59] and the Andalusian influence on maskilic belletristic and philosophical works is clear.[60] As Sorkin notes, the Andalusian tradition's position on rationalism was similar to that of the religious Enlightenment:

> The emphasis on practical knowledge and the repudiation of a contemplative ideal, the endorsement of heteronomy and resistance to historicism, as well as the defense of rabbinic exegesis and the Masoretic text of the Bible were formative ideas [Mendelssohn] maintained throughout his career. Whether addressing philosophy, exegesis, or politics, these ideas allowed Mendelssohn to reconcile faith and reason by rearticulating the Andalusian tradition of practical rationalism in a manner comparable to the Protestant theological Wolffians of the second quarter of the eighteenth century.[61]

59. *GJH* 1:243 and Sorkin *MMRE* xxii. On the seductiveness of the "Golden Age of Spain" for the maskilim, see Eliezer Schweid "Impact" 389–391 and Ismar Schorch, "The Myth of Sephardic Supremacy," *LBIYB* 34 (1989), 47–66. For a more complex and nuanced view, which shows the maskilic usage of the period as evidence for both the possibilities of integration and its failures, see Shmuel Feiner, "Sefarad dans les Representations Historiques de la Haskala—entre Modernisme et Conservatisme," in Esther Benbassa, ed., *Mémoires Juives D'Espagne et du Portugal* (Paris: Centre Nationale du Livre, 1996), 239–250. See also Shmuel Werses, "Geirush sfarad beaspaklaria shel hahaskala," *Peamim* 57 (1994), 48–81, and Mordechai Breuer, "'Hashpaa sfardit beashkenaz besof yemei-habeinayim uvereishit haet hakhadasha," *Peamim* 57 (1994), 17–28.

60. The influence of Andalusian poetry on maskilic poetry is an important subject that awaits full explication. On Andalusian poetry and its usage of classical Jewish texts, see Ezra Fleischer, "The Gerona School of Hebrew Poetry," in Isidore Twersky, ed., *Rabbi Moses Nachmanides (Ramban): Explorations in His Religious and Literary Virtuosity* (Cambridge, MA: distrib. Harvard University Press, 1983), 35–49, as well as Dan Pagis, *Hebrew Poetry of the Middle Ages and the Renaissance* (Berkeley: University of California Press, 1991), 12–13, 31, 35, 62.

61. Sorkin *MMRE* 148.

Indeed, "Mendelssohn's ends . . . assumed an essential harmony between the Andalusian tradition and Wolffian philosophy."[62] For example, Mendelssohn located his refined and reformulated Wolffian/Leibnizian positions on God's existence fairly well within medieval Jewish philosophical positions, though he was occasionally willing to "depart from the line of classical Jewish philosophy" to make his views accord with Leibniz.[63] Mendelssohn also drew heavily on some of these Andalusian figures—Maimonides, Nahmanides, Ibn Ezra, and Judah HaLevi—in his own work.[64] Mendelssohn also politicized this position of limits to rational inquiry, using its implications to preach tolerance of belief.[65] These positions, while locatable within the vast continuum of Jewish interpretive schema, were not organic continuations of current practice.

This is not to say, however, that "current practice" was not changing even before Mendelssohn began to write. In the medieval period, Ashkenazic Talmud study, viewed as significantly more important than study of the Bible,[66] shunned the synthesist, universalist model of medieval Sephardic Jewish philosophy; religious philosophy and the secular sciences, still integrated as they were within Christian scholastic doctrine, found no entry into Ashkenazic academies.[67] Ashkenazic Talmudism, rather, was prone at times to excessive *pilpul*, a hair-splitting anti-literalist approach, as well as an interest in mysticism and Kabbala.[68] However, by the 1730s, a methodological split had occurred be-

62. Sorkin *MMRE* 24. See also *MMRE* 155 and Breuer *Limits* 19.

63. See Alexander Altmann, "Moses Mendelssohn's Proofs for the Existence of God," in his *Essays in Jewish Intellectual History* (Hanover, NH: University Press of New England, 1981), 119–141, 122–126.

64. Sorkin *MMRE* xxiii; see also Chapter Four, esp. n. 132. On maskilic views of Judah HaLevi, see Shmuel Werses, "Hameshorer R' Yehuda Halevi beolama shel hasifrut haivrit hakhadasha," *Peamim* 53 (1993), 18–45.

65. See Arnold Eisen, "Divine Legislation as 'Ceremonial Script': Mendelssohn on the Commandments," *AJSReview* 15:2 (1990), 239–267, 254–256.

66. A shift in priorities once more privileging Bible study would be a mainstay of maskilic polemic: see Halbertal 127–131.

67. See *GJH* 1:16–17, 36–37, 53.

68. See *GJH* 1:56. For more on *pilpul*, see Sorkin *Transformation* 47–48; Peretz Sandler, *Habiur letora shel Moshe Mendelson vesiato: hithavahuto vehashpaato* (Jeru-

tween German and Polish Talmudists, where Germans would sometimes favor emending Talmudic text rather than using *pilpul*,[69] making

> a concerted effort, using rigorous hermeneutic rules, to examine
> these materials in order to derive their meaning . . . the tendency
> [also] arose in the eighteenth century to deal with "metahalachic"
> and general scientific disciplines. This overcoming of the earlier dis-
> tance from science and philosophy . . . is probably also bound up
> with the circumstance that, with the rise of humanism, the sciences
> had emancipated themselves from Christian theology.[70]

As such, Mendelssohnian and maskilic changes already had their
roots in some changing mores in German Jewish intellectual life. Another example of changing mores was the eighteenth-century German
Jewish approach to mystical and esoteric interpretative schema, which
had been part of German Jewish textual study for centuries. Apogees included the twelfth- and thirteenth-century circle of Hasidei Ashkenaz,[71]
and then again in the sixteenth century, where the previously esoteric
Kabbala began to emerge into the public sphere. Lurianic Kabbala grew
increasingly popular in the late seventeenth century in urban centers like
Vienna and Frankfurt, and its influence continued well into the eighteenth century, illustrated by the general popularity of mystical and pietistic customs.[72]

---

salem: Rubin Mass, 1984), 3–4; and Halivni 36–43. For more specific information
on the rejection of certain types of literalist exegesis at the time, see Breuer *Limits*
72. See also Alexander Altmann, "Moses Mendelssohn as the Archetypal German
Jew," in Jehuda Reinharz and Walter Schatzberg, eds., *The Jewish Response to German Culture: From the Enlightenment to the Second World War* (London: University Press of New England, 1985), 17–31, 22–23. See also the perceptive essay of
Amos Funkenstein, *Tadmit vetodaa historit* (Tel Aviv: Am Oved, 1991), 189–198,
esp. 192–194.

69. *GJH* 1:214–218.

70. *GJH* 1:234.

71. On Hasidei Ashkenaz, see Joseph Dan, *Iyunim besifrut khasidei ashkenaz*
(Ramat Gan: Masada, 1975), and idem., *Gershom Scholem and the Mystical Dimension of Jewish History* (New York: New York University Press, 1988), 92–100, 166–
168.

72. *GJH* 1:226–228. See also Dan *Gershom Scholem* 236–237, 248 and Israel
78–80.

Sabbateanism, arguably the ultimate outgrowth of Lurianic Kabbala, affected Germany less than elsewhere, despite limited public opposition. Sabbatai Zevi's failure, however, led to the wide discrediting of the Kabbala among German Jews and a "kind of traumatic anxiety" about the repetition of such mystical leadership, though Sabbatean and Frankist circles and periodicals appeared throughout the eighteenth century.[73] Communal anxiety was unquestionably increased by the Emden-Eybeschuetz controversy, where two of the greatest contemporary Ashkenazic rabbis clashed over amulets with potentially Sabbatean inscriptions.[74] By Mendelssohn's early years, then, interest in Kabbala still existed, but it was waning. As Altmann succinctly phrases it: "The subtle impact of the Enlightenment, which went hand in hand with the slow rise of an industrial age and the breakdown of ghetto exclusiveness, was bound to corrode the mystical spirit."[75]

Mendelssohn's approach to mysticism displays, in microcosm, his general approach to the defense and rehabilitation of the Jewish canon:

> In conversation with enlightened non-Jews, Mendelssohn defended kabbalistic philosophy in its pristine essence as actually quite reasonable.[76] Only when it was adulterated by taking the allegory literally

73. See *GJH* 1:227–233; quote from 233. On links between Lurianic Kabbala and Sabbateanism, see Dan *Gershom Scholem* 291–295 and Tsamriyon 17.

74. For more on the controversy, see *GJH* 1:258–259 and Chimen Abramsky, "The Crisis of Authority within European Jewry in the Eighteenth Century," in Siegfried Stein and Raphael Loewe, eds., *Studies in Jewish Religious and Intellectual History* (University, Alabama: University of Alabama Press, 1979), 13–28, 15–17.

75. Altmann *MMBS* 11. See also Dan *Gershom Scholem* 324 and Shmuel Werses, *Haskala veshabtaut: toldotav shel maavak* (Jerusalem: Zalman Shazar, 1988). See also Gershom Scholem's seminal article, "Redemption Through Sin," in his *The Messianic Idea in Judaism and Other Essays in Jewish Spirituality* (New York: Schocken Books, 1971), 78–141.

76. Mendelssohn may have been drawing on the example of some of the towering rabbinical figures of Jewish history, such as Joseph Caro and the Gaon of Vilna, who combined sound rationalism and mysticism in their own lives and works. I am grateful to Dr. Dov-Ber Kerler for this suggestion. For an important discussion of the links between literalist and mystical interpretative schemas in Jewish history, see Elliot R. Wolfson, "Beautiful Maiden Without Eyes: *Peshat* and *Sod* in Zoharic Hermeneutics," in Fishbane 155–203, esp. 155–159, 167–169, 177–178.

and heaping on imaginative commentaries did it grow into nonsense and fanaticism. His attitude to the Talmud was similar: when studied in the proper manner it was beneficial.[77]

As we will see, later maskilim, who feel themselves to be less on the defensive, will not take quite so moderate an approach.

Of course, impetus for Mendelssohnian change resulted not merely from trends in textual study, but the real life praxis of the dictates of these texts. Scholars like Shohat and Sorkin have focused on contemporary ethical literature (*musar*) to distinguish between ideals and reality: "the *musar* tradition revealed the decay of Jewish society in Germany in the seventeenth and eighteenth centuries . . . In pointing up the shortcomings of the reality, and in suggesting reforms, the musar literature articulated the ideas and themes which the Haskala was to elaborate systematically at the end of the eighteenth century."[78] Indeed, Sorkin frames the role of the Haskala, at least in part, as a radicalization of the ideas in the *musar* literature.[79]

Textually speaking, this first stage of optimism and frustration, exemplified by Moses Mendelssohn and the early contributors to the seminal Hebrew journal *Hameasef* ("The Gatherer," founded Königsberg, 1783), is symbolized by a greater conservatism and a relative fidelity to normative rabbinic Judaism. Much of Mendelssohn's project was rehabilitative: even in his Hebrew works, he was concerned with the negative perceptions of the Jewish community and Jewish texts, and attempted to present them in a manner allowing them to harmonize with the highest tenets of the German Enlightenment. The stage is characterized by mannered, cautious behavior and writing: the Jews, flushed with the possibility of equal and active participation for the first time in modern history, were unwilling to do anything that might rock the boat, even though the injustices in certain spheres of social life were still manifest.[80]

77. Meyer *Origins* 21.
78. Sorkin *Transformation* 45–46, quote from 46.
79. Sorkin *Transformation* 54. See also Sorkin *MMRE* 33.
80. On this harmonization, and the subsequent "expectation of imminent emancipation" aroused in the late 1780s and 1790s, see David Sorkin, "Preacher,

Toward the 1790s:
Radicalization, Assimilation, and Wolfssohn

Obviously, many similarities exist between Mendelssohn's milieu and Wolfssohn's; both writers occupy roughly the same geographical milieu and produce major works within a decade of each other. As a result, much of the background in the previous section pertains here as well. Within a few short years, however, sufficient changes occur to warrant a shift in analytical perspective.

Two factors, the death of Moses Mendelssohn in 1786 and the French Revolution, cause a radical shift in the direction of the Haskala.[81] After the French Revolution, questions of equal Jewish participation in every sphere of social life were being framed for the first time not as requests for the extensions of privileges, but demands for rights.[82] German maskilim saw "that the Jews of France received total emancipation, not as the result of the educational activity of the Haskala movement, and after

---

Teacher, Publicist: Joseph Wolf and the Ideology of Emancipation," in Malino and Sorkin 107–125, 118–119; David Sorkin, *The Berlin Haskalah and German Religious Thought: Orphans of Knowledge.* (Portland, OR: Valentine Mitchell, 2000), 6–9; and Breuer *Limits* 124–131.

81. See Lowenstein *Berlin* 5–6, 70–103.

82. On the French Revolution as the demarcation point for the greater radicalism of the Berlin Haskala, see the important article by Michael, "Hahaskala," as well as Avraham Shaanan, *Iyunim besifrut hahaskala* (Merkhavia: Sifriyat Poalim, 1952), 57–132, esp. 64–82, and Chimen Abramsky, "La révolution française dans les sources hébraïques," in Mireille Hadas-Lebel and Evelyne Oliel-Grausz, eds., *Les juifs et la Révolution française: Histoire et mentalités* (Paris: E. Peeters, 1992), 229–236. For a detailed examination of the wide variety of Jewish literary responses to the French Revolution throughout Europe, ranging from ardent support to virtual disinterest, see Shmuel Werses, "Hamahapekha hatsarfatit beaspaklaria shel hasifrut haivrit," *Tarbiz* 58:3–4 (1989), 483–521. See also Delphine Bechtel, "La Haskalah berlinoise," in Jean Baumgarten, Rachel Ertel, Itzhok Naborski, Annette Wievorkia, eds., *Mille ans de cultures ashkénases* (Paris: Liana Levi, 1994), 354–357, and Moshe Katan, "Dmut hamahapekha beshira haivrit shel yehudei tsarfat beshilhei hamea hayud khet uvereishit hamea hayud tet," *Mahut* 19 (1987), 37–45, esp. 39. For a full listing of all materials on the French Revolution appearing in *Hameasef*, see Janine Strauss, "Yakhasam hashlili shel hamaskilim lemahapekha hatsarfatit," *KOMI* 10B1 (1990), 225–230.

they proved themselves worthy of it, but as the result of a social revolution. They realized that in Prussia, there was no possibility of such a revolution: still they were able to expect similar changes."[83] And for a few years, it seemed as if they might actually receive them. For example, David Friedländer, Prussian Jewry's unofficial leader after Mendelssohn's death, was able to demand and receive the withdrawal of both the body tax (1787) and the doctrine of collective responsibility (1792) from the Prussian government.[84]

Maskilic writers of the period became more willing to take greater literary risk, reflecting the "revolution of rising expectations," to use Steven Lowenstein's wonderful term.[85] In the 1780s, as we have seen, classical texts were used as part of an overarching project of culturally conservative rehabilitation and presentation: it was culturally defensive, whether intended for Jewish or non-Jewish audiences. In the 1790s, these writers' greater radicalism allowed a bit less confinement. They expressed this freedom through engagement in internal dissent, by taking the offensive. As we will see in Wolfssohn's play with its scathing portrait of a hypocritical Hasid, the maskilim of the 1790s are just as concerned with attacking what they perceive to be false and perverted types of Jewish existence, particularly aspects of Eastern European Judaism, as they are with establishing an ideal Jewish existence—perhaps more so.

These attacks against other Jews were primarily still aimed at a Jewish audience; the maskilim were not quite comfortable enough in German society to provide much ammunition to the anti-Semitic forces unquestionably still present. Nonetheless, the expression and vitriol the maskilim allow themselves, the critical spirit, is a new and radical change even within the in-group. The freedom to be accepted—in their own small way—into German society allowed them to differentiate

83. Michael "Hahaskala" 281–282. As just one literary example of the phenomenon, several of the characters in Wolfssohn's play, particularly Yetkhen, use the terminology of rights and demands to justify their positions and choices within the play; see, for example, Yetkhen's speech at the end of Act II.

84. *GJH* 1:344–345, 2:19; Meyer *Origins* 59–62, 80. On Friedländer, see Altmann *MMBS* 350–352.

85. Lowenstein *Berlin* 76.

themselves more sharply from the *Ostjuden*. To be sure, anti-*Ostjude* sentiment had existed before. Yet now, for the first time, literarily speaking, the "united front" breaks down. That breakdown is expressed in textual terms: the Jews of Eastern Europe are accused of engaging in morally opprobrious interpretation of classical Jewish texts.

In short, the maskilic movement of the 1790s, exemplified by Wolfssohn's play *Laykhtzin un fremelay* ("Silliness and Sanctimony"), marks the transformation of the Haskala into the movement that will play such a major role in Eastern Europe: a satirical, critical movement, inveighing against the excesses and corruptions of Hasidism. Contrast this attitude to that of Mendelssohn, the exemplar of the earlier, mannered period, who was largely uninterested in satire. In a paper he delivered before the Wednesday Society, called "Should One Obviate the Spread of Enthusiasm by Satire or by Some External Association?," he opined that "the only means of promoting true enlightenment was not satire but—enlightenment."[86]

This is not to say, however, that there is total discontinuity between the early, Mendelssohnian, Haskala and this more radical one: Wolfssohn's life and work illustrates that though his methods may be more vitriolic and critical, his solutions are in many ways classically Mendelssohnian. Wolfssohn and his contemporaries were truly transitional figures, trying to fit old ideas into new and rapidly changing conditions. They were sufficiently successful that the model of maskilic literature they created would remain the paradigm of maskilic activity for almost a century.

As they were developing this new and more radical approach, however, they were also reflecting on the dangers of wholesale assimilationism and the ambiguous benefits of the full adoption of external culture.[87] Traditional observance had dropped precipitously; by the 1780s, travelers mention "widespread violations of the Sabbath and

86. The paper is reprinted in *JubA* 5:133–137; translation taken from Altmann *MMBS* 665. See also Gilman 108–110 and *MMBS* 36, where Mendelssohn is described as averse to the "flippancy and shallow sarcasm into which the *esprit* of the French *philosophes* had degenerated."

87. On maskilic concerns over this "false enlightenment," see Lowenstein *Berlin* 100–101.

dietary laws," and after Mendelssohn's death in 1786 the abandonment of traditional practice increased even more precipitously.[88] In many cases, though, this was not a result of principled philosophical change, as the maskilim would have it, but simply an uncritical adoption of the "atmosphere of libertinage" which reigned in Berlin under the court of the new Emperor Frederick William II (1786–1797).[89] This included an increased divorce rate, an increase in out-of-wedlock births, and what has been referred to as the *Taufepidemie*, the wave of baptisms that swept through the German Jewish upper classes in the first decades of the nineteenth century.[90]

Another part of this ambivalence stemmed from another important development of the 1790s: the rise of the salon culture, where Jewish women held discussions and parties attracting the elite of both Jewish and non-Jewish society.[91] Shulamit Magnus writes that though "the numbers were miniscule—at its height, salon society numbered one hundred individuals" and though "short-lived—the salons flourished between 1780 and 1806—they were significant, constituting a point of social and cultural intersection between the Jewish and non-Jewish worlds at a time when this was rare."[92] These salonnieres were often in the first wave of converts to Christianity, the threat lying implicitly behind Wolfssohn's play.[93]

88. Lowenstein "Orthodox" 5, 9. See also *GJH* 1:376–378. For more on the demographic shifts and economic transitions during the period, see *GJH* 2:50–89.

89. *GJH* 2:103.

90. See the masterful analysis of the entire phenomenon in Lowenstein *Berlin* 120–176.

91. On salon culture, see Lowenstein *Berlin* 104–110; Deborah Hertz, *Jewish High Society in Old Regime Berlin* (New Haven: Yale University Press, 1988), 7–13, 119–203. For more details, see Petra Wilhelmy-Dollinger, "Emanzipation durch Geselligkeit: Die Salons jüdischer Frauen in Berlin zwischen 1780 und 1830," in Marianne Awerbuch and Stefi Jersch-Wenzel, eds., *Bild und Selbstbild der Juden Berlins zwischen Aufklärung und Romantik* (Berlin: Colloquium Verlag, 1992), 121–138.

92. Magnus "German" 132

93. For a wonderful portrait of the radical changes in the lives of three of the most famous salon leaders, Dorothea Mendelssohn, Rahel Varnhagen, and Henriette Herz, see Meyer *Origins* 91–114; Heidi Thomann Tewarson, *Rahel Levin Varnhagen: The Life and Work of a German Jewish Intellectual* (Lincoln, NE: University

Changing demographic factors were instrumental here as well: the salonnieres generally belonged to the first generation of German Jews who had fully grown up in the age of Enlightenment. As such, they shared a very different set of assumptions and beliefs than their parents. Heidi Tewarson aptly characterizes these women's relationship to the earlier, Mendelssohnian approach to emancipation:

> their understanding of the meaning of Enlightenment, rather than being based primarily on strict and abstract philosophical tenets, was informed by a freer and more flexible individual morality conveyed by the new literature . . . [Mendelssohn] strove for recognition and respect while they demanded full integration into a society they knew was in many ways faulty and retrograde but seemed well on the way to being enlightened.[94]

The maskilim were well aware of this development and its potential dangers as well as its possible benefits, seeing figures like the salonnieres as either proof of the Haskala's success or evidence of its failure. In short, for the first time, the main question of the maskilim was not merely of the possibility for assimilation, but of its consequences. This ambivalence yielded a greater complexity in the maskilic literature of the period, which is also reflected in Wolfssohn's later work.

Early Nineteenth Century Galicia: Joseph Perl

Galicia, that part of Central Europe on the northeastern side of the Carpathian Mountains, serves as an important transition point in the development of the Enlightenment from its beginnings in the age of Mendelssohn and Wolfssohn in late eighteenth-century Prussia to its zenith in Czarist Russia's Pale of Settlement in the mid- to late-nineteenth century.[95]

---

of Nebraska Press, 1998), esp. 25–44, and Hannah Arendt, *Rahel Varnhagen: The Life of a Jewess*, ed. Liliane Weissberg (Baltimore: Johns Hopkins University Press, 1997). Compare, however, Tewarson 3–5 on Arendt's personalized biographical approach to Varnhagen.

94. Tewarson 59–60.

95. For more information on Galicia and Galician Jewry, see Israel Bartal, "'The Heavenly City of Germany' and Absolutism a la Mode d'Autriche: The Rise

For centuries, Galicia had been part of the Polish-Lithuanian Commonwealth, and had thus been subject to the currents and eddies of Jewish cultural development of the late Middle Ages and early modern period there.[96] Thus Galician Jewry shared in the widespread despair in the seventeenth century after an economic downturn, the Chmielnicki massacres of 1648, and the failure of Sabbatai Zevi's messianic movement in 1666.[97] Galicia was also home to a great concentration of traditional Jews, who were far more entrenched in the premodern system of socioeconomic relations than their Western European counterparts.[98] In 1772, a year before Joseph Perl was born, the Partition of Poland annexed Galicia to Austria,[99] and Galician Jews were thrust into an entirely new sociopolitical situation, meaning most Galician maskilic efforts were focused on the Austrian government, both explicitly and implicitly.

As we have said, the progress of Enlightenment and Jewish emancipation differs from one country to the next; at first glance, Austria seems to have been one of the more progressive countries on this front. Indeed, the Austrian Emperor Joseph II's 1782 *Toleranzpatent* led the Prussian maskil Naftali Herz Wessely to write *Divrei Shalom Veemet* ("Words of Peace and Truth"), one of the first maskilic polemics. Austria and Jewish Galicia were thus well positioned politically to serve as a test case for the success of the Haskala.[100] Many fac-

---

of the Haskala in Galicia," in Jacob Katz, ed. *Toward Modernity: The European Jewish Model* (New York: Leo Baeck Institute, 1987), 33–42, and Paul Robert Magocsi, *Galicia: A Historical Survey and Bibliographic Guide* (Toronto: University of Toronto Press, 1983), 227–244.

96. See Avraham Brawer, *Galitsia veyehudeha: mekhkarim betoldot galitsia bemea hashmona esre* (Jerusalem: Mossad Bialik, 1956), 16–22; Katz *Ghetto* 2 and Bartal "Heavenly" 34, 36.

97. On contemporary demographic trends in Eastern Europe, see Brawer 23–33 and Israel 120–121, 165–169. The classic treatment of Sabbatai Zevi remains Gershom Scholem's *Sabbatai Sevi: The Mystical Messiah* (Princeton, NJ: Princeton University Press, 1973).

98. See Brawer 34–39, 46–50.

99. On the partition of Poland, see Brawer 11–15.

100. Galicia was actually not subject to the edict's provisions until 1789; nonetheless, the cultural implications of the decree were avidly discussed in the Jewish world as soon as it was announced. See *GJH* 1:344, 2:16–17. For more on

tors allowed Galicia to serve as a new center for the Haskala, its numerous trade centers, familiarity with European culture, and economic and cultural relations with Vienna and other German cities among them. Maskilim flocked to the large urban centers on Galicia's northeastern border, particularly the three cities of Lemberg, Brody, and Tarnopol.[101]

The close economic relations between Prussia and Austrian Galicia during this period tended to highlight the differences between Jewish life in the two countries. In Prussia, the new economic mobility among the emergent Jewish upper middle class, as well as, more importantly, a sense of social possibility among German Jews, fundamentally conditioned the dynamic of enlightenment, producing a strong drive for cultural assimilation in large segments of the native Jewish population. Few, if any, of these conditions obtained in Galicia; in many cases, the Yiddish-speaking Jews there could not even understand their Polish-speaking neighbors.[102] The political differences were symbolized by the two countries' leaders: while Prussia boasted the "enlightened philosopher" Frederick II, in Austria the Jews had to contend with the more reactionary policies of the Roman Catholic Metternich.

Joseph II and Wessely, see Israel Zinberg, *Di geshikhte fun literatur ba yidn* (Buenos Aires: Altveltlekher yidisher kultur-kongres, 1969), 7:69–76, as well as Bartal "Heavenly" 35; Katz *Ghetto* 66–68, 145–150; and Altmann *MMBS* 355–357. On Wessely's poetic epic "Songs of Glory," see *GJH* 1:312–314; Dan Miron, "Rediscovering Haskalah Poetry," *Prooftexts* 1 (1981), 292–305; and Shmuel Werses, "Hazikot bein hasifrut hayafa levein khokhmat yisrael," *Tarbiz* 55:4 (1986), 567–602, esp. 567–568, which discusses the connection between poetry and scholarship in Wessely's work.

101. On Brody's development as a trade center, see Zinberg 8:198–99 and Brawer 106, 114; on Brody as a maskilic center, see Yisroel Vaynlez, "Yoysef Perl, zayn lebn un shafn," in *Yoysef Perls yidishe ksovim*, ed. Zelig Kalmanovitsh (Vilna: Bibliotek fun YIVO, 1937), ix–xii. For more on the development of the Galician Haskala, see Raphael Mahler, *Hasidism and the Jewish Enlightenment: Their Confrontation in Galicia and Poland in the First Half of the Nineteenth Century* (Philadelphia: JPS, 1985), 1–7, 31–34.

102. As we will see, this lack of concern over non-Jewish reaction to Galician maskilic literary product will allow a greater flexibility in the usage of classical texts.

Austrian policies of tolerance granted by Joseph II, like the freedom of career choice and the ability to invest in manufacturing and real estate, stemmed not so much from an actual recognition of natural rights or universalist sentiment, but from a cold-blooded calculation of possibilities for further economic exploitation of the Jews.[103] As we have seen, though, the Prussian government was hardly acting from more altruistic motives.[104] After Joseph II's death, in 1790, all the rights given to the Jews as a result of his decrees gradually disappeared, and conditions for the Jews worsened throughout the Hapsburg Empire.[105] Jews in Galicia lay "under the double yoke of extreme poverty and governmental exploitation"; at least one-third of them, according to official estimates, were *"luftmentshn* (persons without a definite occupation), who subsisted on odd jobs or who had no trade and often no means of subsistence at all."[106] Residence permits for places like Vienna were hard to come by until 1848. Jews were forbidden to deal in grain, salt, and other foodstuffs. For a long time, Jews were prohibited from building houses in Vienna. Public Purim celebrations were forbidden.[107]

Galician Jews were forced to pay numerous taxes to fill Austrian coffers. Particularly onerous was the candle-tax, instituted in 1795 on the advice of Shlomo Kofler and the approval of Herz Homberg, as well as the infamous "meat tax" on kosher meat. A marriage tax led to many unregistered marriages, creating Jewish "bastards" throughout Galicia. From 1788, Jews faced compulsory military service, though they could not become officers, and though they could attend non-Jewish schools, they were required to sit on special "Jewish benches"; at university, they could only study medicine.[108] The printing of Jewish

103. See Brawer 141–153, 158–168.

104. The hostility of the governmental authority, however, did not stop the editors of Galician maskilic journals like *Bikurei Haitim* ("First Fruits of the Times") from praising it extravagantly. For more on the journal, see footnote 126 *infra*.

105. Bartal "Heavenly" 37.

106. Mahler *Hasidism* 6.

107. Joseph Klausner, *Historia shel hasifrut haivirit hakhadasha* (Jerusalem: Hebrew University Press, 1937), 1:180–183.

108. Klausner 1:183–184.

books without German translation was forbidden in Galicia, which meant either illegal importation of Hebrew-language books from Russia or illegal secret printing.[109]

The Haskala itself was implicated in these restrictive decrees of the absolutist authority. Prussian maskilim, including Herz Homberg and Aaron Miroslav, arrived to oversee the Jewish schools founded as a result of Joseph II's decrees.[110] Homberg's efforts created the feeling among Galician Jewry that the Haskala would lead only to widespread apostasy.[111] Later, in 1820, the Austrian emperor Franz I decreed that only those with a government-issued certificate in both philosophy and Judaism could become rabbis, that all prayers must be said in German or the country's language, and that all non-Jewish subjects must be studied by Jews in non-Jewish schools. Though never carried out in full force, the policy, supported by maskilim, was perceived as an attack by and on the traditional Jewish community. It is hardly surprising that the Haskala was opposed so virulently by traditional Galician Jewry.[112]

Depressed economic circumstances and anti-government sentiment are two strong reasons why Galician Jewry so enthusiastically adopted the pietistic movement of Hasidism.[113] For example, while Brody, in

109. Klausner 1:184–185.

110. Fishel Lachover, *Toldot hasifrut haivrit hakhadasha* (Tel Aviv: Dvir, 1947), 2:2.

111. Bartal "Heavenly" 37; Zinberg 8:198. For more on Homberg (1749–1841), a younger member of Mendelssohn's circle in Berlin, see Klausner 1:186–198 and *GJH* 1:295–7.

112. Klausner 1:185.

113. Most early historiography of Hasidism, possibly influenced by Marxist thinking, portrays the movement as a revolt of the poor against the rich and powerful. Mahler (*Hasidism* 8–10, 23–24) takes a more moderate class-based view, characterizing it as a "middle class . . . and merchant class" movement joined by "prosperous elements of the feudal sphere." Recent work, however, indicates that Hasidism was a movement joined by the wealthy and the powerful almost from the beginning. For more details, see the excellent survey by Morris M. Faierstein, "Hasidism — the Last Decade in Research," *Modern Judaism* 11 (1991), 111–124, esp. 113–114; Gershon David Hundert's important article, "The Conditions in Jewish Society in the Polish-Lithuanian Commonwealth in the Middle Decades of the Eighteenth Century," in Ada Rapaport-Albert, ed., *Hasidism Reappraised* (Lon-

part due to its character as a trade center, had previously been a stronghold of opposition to Hasidism—as early as the 1780s, copies of the early Hasidic work *Toldot Yaakov Yosef* ("The Generations of Jacob Joseph") were burned there—by the early nineteenth century, it had become home to a large Hasidic community.[114] Unlike in Germany, then, Galician maskilim were forced to interact with Hasidim on a daily basis.

The battle for emancipation between maskilim and Hasidim revolved around the maskilic assumption, seen earlier in its Prussian context, that Jewish moral (and social) regeneration was necessary before any rights would be granted or integration would take place.[115] Hasidim were considered by non-Jews and maskilim alike to be far removed from secular society, with their emphasis on mysticism (seen as "superstition"), their pronounced insularity, their social solidarity, and their consequent resistance to cultural integration.[116] Particularly

---

don: Littman Library of Jewish Civilization, 1996), 45–50, which stresses demographic and generational factors, and Immanuel Etkes's "Hasidism as a Movement—The First Stage," in Bezalel Safran, ed., *Hasidism: Continuity or Innovation?* (Cambridge, MA: distrib. Harvard University Press, 1988), 1–26, which admirably sums up previous historiography and ventures new conclusions. For a more detailed look at the development of Galician Hasidism, see Rachel Elior, "Between *Yesh* and *Ayin*: The Doctrine of the Zaddik in the Works of Jacob Isaac, the Seer of Lublin," in Ada Rapoport-Albert and Steven J. Zipperstein, eds., *Jewish History: Essays in Honour of Chimen Abramsky* (London: Peter Halban, 1988), 393–455, 398–399.

114. Zinberg 9:39.

115. See Mahler *Hasidism* 36–39. Meyer Viner couches the conflict between Hasidism and Haskala in the Marxist terms of class struggle: Hasidism represents the feudal order, while the Haskala can represent, at various times, either the petit bourgeois or the democratic socialist order. For Viner, it is this latter tension which explains the maskilic ambivalence toward Yiddish: their attitudes depend on whether they have been seduced by the charms of capitalist society or allowed themselves to serve as unmediated conduits of the popular voice. See Meyer Viner, *Tsu der geshikhte fun der yidisher literatur in 19tn yorhundert* (New York: YKUF Farlag, 1945), 1:26–28. This essay takes a different approach to the question of maskilic ambivalence toward Yiddish, as we will see in Chapters Four, Five, and Six.

116. See Bartal "Heavenly" 36.

odious to the maskilim was the movement within Hasidism later to be referred to as "Zaddikism," a movement imputing special powers and abilities to a particular spiritual leader, abilities normally passed down in dynastic succession.[117] Furthermore, Hasidim actively opposed the maskilim and their efforts, "view[ing] every act of outside intervention as an evil decree. Each time government action threatened the religious and social autonomy of the Jewish body politic, a delegation of Hasidic and other Orthodox leaders headed for the capital while the loyal flock at home crowded into houses of prayer."[118] Is it any wonder that maskilic ire was so implacably focused on the Hasidim?

The maskilim, a small minority surrounded by a hostile Hasidic majority, looked to the government for help. What they failed to realize was that, generally speaking, the reactionary Catholic government had no particular interest in enlightening the Jews; indeed, it was the government's economic policies that were responsible for the Galician Jews' catastrophic poverty.[119] Nonetheless, it is fair to say that the Austrian authorities, over the first half of the nineteenth century, carried out a policy of Germanicization and, broadly defined, Enlightenment-oriented policies, accompanied by vitriolic statements and conceptions of Hasidism as being particularly detrimental to the desired enlightened populace.[120]

117. Mahler *Hasidism* 10–16. See also Immanuel Etkes, "The Zaddik: The Interrelationship Between Religious Doctrine and Social Organization," in Rapoport-Albert *Hasidism Reappraised* 159–167; and, on the particularistic model of Galician Zaddikism at the time, see Elior 400–408, 423–441. Joseph Perl particularly hated Zaddikism and strongly attacked it in his works; see the discussion of his *Megale Temirin* (Chapter Seven) *infra*.

118. David G. Roskies, *Against the Apocalypse: Responses to Catastrophe in Modern Jewish Culture* (Cambridge, MA: Harvard University Press, 1984), 56. These maskilic perceptions of the Hasidic movement were often internalized by Jewish historians and became the archetypal views of Hasidim in modern Jewish history until fairly recently. See Shmuel Werses, "Hakhasidut beeinei sifrut hahaskala," in Werses *Megamot* 91–108, 93, and Israel Bartal, "The Imprint of Haskala Literature on the Historiography of Hasidism," in Rapoport-Albert *Hasidism Reappraised* 367–375.

119. Zinberg 9:40–41.

120. See Mahler *Hasidism* 53–58, 106.

These actions, unsurprisingly, led to a near-worship of the absolutist government on the part of the maskilim and a bitter hatred of the government by the Hasidim. The government's antipathy toward the Hasidim was only mitigated by its recognition of Hasidism's fundamentally conservative character, its unwillingness to too actively destabilize any force that could be counted on to maintain the status quo, and its realization that Jewish communal institutions could be useful in the collection of taxes.[121]

As a result, it is hardly an oversimplification to assert that the literary wing of the Galician Haskala is a reaction to and a struggle against Hasidism,[122] and indeed, this book later argues that Joseph Perl's stylistic and thematic development as a Hebrew and Yiddish writer is directly, though not solely, determined by developments in Hasidic literature, and that his usage of classical texts is heavily influenced by Hasidic literary strategies of textual usage.

More generally, the Jewish literary historian Fishel Lachover describes the Galician Haskala as filled with "a critical spirit," citing its members' attempts to create a philosophy of history, in contradistinction to the Prussian Haskala, whose practitioners he sees as more pleasant, introspective, concerned with ethics and aesthetics.[123] Aside from philosophical differences, a textual difference between the two movements is also evident. For the Prussians, as we will see, the Bible is viewed as a source of universalist dialogue, exemplified by Mendelssohn's Bible translation and commentary. In contrast, the Talmud,

---

121. See Mahler *Hasidism* 69–76.

122. For more on this relationship, see Werses "Hakhasidut" 91–93.

123. Lachover 2:4. On aesthetics and the Prussian Haskala, see Chapters Four and Five. The paradigmatic figure of the philosophical wing of the Galician Haskala is Nachman Krochmal, the Jewish philosopher, neo-Hegelian, and author of the "Contemporary Guide to the Perplexed" (published posthumously in 1851); the standard work on Krochmal and his thought is Jay Harris, *Nachman Krochmal: Guiding the Perplexed of the Modern Age* (New York: New York University Press, 1991). On Galician maskilic efforts to create a science of history, see Shmuel Feiner, *Haskala vehistoria: toldoteha shel hakarat-avar yehudit modernit* (Jerusalem: Zalman Shazar, 1995), esp. 105–209, now translated as *Haskala and History: The Emergence of a Modern Jewish Historical Consciousness* (Oxford: Littman Library of Jewish Civilization, 2002), esp. 71–156.

regarded with suspicion by the non-Jewish public, was often treated by the Prussian maskilim as a text to be defended and protected, but not studied and shared. Conversely, Galician maskilim, coming from a more traditionalist society, maintained the traditional emphasis on the Talmud as the textual center of Jewish higher culture, occupying themselves less with Biblical criticism than with Talmud criticism.[124]

The literary wing of the Galician Haskala is heavily influenced both thematically and linguistically by the Prussian Haskala;[125] for example, the prime Austrian maskilic journal, *Bikurei Haitim* ("First Fruits of the Times," 1821–1832), was explicitly founded as a successor to *Hameasef*, and was often a near-copy of the earlier periodical, reprinting articles and providing summaries.[126] Galician maskilim like Mendl Lefin spent significant periods of time in Prussia, and brought back the lessons of that milieu with them to their home region.[127] Nonetheless, the Galicians carved out a literary space all their own. Galician poetry, exemplified by Meir HaLevi Letteris, reaches greater artistic heights than the Prussian pastorals, and the genres of the ballad and the historical play are significantly developed.[128] These genres, which merit separate study, commonly feature aggadic and midrashic material as the basis for their creative inspiration, reflecting the greater freedom with classical texts we see in the Galician Haskala as a whole.

Most importantly for our purposes, though, the Galician Haskala is generally considered to have developed the Hebrew prose satire. Predecessors such as Isaac Euchel exist in the Prussian Haskala, certainly, but it is in the hands of the Galician maskilim, particularly Joseph Perl and Isaac Erter, that the genre reaches a new maturity and quality.[129] Baruch Kurzweil suggests that satirists "can only flour-

124. Lachover 2:4–5.

125. See Lachover 2:2–4.

126. Zinberg 9:35–37. *Bikurei Haitim*, published in Vienna, was located in Austria proper, but drew upon the traditional communities of Galicia, Bohemia, and Hungary. On Shalom Hacohen, the journal's founder and an important transitional figure between Berlin and Galicia, see Klausner 1:244–257.

127. For more on Lefin, see Chapter Six.

128. See Lachover 2:6–11.

129. It is a source of some debate among literary historians as to which figure, Perl or Erter, is the greatest satirist of the Galician Haskala. Earlier critics, with

ish in times of spiritual and metaphysical crisis"; their utopian visions arise from their extreme dissatisfaction with the current condition. It is no wonder, then, in light of the historical context discussed earlier, that satire was a hallmark of the Galician Haskala.[130] Much of this satire was aimed at the Hasidim, naturally, and often combined attempts at entertainment with attempts at edification.[131]

Though Perl's satirical prose style is discussed in more detail later, his work allows us to look at an important development of the Galician Haskala: a greater linguistic flexibility. Perl breaks sharply with the received wisdom of what a maskilic writer's prose ought to look like. The general vision of Hebrew prose, codified by the Prussian Haskala from the first writers of *Hameasef,* can be roughly characterized as *melitsa*—the stringing together of mostly Biblical phrases and fragments to form mosaic sentences. *Melitsa* evolved from a combination of the maskilic regard for Biblical Hebrew as linguistically "pure" on the one hand, and a linguistic theory that distinguished between "pure" and "corrupt" languages on the other. Though the actual picture is more complex than most previous scholars have suggested,[132] most maskilim certainly adopted the theory to attack the "corrupt" language of Yiddish, particularly the Eastern European Yiddish "adulterated" with Slavicisms. It was an article of faith among Prussian maskilim that polemical

the notable exception of Baruch Kurzweil, seem to have favored Erter; however, Perl's playfulness with levels of textuality and intertextuality and complex narratological structures may well cause the pendulum to shift in a generation of scholars more enamored with these issues. For an earlier survey of comparative criticism, see Baruch Kurzweil, "Al hasatira shel Yosef Perl," in his *Bemaavak al erkhei hayahadut* (Schocken: Jerusalem, 1969), 55–85, 70–72.

130. Kurzweil "Al hasatira" 55–61.

131. For some general remarks on the literature of the period, see Shmuel Werses, "On the History of the Hebrew Novella in the Early Nineteenth Century: Studies in Zahlen's 'Salmah mul Eder,'" in Joseph Heinemann and Shmuel Werses, eds., *Studies in Hebrew Narrative Art Throughout the Ages* (Jerusalem: Hebrew University, 1978), 107–124, 108–109. For examples of Galician anti-Hasidic work, like Mieses' *Kinat Emet,* see Zinberg 9:41–48.

132. See the sources cited in Chapter Two, notes 16–18 and the discussions of Mendelssohnian and Wolfssohnian attitudes toward Yiddish in Chapters Four and Five.

works should not be written in Yiddish, and should be written in the *melitsa*-based Hebrew of Mendelssohn's circle.

However, this book stresses that the Haskala's aesthetic and linguistic ideology was hardly monolithic; what may have been absolutely taboo in cosmopolitan Berlin or Königsberg may have been necessary in Galicia. Perl is a prime example of this point. Social and cultural considerations, particularly the power and influence of Hasidic texts and interpretations, force him to create polemical literature in a form of Hebrew different from that adhered to by most of the maskilim who preceded him. The same sociological exigencies force him to consider the most radical decision a maskil could make in the early nineteenth century—to compose in Yiddish. In Galicia, more than in other areas, the maskilim sacrificed certain aesthetic and literary principles to ideological necessity. This was Perl's reason for writing in a language he was ideologically opposed to using; this is why his Hebrew and his Yiddish works take the shape they do. And, as we will see, this is why his usage of classical texts is significantly more flexible and radical.

In summary, the socioeconomic and political situation of Galician Jewry is such that the contours and outlines of the struggle over emancipation in Galicia are much starker than in the semiofficial, semineutral public spheres of cosmopolitan Prussia. The battle lines are drawn more clearly; friends and enemies of emancipation are easier to spot. No wonder that strategies of secrecy and subversion were resorted to; no wonder that barbed satire flourished as strongly as it did in Galicia; no wonder that Perl was willing to try anything to win over his hostile audience; no wonder an audacious and flexible literature flourished as a result.

Now that this background has been provided, we can turn to an individual examination of the authors under discussion.

Part Two   Prussia

Four   Moses Mendelssohn

Introduction

Though Moses Mendelssohn's legacy seems to change based on the historian who analyzes him—he has variously been idolized as the progenitor of a new epoch in Jewish history, used to symbolize changing social and cultural dynamics, and identified as a precursor of the real emancipation symbolized by the French Revolution[1]—there is widespread critical consensus on his iconic role in modern Jewish history. Precursors such as Israel of Zamosc existed,[2] but none had Mendelssohn's influence, as an ideal, on Western and Eastern European maskilim: most Prussian maskilim had either directly encountered Mendelssohn or revered his thought, and the Eastern Europeans, faced only with his powerful image, often hagiographized him further, a process that continued until a critical reexamination a century after his death.[3]

1. These perspectives are adumbrated in Mendes-Flohr *Modern World* 4. For a recent general overview, see Michael L. Morgan, "Mendelssohn," in Frank and Leaman 660–681.

2. On Israel of Zamosc, see Sorkin *Berlin Haskalah* 50–52.

3. Works on Mendelssohn's reception in Jewish Europe by both traditional and maskilic Jewry include: Meir Hildesheimer, "The Attitude of the Hatam Sofer Toward Moses Mendelssohn," *PAAJR* 60 (1994), 141–187; idem, "Moses Mendelssohn in Nineteenth Century Rabbinical Literature," *PAAJR* 55 (1989), 79–133; and Barzilay "Smolenskin" 11–48. On the establishment of the genre of Haskala biography/hagiography through biographies of Mendelssohn, see Moshe Pelli, "Moshe Mendelson kidmut hayehudi hekhadash bemoral biografi shel Yitzkhak Aykhl," *Bizaron* 45–48 (1990–91), 118–127, and Pelli, "Habiografia kezhanr behaskala: dmuto shel Yitzkhak Abravanel kemaskil hamegasher bein shtei tarbuyot," *Mekhkerei yerushalayim besifrut ivrit* 17 (1997), 75–88, later revised in Pelli *Sugot vesugyot*

Any discussion of maskilic literature and strategy must thus begin
with Mendelssohn, because his image "served German Jewry as a
model upon which to form itself . . . and as an assuring symbol of
what it stood for."[4] It was him the ideologues dreamed of becoming;
he thus influenced a century of ideological literature.[5] Even recent re-
examinations of Mendelssohn's influence on later maskilim, which
suggest more complex models that are less Mendelssohn-centric,[6]
nonetheless acknowledge that Mendelssohn's *image* became a model
and myth for the maskilim: "The admiration for Mendelssohn's
unique personality . . . did give the maskilim a kind of reference point:
Mendelssohn could serve as a cultural hero, a successful example of a
Jewish man of the European Enlightenment, whose 'glory among the
nations' raised the Jews' image in the eyes of the Christian world and
provided a source of self-respect and security for his disciples."[7] More
than anyone else, he balanced internal and external demands and
claims, providing a model for later maskilim and Jewish thinkers:
Franz Rosensweig called him "'the first German Jew,' as the first to
bear 'both words,' German and Jew."[8] His ideological positions were

---

237–266. For one contemporary biographical treatment, see Solomon Maimon,
"Recollections of Mendelssohn," in Ritchie Robertson, ed., *The German-Jewish
Dialogue: An Anthology of Literary Texts, 1749–1993* (Oxford: Oxford University
Press, 1999), 46–53.

4. Altmann "Archetypal" 17.

5. See *GJH* 1:280.

6. See Shmuel Feiner's "Mendelssohn and 'Mendelssohn's Disciples': A Reexamination," *LBIYB* 40 (1995), 133–167. Feiner correctly notes (137, 143) that the
"attempt to portray [later maskilim] as a united group of disciples is largely artificial . . . the young 'Haskalah family' found its organizational framework and its
direction without Mendelssohn's guidance." Compare the article's Hebrew version: "Mendelson ve'talmidei Mendelson': bekhina mekhadash," *KOMI* 11B2
(1994), 1–8.

7. Feiner "Mendelssohn" 152. Despite the cultivation of Mendelssohn's image
by the maskilim of the 1790s, it was *their* work, argues Feiner, that truly laid the
foundations for the new Haskala. Wolfssohn's development, discussed in Chapter Five, seems to bear this out.

8. See Paul Mendes-Flohr, "Mendelssohn and Rosensweig," *JJS* 38:2 (1987),
203–11, 203–206. See also Jacob Katz, "The Unique Fascination of German-Jewish
History," *Modern Judaism* 9:2 (1989), 141–150, and Scholem's comments in Dan
Gershom Scholem 6–7.

neither lasting nor universally adopted; a generation later, maskilim advocated significantly more radical positions than his essentially conservative traditionalism. But Mendelssohn opened the door.

Mendelssohn's output and influence have been so vast that he has often resisted previous attempts to treat him in totality. Efforts have been made to divide his work by language, genre, and chronology. All these approaches have their benefits, but division itself often yields dichotomies unwarranted when Mendelssohn's work is carefully examined in a translinguistic, synchronic context.[9] For example, much has been made in recent scholarship of the distinction between the "public" and the "private" Mendelssohn. All too often, we are told, Mendelssohn presents a face for public consumption radically at odds with his true feelings. Interestingly, critics debate over the nature of the "private" face—whether Mendelssohn was more traditionalist than his public love of non-Jews and Enlightenment would suggest, or, conversely, whether he was a radical deist merely posing as a traditionalist to find legitimation within the traditional Jewish community.

The former position is expressed by, among others, David Patterson, who writes that "Mendelssohn's standpoint was conditioned by three separate facets of his personality, namely, the loyal Jew, the aspiring German, and the confirmed rationalist."[10] By contrast, those who claim Mendelssohn as a deist, secretly denying the tenets and doctrines of traditional Judaism, seem to focus more on his philosophy than his personality.[11] In fact, the public/private distinction so often marshaled to support their case may well show that the statements they seize on stem largely from public circumstances. For example, the passage Allan Arkush cites to illustrate Mendelssohn's supposed anti-

9. See Tsamriyon 44 and Sorkin *MMRE* 154, and, more recently, David Sorkin, "The Mendelssohn Myth and Its Method," *New German Critique* 77 (Spring-Summer 1999), 7–28, on the influence of Mendelssohn's German writings over his Hebrew ones on scholars and critics.

10. David Patterson, "Moses Mendelssohn's Concept of Tolerance," in Alexander Altmann, ed., *Between East and West: Essays Dedicated to the Memory of Bela Horovitz* (London: Horovitz Publishing Co., 1958), 149–163, 149.

11. See Arkush *MME* 266–270, and, more recently, Allan Arkush, "The Questionable Judaism of Moses Mendelssohn," *New German Critique* 77 (Spring-Summer 1999), 29–44, esp. 35–38.

nomian tendencies, a discussion of the "yoking and binding" of law, is from *Jerusalem,* perhaps Mendelssohn's most public statement, and thus may be taken with a grain of salt.[12]

In reality, Mendelssohn was a greater traditionalist and foe of universalism than his public works seem to indicate, his belief seeming to result more from personal conviction than ideological necessity. Extensive scholarly work has documented this private traditionalism;[13] Mendelssohn believed Ecclesiastes to be written by King Solomon under divine inspiration, and believed in the resurrection and the world to come.[14] He even wrote in a letter to Elkan Herz,

> I am far removed from declaring a single utterance of our sages, of blessed memory, to be a *Scharteke* [trashy volume], God forbid. There is not a single Gentile scholar who has leveled this charge against me or misinterpreted my words to this effect. Had this been my opinion, I would have had to declare myself a Karaite, not a rabbinite.[15]

Mendelssohn's traditional observance was well known within the Jewish community and accepted as genuine: Meir Hildesheimer points out that

> the controversy which raged in regard to Mendelssohn and his work cannot overshadow the very basic fact that Mendelssohn was never entirely rejected by all rabbinical circles. He remained within the camp. The haskamot [approbations] granted by the rabbis for the various editions of [his] translation and Bi'ur, the laudatory remarks written about him, and the references made to his work, supply ample proof that this was so, although they do not necessarily indicate an unconditional acceptance of his ideas and viewpoint.[16]

12. Arkush *MME* 254–257. For a different interpretation of the passage, see the discussion of *Jerusalem infra*.

13. See *GJH* 1:281; Zinberg 7:25; Edward Breuer, "Of Miracles and Events Past: Mendelssohn on History," *Jewish History* 9:2 (1995), 27–52, 31–32; Tsamriyon 49–50; Schweid 389–392; and Altmann *MMBS* 96.

14. Arkush *MME* 182.

15. *JubA* 19:142; translation taken from Altmann *MMBS* 250. See also Altmann "Archetypal" 22 and *MMBS* 719–720.

16. See Hildesheimer "Nineteenth Century" 117–129; quote from 129.

A grateful Berlin community's release of Mendelssohn from the requirement to pay taxes in 1763 and his service, starting in 1780, as one of the Tovim, a member of the communal governing board, further serves to confirm this acceptance.[17] While it is certainly possible that Mendelssohn managed to deceive the entire surrounding community, the burden of proof certainly lies on the scholar to prove such deception.

This is not to say that Mendelssohn's position as preacher of reform within the traditional Jewish community was not precarious. The religious Jewish community had little tolerance for any form of religious impropriety, and topics Mendelssohn dealt with daily were ideologically sensitive. Mendelssohn well knew that his presentation of texts and his positions on Judaism to his non-Jewish audience, to say nothing of his personal behavior, needed to satisfy the Jewish community as well. His keen awareness of that pressure can be seen in his description of Socrates in one of his philosophical works; Mendelssohn's comment that "the feeble understandings of his fellow citizens required to be managed with great tenderness that he might draw no reproaches upon himself, or lessen the influence which the poorest religion has on the morals of weak minds" may well have been aimed at Berlin as well as Athens.[18]

There seems, then, to be no real historical or biographical evidence for the assertion that Mendelssohn was a deist, and there seems to be more compelling explanation for the absence of such evidence than deception.[19] Nonetheless, critics often distinguish between the "public" and "private" Mendelssohn along the simple axes mentioned above, particularly language, to make these and other arguments about Mendelssohn. Careful analysis of Mendelssohn's work *in toto*, however, locates the relevant distinction, quite reasonably, between "public" and

17. Lowenstein "Social Dynamics" 340.

18. Moses Mendelssohn, *Phaedon, or the Death of Socrates*, trans. Charles Cullen (London: J. Cooper, 1789), ix.

19. Mendelssohn and other maskilim were certainly well aware of and influenced by deist thought, however; see Pelli *Age* 7–32, and Moshe Pelli, *Moshe Mendelson: bekhavlei masoret* (Israel: Hotzaat sefarim aleph, 1972), 18–20, 75–78, 120–137, which argues against Mendelssohn as deist.

"private" forums themselves: when Mendelssohn writes for public consumption, *regardless of the language in which he writes*, his attitudes toward Judaism—at least as exemplified in his usage of classical Jewish texts—are identical. These attitudes, and this usage, differ from those in his writings for private audiences or those writings he chose to keep unpublished.[20] Mendelssohn's private correspondence, written in, among other languages, Yiddish, is particularly in need of further study.[21]

Though this chapter, for reasons of space, is unable to address the private side of Mendelssohn's output, it will attempt to illuminate the "public" side of his work.[22] In comparing samples of Mendelssohn's public work from the beginning and end of his public career, we will see him adopt identical strategies for using classical texts, regardless of audience, language, and time—strategies that prove influential on both the polemical approach and literary style of later maskilic work. This chapter limits itself to detailed discussion of two published texts, one widely read—the German *Jerusalem*, the culmination of Mendelssohn's political philosophy and his (at least public) position on Judaism,[23] and one less widely read—the Hebrew *Kohelet Musar*, a short

20. For an example of an unpublished polemic anti-Christian manuscript, see Sorkin *MMRE* 25–28. A few examples of a greater flexibility in Mendelssohn's use of classical texts in his letters appear in *JubA* 19:109–111 (letter 90), 115 (letter 91), 118–119 (letter 98), 138 (letter 117), 150–151 (letter 127), 203–204 (letter 179), 204 (letter 180), 212–213 (letter 188), 230 (letter 208), 241 (letter 211), and 278 (letter 248). In the last letter, for example, Mendelssohn uses the exalted language of the Song of Songs and Psalms to refer ironically and self-deprecatingly to himself and his modest state in a fresh way that is not apparent in his public work.

21. For a discussion of Mendelssohn's attitude to Yiddish, see *infra*. For more on the letters, see Efraim Shmueli, "Khavlei tarbut—khavlei lashon: Moshe Mendelson ubeayat ribui haleshonot besifrut yisrael," *Kivunim* 33 (1987), 129–152, 141–144; Zinberg 7:18; Marianne Awerbuch, "Moses Mendelssohns Judentum," in Awerbuch and Jersch-Wenzel 21–41, 27–30; Altmann *MMBS* 95; and Werner Weinberg, "Language Questions Relating to Moses Mendelssohn's Pentateuch Translation," *HUCA* 55 (1984), 197–242, 239–240, particularly on Mendelssohn's flexible and adaptable Yiddish and Hebrew epistolary style.

22. See Pelli *Moshe Mendelson* 13.

23. Mendelssohn's *Jerusalem* was partially translated into Hebrew as early as Euchel's 1788 Mendelssohn biography (*Toldot rabeinu hakhakham moshe ben menakhem* (Berlin: 1788)); most contemporary maskilim read German, however.

set of Hebrew pamphlets written by Mendelssohn at the very beginning of his public career.

Certain other aspects of Mendelssohn's Hebrew writing, particularly his Biblical translation and commentary, have been excellently
dealt with in recent scholarship; these works, briefly discussed here,
provide a solid touchstone for this further exploration of other parts
of Mendelssohn's oeuvre. This comparison of two Mendelssohnian
works will hopefully illuminate Mendelssohn's perspective on Jewish
texts, as well as illustrate a trend in the development of Jewish literature that is continued in later chapters.

Biographical and Social Notes

Before moving to Mendelssohn's work, some relevant biographical
details should be mentioned, though Altmann's magisterial biography
has precluded the need for a larger biographical study.[24] Mendelssohn
grew up in Dessau, a locus of "modern" Jewish book production
where, in the first half of the eighteenth century, new books about hu-
manistic disciplines in Hebrew—dictionaries, writings on Hebrew
linguistics and grammar, and popular scientific treatises—appeared
from the same presses that published traditional rabbinic works.[25]
Mendelssohn's first biographer, Isaac Euchel, "reports that at the age
of six Moses had already begun to study 'Halakha and Tosafot,' i.e.,
the Talmud with its commentaries and codes."[26]

While most Jewish educational institutions stressed familiarity
with the Talmud at the expense of the Bible and its commentaries,

24. On Altmann, see Allan Arkush, "The Contribution of Alexander Altmann
to the Study of Moses Mendelssohn," *LBIYB* 34 (1989), 415–420.

25. *GJH* 1:222–226, 235–238. On Dessau, see Sorkin *MMRE* 3, particularly on
the important republication of Maimonides' *Guide to the Perplexed*, a vital text to
maskilic thought; see also Shohat 207; Dov Rafel, "Khanut hasfarim kemosad
khinukhi lemaskil yehudi," in Dov Rafel, ed., *Mekhkarim bamikra uvekhinukh mugashim leprofesor Moshe Arend* (Jerusalem: Touro College, 1996), 336–344; and
Menachem Schmelzer, "Hebrew Printing and Publishing in Germany 1650–1750—
On Jewish Book Culture and the Emergence of Modern Jewry," *LBIYB* 33 (1988),
369–383, 372–373.

26. See Altmann MMBS xiii.

Mendelssohn from an early age was enamored with the Bible, becoming "so well versed in it that he came to know large portions of the Hebrew text by heart . . . the fondness for the Bible and for Biblical studies, which led him to his German translations of the Hebrew texts of the Psalms, Canticles, and above all the Pentateuch, goes back to the strong attachment to the Bible that he developed as a child."[27] Indeed, Mendelssohn himself became sufficiently familiar with Hebrew to use it as at least a partial cognitive base: he later wrote that "[s]ince . . . I received my first tuition in the Hebrew tongue, I used to translate in my mind every significant term that I read or heard in another language into Hebrew."[28]

Mendelssohn also learned the Palestinian Talmud and midrashic material generally not taught to German Jews, also encouraging his later independence within the canonical system.[29] Mendelssohn's rabbinic knowledge was sufficiently developed that he felt himself capable of arguing Jewish law with Rabbi Jacob Emden, the generation's leading jurist, and writing what was essentially a responsum on the controversial subject of early burial that appeared in the maskilic journal *Hameasef*.[30] In his response, Emden accuses Mendelssohn of the same sort of casuistry the latter inveighs against—as we will see, not a charge entirely without justification.

Early burial provides a good example of Mendelssohn's position on law and interpretation: Mendelssohn supported subtle changes in Jewish society and law, but believed these changes to be within the continuum of Jewish legal possibility. To provide another example:

27. Altmann *MMBS* xiii, 10.

28. *Gesammelte Schriften* 2:326; translation from Altmann *MMBS* 681.

29. See Altmann *MMBS* 13.

30. *Hameasef* 2:155. For discussion, see Falk Wiesemann, "Jewish Burials in Germany—Between Tradition, Enlightenment, and the Authorities," *LBIYB* 37 (1992), 17–31, esp. 21–22; Pelli *Moshe Mendelson* 48–52; Sorkin *MMRE* 97–101; Katz *Ghetto* 144–145; and Altmann *MMBS* 288–294, 347–350, where Mendelssohn's and Emden's arguments are detailed. On the relationship between Mendelssohn and Emden, see Theodor Dreyfus, "Yakhaso shel Moshe Mendelson el R' Yaakov Emden," in Moshe Khalamish and Moshe Schwartz, eds. *Hitgalut, Emuna, Tevuna: Kovets Hartsaot* (Ramat Gan: Bar-Ilan University, 1996), 99–112.

Mendelssohn was even more liberal about religious practice than the philosemitic Von Dohm when it came to participation in the Prussian military service. Von Dohm, in his *On the Civil Improvement of the Jews*, cites a Jewish scholar (obviously Mendelssohn) who discusses changing the current law dramatically if done in conformity with Talmudic tradition (e.g., authorizing military service on the Sabbath).[31] Nonetheless, Mendelssohn grounded his flexibility and reinterpretation of legal matters in terms of a recognized and traditionalist interpretive and juridical process, though still in a highly formalized and traditional context.[32]

Mendelssohn's background allows him to use the entire classical Jewish canon with a master's ease, both for private, resonant "in-jokes" with members of his subgroup, and to polemically challenge non-Jewish slanders and calumnies resulting from textual misinterpretation. Mendelssohn does not, however, always hew to traditionalist interpretations, even when claiming to do so. His representation of the Jewish canon, smacking of literary artistry, appears in his earliest published works and remains consistent until works published at the end of his life.[33]

Tensions clearly evident in Mendelssohn's life, but often unmentioned in analyses of his work, must also be noted. Mendelssohn is often presented as a welcome guest in Berlin society, and he unquestionably received honors that had come to few if any Jews before him.

31. Arkush *MME* 274. For more on Von Dohm and his views on Jewish emancipation, see Sorkin *Transformation* 24–27; compare with Johann David Michaelis's anti-Semitic approach in Jacob Katz, "'A State Within a State': The History of an Anti-Semitic Slogan," in Katz *Emancipation* 47–76.

32. See Pelli *Age* 39–47 and *Moshe Mendelson* 32–48, and esp. Kenneth Hart Green, "Moses Mendelssohn's Opposition to the Herem: The First Step Towards Denominationalism?" *Modern Judaism* 12:1 (1992), 39–60, 49–50.

33. This is not to imply Mendelssohn remained static as a thinker. His philosophical positions shifted, particularly in the sphere of metaphysics. An example illustrative of both Mendelssohn's changing views and his attempts to synthesize medieval Jewish philosophy and Leibnizian optimism is his discussion of miracles; see Alexander Altmann, "Moses Mendelssohn on Miracles," in Altmann *Essays* 142–153, 142–146.

However, even Mendelssohn's non-Jewish friends were often sympathetic to him as an extraordinary individual but not to the Jewish community as a whole,[34] and many, including the pamphleteer who inspired Mendelssohn to write *Jerusalem*, felt this social acceptance was merely a step in Mendelssohn's eventual conversion to Christianity. Lavater's outspoken plea for Mendelssohn to convert was considered by much of the non-Jewish community as a "tactless gesture," but no worse than that.[35]

As an "extraordinary Jew," Mendelssohn lived in Berlin on the king's sufferance, and was forbidden to pass on his right of residency to his children.[36] His candidacy for the Royal Academy of Science was rejected in 1771 by King Frederick II, the "Enlightenment king," whose actual attitude toward the Jews was somewhat less enlightened.[37] At his synagogue, a Christian professor attended the service to prevent congregants from saying the phrase in the *Aleinu* prayer describing the futility of idol worship, believed to be an expression of anti-Christian sentiment.[38] At the theater, the few philosemitic portraits of the individual Jew in his friend Lessing's plays were vastly outnumbered by the appearances of the stock comic Jewish character, a theatrical fixture.[39] Jews were often believed to be thieves, since the

34. *GJH* 1:144.

35. Katz *Ghetto* 52. For a further discussion of the Lavater affair, as well as the later public urgings of the then-anonymous pamphleteer of "The Search for Truth and Light," August Cranz, and Balthasar Kolbele, see Katz *Ghetto* 52–54 and Pelli *Moshe Mendelson* 14–23. Cranz's pamphlet is discussed in greater detail in the section on *Jerusalem infra*.

36. See GJH 1:102–103, 136–137, 149.

37. See Holland 31; Katz *Ghetto* 56–57; *GJH* 1:147–150; Altmann *MMBS* 462–464.

38. The phrase is "For they bow down to vanity and emptiness, and pray to a god who does not help." The law, issued in 1703 by Frederick I, was still in effect as late as 1788 in Königsberg—six years after the publication of *Jerusalem*. See *GJH* 1:157–158. On Mendelssohn's efforts to end this practice, see Sorkin *MMRE* 102–103 and Altmann *MMBS* 308–309.

39. Anti-Semitic images had appeared in Christian plays as early as the thirteenth century; see *GJH* 1:48 and Katz *Ghetto* 86. On sympathetic Jewish characters, see Meyer *Origins* 16. See also Wolfgang Marten, "Zur Figur eines edlen Juden im

thieves' cant of the period, *Rotwelsch*, bore "a number of very clear Jewish lexical traces."[40] Mendelssohn certainly recognized this generally hostile sentiment; in his 1782 preface to the reprint of Manasseh Ben Israel's *Vindiciae Judaeorum*, he wrote, "Now we are reproached for superstition and stupidity; a lack of moral feeling, taste, and good manners; the inability to engage in arts, sciences, and useful occupations, principally in the service of the state; an incorrigible propensity to deceit, usury and lawlessness."[41]

On a more personal level, Mendelssohn's precarious financial situation meant he occasionally had to sell *etrogim* and make matches to make ends meet,[42] and his home was filled with twenty large china monkeys, forced purchases resulting from Frederick II's new legislation requiring Jews to bail out the "not very profitable royal manufactory . . . [d]istributed throughout his home, they must have served as a constant reminder of his inferior status."[43]

It is perhaps unsurprising, then, that when Joseph II's *Toleranzpatent* appeared, Mendelssohn greeted it skeptically, claiming the decree was probably a veiled attempt at religious proselytism.[44] To Mendelssohn, political change was simply a further continuation of religious polemics, and Mendelssohn's literary activity must thus also

---

Aufklärungsroman vor Lessing," in Jacob Katz and Karl Heinreich Rengstorf, eds., *Begegnung von Deutschen und Juden in der Geistgeschichte des 18. Jahrhunderts* (Tübingen: Max Niemayer Verlag, 1994), 65–77, esp. 68–70. See also Jacob Katz's article in the same volume, "Frühantisemitismus in Deutschland," 79–89. On Mendelssohn's friendship and collaboration with Lessing, see Altmann *MMBS* 36–50.

40. *GJH* 1:248. See also Gilman 68–70, 76–77 and Dovid Katz, "Notions of Yiddish," in Abramson and Parfitt 75–92, 81–82.

41. *JubA* 8:6; translation from Sorkin *MMRE* 113.

42. Zinberg 7:21–22; Tsamriyon, 41–47. See David Friedländer's account of Mendelssohn's home environment cited in Meir Gilon, *Kohelet Musar leMendelson al reka tkufato* (Publications of the Israel Academy of the Sciences and Humanities: Jerusalem, 1979), 18–20.

43. Tewarson 19.

44. See Altmann *MMBS* 462–464; Barzilay "Smolenskin" 23–25; and Isaac Eisenstein-Barzilay, "Early Responses to the Emancipation in Hebrew Haskalah Literature," *Judaism* 38:4 (1989), 517–526.

be understood in polemical terms. However, much of Mendelssohn's ambivalence was expressed privately, and, when added to the fact that Mendelssohn was a genuinely patriotic Prussian citizen and certainly wished to be identified as a German, even translating a special prayer for the Prussian forces into German during the 1756 war among Prussia, Austria, and Saxony, his position becomes too complicated to characterize easily.[45]

Perhaps Mendelssohn's sentiments can be expressed in martial metaphors: as in ages before, Mendelssohn still felt that there was a battle to be fought, a battle against the forces of ignorance and hatred, and that society needed to be transformed. But, for the first time, the conditions of that battle—the field of engagement and the weapons employed—had changed, and Mendelssohn and others like him felt there was a possibility of winning this new battle. But the battle had to be fought; Mendelssohn's works are reports from the front.

The Early Years: The Philosophical Writings and Kohelet Musar

Mendelssohn published very little that can be considered belletristic, though many of his philosophical works are, in the spirit of the time, framed in quasiliterary form, particularly in the form of the pastoral dialogue.[46] Though the *Philosophical Writings*, which brought him fame in non-Jewish intellectual circles, are generally unrelated to Jewish themes, Mendelssohn very occasionally cites the Jewish canon in

45. See Altmann *MMBS* 67.

46. For an example of Mendelssohn's aesthetic output in Hebrew, see the parables reprinted in Lachover 1:59 and the poems in *JubA* 14:283–284. On the genre of the parable in maskilic literature, see especially Pelli *Sugot vesugyot* 116–137 and also Gideon Toury, "Shimush muskal bemashal maskili: Kristin Firkhtgut Gelert besifrut haivrit," in Shamir and Holzman 75–86, which also discusses the time lag between the popularity of a genre in the Enlightenment and its adaptation by the Haskala. On the pastoral dialogue as popularized by Italian proto-maskilim in the seventeenth and eighteenth centuries, see Ariel Rathaus, "Hashira hapastoralit haivrit beitalia bemeot hayud zayin vehayud khet," *Italia Judaica* 3 (1989), 111–120, and Gilman 134.

ways seemingly extraneous to his discussion—unless his additional political agenda, of legitimating Biblical and rabbinic tradition to his non-Jewish audience, is taken into account.[47]

Altmann's comments on the matter are, as always, directly on point:

> Rabbinic phrases are quoted, although not always identified. . . .
> No doubt there was a certain deliberateness in quoting Hebrew phrases of this kind. They were obviously meant to show the poetic flavor or simply, the "wisdom" to be found in Jewish literature. Prejudice might slowly be defeated in this unobtrusive way.[48]

Altmann's point is borne out through a brief look at the few Jewish references in these early works of Mendelssohn's.

At the end of the Socratic dialogue *On the Sentiments* (1755), a general treatise on aesthetics, a character with the Hellenistic name of Theocles cites a Talmudic statement. Mendelssohn notes the phrase's Jewish origins without revealing it as a rabbinic source, referring to it only as the work of "the Hebrew poet," perhaps even implying a Biblical setting, since the Talmud was not known for its poetry.[49] Notably, the phrase, "mountains hanging on a hair," is there used to attack the kind of hair-splitting pedantry that so characterized contemporary rabbinic thought. Mendelssohn's reticence to force his readers into a direct confrontation with issues of rabbinic interpretation and value is understandable: these are not polemical pieces, they are discussions of aesthetics. It is unsurprising, then, that Mendelssohn's citations here serve primarily aesthetic purposes.[50] References to rabbinism are far more explicit in a polemical work like *Jerusalem*. Furthermore, early in his career, Mendelssohn—though his opinion on the use and presentation of classic Jewish texts is identical to his later position—is hardly

47. The citations are eminently noticeable to the alert observer. See Katz *Ghetto* 49.

48. Altmann *MMBS* 196. See also Meyer *Origins* 22.

49. *JubA* 1:302 (*PW* 69): the quote is from *BT Khagiga* 10a.

50. Though for Mendelssohn, of course, the aesthetic was also polemical: "The arts could play a helpful role in promoting morality by arousing sentiments and stimulating the imaginative faculty. Rational arguments were able to convince the intellect of the excellence of virtue but belles-lettres and the arts compelled the approval of imagination." Altmann *MMBS* 129.

a household name, and does not wish to polemicize without cause. To throw clearly designated rabbinic texts into a general work of philosophy might cause the non-Jewish world to throw out the philosophical baby with the rabbinic bathwater.

Instead, he contents himself with veiled allusions to rabbinic sources and the subtle accentuation of Biblical universalism. All other references to classical Jewish texts in the *Philosophical Writings* are Biblical; Mendelssohn cites Genesis and the Psalms to illustrate points concerning the sublime,[51] and drops the merest hint that Jewish tradition might illuminate the matter. When provoked, though, Mendelssohn defends Jewish tradition more explicitly, as we will see.

At exactly the same time he composed the *Philosophical Writings*, Mendelssohn similarly "harmoniz[ed] the sensual and the rational" for another audience.[52] His *Kohelet Musar* ("The Preacher of Morals") is one of the first, if not the first, modern Hebrew writings imbued with the spirit of the Enlightenment, written to encourage traditional Jewish audiences to adopt Enlightenment positions on various topics.[53] Though Hebrew-reading Orientalists such as Johann David Michaelis did exist—in fact, their opinion was highly prized, since for maskilim they were the "objective" gatekeepers into German society, judging whether the Jews' literary product rendered them worthy of social emancipation[54]—it is absurd to contest that *Kohelet Musar* was written for non-Jews. The fact that Mendelssohn's strategies of textual citation and usage are identical between this polemic and his later polemic *Jerusalem,* then, reveals much about Mendelssohn's own public/private distinction and the dynamics of maskilic writing.

---

51. See *JubA* 1:462, 465, 470 (*PW* 200, 202, 208), and the discussion of Psalms *infra*.

52. Altmann *MMBS* 658.

53. For comparisons between *On the Sentiments* and *Kohelet Musar*, see Gilon 71–80.

54. For more on Michaelis and his complicated and problematic relationship with Mendelssohn, see Anna-Ruth Löwenbrück, "Johann David Michaelis und Moses Mendelssohn: Judenfeindschaft im Zeitalter der Aufklärung," in Albrecht, Engel, and Hinske 316–332, esp. 318, 329, and Karlfried Gründer, "Johann David Michaelis und Moses Mendelssohn," in Katz and Rengstorf 25–50, esp. 26–31. See also Altmann *MMBS* 242–244.

As we have said, maskilic usage of these texts is Janus-faced: they must present classical Jewish texts in accordance with (or, at the very least, not doing violence to) classical Jewish interpretations of those texts, while simultaneously rehabilitating them and presenting them to the non-Jewish reader—all, of course, while using them to make their potentially subversive polemical points. Theoretically, the maskilim could simply present two different sets of interpretations to their two audiences.[55] Mendelssohn, however, does not do so; the strategies used in *Kohelet Musar* are identical to those of *Jerusalem*, and differ from those employed in his private letters.

The dating and authorship of *Kohelet Musar* are discussed at great length elsewhere, and are largely irrelevant to our discussion here.[56] Though it is likely that only half of *Kohelet Musar* was written by Mendelssohn, this chapter discusses the entire document for two reasons. First, even if Mendelssohn did not write the entire work, he was heavily involved with its production and publication, and presumably approved of the strategies of textual citation throughout.[57] Second, many of the readers whom the work influenced were seemingly unaware of which parts were written by Mendelssohn and which parts were not; as Altmann writes, "A single voice speaks throughout [*Kohelet Musar*], and it is the voice of Mendelssohn."[58]

Kohelet Musar was modeled on the "moral weeklies," a type of German newspaper generally dedicated to spreading Enlightenment ideals and expressing the opinions and ideals of the new bourgeoisie.[59] *Kohelet Musar* exemplifies the genre, with its name ("The Preacher of Morals"),

55. See the discussion of Wolfssohn's *Jeschurun* in Chapter Five.

56. Gilon's dating of the work, from the middle of 1755 or beginning of 1756, seems conclusive, as does his determination of which sections were composed by Mendelssohn and which by Tuvia (9–17, 83–87).

57. On stylistic differences between Tuvia and Mendelssohn, see Gilon 95–96; their strategy of polemical citation of classical texts seems to be very similar, if not identical.

58. Altmann *MMBS* 87.

59. For Mendelssohn's contributions to an earlier (German) moral weekly, *Der Chameleon*, see Altmann *MMBS* 78–80. For more on the moral weekly, and its generally marginal status in German culture, see Sorkin *Transformation* 15–16 and Gilon 22–36.

its advocacy of Enlightenment ideals such as natural religion based on reason, its contributors' anonymity and its featuring of a fictitious authorial persona and invented social gatherings—the only difference is, as Gilon puts it, that this one was written for "an audience composed of yeshiva students."[60]

Altmann notes that "no antagonism to tradition was consciously implied in the modest undertaking of the two young men,"[61] and the communal opposition that closed down the journal after two issues appears to have stemmed merely from its publication without the previous receipt of consent from the rabbinical authorities.[62] This said, the work "did constitute a shift in accent: from the closed, isolated circle of the old, normative patterns of Jewish thought into a new sphere— one the traditionally-oriented Jew, consciously or unawares, had ignored until then."[63]

However, Mendelssohn's shift is subtle, and while he creates the appearance of traditionalism through his judicious and careful use of classical texts, the picture created by his usage of those texts differs substantially from previous Jewish writings. As Sorkin phrases it: "Mendelssohn attempted to activate the textual heritage, applying texts in a manner entirely foreign to the world of Talmudic dialectics to issues he thought significant to any educated Jew."[64] Meir Gilon employs the wonderful image that in *Kohelet Musar*, Enlightenment ideas are like the apodictic statements of the Mishna, and the Jewish canonical texts are like the explanatory attempts of the Talmud and the later commentators.[65] An analysis of the two issues of *Kohelet Musar* themselves, each divided into three letters, amply bears out these statements.

60. See Gilon 37–53; citation from 48. For a formal, stylistic, and ideological comparison with an internal genre, contemporary Jewish ethical literature (*musar*), see Gilon 110–139.

61. Altmann *MMBS* 83.

62. *GJH* 1:278. See also Gilon 87–88, 97–101, on the different types of censorship in contemporary Germany.

63. *GJH* 1:276.

64. Sorkin *MMRE* 18.

65. Gilon 50. See Gilon 50–57 for a discussion of Biblical and Talmudic proofs brought in *Kohelet Musar*.

The first issue of *Kohelet Musar,* which focused on propagating the Enlightenment ideal of "the ennobling effect of the beauties of nature upon man,"[66] opens with Biblical language from the book of Ecclesiastes and a clearly demarcated rabbinic statement expressing the rabbis' love of nature.[67] In doing so, Mendelssohn both legitimates the Enlightenment love of nature to his traditional audience by grounding it in a rabbinic prooftext, and presents the rabbis as proto-Enlightenment figures, possessors of natural wisdom; in fact, in this letter, the rabbis are called "pillars of the world" (*amudei haolam*),[68] implying that their teachings are worthwhile for a universal audience, in accordance with the Enlightenment principle that all who practice the religion of reason have things to teach each other.[69] In this vein, Mendelssohn never, in any Jewish or non-Jewish public context, presents the rabbis as performing any action or expressing any thought contrasting with Enlightenment tenets.

However, Mendelssohn's presentation of the rabbis as lovers of nature is but one facet of a significantly more complex and ambiguous rabbinic attitude toward nature—expressed most notably in the Talmudic statement, located near the one he cites, that if one stops in the middle of prayer to admire God's handiwork, one is liable to death.[70]

66. Halkin *Modern Jewish* 51.

67. See Gilon 157; 1:1–2, 4. (References to *Kohelet Musar* refer to the pagination and numbering in Gilon's critical edition.) Mendelssohn calques Ecclesiastes 4:1,7 and 3:14. The rabbinic source is *BT Berakhot* 43b, which reads: "Rab Judah says: If one goes abroad in the days of Nisan [spring time] and sees the trees sprouting, he should say, 'Blessed be He who hath not left His world lacking in anything and has created in it goodly creatures and goodly trees for the enjoyment of mankind.'" Translation Soncino *Zeraim* I:264. Both Gilon and Borodianski, in *JubA* 14:xii–xvi, have attempted to gloss *Kohelet Musar*. Neither work is complete, perhaps a necessity in attempting to gloss a work where every word may be a reference, either directly or a calque. I have used both lists and added glosses of my own; needless to say, this is not a complete list, either.

68. Gilon 159 1:48.

69. See Sorkin *MMRE* 59–60.

70. *Mishna Avot* 3:8. The rabbis did not have a negative view of nature, but they did view it as subordinate to religious values. For more on this topic, q.v. "Nature," *EJ* 12:888–891, and, more recently, compare David Ruderman, *Jewish Thought and*

Mendelssohn, of course, refrains from mentioning that view. These essays are polemical works, and Mendelssohn presents his view as if it were rabbinic totality, as any good ideologue would.

Biblical texts seemingly used for purely stylistic purposes will not be focused on here,[71] since it is difficult to tell where linguistic necessity ends and thematic commentary begins. However, the citations from Psalms and the "Psalmist,"[72] the Jewish book of nature *par excellence*, and the selections from Genesis reminding the reader of man's triumph over nature, seem to have thematic as well as stylistic resonance.[73] Further proofs of this Enlightenment approach to the triumph over nature are brought from the Talmud and Maimonides, the noted rationalist.[74]

The second letter is more polemical, dealing with a specifically Jewish subject, albeit in Enlightenment-influenced terms. The section attempts to demonstrate the essential superiority of the Hebrew language and its fitness to express literarily the range of emotions. As previously noted, historical trends in non-Jewish scholarship made the first part of this position not merely an idle boast of Jewish chauvinism but conventional wisdom, at least in Biblical terms. Could the same superiority, or at least equality, of Hebrew of the Biblical period be applied to Hebrew today, and then synecdochically to its speakers? Once the grounds of the first statement are accepted, the second becomes open to debate.

In *Kohelet Musar*, Mendelssohn does not merely require his Jewish audience to acknowledge the theoretical superiority of Hebrew (presumably, most would already do so), but its *actual* superiority; he urges a more active adoption of the Hebrew language, certainly in

---

Scientific Discovery in Early Modern Europe (New Haven: Yale University Press, 1995), 17, 375–382.

71. Texts quoted or referred to in the section include Hosea 6:3, Ezekiel 45:20, and Isaiah 67:11.

72. "*Hameshorer*"; the citation is from Psalms 104:24. Other references to Psalms in the section include Psalms 50:11 and 80:14. Gilon 159 1:56–57.

73. Genesis 1:21, 21:15. Gilon 159 1:39, 43.

74. *BT Rosh Hashana* 2a, *BT Khulin* 60a (Gilon 159 1:51–52), *Guide to the Perplexed* 2:30 (Gilon 159 1:52–55).

contrast to Yiddish and possibly even as a particularistic counterpart of or complement to German. This would be accomplished through study, then active usage, of Biblical Hebrew. A polemical argument is particularly necessary here because, perhaps contrary to expectations, the Jewish community—even and especially the traditionalists—did not actively study Biblical Hebrew, partially as the result of their interpretation of Rashi's commentary on the Talmudist Rabbi Eliezer's deathbed demand to "keep your children from meditation (*min'u bneikhem min hahigayon*)."[75]

In arguing for Hebrew's essential and practical superiority, Mendelssohn draws on many Jewish sources, necessary to prove to his audience that all strata of Jewish law agree on the superiority of Hebrew and the necessity of active usage, quoting Judah HaLevi's *Kuzari*,[76] Maimonides' *Commentary on Ethics of the Fathers*,[77] and even the midrashic *Mekhilta,* the last to show that even in the exile of Egypt, the Jews did not forget their language.[78] In rebutting the current traditionalist position toward Biblical Hebrew study, he refers to Maimonides' definition of the phrase,[79] arguing that most people misunderstand Rashi's intent, which is merely to decry the phenomenon of learning without ethical practice. To prove his point, he cites another statement of Rashi's, fighting text with text, interpretation with interpretation.[80]

Mendelssohn addresses another question in the same letter: is everything God does for good? Clearly attempting to fit his optimistic Leibnizian philosophy into a Jewish context, Mendelssohn labors tirelessly to prove that Jewish thought and traditional texts, particularly rabbinic texts, harmonize with the latest German philosophy.[81] In the

75. See *BT Berakhot* 28b and Rashi *ad loc.* For a full discussion of Mendelssohn's responses to this issue, see Edward Breuer, "Hahaskala vehamikra: iyun bikhtavav hakedumim shel Moshe Mendelson," *Zion* 59:4 (1994), 445–463. See also Breuer *Limits* 116–117; Altmann *MMBS* 88–90; and Parush "Mabat akher" 87.

    76. *Kuzari* 4:25; Gilon 160 2:7–11.

    77. 2:1; Gilon 160 2:17–19.

    78. Bo 5; Gilon 160 2:23–24.

    79. Maimonides, *Milot Hahigayon*, Chapter 14 (Gilon 161 2:28–29).

    80. See Rashi's commentary to Deuteronomy 11:19. (Gilon 161 2:34–36).

    81. See Sorkin *MMRE* 16, and *Berlin Haskalah* 53–54, 106.

motto framing the discussion, another common feature of the moral weekly, he quotes the Talmudic statement that "[e]verything that God [lit. The Merciful One] does, He does for good,"[82] and, after discussing the story of Jonah, relates an anecdote, newly written but cast in traditionalist form, concretizing the problem in quasiliterary terms.[83]

Throughout the letter, snippets and sections of Biblical verses appear, often seemingly used as a matter of linguistic necessity,[84] but occasionally one extrudes sufficiently to display thematic connections to the issue discussed. For example, Mendelssohn uses the phrase from Esther 4:14, *revakh vehatsala* ("relief and deliverance"), highly resonant to readers from the annual reading of Esther on Purim.[85] The sentiments expressed in the Biblical passage, that the difficult position Esther now faces has been arranged by God for the benefit of the entire Jewish people, that this temporary suffering is part of the Divine plan, are so perfectly in accord with the tenets of Leibnizian (and maskilic) optimism that the modern reader suspects that Mendelssohn intended this as a subtle ideological and political point, not merely a felicitous turn of phrase. At times, the usage of Biblical language can be explicitly homiletic as well, such as when Mendelssohn cites Psalms 104:31, which says that "God rejoice[s] in his works," as a prooftext for God's goodwill toward His creatures.[86]

---

82. *BT Berakhot* 60b (Gilon 162 2:50). Gilon (48–49) notes that of the four mottos appearing in the text, three are Talmudic and one is Biblical. Were we not aware of Mendelssohn's need to cast the rabbis as proto-Enlightenment figures, this emphasis on rabbinic texts might be odd.

83. Jonah appears in Gilon 162 2:55ff; the anecdote in Gilon 162–163 2:74ff. The protagonist's name is Biblical (1 Samuel 14:3, 22:9), though in this case, the name *Akhitov*, literally meaning "my brother is good," seems merely to be a playful attempt to identify the subject of discussion with the object of discussion. On names in *Kohelet Musar*, see Gilon 49.

84. For example, this section quotes, among others, selections from Micah (2:8), Ezekiel (21:20), Isaiah (3:3, 8:22, 38:17, 41:7), Proverbs (16:20, 25:2, 28:17), Ecclesiastes (5:5, 7:11), Psalms (49:14, 78:41), Song of Songs (6:5), Job (7:15), 2 Chronicles (28:15), and Jeremiah (23:31, 10:11).

85. Gilon 162 2:69.

86. Gilon 163 2:99.

   This letter illuminates Mendelssohn's hierarchy of legitimation, one that subtly betrays an Enlightenment-influenced attitude toward the various strata of Jewish texts. After a preliminary rabbinic statement to set the tone, the first set of arguments are grounded in reason and anecdote, a universally accessible medium for proof. Realizing this audience's particular needs, Mendelssohn subsequently turns to Jewish prooftexts, but still places the more universalist and partially Enlightenment-based Biblical proofs before the rabbinic proofs. Only after the Bible has been explored does Mendelssohn write: "And many of the sayings of our sages, may their memory be for a blessing, agree with these words."[87] Mendelssohn presents the rabbis as merely in step with the pure and ideologically irreproachable Biblical statements, as wise men who lived in harmony with the teachings of the Bible, which, in turn, are in accord with reason.

   Mendelssohn then proceeds to cite two rabbinic proofs: the Talmudic story where Ulla dismisses as blasphemy a rabbinic attempt to comfort the bereaved Rabbi Samuel ben Judah through reference to human insignificance in the face of an uncaring God, implying that everything God does is good,[88] and a midrashic source that he calls "even more wondrous," where an exegetical interpretation equates the creation of death with the Biblical phrase "and God saw it was very

---

87. Gilon 164 2:109.

88. Gilon 164 2:110–119; *BT Bava Kama* 38a:

> When R. Samuel b. Judah lost a daughter, the rabbis said to Ulla: "Let us go in and console him." But he answered them: "What have I to do with the consolation of the Babylonians, which is blasphemy? For they say 'What could have been done,' which implies that were it possible to do anything, they would have done it."

Translation from Soncino edition, Dr. I. Epstein, ed. (London: Soncino Press, 1935), Vol. *Nezikin* I, pp. 215–216. See also *Nimukei Yosef* ad loc. The Talmudic story is both cited in Aramaic and subsequently translated into Hebrew for the audience's benefit; this Mendelssohnian decision can serve as one example to use in pinpointing levels of audience knowledge and differentiation. A more detailed effort at audience phenomenology is seen in Chapter Seven in the discussion of *Megale Temirin*.

good."[89] Even death is for the best. Mendelssohn, in his citation and translation, skips certain sections of the Talmudic story. Though possibly doing so for simple narrative felicity, the omissions may also be symptomatic of Mendelssohn's effort to reshape the Jewish canon to fit his ideological positions, whereby narrative sections that do not accord are excised.

The third letter continues to discuss the problem of evil and to attempt to synthesize Jewish thought with current German philosophy. In this letter, classical and particularly Biblical texts appear primarily for stylistic purposes,[90] but there are two notable exceptions. The first is the opening rabbinic motto quoting the rabbinic requirement for an individual to make a blessing even upon experiencing bad events.[91] The rabbis understood, insinuates Mendelssohn, that seemingly bad events were also part of an inherently good world order.

The second exception occurs in a footnote, where Mendelssohn painstakingly explains his system of punctuation, afraid that traditional readers might be unfamiliar with it. Even this minor change, though, needs to be justified and legitimated in traditional terms.[92] First, Mendelssohn compares the (modern) style of punctuation to the *trop*, the masoretic cantillation notation, writing, for example, *bet nekudot bimkom etnakhta*, that a colon is used as an analogue to the traditional *etnakhta*, the masoretic note that functions as a comma in a Biblical verse. But Mendelssohn goes further: he justifies this apparent innovation on the grounds that canonized Jewish authorities also used punctuation, citing Maimonides' *Yad Hakhazaka* and Isaac Abarbanel's Pentateuch commentary as examples.

89. Gilon 164 2:120–124; *Bereshit Raba* 9:5: "In the teaching of Rabbi Meir, it was found to be written: 'and behold, it was very good *(tov meod)*—and behold, death is good *(tov mavet)*." J. Theodor, ed., *Bereschit Rabba mit kritischem Apparat und Kommentar* (Berlin 1912), 70.

90. References include Genesis (42:29, 43:28, 49:23), Isaiah (58:4), Exodus (17:7), 2 Samuel (3:25), Psalms (131:2), Ecclesiastes (12:5), Lamentations (3:26), Psalms (37:7), Job (11:12), and Proverbs (4:26, 9:4, 17).

91. Motto appears on Gilon 165 3:1; *BT Berakhot* 54a.

92. Gilon 168 3:80–82. As we will see in the chapters on Joseph Perl, however, typography can be a flashpoint for traditionalist opposition or a prime source for subversion. See Chapters Six and Seven *infra*.

All the modern belletristic or essayistic works of the Aufklärung were punctuated; to bring Hebrew printing and orthography into the eighteenth century, Jews needed to follow suit. That even this limited type of change needed legitimation shows the magnitude of the maskilic task in general. Mendelssohn's note suggests that the audience was either so unfamiliar with non-Jewish books that they needed to be taught the meaning of punctuation, or was so conscious of the distinction between Jewish *sforim* and non-Jewish *bikher* that they had real problems accepting the style of one in the other, or that different subgroups of Mendelssohn's audience existed with each of these problems. An interesting perspective on this legitimative strategy can be seen by examining the editions of the works Gilon identifies as Mendelssohn's prooftexts in the matter of punctuation: the Amsterdam 1702 edition of the *Yad Hakhazaka* and the 1710 Hanau edition of Abarbanel's Pentateuch commentary.[93] Examination of these editions reveals that though a rudimentary schema of punctuation exists in each, it is a different and less developed one than Mendelssohn suggests. Presumably, the image of legitimation is more important than actual mimesis.

The fourth letter of *Kohelet Musar*, the beginning of the second issue, marks a turn for the literary: Mendelssohn begins to play with the notions of persona, frame narrative, and external epistolary devices that will be crucial to the development of maskilic literature. Expertly, Mendelssohn defuses opponents' potential criticisms by writing that he, the author, was delivered a letter asking him to stop writing letters of moral reproof and so allowing them to engage in the guiltless pursuit of pleasure.[94] Here, where the text moves from the essayistic to the narrative, Mendelssohn's Biblical language becomes highly resonant, commenting on mood and action, offering commentary as well as additional emotional shading.

To mention only two related examples: first, the letter writer uses imagery taken from the story of the Golden Calf in order to characterize his own merrymaking, like that of the Israelites around Mount

93. Gilon 155.
94. Gilon 168–169 4:1–36.

Sinai, as lacking any moral component.[95] Second, the author—Moses—playfully puts the letter writer in the place of the earlier, Biblical Moses; his reaction to the author's earlier letters is to cite Moses' words when confronted with the public revelation of his slaying of the Egyptian: *akhen noda hadavar* ("Certainly, the thing is known").[96]

Mendelssohn answers his opponent's charges, not surprisingly, by using classical texts. He uses numerous Biblical phrases to show that he, too, loves pleasure, but his pleasure is a more rarefied one, based on intellectual and rational apprehension of God's power and man's distinguished place in the chain of being: he writes, "Tell me if you know a greater pleasure than the pleasure of this intellectual examination?"[97] In this vein, his citation of Jeremiah 9:22 is particularly noteworthy, stating that a person should not exult in his own wisdom, for all wisdom—and the pleasure derived therefrom—comes from God.[98] Mendelssohn's language, such as *bekhina* ("aspect"), *taanug haamiti* ("true pleasure," defined as resulting from use of the rational faculty), and *shlemut* ("perfection"), demonstrate his familiarity with the Maimonidean terminology of the *Guide to the Perplexed*,[99] and constitute another attempt to ground this aspect of Enlightenment ideology in a Jewish philosophical framework.

Mendelssohn moves from discussing pleasure and perfection on an individual level to treating the mutual relationship of friendship, a trope necessarily popular considering the dialogic style favored by Enlightenment philosophy. He illustrates the Enlightenment ideal of friendship by appealing to the Biblical model of friendship *par excellence*, David and Jonathan. Further, he even shows that the rabbinic characterization of

95. Gilon 169 4:21–22. See Exodus 25:18.

96. Exodus 2:14; Gilon 169 4:27. Quotations also appear in this section of the letter from Psalms (2:10, 94:8), 1 Kings (20:40), Genesis (23:6), Ecclesiastes (2:1), Job (39:21), and Proverbs (31:4).

97. Gilon 170 4:62–63. Also particularly noteworthy here are the Biblical references in this section of the letter from Proverbs (1:22, 27:7), Isaiah (6:10, 59:13, 63:1), Lamentations (4:21), Samuel (26:23), Jeremiah (15:19), Deuteronomy (32:24), and Job (5:27, 28:16).

98. Gilon 171 4:79.

99. From, respectively, Gilon 170 4:63, 170 4:70, and 171 4:85, 96.

this optimal friendship perfectly accords with Enlightenment tenets, quoting the sages' statement that David and Jonathan's love was "a love not dependent on anything,"[100] a rarefied, pristine friendship based on recognition of the other's perfect qualities—particularly their rational and intellectual perfection. Mendelssohn's final words on the subject both rehabilitate the rabbis and reveal himself as a member of the Religious Enlightenment: he cites the Talmud to demonstrate that the pleasure gained from using one's rational and intellectual faculties is what is called *ahavat hashem* ("love of God") in traditional sources.[101]

The fifth letter is dedicated to propounding the Enlightenment notion of productive labor, though Mendelssohn, unlike later maskilim, does not discuss productivization or the value of manual labor. By "productive labor," Mendelssohn merely means that a life of study is insufficient unless properly balanced with some sort of work. The letter's legitimation strategies are identical to those of previous letters: the anecdote,[102] Biblical prooftexts, and the occasional rabbinic citation. As in the previous letter, a major proof is taken not from Biblical or rabbinic sources, but rather medieval Jewish philosophy. Mendelssohn writes about the necessity of work: "And these ideas are ancient: those who feared God, and our wise sages, spoke of them. And after them, those who edified/rebuked the nation (*mokhikhei haam*) came to the fore: the sages and the *geonim*."[103] Mendelssohn then cites the *Kuzari* to illustrate the importance of work.[104]

Mendelssohn continues to use the earlier strata of the Jewish canon, of course. He cites a rabbinic statement that sacrificing a sin-offering without making restitution is not acceptable to God, using it to indicate that duties to mankind (one's labor) are more pleasing to God

100. *Mishna Avot* 5:17. See Gilon 171–172 4:98–104.

101. *BT Sota* 31a. Discussion takes place in Gilon 172 4:109–119.

102. Gilon 173–174 5:15–50. Characters in Mendelssohn's anecdotes here are named *Elzabad*, *Yedaya*, and *Asael;* all are Biblical names (taken from 1 Chronicles 26:7; Zechariah 6:10, Ezra 2:36, Nehemiah 11:10; and 2 Chronicles 17:8, 31:13 respectively), though none seem to refer to their Biblical counterparts.

103. Gilon 174–175 5:51–52.

104. Gilon 175 5:52–55. *Kuzari* 2:50.

than, and primary to, direct divine service.[105] And again, this letter incorporates many fragments of Biblical verses for primarily stylistic purposes.[106]

In the final letter of *Kohelet Musar*, Mendelssohn further develops the frame narrative last seen at the beginning of Letter Four: the author receives another letter, this time from an admirer, which informs him of the existence of a group of like-minded individuals.[107] Mendelssohn's author has developed from a prophetic voice crying in the wilderness[108] to the representative voice of an alternative community. If these others can validate the author, the letter seems to imply, so can the reader. The letter as a whole does not contain many citations of classical texts,[109] dedicated as it is to Mendelssohn's previous assertion that Hebrew is a vehicle capable of expressing a range of modern emotions. The prooftext here, unsurprisingly, is not a classical Jewish text, but a secular one; Mendelssohn translates a selection of "Night Thoughts" by the English poet Edward Young.[110] It is this translation that, for all intents and purposes, closes the work.

105. Gilon 175 5:57–58. Though Mendelssohn introduces the statement as a direct quote, there is no such quote in rabbinic literature; the closest analogous statement is *BT Bava Kama* 111a. Mendelssohn either relied on memory in providing the quote, or subtly revised the statement to make his point more powerfully.

106. Calques and citations in the letter include references to Genesis (19:15, 33:13), Psalms (10:10, 35:17, 37:3, 55:11, 89:40), Ecclesiastes (1:17, 2:12, 8:1), 2 Kings (12:15), Daniel (11:24), Isaiah (5:13, 30:7, 30:19, 49:10, 57:10, 58:5), Ezekiel (13:19, 18:7, 29:18), Jeremiah (10:14, 43:10, 49:7), Job (15:17, 30:5, 31:39, 34:25), and Proverbs (7:16, 11:10).

107. Gilon 176–177 6:1–21.

108. The number of quotations from prophets in *Kohelet Musar* may, among other things, indicate Mendelssohn's literary identification with the prophetic archetype.

109. Though Biblical phrases again appear for stylistic purposes: Job (4:14, 20, 6:9, 13, 28, 7:14, 27:5, 33:17, 35:11, 38:7), 2 Kings (12:12, 22:5, 9), Isaiah (11:11), and Psalms (35:14).

110. Gilon 178–180 6:34–72. On this translation, see Gideon Toury, "Translating English Literature Via German—and Vice Versa: A Symptomatic Reversal in the History of Modern Hebrew Literature," in Harald Kittel, ed., *Di literarische Übersetzung: Stand und Perspektiven ihrer Erforschung* (Berlin: Erich Schmidt Ver-

This last section throws the whole project sharply into another perspective: when a group of like-minded, free-thinking Jews congregate to discuss the future of Hebrew, the test of its survival is its ability to harbor an English poem, its capability to bear the weight of other literature, other values; the unstated assumption is that these values are the crucial ones. All the other efforts, how rabbinic texts are rehabilitated, efforts to prove Enlightenment dogma, all fall into place. Even the revitalization of Hebrew, the one topic in *Kohelet Musar* whose source seems internal rather than external and which could potentially become a source of autonomous pride, is revealed as externally contingent, based on foreign aesthetic principles.

The final lines of *Kohelet Musar* offer poetic proof that Mendelssohn's efforts were aimed at shaping Jewish tradition to fit Enlightenment values. This stemmed not merely from the desire to gain non-Jewish recognition and social emancipation, but also from the true internalization of those values and the feeling that Jewish tradition can, and must, be shaped and re-presented to fit them. At least, this is the position he takes in public.

Brief Notes on the Middle Years

As we have said, the main focus of this chapter is to discuss *Kohelet Musar* and *Jerusalem*; nonetheless, a number of other Mendelssohnian projects are substantially important to our understanding of Mendelssohn's usage of classical Jewish text, and though we lack the space to discuss them in full, they do merit brief consideration.

In 1759, Mendelssohn, reviewing a German translation of the Mishna in a German journal, posed as a Christian consulting a Jewish rabbi to illustrate that the conclusions reached by a "reasonable" "Christian"

---

lag, 1988), 139–157; Altmann *MMBS* 91; Lawrence Marsdale Price, *English Literature in Germany* (Berkeley: University of California Press, 1953), 36–51, 113–121, esp. 118; and now, Jeremy Dauber, "New Thoughts on 'Night Thoughts': Mendelssohn and Translation," *Modern Jewish Studies* 2:2 (2003), 132–147, for a much fuller discussion of the topic.

can be identical to those reached by a reasonable Jew;[111] such playfulness with persona and identity by Mendelssohn notably continues a trend first seen in *Kohelet Musar.* Mendelssohn's rabbi, aware of widespread Christian anti-Talmudic sentiment, partially casts the blame on Jewish scholars who "were unwilling or unable to offer an articulate response that Christians could understand."[112] The implication, of course, is that if such a response were to be offered, the Christians would change their minds. The review mentions the problematic *aggadot* which were the most serious source of anti-Semitic attack, but defuses criticism by writing that "'Those matters,' said the rabbi, 'which at first glance should appear absurd, constitute about a fifth of the Talmud,'" and even these sections contained wisdom. A better snapshot of Mendelssohn's defense of the Talmud cannot be imagined.

Mendelssohn is not best known for his work on the Talmud, however; rather, it is his Bible translations, notably of the Pentateuch, the Song of Songs, Psalms, and Ecclesiastes, and the *Biur*, the German-language Bible commentary he organized, that occupy pride of place in his maskilic writings.[113] The translation was "expected to sweep aside all mystic and allegoric interpretations of the Scriptures and introduce the rational and scientific method,"[114] and was one of the earliest maskilic projects to generate conflict between the maskilim and the traditional Jewish community.[115] Mendelssohn's project of Bible

111. The review can be found in Moses Mendelssohn, *Gesammelte Schriften*, ed. G.B. Mendelssohn (Leipzig: 1843–1845) 4.1:529–531. Translation appears in Breuer *Limits* 140–141; see also Altmann *MMBS* 196–197.

112. Breuer *Limits* 140.

113. The *Biur* was a communal effort; for ascriptions of authorship of various parts, see Silberschlag 82n20 and Sorkin *MMRE* 36–40. For details concerning the *Biur*'s publication in Berlin 1783, see Sandler 160–163. On later, "corrected" editions, see Sandler 184–186.

114. Nachum Slouchz, *The Renascence of Hebrew Literature* (Philadelphia: JPS, 1909), 31; see also Altmann *MMBS* 372.

115. On opposition to the *Biur*, see Sandler 194–218 and Altmann *MMBS* 382, as well as Jacob Katz, "R' Raphael Cohen, yerivo shel Moshe Mendelson," *Tarbiz* 56:2 (1987), 243–64. Ironically, the *Biur*, under the title *Sefer Netivot Hashalom* ("The Book of the Paths of Peace") eventually became a religious text in Eastern Europe. See Sorkin *MMRE* 88–89.

translation and commentary, and the congruence of his translation choices with maskilic aims, has been discussed at great length elsewhere;[116] a few points will be extracted from the scholarly discussion relevant to this essay.

A good overview of Mendelssohn's own approach to translation can be seen in the approbation he gave to the 1777 commentary on Job *Pesher Davar* ("The Interpretation of a Matter"),[117] where he notes approvingly that the work is both based on literalist interpretations of Jewish texts and is in agreement with the moral teachings of the sages.[118] Mendelssohn's comments on his own interpretations are also illuminating: "I did what all commentators do. I offered an interpretation that somehow agrees with the meaning of the words, and the reader has to be satisfied with this."[119] These guidelines have served him well in the past and continue to do so in his own work of Biblical translation and commentary.

Ideologically, Mendelssohn's reasons for turning to the Bible, the ultimate universal legitimating force for Jew and non-Jew alike, are clear. Mendelssohn wrote that one reason for producing a new translation was that extant German translations, used also by German-speaking Jews, were eminently christological.[120] Mendelssohn's comments on contemporary Jews' choice of Biblical translations are noteworthy:

> In their narrow straits they "turn to vainglory and alluring deception," that "changes into wormwood" the law of our God. They supply themselves with the works of the gentiles, using the translations of the non-Jewish scholars who disdain the trusted interpretations

116. See, for example, the works by Altmann, Breuer, Lowenstein, Sandler, Sorkin, and Weinberg cited in this chapter. On Ecclesiastes as wisdom literature with universalist appeal, see Sorkin *MMRE* 35–36. Maskilic translation was not limited to the Bible, of course; see Silberschlag 98–102, esp. n.79, for a good overview of early maskilic translation.

117. The book, authored by Zeev Wolf b. Abraham Nathan of Dessau, was published in Berlin. Its title is taken from Ecclesiastes 8:1; "Who is like the wise man and who knows the interpretation of a matter?"

118. Discussion taken from Hildesheimer "Nineteenth Century" 80–81.

119. *JubA* 12.2:23. Translation taken from Altmann *MMBS* 275.

120. See Sorkin *MMRE* 53 and Tsamriyon 45.

of our sages of blessed memory and who refuse to accept their un-
blemished tradition, while interpreting Scripture according to their
own fancy and spoiling the vineyard of the Lord of Hosts.[121]

As such, Mendelssohn's translation served its own polemical purpose,
accusing non-Jews of interpretive excess and attempting to offer a universally accessible and mutually agreeable alternative, one based on
the rationalist "plain meaning" of the text.

Mendelssohn had an additional, more subtle agenda: a reemphasis
on the Bible, sparked by a new translation and commentary, could
serve as a flashpoint for a renaissance of Hebrew among eighteenth-
century German Jewry, where a general decline in Hebrew knowledge, beginning at the end of the last century, had reached new
depths, and Biblical study was rare.[122] Mendelssohn, well aware of this
phenomenon, writes in the Hebrew prospectus to his translation:
"For the ways of our holy tongue have been forgotten in our midst;
the elegance of its phraseology [*tsachut melitsoteha*] eludes us; and the
loveliness of its poetry is hidden from our eyes."[123] Indeed, the aspira-
tion to revitalize Hebrew—the primary language of Jewish canonical
text—will play a central role, implicitly or explicitly, throughout
Mendelssohn's work.[124]

Lowenstein and Weinberg have done excellent work on the audience of Mendelssohn's Bible translation and have perceptively noted
that the work is largely aimed at people knowing German but not Hebrew; the introductions to the *Biur* state its aim is to teach Hebrew to
German speakers, not vice versa,[125] and the financial support for
Mendelssohn's *Biur* was much stronger among the upper class, among

121. *JubA* 14:327; translation from Altmann *MMBS* 375.

122. See *GJH* 1:219 and Breuer *Limits* 19.

123. *JubA* 14:242; translation from Altmann *MMBS* 369.

124. On the Berlin Haskala's "practical intention from the outset . . . to create
and propagate 'a new Hebrew language' to function alongside other languages,"
see Yaacov Shavit, "A Duty Too Heavy to Bear: Hebrew in the Berlin Haskalah,
1783–1819: Between Classic, Modern, and Romantic," in Glinert 111–128, esp. 111.
See also Pelli *Age* 73–90; Yedidia Yitzchaki, "Sifrut khaya bilshon meta," *Bikoret
ufarshanut* 25 (1989), 89–100, 91–93; and Shmueli 135–136.

125. Weinberg 203–205.

new communities, particularly Berlin, and newer generations.[126] In fact, the elite who were Mendelssohn's audience had long acquired good knowledge of German, despite their greater comfort with the Hebrew alphabet. German language education was increasing rapidly, thanks to governmental decrees and new types of Jewish schools.[127] Weinberg even states that "Mendelssohn's German was much too highbrow, too sophisticated to be considered of any pedagogical value for teaching the language to beginners" and that "if . . . any reproach should be attached to Mendelssohn's translation at all, it would be the charge of elitism. His translation was not accessible to and, indeed, not intended for the masses of Jews, especially those who lived in smaller towns or in rural areas."[128]

By providing a German translation for German speakers and a Hebrew commentary for further study, Mendelssohn may have hoped to use the expected renaissance of Hebrew as a basis for the (re)creation of an autonomous and authentic Jewish culture that could stand on an equal basis to the cultures of Europe—and would thus render the Jews equally worthy of social emancipation. Mendelssohn's linguistic deliberations, however, did not merely limit themselves to Hebrew and German. Mendelssohn also writes of his hope that his translation would replace extant Yiddish Bible translations.[129] Though some scholars have argued that the *Biur* is Mendelssohn's attempt to wean Jews from the Yiddish language,[130] this does not seem to be the case: Mendelssohn's relationship to Yiddish is more complicated than straightforward opposition.

126. See Steven Lowenstein, "The Readership of Mendelssohn's Bible Translation," in *The Mechanics of Change; Essays in the Social History of German Jewry* (Atlanta: Scholars Press, 1992), 29–64, and "Social Dynamics" 340–345. See also Altmann *MMBS* 377 and Breuer *Limits* 26.

127. Weinberg 226–227. For a detailed overview of the educational system during this period, see Weinberg 228–234.

128. Weinberg 208, 206.

129. For Mendelssohn's comments on earlier Yiddish translations, see *JubA* 14:232–243, esp. 242–243.

130. See, for example, Sandler 6–15 and the more nuanced approach taken by Gilman (90–100).

The maskilic hatred of Yiddish, generally speaking, is well known, though, as we will see throughout this book, that hatred is not as monolithic as it is often presented to be.[131] As with so many ideological issues of the Berlin Haskala, this linguistic ideology was conditioned as much externally as internally: the attitude toward Yiddish in Germany in the 1780s and the 1790s is analogous to the debate over the relationship between *Hochdeutsch* and other dialects of German within the general German-speaking community—the division of languages into "pure" and "corrupt."[132] Steven Aschheim notes perceptively that the opposition to Yiddish was not because of its alienness, but because "it was widely regarded as a corrupt and lowly derivation of German itself. Elsewhere Yiddish sounded merely strange, but in Germany it was precisely its familiarity that bred contempt."[133]

The notion of Yiddish was also intimately connected with the question of the *Ostjuden*; often, the view of Yiddish as expressed in *Hameasef* is based on the notion of an Eastern European Yiddish—that is, one filled with Slavicisms, and therefore, to the maskilim, particularly distant from "pure" German and thus "corrupt."[134] Indeed, it was the Eastern European Yiddish that the *Mauscheln,* the stock Jewish characters in the German theater, spoke for the amusement of anti-Semitic audiences.[135] Notably, the word referred not merely to the stock characters, but to their stock mannerisms as well, which include "the per-

131. An excellent and nuanced overview of the changing attitudes toward Yiddish throughout the Haskala appears in Shmuel Werses, "Yad yamin dokhe yad smol mekarevet: al yakhasam shel sofrei hahaskala lelashon yidish," *Khulyot* 5 (1998), 9–49. Another major treatment of this issue appears in Dan Miron's *A Traveler Disguised* (Syracuse, NY: University of Syracuse Press, 1996), esp. 34–45.

132. See Peter Freimark, "Language Behaviour and Assimilation: The Situation of the Jews in Modern Germany in the First Half of the Nineteenth Century," *LBIYB* 24 (1979), 157–177, 159–160, 163–166. For a full treatment of the German attitudes toward Yiddish, see Jeffrey A. Grossman, *The Discourse on Yiddish in Germany: From the Enlightenment to the Second Empire* (Rochester, NY: Camden House, 2000), esp. 75–90, 110–111.

133. Aschheim 8.

134. Werses "Yad" 10–12.

135. For more on the *Mauscheln*, see Gilman 139–140, 155–157, and Strauss 236 and the sources cited there.

sistence of errors in syntax and pronunciation, characteristic intonations, occasional Yiddish words, and hand gestures."[136]

Mendelssohn accepted the distinction between "pure" and "corrupt" languages;[137] this may have led to his ambivalence toward Yiddish in a public sphere, as he felt that Yiddish, particularly the Yiddish of the *Ostjuden* which was "adulterated" with Slavicisms, was a "corrupt" language and unsuitable for philosophical or political expression. This would explain Mendelssohn's famous opposition to the use of Yiddish to take oaths in judicial contexts, when he writes, "I am afraid that this jargon has contributed not a little to the immorality of the common people, and I expect some very good results from the use of the pure German way of speech that has been coming into vogue among my brethren for some time."[138] The rhetoric of purity, given our discussion, must be taken as significant. Nonetheless, as Weinberg writes,

> this does not mean that he spearheaded a concerted effort to dislodge
> Judeo-German. What he wanted to eradicate were the Judeo-German
> Bible translations, as much for their word by word translation
> method—which prevented syntactical understanding on the side of
> the pupils[139]—as for the fact that the young generation of his time
> understood German well. Concerning Judeo-German, however, as an
> informal and unpretentious vehicle of oral and written communica-
> tion among Jews—he was perfectly at ease with it. No better testi-
> mony is needed than his own letter writing habits.[140]

Mendelssohn's Yiddish writing was certainly not intended for public consumption and cannot be considered literature in the public sense *per se*. However, this very dynamic—writing in Yiddish but refusing to publish in it—epitomizes the maskilic position toward Yiddish in 1780s

136. See *GJH* 2:204.

137. See *GJH* 1:309.

138. *JubA* 7:279; translation taken from Altmann *MMBS* 499.

139. On previous Yiddish Bible translations, see *GJH* 1:220 and Marion Aptroot, "Blitz un vitsenhoyzn: naye penimer fun an alter makhloykes," *Oksforder yidish* 1 (1990), 3–38. On other non-Yiddish translations, see Sandler 37–41.

140. See Weinberg 236–241; citation from 239. See also Tsamriyon 38–39.

Berlin; this was thus the "Age of Mendelssohn" in terms of attitudes toward Yiddish as well.

Mendelssohn's methods for achieving his goals, however, stirred up nervousness among traditional circles: "The printing of the German version side by side with the Hebrew text seemed an intrusion of the profane into the realm of the sacred. It was all the more necessary to show . . . that there was nothing heterodox in either the translation or the Hebrew commentary."[141] Indeed, despite the traditional opposition, Mendelssohn's translation and commentary fall firmly into the same liminal position previously noted: his famed comment that his Bible translation is the "first step to culture" may have implied an embrace of *Bildung*, but hardly constituted an attack on orthodoxy.[142]

As just one example of his traditionalist perspective, his entire work of Biblical translation and commentary can be seen as a defense of the traditional masoretic text in the face of contemporary Biblical criticism, much of which was overtly polemical, challenging Jewish traditions concerning the masoretic text, rejecting midrash, and focusing solely on the literalist sense of the text.[143] For Mendelssohn, the defense of these texts was not merely a matter of scholarly authenticity, but legal stability: Jewish law was based on these texts.[144]

Notably, the defense is largely an argument from absence; Mendelssohn makes no mention in the *Biur* of contemporary Biblical scholarship. The Biblical criticisms of Spinoza or the Protestant neologists such as Spalding and Reimarus are rarely directly addressed in any of Mendelssohn's work, though some view *Jerusalem* as a kind of

141. Altmann *MMBS* 374.

142. Cited in Meyer *Origins* 43.

143. See Mendelssohn's strong defense of the masoretic text in his introduction to the *Biur*, *Or Letiva* (*JubA* 14:213–228). Breuer has written extensively on this topic; see *Limits* 77–175, esp. 95–99, 111–115, 121–122, 147–175; Breuer "On Miracles" 28; Sorkin *MMRE* 80–81; Sandler, 34–37, 85–89; and Raphael Jospe, "Biblical Exegesis as a Philosophic Literary Genre: Abraham Ibn Ezra and Moses Mendelssohn," in Emil L. Fackenheim and Raphael Jospe, eds., *Jewish Philosophy and the Academy* (Teaneck, NJ: Farleigh Dickinson Unversity Press, 1996), 48–92, 60.

144. See Breuer *Limits* 161–166; Breuer "Rabbinic Law" 316; and Jospe 51–52.

"counter-Theologico-Politico-Treatise."[145] Breuer cites this as an indication of Mendelssohn's "tenuous position in the intellectual life of eighteenth century Germany" and that his primary goal was "less a substantive response to European scholars than the desire to make a German translation available to fellow Jews."[146]

Nonetheless, Mendelssohn's translation and commentary boasted something different from previous traditionalist works: the adoption of a potentially universalizable approach to Jewish texts which, though locatable within the canon, was not the approach currently in vogue among traditional German Jewry.[147] The development of Jewish literalist (*peshat*-based) exegesis has been examined at length elsewhere;[148] Breuer discusses the use of the medieval literalist exegetes in the *Biur*, particularly Rashi, Rashbam, Ibn Ezra, and Nahmanides, at great length.[149]

Mendelssohn further develops the traditional literalist approach, stressing a literalist notion of connectedness; highly valuing the logic, context, and structure that constitute units of meaning, he still attends to the "variety of linguistic subtleties and anomalies" within the Biblical text.[150] Mendelssohn was willing to introduce interpolations and novel interpretations when he believed them more sensible,[151] and

145. See Arkush *MME* xiv, 21–27, 134–139, 148–154, 178, 230, and Michael L. Morgan, *Dilemmas in Modern Jewish Thought: The Dialectics of Revelation and History* (Bloomington: University of Indiana Press, 1992), 14–26. On Reimarus, see Gerhard Alexander, "Die Einfluß von Hermann Samuel Reimarus auf Moses Mendelssohn," in Katz and Rengstorf 17–24, as well as Altmann *MMBS* 332–340.

146. *Limits* 173–174.

147. See Altmann *MMBS* 376.

148. See Breuer *Limits* 33–76, esp. 54–60. On the balance of *peshat* and other types of interpretation in the work of literalist exegetes, see Eliezer Segal, "Midrash and Literature: Some Medieval Views," *Prooftexts* 11 (1991), 57–65, esp. 57.

149. Breuer *Limits* 177–222. See also Altmann *MMBS* 375. On Nahmanides, see Bernard Septimus, "'Open Rebuke and Concealed Love': Nahmanides and the Andalusian Tradition," in Twersky 11–34, esp. 18.

150. The latter is Mendelssohn's interpretation of the exegetical method known as *derash*; see Breuer *Limits* 190–196, 201; citation from 196. For Mendelssohn's explanation of the four levels of Jewish exegesis, see his introduction to Ecclesiastes (*JubA* 14:148–151). See also Sandler 41–57.

151. Sorkin *MMRE* 71–72; Sandler 77–79.

clearly downplayed the popular mysticist exegetical techniques of *re-mez* and *sod*,[152] writing: "Long enough has the clear meaning of Scripture been obscured by mystical casuistry."[153] Despite these innovations, Mendelssohn and his collaborators clearly functioned within a traditionalist framework, willing to translate according to rabbinic tradition over *peshat* if the consequences were deleterious for Jewish law or dogma.[154] In doing so, however, Mendelssohn insisted that the attention the rabbis gave to their exegetical interpretations "did not imply that they eschewed or belittled the value of *peshuto shel mikra* [the literal meaning of the text]: it was, rather, so thoroughly assumed by them as to be taken for granted."[155]

Mendelssohn follows the same strategies in the *Biur* that we have seen him employ in *Kohelet Musar* and his other works. Citing from a variety of sources, including rabbinic sources, Mendelssohn sets out to rehabilitate Jewish interpretation in general and rabbinic interpretation in particular, both polemically, against the perceived irrationality of non-Jewish (christological) interpretations, and subversively, to appeal to universalistic and reasonable conceptions of what Biblical interpretation should be, allowing non-Jews to validate Jewish cultural product.[156]

Jerusalem

Though this chapter does not intend to discuss Mendelssohn's general philosophy and its relation to general Enlightenment philosophy,[157]

---

152. See Breuer *Limits* 184–187 on Mendelssohn's (somewhat unnormative) definition of these terms. On Mendelssohn's "passive opposition" to mysticism, see Dov Schwartz, "Hahitpatkhut shel hamin haenoshi bemishnato shel Mendelson—perek betoldotav shel haraayon hameshikhi," *Daat* 22 (1989), 109–121.

153. *JubA* 13:109; translation taken from Altmann *MMBS* 242.

154. See Breuer *Limits* 205.

155. Edward Breuer, "Between Haskalah and Orthodoxy: The Writings of R. Jacob Zvi Meklenburg," *HUCA* 66 (1996), 259–87, 284–285.

156. Compare Breuer *Limits* 201 and Sorkin *MMRE* 47.

157. For an excellent introduction and overview of this issue, see Altmann *Introduction* 3–29, as well as sections of his commentary (143–240, hereafter *Commentary*), as well as Arkush, *MME, passim*.

the chapter's final section will analyze his most famous philosophical work, *Jerusalem*. *Jerusalem*, the culmination of Mendelssohn's writings, is a prime example of the Mendelssohnian polemic, and uses canonical Jewish texts in the same manner and for the same purposes that we have seen throughout our discussion of the Mendelssohnian oeuvre.

Jerusalem is unique among the works discussed in detail in this book in that though other works of Mendelssohn's, such as his Bible translation and commentary, were certainly written with an eye toward non-Jewish approval, and this one was secondarily intended for a Jewish audience, it is the only one addressed directly to the non-Jewish community.[158] However, the influence of its citative strategies on later maskilic literature, as well as its importance to understanding Mendelssohnian—and thus general—maskilic strategy, makes a discussion of its usage of sources imperative.[159]

Briefly summarized, *Jerusalem* argues that the state should concern itself with the temporal sphere of power, and the church[160] with the religious sphere; the state has no coercive right where matters of belief are concerned. Mendelssohn bases his argument on the premise, which was (at least nominally) universally assumed, that any religion in accord with the dictates of reason must be tolerated, including Mendelssohn's rational Judaism.[161] It must be said, however, that Mendelssohn still felt Judaism to be the most rational religion, a sentiment

158. See Arkush *MME* 194–196 and Altmann *MMBS* 528–532.

159. Citations refer to both the edition in the *Jubiläumsausgabe* (*JubA* 8:103–204) and to Arkush's translation. On the powerful effect that *Jerusalem* would nonetheless have on Jewish circles, see Lionel Kochan, "Moses Mendelssohn as Political Educator," in Abramson and Parfitt 299–306, 300.

160. Mendelssohn uses the words "church" and "religion" interchangeably throughout the book, possibly indicating Christian cultural pressure in framing the very terms of the field of argument.

161. Mendelssohn's argument builds upon the philosophies of Leibniz, Wolff, and Spinoza, as well as the political-philosophical work of other deists such as Toland, Tindal, and Locke. See *Introduction* 21–23. For a closer look at the relationship (perhaps the anxiety of influence) between Mendelssohn and Spinoza, see Patterson "Moses Mendelssohn" 159; Michael L. Morgan, "Mendelssohn's Defense of Reason in Judaism," *Judaism* 38:4 (1989), 449–459, 454; Awerbuch 38; and Altmann *MMBS* 33.

that finds greater but still implicit expression in the second section of the work.

In its second section, *Jerusalem* also features Mendelssohn's most powerful articulation of his philosophy of Judaism: the laws and commandments of Judaism are based on the society of ancient Judaism, which therefore no longer confers legislative obligations, only moral ones, on contemporary Jews.[162] The right of punishment thus should not lie within the aegis of the current Jewish community—it was allowed only when the state and the religion were one, in ancient Jewish society. Currently, all that remains are practical commandments, the fulfillment of a moral consciousness, which Jews should follow; generally speaking, Jews are obligated to obey the laws of the regime in which they find themselves.[163] This does not imply, however, that Mendelssohn denied the concepts of Jewish covenant and special destiny; on the contrary, he connected revelation with the special destiny of the Jewish people.[164]

In both *Jerusalem* and its 1782 precursor, his "Preface" to the reprinting of Manasseh Ben Israel's *Vindiciae Judaeorum*, Mendelssohn uses Biblical and rabbinic prooftexts to locate these notions of religion and philosophy in a specifically Jewish grounding, as opposed to what he himself would have characterized as a value-neutral, sterile deism;[165] in his review of *Jerusalem*, Michaelis remarked that even

162. See Breuer "Rabbinic Law" 299–300. On the link between the two parts of *Jerusalem*, see Altmann *MMBS* 552.

163. Interestingly, in discussing the question of obligation to the laws of current non-Jewish society, Mendelssohn does not cite the classic Jewish formulation of *dina demalkhuta dina* ("the law of the land is the law"), seemingly perfect for his needs, but instead cites the New Testament passage concerning God and Caesar. *Jerusalem* 132 (*JubA* 8:197). The concept of *dina demalkhuta dina* is cited in *BT Nedarim* 28a; see *Commentary* 234–235 for further discussion, as well as Amos Funkenstein, *Perceptions of Jewish History* (Berkeley: University of California Press, 1993), 224.

164. See *Introduction* 18–19.

165. Though I will discuss neither *Vindiciae Judaeorum* nor Mendelssohn's preface to it in detail, Manasseh notably uses a strategy of selective citation similar to Mendelssohn's; see Altmann *MMBS* 491 for more details. In his Preface (reprinted

Mendelssohn's discussion of natural law is guided by "his native rabbinic tradition."[166]

As before, the usage of Jewish prooftexts in this book, dedicated to non-Jewish audiences, is not merely the result of Mendelssohn's desire to draw upon the wisdom of his own tradition. *Jerusalem* was written in response to a June 1782 pamphlet by August Cranz, who challenged Mendelssohn's support in the "Preface" for the abolition of the coercive power of the Jewish communal authorities. Cranz claimed that Mendelssohn had removed one of the cornerstones of Judaism and, if he was determined to undermine his religion in this way, he should simply convert. Though Mendelssohn generally avoided engaging in public polemic, this was a challenge that could not go unanswered, particularly since the pamphlet was issued anonymously, and Mendelssohn believed it to be written by a different author, Joseph Baron von Sonnenfels, a supporter and patron of Mendelssohn's.[167]

Cranz used Jewish sources to buttress his claim, continuing the pattern set by Eisenmenger, Wagenseil, and others of non-Jews misusing classical Jewish texts for polemical purposes.[168] This meant that any

---

in *JubA* 8:1–25), Mendelssohn uses the same strategies we have seen throughout his work, quoting King Solomon's dedication prayer at the Temple (1 Kings 8:41–43) and a Talmudic source (*BT Khulin* 5a) to prove that the rabbis and the Biblical kings never "did pretend to any such right as excluding individuals from religious exercise" (*JubA* 8:22). For more on Manasseh ben Israel, see Sorkin *MMRE* 112–114.

166. See *Introduction* 6–7, 15 and Mendes-Flohr 44–47, 87–89.

167. See Jacob Katz, "Lemi ana Mendelson bi'Yerushalayim' shelo?" *Zion* 29 (1964), 112–132; 36 (1971), 116–117. For a translation of selections of Cranz's letter, and the even more polemical postscript by David Ernst Moerschel, see Mendes-Flohr 91–96; the pamphlet as a whole is reprinted in *JubA* 8:73–88; see esp. 84–85. A complicated philosophical background also lies behind the writing of *Jerusalem*, revolving around Lessing's death and his possible identification as a Spinozist; this topic is admirably summarized and explicated in Morgan "Mendelssohn's Defense" 450–456.

168. See Chapter Three and Katz *Ghetto* 53. Further background on the writing of *Jerusalem* can be found in Patterson "Moses Mendelssohn" 149–153. The title *Jerusalem* is itself a reference to a New Testament verse cited by Cranz; see Altmann *MMBS* 514.

response Mendelssohn would give needed to be, even more than his other works, a defense of Jewish text. Specifically, the pamphlet "repeatedly drew attention to what it perceived to be the particular problem of rabbinic law," and so issues of rabbinic rehabilitation were of particular importance here.[169] We have seen this same pattern of balancing tradition and innovation throughout Mendelssohn's work;[170] here, though, at the end of his life, and with the eyes of all Prussian society on him, this may have been his most important hour.

Mendelssohn uses classical texts themselves to indicate his awareness of the polemical role textual material occupies between Jews and Christians in general, and here in particular. (Obviously, to a certain extent, Mendelssohn denies that he is polemicizing, but a certain degree of disingenuousness is natural in this context.)[171] Concerning the argument the anonymous Christian pamphleteer makes urging him to convert to Christianity, Mendelssohn writes, "Now, if this were the truth, and I were convinced of it, I would indeed shamefully retract my propositions and *bring reason into captivity under the yoke of*—but no! Why should I dissimulate?"[172] Mendelssohn's use of the emphasized phrase, a reference to a New Testament passage (2 Corinthians 10:5), indicates cleverly that the battle over religions and over religious approaches can be characterized as a battle over texts and their interpretations.

In the next sentence, Mendelssohn writes that even were he to accept the other's arguments, it would not ultimately matter, because the true arguments will

> nevertheless, reappear in the most secret recesses of my heart, be
> transformed into disquieting doubts, and the doubts would resolve
> themselves into childlike prayers, into fervent supplications for illu-
> mination. I would call out with the Psalmist: *Lord, send me Thy light,*

169. Breuer "Rabbinic Law" 304–12. Citation from 304.

170. The subtlety of Mendelssohn's performance here has allowed various scholars to draw differing conclusions about *Jerusalem's* traditionalism: compare Morgan "Mendelssohn's Defense" 449 and Eisen "Divine Legislation" 243.

171. See, for example, *Jerusalem* 88–89 (*JubA* 8:155).

172. *Jerusalem* 85 (*JubA* 8:153), emphasis mine.

Thy truth, that they may guide and bring me unto Thy holy mountain, unto Thy dwelling place![173]

The non-Jewish authorities pervert and misinterpret Jewish texts; Mendelssohn's call for truth, though, eventually expresses itself in a call (itself expressed in textual terms)[174] for the true interpretation of these arguments—that is to say, these texts.

For Mendelssohn, *Jerusalem* is thus the continuation of a Jewish/Christian debate that has taken place for centuries. However, with the widespread acceptance of Enlightenment tenets, Mendelssohn believes victory in the debate can be his, if he can only show his set of texts and interpretations to harmonize better with the tenets of the (theoretically) secular, rational, and deist Enlightenment than his opponents'. In his reference to the passage from 2 Corinthians, he implies that to accept Christian doctrine and Christian text is to accept unreasonable, unnatural ideas;[175] to accept Christianity, one has to enslave that force which the entire Enlightenment period has been dedicated to liberating.

The rhetoric of binding and yoking in the New Testament passage resonates with images of medievalism, of serfdom, which is, of course, precisely what modern thinkers reject. Mendelssohn, then, offers the alternative of the "classical" Jewish (here Biblical) texts, whose true interpretations have been forced underground throughout the medieval period through the Christian forces of unreason, and have now burst forth in the form of "fervent supplications for illumination." Of course, the identification of the exact words of the textual passage with Enlightenment tenets is simple; the author explicitly asks for light and truth. Indeed, Mendelssohn's quotations from Psalms throughout *Jerusalem* present the universally accepted Psalmist as the model of

173. *Jerusalem* 85–86 (*JubA* 8:153), emphasis Mendelssohn's; quotation is from Psalms 43:3.

174. Notably, in the German text, Biblical and rabbinic sources function solely as prooftexts; the issues of linguistic necessity or stylistic facility we have discussed in previous chapters are obviously not involved here.

175. Importantly, Mendelssohn merely refers to the New Testament passage; he does not bestow upon it the legitimacy of a direct quotation.

enlightenment[176] and use him, variously, to illustrate the triumph of simple reason over sophistry,[177] to support the religious Enlightenment's conception of a limited reason that cannot be transcended,[178] and to help summarize his definition of Judaism.[179] This text from Psalms, then, quoted by Mendelssohn in its entirety, serves as a prime example of Mendelssohn's rehabilitation of the classical Jewish approach to texts and portrayal of Judaism as the reasonable, enlightened alternative to Christianity.

Mendelssohn similarly compares the two traditions to portray Judaism as the rational religion when he asserts that "according to the concepts of true Judaism, all of the inhabitants of the earth are destined to felicity; and the means of attaining it are as widespread as mankind itself. . . ."[180] Here, seemingly, is another sign of the universality, ecumenicism, and rationalism of Judaism—the mark of the perfect Enlightenment religion. By contrast, in the previous paragraph, Mendelssohn savagely attacks the Christian notion of the necessity of revelation for salvation, noting the theological challenge to that doctrine of the discovery of whole continents of people who had never heard the Word. Christianity has committed the worst sin of all—it has put forth a doctrine incompatible with reason and universalism.

However, as Mendelssohn well knew, this doctrine has appeared in Judaism as well, particularly during the medieval period. No less a noted authority than Maimonides ruled that a "righteous heathen" will only obtain a portion in the world to come if he observes the laws given to Noah and his descendants as divinely revealed laws. Con-

---

176. See Sorkin *MMRE* 129 and Tsamriyon 53–54.

177. *Jerusalem* 95 (*JubA* 8:161) "Very often, as the Psalmist says, *the babbling of children and infants will suffice to confound the enemy.*" Psalms 8:3.

178. Mendelssohn writes, following Psalms 73:17, "Who can say: I have entered into God's sanctuary, looked over the whole of his plan, and am able to determine the measure, goal, and limits of his purposes?" *Jerusalem* 118 (*JubA* 8:184); the passage is used again in a similar context on 133 (*JubA* 8:198).

179. Psalms 19:1–5, 103:2–4; see *Jerusalem* 126–127 (*JubA* 8:191–192).

180. *Jerusalem* 94 (*JubA* 8:161).

cerning this ruling, Mendelssohn wrote to Rabbi Jacob Emden on Oct. 26, 1773:

> These words are harder to me than flint. Are, then, all dwellers on earth . . . except for us, doomed to perdition if they fail to believe in the Torah that was given as an inheritance only to the congregation of Jacob? . . . What, then, is expected of the nations unto whom the light of the Torah did not shine and who received no tradition either, except from ancestors not to be relied upon?[181]

Mendelssohn makes the same claim against the Jewish tradition in intra-communal critique as he does against the Christian tradition when engaging in inter-communal polemic. He engages in an act of re-creation—but not merely for polemical purposes, though that is, of course, crucial. Equally important is the fact that Mendelssohn challenges Christianity with his vision of "'true' Judaism," which to him "is identical with the 'ancient' Judaism in its pristine purity, free from 'human additions and abuses'."[182] Mendelssohn thus argues against Christian doctrine and philosophy as it is with Jewish doctrine and philosophy as he would like it to be, and, on some level, believes it "truly" is. Mendelssohn's rehabilitation of Judaism is thus not merely for external purposes, but the result of honest belief and desire for change on his own part.[183]

A similar dynamic is apparent in Mendelssohn's discussion of revelation: Mendelssohn feels the obligation to preserve some sense of

181. The quote from Maimonides is from *Yad Hakhazaka, Hilkhot Melakhim* 8:10–11. Letter appears in *JubA* 19:178, translation from *Commentary* 209. On Mendelssohn's ambivalent relationship with Maimonides, see Sorkin *MMRE* 63; Altmann *MMBS* 141; and Eisen, 250–253. On Mendelssohn and Emden, see the sources cited in note 30 *supra*, as well as Altmann *MMBS* 210, 216–217, 294–295.

182. *Commentary* 210. Mendelssohn constantly emphasizes in the second section of *Jerusalem* that he is interested in the "true," "original" Judaism. *Introduction* 15.

183. On Mendelssohn's defense of the "liberal" Jewish tradition on the salvation of the Gentiles as a misreading of the relevant texts, see Arkush *MME* 200–204. Based on Mendelssohn's excellent knowledge of traditional sources, this misreading can only be seen as willful and dictated by polemic and ideological exigencies.

revelation and particularist Jewish chosenness both to maintain communal legitimacy and from honest belief and thus treats the Sinaitic revelation as a historical event.[184] Conversely, his need to present Jewish tradition as universalist and ecumenical means that revelation's benefits cannot be so extreme as to remove the possibility for the rest of the world, who have not received this revelation, to achieve moral perfection, since moral perfection is, in the Enlightenment conception of the phrase, based on one's ability to use reason to apprehend the moral good and to follow it. Moral perfection must be within the grasp of all reasonable beings, not merely those who have received revelation's blessing. And polemically, to deny such perfection would put the Jewish tradition on much the same footing as the Christians who denied salvation to those who had not heard the Word.

Mendelssohn thus limits the revelation in Judaism to one concerning only legislation, and, as we have seen, ignores any canonical possibility of a particularistic notion of salvation based on revelation. In fact, Mendelssohn uses the Biblical text surrounding the Sinaitic revelation to characterize the revelation as merely "a historical truth, on which this people's legislation was to be founded, as well as laws, was to be revealed here—commandments and ordinances, not eternal religious truths." This interpretation of the Sinaitic revelation is, at best, disingenuous.[185] Notably, Mendelssohn's explanations of the text in his *Biur* accord with his statements here; again, Mendelssohn's strategies and arguments remain constant whether his audience is Jewish or non-Jewish.[186]

Parenthetically, the entire question of revelation, a question that resonates throughout *Jerusalem,* is at heart a question about text and its epistemological status: was the text itself divinely revealed? And if

184. Despite Mendelssohn's famous statement that "I was of the opinion that a man who has no country could not expect any advantage from [the study of] history" (*JubA* 12.1:120, translation from Altmann *MMBS* 107), Mendelssohn's attitude toward the subject is fairly complex; in David Sorkin's words, "Mendelssohn was historical without being historicist: he acknowledged history in the Pentateuch rather than the Pentateuch as a product of history." Sorkin *MMRE* 85. See also Breuer "Of Miracles" 33, 41–45.

185. *Jerusalem* 98 (*JubA* 8:164–165). The textual citation is from Exodus 20:2.

186. *JubA* 16:185–186. See also *Commentary* 213–215 and Arkush *MME* 261.

so, what resulting claim should that exercise on its readers, both Jewish and non-Jewish? In discussing the status of revelation and the *meaning* of the texts discussing that revelation, Mendelssohn has still managed to make a subtle and almost unrecognized point about the text's *nature*. The argument, so far as Mendelssohn is concerned, has still remained about the proper way to read the word of God.

Mendelssohn does attempt to consider the nature of the text itself in *Jerusalem*; as mentioned earlier, questions concerning the Biblical text were part of an increasingly important contemporary debate between Jews and Christians. Some Biblical scholars argued that what the text *said* may have been unimportant if the text itself was historical, corrupted or shaped by Jewish ideologues to make Jewish ideological points.[187] As in his Bible translation and commentary, however, Mendelssohn dismisses this view almost entirely, assuming the masoretic text to be correct and divine, and the Bible to be universally accepted as a source of truth (which, except among certain Biblical critics, was generally true).[188]

Though Mendelssohn did attempt to rehabilitate rabbinic texts, as we have seen, his discussion of revelation and text in *Jerusalem* can also be seen to confirm and reinforce the polemical value of the universal Biblical text in contradistinction to the challenged rabbinic text. Ancient Biblical Judaism provides lessons from the unmediated word of God apprehensible to pure reason; the lessons of the rabbis are the later accretions of an oral, essentially non-textual tradition that, even according to Mendelssohn, could be subject to corruption. It may be that some of the maskilic idealization of the Bible and of Biblical Hebrew stems from the complicated circumstances surrounding the notion of revelation in Mendelssohn's thought.

Returning to Mendelssohn's strategies of textual citation, Mendelssohn occasionally displays the polemic power of these ideal Biblical texts by citing several of them in concert to make polemic points. For example, to prove that Judaism does not coerce belief—an important sign of its ecumenicism—he cites several verses to prove the word

187. See Arkush *MME* 180 and Israel 218–219, 232.
188. See *Jerusalem* 105–115 (*JubA* 8:173–182).

heemin or *emuna* actually means "trust, confidence, and firm reliance on pledge and promise," and that "whenever it is a question of the eternal truths of reason, it does not say *believe,* but *understand* and *know*."[189] Once again, Mendelssohn's dual goals of a literalist interpretive framework and of polemical ideological necessity are both met, as his argument is grounded in universally acceptable interpretations of a universally accepted text.

However, Mendelssohn's goal is once more achieved at the cost of selective citation of normative Jewish tradition, as commentators in the classical literature certainly exist, most notably Maimonides, who interpret these passages to command belief. In this vein, Mendelssohn's comments on Maimonides' articles of belief in *Jerusalem* are worth mentioning.[190] His argument there—that since conflicting catechisms of Jewish belief exist, none of which have been branded heretical by the general populace, none are obligatory dogma—has some merit, but is slightly disingenuous: these systems can easily be seen as differing not over the requirement or substance of belief, but merely nomenclatural categories about how the same beliefs should be reduced to basic principles.[191]

Despite this idealization of the Biblical text, Mendelssohn does not restrict his citation of classical Jewish texts to the Bible. Several pages into the first section—the section claimed by contemporaries and later scholars to refer solely to general philosophy and not to reflect a Jewish sensibility—Mendelssohn writes the following concerning the importance of man's eternal welfare:

> It is necessary for man to be reminded constantly that with this life all does not end for him; that there stands before him an endless future,

189. *Jerusalem* 100 (*JubA* 8:166–167; citation from 166). No attempt is made to deal with every instance of the word's appearance in the Bible, unlike similar lexicographical analyses in the Mendelssohn-influenced journal *Hameasef*. This may be because the word is so common that such an effort would have been literarily unwieldy. The passages quoted are Genesis 15:6, Exodus 14:31, Deuteronomy 4:39 (cited twice), and Deuteronomy 6:4—certainly some of Pentateuch's most important passages concerning faith and eternal truth.

190. *Jerusalem* 101 (*JubA* 8:167).

191. A further discussion of this section appears *infra*.

for which his life here is a preparation, just as in all creation every present is a preparation for the future. This life, say the rabbis, is a vestibule in which one must comport oneself in the manner in which one wishes to appear in the inner chamber.[192]

In this statement, Mendelssohn again opposes himself to a Christian tradition, advocated by Locke, of a radical separation between temporal and eternal welfare. Besides the significance of Mendelssohn's use of a Jewish text in a section often considered a generalist work of political philosophy,[193] Mendelssohn's use of a rabbinic source once more illustrates his strategy of citing texts from the rabbinic canon to represent the rabbis as ecumenical and universalist, dispensing wisdom in tune with the Enlightenment. This passage is taken from the Ethics of the Fathers, a book containing numerous general ethical teachings, and discusses the theme of *memento mori*, a common trope among both Jewish and non-Jewish thinkers of the period.

Mendelssohn similarly employs the other rabbinic texts cited throughout *Jerusalem*. Discussing financial remuneration for religious teachers, he cites a Talmudic passage which, interpreting Deuteronomy 4:5, suggests that a salary should not be taken for this sort of teaching.[194]

192. *Jerusalem* 39 (*JubA* 8:109). The citation is from *Mishna Avot* 4:16. See also Alexander Altmann, "The Philosophical Roots of Mendelssohn's Plea for Emancipation," in Altmann *Essays* 154–169, 160.

193. Other statements in the first section reveal the influence of Jewish juridical principles on Mendelssohn's thought. See *Commentary* 171 and 194 for, respectively, discussion of examples of coercive levying of charitable fines and oath taking. Other examples not mentioned by Altmann appear, however, such as the concept of *kinyan*, which is not explicitly mentioned but obviously referred to in *Jerusalem* 54 (*JubA* 8:123). There are also, of course, simple factual allusions to religious law throughout the book that do not involve direct textual citations: for example, Mendelssohn notes in discussing the role of miracles in Judaism that performance of a miracle by a person is insufficient grounds to obey a claim to abrogate traditional law, referring to, though not citing, the discussion in Deuteronomy 13:2–6; *Jerusalem* 99 (*JubA* 8:165). Parts of the first section also reveal the influence of Jewish philosophical thought, particularly in the discussion of one's duties to God. See *Jerusalem* 58 (*JubA* 8:126) and *Commentary* 184–185.

194. *BT Nedarim* 37a, *BT Bekhorot* 29a; see *Jerusalem* 60 (*JubA* 8:128–129) and *Commentary* 187. See also Lawrence Kaplan's "Supplementary Notes on the

Mendelssohn's citation of the text and his subsequent interpretation are significant and will be quoted here in full:

> But if the church has no property, who is to pay the teachers of religion? Who is to remunerate the preachers of the fear of God? Religion and pay—teaching virtue and salary—preaching the fear of God and remuneration. These notions seem to shun one another. What influence can the teacher of wisdom and virtue hope to have when he teaches for pay and is for sale to the highest bidder? What impression can the preacher of the fear of God expect when he seeks remuneration? *Behold, I have taught you laws and ordinances, as the Eternal, my God,* [commanded] *me* (Deut. 4:5). According to the rabbis' interpretation [the words] *as . . . my God . . . me* signify: *Just as He taught me without* [exacting] *payment, so do I teach you* [gratis], *and so should you teach* those in your care. Payment and remuneration are so contrary to the nature of this exalted occupation, so incompatible with the way of life which it demands, that the slightest proclivity towards gain and profit seem to degrade the profession.[195]

Again, the rabbis are portrayed here as offering universal reasonable wisdom applicable in an ecumenical context: Mendelssohn's original, reasonable explanation is confirmed by the words of the sages.

Mendelssohn cites the rabbis to express a universalist concept on another occasion, when he defines the "quintessence of Judaism" by citing the story of Hillel, who, when asked by a "heathen" to be taught the entire Torah while standing on one foot, replies to "love thy neighbor as thyself."[196] As Altmann notes, the Talmudic story uses a different, negative formulation of the Golden Rule; Mendelssohn uses the

---

Medieval Jewish Sources of Mendelssohn's *Jerusalem*," *JQR* 87:3–4 (1997), 339–342, 340, which notes the Maimonidean tradition implicitly referred to here (*Commentary to Avot* 4:6, *Hilkhot Talmud Tora* 1:7, 3:10–11, and *Commentary to Nedarim* 4:3).

195. *Jerusalem* 60 (*JubA* 8:128–129). On Mendelssohn himself as a preacher, see Altmann *MMBS* 68, where a 1757 sermon he wrote is cited as the earliest example of modern Jewish preaching in German. See also Alexander Altmann, "The New Style of Preaching in Nineteenth Century Germany," in Altmann *Essays* 190–245, esp. 192. On the homiletic style of eighteenth-century preaching in general, see Katz *Tradition* 146–147.

196. *Jerusalem* 102 (*JubA* 8:168). Story appears in *BT Shabat* 31a.

Biblical formulation.[197] The reason for Mendelssohn's change may be both a wish to identify the rabbis with the Bible even further as well as to avoid the negative formulation because of its more legalistic phrasing. Mendelssohn wished to move away from the image of Judaism as essentially legalistic and hoped to present the essential nature of Judaism, especially rabbinic Judaism, as predicated on the universalistic sentiment of love for others.[198]

This process indicates the complexities of Mendelssohn's position in reference to the rabbinic tradition. On the one hand, succumbing to the external blandishments of Christian and modern historiography, he had begun to view certain aspects of the rabbinic period as accretions on the classical, "good" Judaism.[199] Mendelssohn certainly emphasizes the Bible as opposed to the Oral Law,[200] and he does seem to express some ambivalence toward the creation of the rabbinic writings. Mendelssohn cites Biblical and rabbinic texts in order to characterize this development—termed "the destruction of the law"—as demarcating a transition between classical, spiritual, living Judaism and later ossified rabbinism.[201]

On the other hand, Mendelssohn was engaged in a project to rehabilitate Jewish law, not destroy it, as we have seen. Faced with opponents who would seize upon any critique of rabbinism as an excuse to attack the entire system of rabbinic—and thus contemporary—Judaism, Mendelssohn needed to rehabilitate Jewish rabbinism by portraying the rabbis as enlightened figures making statements in accord

197. Leviticus 19:18; see *Commentary* 219–220 for a fuller discussion of the various formulations.

198. It is also possible, however, that this conflation of various versions of the story stems from a greater familiarity with and sensitivity to the Biblical text than the other formulations on Mendelssohn's part; see note 209 *infra*.

199. On the difference between Jewish and Christian notions of history and progress as symbolized by Mendelssohn and Lessing, see Sorkin *MMRE* 131; Meyer "Modernity" 159; and Altmann *MMBS* 539.

200. Though this emphasis could be due to the polemical needs of the work, as previously discussed.

201. Sources cited are Psalms 119:126, *BT Gitin* 60b, and *BT Temura* 14b; see *Jerusalem* 102 (*JubA* 8:169).

with reason. This is why Mendelssohn takes such pains to quote the rabbis in contexts where their message is obviously and immediately intelligible in an ecumenical, conventionally rational context. Finally, the Mendelssohnian effort to reform rabbinism was an *internal* effort; it could not and should not, according to principles of toleration, be forced upon the Jewish community by non-Jewish critique. This would be the case even if non-Jews were making appropriate critiques of rabbinism, which, in Mendelssohn's eyes, they were not. As such, Mendelssohn needed to engage in a defense of rabbinism for external reasons.

Of course, Mendelssohn's rabbinic rehabilitation can only be a partial one at best. Many rabbinic statements do violence to both grammar and semantic meaning, and reach conclusions neither ecumenical nor universal. Mystical and superstitious readings must be glossed over. It is clear from reading *Jerusalem* that texts are being marshaled for a particular purpose and a particular set of strategies.

For example, if we search the entire book for mystical references—a mainstay of Jewish exegesis—we find but two oblique allusions to the entire Jewish mystical endeavor. The first reference is Mendelssohn's mention of the year 2240: "And yet from time immemorial men have acted in opposition to these self-evident principles. Happy will they be if in the year 2240 they cease to act against them." Mendelssohn clearly chooses this date in reference to the mystical and eschatological Talmudic statement that the world will end in the Jewish year 6000—2240 in the secular calendar.[202] Mendelssohn is either simply being flippant here, or attempting to strike a certain ecumenical chord with Christians studying eschatological matters, as the Talmudic doctrine had been adopted by certain Christian milleniarists.[203]

Another potential hint of mysticism in *Jerusalem* is when, in explaining the inherent connection between Jewish laws and eternal

202. *Jerusalem* 59 (*JubA* 8:127). See *BT Sanhedrin* 97a and *BT Avoda Zara* 2b.
203. See *Commentary* 185 on Christian eschatological support for this Jewish concept. See also Green 51–52. On Christian mysticism and its links to Jewish mysticism in the Renaissance and early modern period, see Dan *Gershom Scholem* 236–237.

truths of reason, Mendelssohn refers to what he claims to be a rabbinic statement: "Hence, our rabbis rightly say: the laws and doctrines are related to each other like body and soul."[204] As Altmann notes, Mendelssohn's statement may refer to a Zoharic description of the commandments as *gufei tora*, the "bodies of Torah" wrapped in the Biblical narrative that serves as clothing.[205] However, the likelier explanation is that Mendelssohn was playing on the popular saying that "prayer without devotion is like body without soul," and was not referring to mystical texts here. Later in the same passage, Mendelssohn employs a metaphor of veiled feminine beauty that "recalls the allegory of the beautiful maiden employed by the Zohar."[206] Even if Mendelssohn were referring to these texts, however, mystical references are so few and so oblique compared to the other textual citations in *Jerusalem* that it is certainly reasonable to speak of mystical aspects of Judaism as sublimated in the work, if not absent altogether, sensible in light of Mendelssohn's desire to purge his presentation of Judaism of mystical elements.

Kabbalists themselves are mentioned once in *Jerusalem*, during a discussion of the possible existence of religious doctrines in Judaism. The continuum of answers examined ranges from Mendelssohn's, who says there are none, to that of "still others, especially Luria and his disciples, the latter-day Kabbalists, [who] do not wish to recognize any fixed number of fundamental doctrines, and say: In our teaching, everything is fundamental."[207] Two conclusions emerge from this passage: first, Mendelssohn was acquainted with the work of the Lurianic kabbalists; second, he had very different opinions than they did about Judaism.

Even here, though, the animus toward mysticism appearing in later maskilic work is absent:[208] Mendelssohn's principles of tolerance and pluralism remain, and he grounds these principles in a set of rabbinic

204. *Jerusalem* 99 (*JubA* 8:166).
205. *Commentary* 215–216; citation is from *Zohar* III:152a.
206. *Commentary* 216.
207. *Jerusalem* 101 (*JubA* 8:167).
208. See Chapters Five through Seven on Wolfssohn and Perl.

statements that may be the most important citations in the entire work. In characterizing the discussion as a whole, he notes approvingly that "this debate was conducted as all controversies of this kind should be: with earnestness and zeal, but without animosity and bitterness," and cites "the important dictum of our sages" that "we have not yet disregarded . . . *Although this one loosens and the other binds, both teach the words of the living God.*"[209] Mendelssohn's use of the first person plural here is not merely a rhetorical flourish; he does not relate to these rabbinic statements as part of an alien textual corpus to be dissected and analyzed, but as the living words of a community to which he belongs.

This statement seems to be a perfect model for the debate over religion and its place in society, a model Mendelssohn clearly hopes will also be adopted in a secular context. Mendelssohn dismisses as a "pedant" anyone who perversely interprets this passage to imply that the rabbis had no concept of contradiction; quite the contrary, he feels that argument or dialogue held between individuals or groups who have proper respect for their own spheres of action is the optimal

209. *Jerusalem* 101 (*JubA* 8:168). There may be a slyly polemic literary contrast here: Mendelssohn's text referring to the essential nature of Jewish belief contains language of both binding and loosening, while the passage he alludes to from 2 Corinthians to describe the process of Christianization, discussed above, is simply restrictive ("yoking"). Mendelssohn's quotation here conflates two rabbinic passages, *BT Yevamot* 13b and *BT Eruvin* 13b. Mendelssohn makes no mention of this conflation, an absence that may be merely for polemic purposes, but may raise an interesting question about the nature of Mendelssohn's citative methodology. Was it a careful, academic citation based on careful analysis or observation of the classical texts? Or were the sources that Mendelssohn cited for this polemical work based on his prodigious memory for the classical Jewish works that he had learned as a youth? This conflation, as well as the somewhat non-systematic presentation of quotations and rabbinic dicta and ideas in the book (see notes 105, 183, and 198 *supra*), seems to suggest the latter. This is not to say that Mendelssohn was incapable of, or unwilling to, engage in a systematic look at the Jewish classical corpus, of course; by definition, this is what he did in his translations and commentaries on particular works. However, when it comes to a polemical work where the emphasis is to draw out aspects of the Jewish tradition that agree with the general ideological principles that he is trying to elucidate, Mendelssohn's methodology of citation might well be different.

means of reaching true enlightenment. Though Mendelssohn is currently writing a polemic piece, he hopes that doing so is only a temporary necessity. Once more, the rabbis are presented as ideal Enlightenment figures.

We have seen both Mendelssohn's idealization of the Biblical texts for its universal claims and his rehabilitation of rabbinic texts to present them as universal. This does not mean, however, that it is only the rabbinic doctrines that require rehabilitation in the name of universality. Even the seemingly universal Bible may require a similar process. In a note to this discussion of the proper form of dialogue for considering the question of Jewish doctrine, Mendelssohn cites the prophecy in Zechariah 8:19 describing the transformation of Jewish fast days into "days of joy and gladness if you but love peace."[210] Eisen notes that the text is also the one with which the prayer leader on the High Holy Days finishes when asking God to be worthy of pleading before the congregation; he neatly compares this to Mendelssohn's desire to be found worthy of pleading his interpretation of Judaism before Jews and Gentiles alike.[211]

Examining the citation's context, however, yields new subtleties. Mendelssohn prefaces the citation with a universalist statement: "I hope to see the day when all the peoples of the earth will admit this. . . ." This is a standard universalist presentation of the utopian theme, especially since the arrival of the utopian state seems to be contingent on toleration ("loving peace"). Indeed, referring elsewhere to the utopian period, Mendelssohn uses the language of Isaiah to decry the idea that ideally only one religion should exist:

> There are some who want to persuade you that if only all of us had one and the same faith we would no longer hate each other for reasons of faith . . . that the scourge would be wrested from the hand of hypocrisy and the sword from the hand of fanaticism, and the happy

210. *Jerusalem* 101, author's note (*JubA* 8:168). Mendelssohn cites the same prophecy in *Jerusalem*'s utopian ending, though the verse cited there is 8:29; *Jerusalem* 139 (*JubA* 8:204). Altmann (*MMBS* 419) notes that this ending is the same as the ending to the introduction to the *Biur, Sefer Or Lanetiva*.

211. Eisen 262.

days would arrive, of which it is said, *the wolf shall lie down with the lamb, and the leopard beside the kid.*[212]

The predatory language of the passage, however, especially in the curtailed version quoted by Mendelssohn—the rest of the verse, "and they shall not be afraid," is not cited—provides a sly comment on the nature of any process yielding such unanimity. Mendelssohn is, of course, polemicizing here: if there were to be but one faith in Europe, it was clear to all what that faith would be and what illiberal means would be used to attain that unanimity. Generally, however, the passage is cited (though negatively) to lend support to the idea that any utopia would necessarily involve a pluralistic model of religious diversity.

However, the first passage cited by Mendelssohn refers to a particularistic utopia marked by a particular transformative event in Jewish history—the transformation of these fast days, currently commemorating the destruction of the Jewish temple and thus the destruction of Jewish theocratic autonomy, into feast days after the arrival of the Jewish messiah and the rebuilding of that temple. Arguably, this is one of the more particularistic passages in the Bible—one that admits the least universalistic interpretation, certainly if one applies Mendelssohn's generally held principle of literalist interpretation.[213]

Particularistic aspects are even more strongly evoked by Mendelssohn's usage of traditional language reminding the traditional reader of the *Aleinu* prayer, both the final passage ("And it is written: that the Lord will be king over all the land, *on that day* the Lord will be one and his name one") as well as the earlier part of the prayer speaking of "all the peoples of the earth" recognizing God's kingship and serving Him.[214] Any citation or reference to the *Aleinu* prayer is intensely polemical, playing into the contemporary historical debate over the inclusion of a controversial passage in the prayer previously mentioned.[215] The more oblique referentiality here may reflect Mendels-

---

212. *Jerusalem* 136 (*JubA* 8:201); citation from Isaiah 11:6.

213. Altmann (*MMBS* 416) notes this dissonance, but does not address it in detail. For a rabbinic discussion of this passage, see *BT Rosh Hashana* 18b.

214. Zechariah 14:9.

215. See *supra*.

sohn's complex personal position on the question of particularistic Jewish messianism, or at least a return to Israel and a restoration of a Jewish state: desirable but unlikely, and certainly not to be mentioned because of current political exigencies.[216] Still, even this subtle reference to the prayer marks a polemic stance against what must have been viewed by Mendelssohn as public intrusion into the private sphere of religion.

The theme of Christian misunderstanding of Jewish intent (at least, according to Mendelssohn) concretized in the *Aleinu* controversy can also be seen in *Jerusalem*'s other reference to the destruction of the Temple. Several pages later, Mendelssohn refers to the midrash that "in plundering the Temple, the conquerors of Jerusalem found the cherubim on the Ark of the Covenant, and took them for the idols of the Jews. They saw everything with the eyes of barbarians, and from their point of view."[217] While Mendelssohn is unquestionably referring to pagans here, the sentiment can easily be metaphorically applied to the current cultural context, particularly in the reaction to works such as Eisenmenger's *Entdecktes Judentum* which grievously misrepresented the image of Judaism. Similarly, the quotation from Hosea which marks the reversed hierarchies of idolaters can be seen to subtly criticize non-Jews who still sublimate reason to coercive theological attacks, Cranz, the "inspiration" for *Jerusalem*, being a prime example.[218]

Nonetheless, even this reference to the *Aleinu* prayer—a prayer viewed by the non-Jewish authorities as the most problematic, the most blasphemous, the most particularistic part of Judaism—has been subverted by Mendelssohn into evidence of a sincere Jewish hope for a universalist ecumenical utopia. In using this passage, Mendelssohn says that his readers need not worry about the *Aleinu*, or the particularistic desires for a superior Jewish messianism for which it stands— in truth, what is hoped for is universal enlightened redemption.

216. See also the discussion on Jewish settlement outside Israel in note 230 *infra*.

217. *Jerusalem* 114 (*JubA* 8:180); midrash from Lamentations Rabbah 9.

218. *Jerusalem* 116 (*JubA* 8:182); quote from Hosea 13:2.

Sometimes Mendelssohn even cites rabbinic texts to rehabilitate Biblical texts. Mendelssohn cites the Talmudic interpretation of the process surrounding the death penalty to downplay the excessively strict, legalistic image of Judaism that here emerges from a reading of the Biblical text, and to provide the impression that the Jewish courts were much less strict than believed to be. Doing so would be of particular importance in a social context where any Christian thought of a Jewish court would be inextricably connected with the Sanhedrin that passed a sentence of deicide against Jesus. Mendelssohn writes: "Indeed, as the rabbis say, any court competent to deal with capital offenses and concerned for its good name must see to it that in a period of *seventy* years not more than one person is sentenced to death."[219]

Mendelssohn, in a by now familiar strategy, changes the formulation slightly, yielding a major change in resonance. The original text reads that any court executing more than one person in seventy years is called a "murderous court." Aside from the term's unpleasant resonances, which ascribe to the Jewish courts all the tendencies Christians had been imputing to Jews for years, the rabbinic language also implies that past courts may indeed have exceeded this limit. No such impression is given in Mendelssohn's formulation. In this case, the rabbinic interpretation of the Bible is accepted wholeheartedly by Mendelssohn, even though no evidence whatsoever exists for it in any strictly literalist reading of the Biblical text.[220]

In fact, Mendelssohn is even selectively citing from the rabbinic text to present the courts in the best possible light. The full text reads "A Sanhedrin that effects an execution once in *seven* years is branded a bloody tribunal; R' Eleazar b. Azariah says: once in seventy years. R' Tarfon and R' Akiva say: were we members of the Sanhedrin, no person would ever be put to death. Thereupon Rabbi Simeon b. Gamliel remarked: [Yea,] and they would also multiply shedders of blood in Israel!"[221] It is the unattributed statement—in this case, the one that

---

219. *Jerusalem* 130 (*JubA* 8:195). Citation from *BT Makot* 7a, emphasis author's.

220. *Jerusalem* 129 (*JubA* 8:195).

221. Translation Soncino's, emphasis mine.

most strongly presents an image of a judicial system considerably more prone to capital punishment—that is generally considered to be the normative statement in Talmudic study. If so, Mendelssohn is once again adopting the less normative interpretation for polemical purposes. And once again, a Biblical text serves as a capstone to Mendelssohn's intentions; he reminds his audience that the Bible, that pristine classical text, remarks that "an executed man is a reproach to God."[222]

This is not to say that Mendelssohn accepts the current rabbinic judicial system: Mendelssohn, again selectively citing from rabbinical history and tradition, writes that the Jewish community stopped using its punitive powers after the loss of its political independence, which is clearly untrue, in order to justify his larger point about the necessity for abolition of coercive powers by the state in religious matters.[223] Again, we see Mendelssohn opposing the Christian system as it is with the Jewish system as he would like it to be.[224]

A longer and more complicated example of Mendelssohn's rehabilitation of the Biblical text comes in his retelling of the story of the Golden Calf. Mendelssohn restates the opinion of his own *Biur*, which itself follows Judah HaLevi's *Kuzari*, and presents Israel as requesting not an idol, but an imagic representation of God which they can worship, thus presenting them as less ungrateful to their Divine deliverer. Both HaLevi and Mendelssohn were clearly moved, in polemical works, to provide a polemical interpretation that, though

222. Deuteronomy 21:23.

223. *Jerusalem* 130 (*JubA* 8:195). Mendelssohn writes: "[T]he rabbis expressly state [that] with the destruction of the Temple, all corporal and capital punishments and, indeed, even monetary fines, insofar as they are only national, have ceased to be legal." The actual rabbinic source for this is unclear; throughout the medieval and early modern period, Jewish communal bodies exercised punitive measures, as Mendelssohn well knew. See *GJH* 1:167–168; Katz *Tradition* 79–87; and Sorkin *MMRE* 116, 138. On the cessation of the excommunicatory ban as a credible threat, see Meyer "Modernity" 153; Alexander Altmann, "Mendelssohn on Excommunication: The Ecclesiastical Law Background," in Altmann *Essays* 170–189; and David Biale, *Power and Powerlessness in Jewish History* (New York: Schocken Books, 1986), 109–110, 116–117.

224. See Green 42–44, 46, 49.

found in traditional sources, certainly does violence to the literal meaning of the text.[225]

More importantly, Mendelssohn selectively cites and translates the remainder of the story to give the image of a merciful God; the passages known in Jewish tradition as the Thirteen Attributes of Mercy are cited in full, and Mendelssohn continues: "What man's feelings are so hardened that he can read this with dry eyes? Whose heart is so inhuman that he can still hate his brother and remain unforgiving toward him?"[226] This presentation of the Biblical narrative provides an image of Judaism diametrically opposed to the one in the minds of non-Jewish readers: the God of the Bible is not harsh and unforgiving, but rather compassionate.[227] It also, of course, subtly prescribes a model of conduct for the non-Jews toward their Jewish brethren.

Significantly, Mendelssohn's presentation omits any mention of the exile in the wilderness, the direct result of the sin of the Golden Calf. Besides his desire to present a more modern, enlightened image of the Jewish God, Mendelssohn had another reason to excise that section: he was mindful of the strain of opposition to Jewish emancipation that based its arguments on the perceived dual loyalties of Jews, claim-

225. See *Jerusalem* 120 (*JubA* 8:185–186) and *Commentary* 227. Source taken from *Kuzari* I:92–98. However, see Kaplan's comments on 341–342.

226. *Jerusalem* 122–123 (*JubA* 8:188); passages cited in the section range selectively from Exodus 33:15–34:10.

227. This assertion requires some further development, since Mendelssohn does also quote the passage that God allows nothing to go unpunished; he may have felt it was better to cite this latter passage in order to explain it and defuse potential criticism. Mendelssohn explains away its connotations by quoting the "rabbis" that "this too is a quality of divine love that for man nothing is allowed to go entirely unpunished." *Jerusalem* 123 (*JubA* 8:188). Mendelssohn may be stretching his definition of "rabbinic" literature here: though this interpretation appears in Ibn Ezra and Nachmanides, it is not to be found in the Talmud or any early rabbinic literature (though Mendelssohn, in his *Biur*, suggests that Ibn Ezra relies on *BT Avoda Zara* 4a, which states that God in his mercy distributes punishment over a long period of time, rather than all at once). See *Commentary* 228. However, Mendelssohn is hardly making the same point as the rabbinic sages; he, once again, re-presents the rabbis as in line with the messages of his day. See also Arkush *MME* 184–185.

ing Jews viewed themselves as exiles, not loyal citizens, who would one day leave the state and return to the Land of Israel. Michaelis, for example, responded to Dohm's plea for Jewish emancipation by saying that the expectation of a return to Palestine when the Messiah comes "casts doubt on the full and steadfast loyalty of the Jews to the state and the possibility of their full integration into it."[228] Any mention of exile, then, was either to be avoided entirely, or addressed head on in a polemical context.

Mendelssohn employs the latter strategy as well: several pages later, Mendelssohn proactively cites some Biblical verses that might be construed as problematic—they say that "he who must sojourn outside the land serves foreign gods"—and interprets them so as to remove any potential objection, mentioning that "this [statement which occurs] several times in Scripture cannot be taken in a literal sense. It actually means no more than that *he is subject to alien political laws which, unlike those of his own country, are not at the same time a part of the divine service.*"[229] Here, polemic exigencies force the literalist Mendelssohn to retreat from the plain meaning of the text. In the process, Mendelssohn also reiterates the point, so vital to his argument, that many of the Biblical passages and ideas contained therein referred to a period when the religion and the state were one—a time that lay in the distant past and that has no bearing on the current political situation.[230]

Finally, in order to explicate a theological point concerning Divine punishment, Mendelssohn brings two long quotations from Psalms,

228. Cited in Arkush *MME* 263. See also *Commentary* 235; Katz *Ghetto* 97–98; Biale *Power* 112; and note 31 *supra*.

229. *Jerusalem* 129 (*JubA* 8:194), emphasis Mendelssohn's; citations are from Deuteronomy 18:2, 10:9.

230. Conversely, Altmann (*Commentary* 231) cites the passage from *BT Ketuvot* 110b that a Jew living outside the land of Israel is considered an idolater. This Talmudic text is a perfect example of the type of rabbinic passage that could have been employed by non-Jews to challenge new models of Jewish emancipation. It is hardly surprising that Mendelssohn does not proactively mention it, though presumably he could have dealt with it in exactly the same way as he does the Biblical passage. However, the Bible was easier to rehabilitate than the rabbis, who were already viewed as suspicious by the non-Jews, which may account for Mendelssohn's treatment of the issue from a Biblical and not rabbinic perspective.

one of which quotes from the passage from Exodus previously mentioned.[231] This hints at a previously undiscussed strategy of looking at problematic Biblical texts: through the lens of later Biblical texts. This is an interesting way of preserving the traditional *method* of Jewish interpretation without relying on the rabbinic school of interpretation. While Mendelssohn certainly defends the rabbinic writings through his method of rehabilitation, as we have seen, he feels himself to be on constantly challenged ground whenever he uses them as prooftexts. However, if he can adduce the same principles from a Biblical text, his claims must be taken more seriously by a non-Jewish audience that claims the same reverence for the Bible that the Jews do.

This intra-Biblical intertextuality also reasserts the emphasis on the essential unity of the Bible, a possible response to the schism between the Old and New Testaments, since the interpretation adduced here is not in any way prefigurational but rather organically explicative. Mendelssohn's note to the citation of Psalm 103 is particularly interesting: he stresses that "the contents of this *entire* Psalm are altogether of the utmost importance. Interested readers will do well to peruse it *in its entirety* with attention."[232] The comment and the citation themselves remind readers of a facet of the argument between Jews and Christians over textual interpretation. It is difficult to make that point generally in a work such as *Jerusalem*, where so many topics are being discussed, so Mendelssohn, near the end of the book, finds it vital to do so once more.

Conclusion

In his *Jerusalem*, Mendelssohn engages in the same strategy we have seen throughout his work, regardless of language, regardless of audience: he uses a complicated series of strategies in order to achieve a main goal of what may be called rehabilitation. Anxious to prove the

---

231. *Jerusalem* 125 (*JubA* 8:190); quotations are from Psalms 62:12–13 and the entire Psalm 103.

232. *Jerusalem* 125 (*JubA* 8:190), author's note; emphasis mine.

merits of Judaism as a rational religion in the face of an external authority that claims to judge on a set of rational principles, Mendelssohn cites, translates, and interprets selectively in order to present an
image in line with that external valuation, regardless of whether he is
addressing Jews in Hebrew or non-Jews in German. Mendelssohn's
cautious and mannered usage of texts reflects the precarious political
position of Jews in the 1780s, unwilling to submit their claims for
emancipation too radically but newly optimistic about opportunities
for non-Jewish acceptance of a properly presented Judaism. This sublimation of an independent tradition to external valuations will have
grave consequences later for the German Haskala, and may well be the
reason that the hermeneutical tightrope Mendelssohn walked was
truly only an ephemeral solution.[233]

233. Phrase is Meyer's; see *Origins* 29.

Five   Aaron Halle-Wolfssohn

Introduction

Aaron Halle-Wolfssohn (1754–1835) is one of the most important figures of the Haskala in the period after Moses Mendelssohn's death. Both his life and work symbolize crucial developments in German and Jewish culture facing the maskilim during the 1790s: in the aftermath of both Mendelssohnian conservatism and the French Revolution, facing major changes in Jewish social and cultural life, Wolfssohn and the maskilim attempted to radicalize the fairly conservative dynamic of the Haskala while simultaneously remaining ambivalent about its ultimate destination.

Wolfssohn's German-Yiddish play *Laykhtzin un fremelay* ("Silliness and Sanctimony") is an especially noteworthy symbol of this process, particularly when these questions of assimilation and traditionalism are examined through the lens of Wolfssohn's usage of classical Jewish texts in the play. Wolfssohn often continues Mendelssohn's fairly conservative strategy of rehabilitation of traditional texts, but his attacks on a different type of Jewish interpretation—that of the *Ostjuden*, the Eastern European Jews—marks the beginning of a strategic shift by the Jewish Enlighteners from external defensiveness to internal critique that reaches its apogee in the Eastern European Haskala of the nineteenth century. Additionally, the presence and absence of classical Jewish texts in the speech of various characters portrays powerfully Wolfssohn's concerns about assimilation.

As *Laykhtzin un fremelay* is Wolfssohn's most important work and is crucial to the development of the Yiddish theater, a contextualization and analysis of the play constitutes the majority of the chapter. However, some of Wolfssohn's other works are also briefly considered to illustrate the role of classical textual citation in a variety of genres for a maskil of the 1790s.

Wolfssohn's Life and Work

Aaron ben Wolf was born in the Prussian city of Halle in 1754, to a family that had already begun to assimilate and accept Enlightenment tenets.[1] Wolfssohn's grandfather was "a comparatively wealthy merchant with a strong interest in learning and the affairs of the Jewish community"; his father, while studying Talmud, also studied medicine at Halle, an Enlightenment-inspired course of action fairly rare among Jews of his generation.[2] The radicalism expressed in some of Wolfssohn's works may thus be traced, at least in part, to his (qualified) second-generation maskilic status.[3] Wolfssohn's father wrote to Mendelssohn that "it seems likely that [he] already became acquainted with many maskilic writings while he was still living at his parents' home,"[4] and Wolfssohn grew up speaking German, not Yiddish.[5]

1. Practically the only modern research on Aaron Wolfssohn and *Laykhtzin un fremelay* is Jutta Strauss's doctoral dissertation ("Aaron Halle-Wolfssohn: A Trilingual Life," D.Phil. thesis, University of Oxford, 1994, hereafter "Strauss"), which provides excellent biographical and bibliographical data, but does not devote itself to a literary analysis of Wolfssohn's work; see also her "Aaron Halle-Wolfssohn: ein Leben in drei Sprachen," in Anselm Gerhard, ed. *Musik und Ästhetik im Berlin Moses Mendelssohns* (Tübingen: Niemeyer, 1999), 57–75. This book, conversely, focuses primarily on literary considerations. See also Dan Miron's excellent "Al aharon volfson vemakhazehu 'kalut dat utseviut' (r' henokh verav yosefkhe)," in Aaron Halle Wolfssohn, *Kalut daat utseviut* (Israel: Sman Keriah, 1977), 5–55. Miron's essay serves primarily as an introduction to his edition of the earlier unpublished Hebrew version of *Laykhtzin un fremelay* (see n. 70 *infra*), and thus necessarily offers different perspectives from the analysis of the Yiddish/German work discussed here. Another important but highly tendentious essay is Max Erik's introduction to the period in *Di komedyes fun der berliner oyfklerung* (Melukhe-Farlag: Kiev, 1933), 5–67.

2. Strauss 40.

3. Zalman Reyzen, *Fun Mendelson biz Mendele* (Warsaw: Farlag Kultur-Lige, 1923), 25. See the genealogical table in Strauss 37.

4. Cited in Strauss 44.

5. Strauss 239–240.

Like many early Prussian maskilim, Wolfssohn moved to Berlin to join Mendelssohn's circle of Jewish intellectuals. Arriving there in 1785, he quickly became involved in both major maskilic projects of the time: the translation of the Bible into German with Hebrew commentary, begun by Mendelssohn and Solomon Dubno, and *Hameasef*, the monthly designed as a Hebrew counterpart to the German *Berlinische Monatsschrift* and dedicated to the dissemination of maskilic ideals.[6]

Wolfssohn's work on the Bible commentary began in 1788, when, together with Joel Bril, he published Mendelssohn's German translation of the Song of Songs, accompanied by their own commentary.[7] In 1789, Wolfssohn produced German translations of Lamentations, Ruth, and Esther.[8] In 1791, he translated the book of Job, and, in 1800, the book of Kings; all these later works are accompanied by an original Hebrew commentary by Wolfssohn. In 1790, along with Euchel, Friedlander, and a dozen other maskilim, he translated the Haftorot into German.[9] Wolfssohn's work here is directly influenced by the general considerations of the early Mendelssohnian Haskala: a "renewed interest in the study of the Bible" and an "endeavor to show the validity of much of traditional Jewish exegesis, that is, medieval

---

6. The most detailed treatment of this seminal journal is Tsemach Tsamriyon, *Hameasef: ktav haet hamoderni harishon beivrit* (Tel Aviv: University Publishing Press, 1988). See especially the charts of appearances of features and biographies of contributors (44–59), and the discussion of the maskilic attitude toward the Bible, Yiddish, and the *Ostjuden* (72–90). See also Moshe Pelli, *Dor hameasfim beshakhar hahaskala: terumatam hasifrutit shel khalutsei "Hameasef," ktav-haet haivri harishon, lehaskala haivrit bereshita* (Tel Aviv: Hakibutz hameuchad, 2001), *passim,* and Miron "Volfson" 9–12.

7. Moses Mendelssohn, *Megilat shir hashirim meturgemet ashkenazit al yedei harav rabeinu moshe ben menakhem zs'l venilve eilav beiur hamilot meet aharon ben-volf umar'ehu yoel bril* (Berlin: 1788).

8. Aaron Wolfssohn, *Megilat rut im targum ashkenazi vebeiur* (Berlin: 1789); *Megilat eikha im targum ashkenazi vebeiur* (Berlin: 1789); *Megilat ester im targum ashkenazi vebeiur* (Berlin: 1789).

9. *Haftorot mikol hashana im targum ashkenazi vebeiur* (Berlin: 1790). A full list of the contributors to the work is provided in Feiner "'Mendelssohn's Disciples'" 144.

Scriptural interpretation and its handling of Talmudic and midrashic literature, for a contemporary scholarly approach."[10]

The year 1788 also marks the beginning of Wolfssohn's writing in *Hameasef*, though he is listed as an editorial assistant as early as 1785. Wolfssohn wrote on numerous subjects: analyses of Hebrew and Aramaic words,[11] essays on natural history,[12] book reviews and announcements,[13] and mathematics.[14] He also tried his hand at some of the genres popular in contemporary German literature: ethical fables[15] and occasional poems.[16] In all cases, Wolfssohn attempts to strike a

10. Reyzen 26. Traditional commentaries cited by Wolfssohn include Rashi, the Radak, and Gersonides. See Strauss 131.

11. *Hameasef* 4:17–18, 21–24 (on the word *nekhmata*); 6:9–11 (letter to Bril about attempts to explain difficult Biblical passages); 6:249–253 (letter to David Theodor on the concept of "Jewish names"); 6:356–357 (question on interpretation of Joshua 17:14–18).

12. *Hameasef* 4:49–57 (on the lion); 5:234–240 (on the beaver); 5:289–291 (on the hippopotamus); 5:291–293 (essay explaining certain Biblical passages about animals in light of modern biology); 6:73–80, 108–122 (dialogue explaining the phenomenon of the tides); 7:274–80 (on the elephant).

13. *Hameasef* 5:245–249 (reviewing Joel Bril's translation and commentary to Jonah); 5:373–77 (announcement of his new Hebrew schoolbook); 6:177–186 (book review of book on ethics); 6:190–191 (announcement of Wolfssohn's new book *Avtalyon*); 6:224 (announcement of error found in *Avtalyon*); 7:175–179 (notice about letter unintentionally printed in *Hameasef*); 7:251–266 (review of Isaac Satanow's pseudo-wisdom literature text *Mishlei Asaf*); 7:304–360 (answer to a writer who had criticized *Hameasef*).

14. *Hameasef* 5:307–312 (various letters dealing with the statistical phenomenon of attaining majorities and representations as they are expressed in the Talmud); 5:354–355 (playful poem on the zero); 7:111–117 (essay on parallel lines).

15. *Hameasef* 4:80, 4:95–6 (ethical fables: "The woman and the sea-serpent," "The woman and the bee"); 4:172 (rhymed answer to an earlier riddle; the answer is "time"); 4:175–176 (ethical fables: "Rekhavam the wicked one," "Amnon the youth," "Aviezer the shepherd," "Avner the vintner"); 5:158 (untitled ethical fable concerning circumspection); 7:21 (ethical fable concerning sin and punishment). See Lachover 1:78–80; Joseph Klausner, *Hanovela besifrut haivrit* (Tel Aviv: J. Chachik, 1947), 122–124; Miron "Volfson" 10–11; and Moshe Pelli, "Hasuga shel hamashal besifrut hahaskala haivrit begermania: giluyei hamashal beHameasef," *KOMI* 11C3 (1994), 45–52.

16. *Hameasef* 5:161–164 (poems in honor of Purim); 6:160 (poem expressing Job's question and answer); 6:221 (poem written on the tombstone of a

fairly Mendelssohnian balance between traditional forms and concepts and modern sensibilities and ideals.

Wolfssohn's editorial role in *Hameasef* steadily increased throughout the 1790s, in directly opposite proportion to the journal's success. As of 1790, *Hameasef*, which had been decreasing in subscriptions on a monthly basis, announced its cessation of regular publishing and its transformation into an occasional journal under Wolfssohn's editorship. The next volume appeared in 1794, edited jointly by Wolfssohn and Bril; one volume appeared each subsequent year until 1797.[17] By 1797, it seemed as if Wolfssohn was writing most of the journal himself. His most notable contribution was *Sikha beeretz hakhayim* ("A Conversation in the Land of the Living"), an imaginary dialogue between Moses Mendelssohn, Maimonides, and an unnamed *Ostjude* set in the "World to Come," where maskilic ideology and interpretive approaches to the Jewish canon are vindicated and the mystical, irrational interpretations of the *Ostjuden* are excoriated.[18]

A selected exchange between the *Ostjude* and Wolfssohn's Maimonides will serve to indicate the nature of the polemic. Maimonides has just dismissed a question by the Polish Jew about his law book, the

---

friend's wife); 6:256 (aphorism); 7:14–19 (poems honoring the birthday of David Friedländer).

17. Reyzen 27. The 1797 volume marked the end of *Hameasef* for twelve years; though the journal appeared again in Berlin in 1809, Altona in 1810, and Dessau in 1811, this was, at best, a coda to its main activity.

18. *Sikha beeretz hakhayim* appeared in *Hameasef* 7:54–67, 120–55, 203–28, 279–98. See Pelli *Sugot vesugyot* 48–72; GJH 1:318–19; Miron "Volfson" 12; Shmuel Aviezer, *Hamakhaze vehateatron haivri vehayidi: kerakh aleph: mereshitam vead sof hamea hayud tet* (Jerusalem: Reuven Mass, 1996) 62, 80; Meir Gilon, "Hasatira haivrit bitkufat hahaskala begermania—anatomia shel mekhkar," *Zion* 52 (1987), 211–250, 246–250; and Yehudit Tsvik, "Reshit tsmichato shel ha'sipur' behaskala hagermanit: hatakhbula hadialogit," *KOMI* 11C3 (1994), 53–60. On Maimonides' role in the work and in the Haskala in general, see Yehuda Friedlander, "HaRambam veElisha ben Avuya kearkhetipusim besifrut haivrit hakhadasha," in Nash 271–282, esp. 271–275, and idem., "Mekomo shel hahalakha besifrut hahaskala—hayakhas leRambam keposek," *Mekhkerei yerushalayim bemaskhshevet yisrael* 5 (1986), 349–392.

Yad Hakhazaka, by indicating that the answer appears in detail in the section of the *Yad Hakhazaka* dedicated to ethics and metaphysics, *Hilkhot Deot* (lit. "The Laws of Beliefs"), which serves as a preface to the book as a whole. The anonymous Jew replies that he has only read the sections of the work dedicated to actual law: "For what do I care of these matters about which you have asked me; what do I gain if I know them and what do I lose if I do not know them? This is why I did not learn *Hilkhot Deot* at all."[19] As we will see in our discussion of Wolfssohn's Hasid Reb Yoysefkhe, the *Ostjuden* are portrayed as engaging in textual learning without interest in its moral or philosophical dimensions. It is no wonder their interpretations are portrayed as incorrect and irrational; to the maskilim, they lack the foundational moral and philosophical grounding on which to base those interpretations.

Maimonides' response, on the other hand, indicates both the maskilic antipathy toward these approaches and their commitment to rectifying them:

> [N]ow the mask has been removed from him and he has been revealed before me as naked as when he emerged from his mother's womb. But what should I do now? Leave and let him continue on his own way? Then will he not persist in his treacherous and false opinions? It shall not be! For the honor of God I will stay and enlighten him in the proper manner on which to go; perhaps his heart will understand and return and be healed.[20]

The rest of the debate continues in similar fashion.

Wolfssohn's work in the 1790s was not limited to contributions to *Hameasef* and Bible translations and commentaries; it included pedagogical innovation as well. *Avtalyon* (1790) marked the first attempt to create a Hebrew textbook for students based on Enlightenment

---

19. *Hameasef* 7:65. All translations from Hebrew and Yiddish in this chapter are mine unless otherwise noted, with the exception of translations from *Laykhtzin un fremelay,* taken from the translation by Joel Berkowitz and Jeremy Dauber.

20. *Hameasef* 7:66.

pedagogical principles.[21] In the "Tidings of new books" section of *Hameasef* in Elul 1789, Wolfssohn writes:

> You know well the custom among us, that from the day that a child is able to lisp words and letters in the prayer books, he is taken to the schoolhouse to learn the Torah of Moses, the man of God, from the schoolmaster, from its beginning to its end. And who among you, my brothers and friends, does not know that the Torah is very deep, without end . . . and if so, then tell us: how can the child, who until now has not known a single word on the Hebrew tongue, how can this child begin to learn from this holy book immediately? . . . For what will the child remember first, if the words are taught at the same time as the explanations, the words themselves, or the explanations?[22]

This radical project, though, is phrased cautiously in traditional terms:

> And our sages, may their memories be for a blessing, also realized with their pure intellect the difficulties of learning, and as a result they apportioned a great deal of time—five years—for study of the Bible, as it says in the Tractate of the Ethics of the Fathers: "Five years old for the Bible, ten years old for the Mishna."[23] And there as well they established the time for learning only from five years and above, and not, as the way that we do it now, to instruct them from the day that they are able to speak, since their intent was to instruct them previously in simple subjects and to bring them in so doing to this holy book gradually.[24]

21. On *Avtalyon*, see also Strauss 73–120; the edition cited here was published in 1814 in Vienna by Anton Schmid. On the contemporary Philanthropinist movement's influence on Wolfssohn, see Strauss 246. An early but still valuable treatment of the Jewish educational system can be found in Max J. Kohler, "Educational Reforms in Europe in Their Relation to Jewish Emancipation—1778–1919," *PAJHS* 28 (1922), 83–132, particularly 90–96, 103–105. For a more recent survey, see Yaacov Iram, "L'éducation juive moderne de l'époque de la Haskala à la fondation de l'État d'Israël," *La société juive a travers l'histoire* II (1992), 351–381, esp. 358–359.

22. *Hameasef* 5:374; the entire article runs from 5:373–377.

23. *Mishna Avot* 5:24.

24. *Hameasef* 5:375.

As a result, Wolfssohn intends to write a book called "Introduction to Learning" (*Mevo Halimud*), a book that would eventually become *Avtalyon*.

These passages clearly illustrate Wolfssohn's Mendelssohnian strategies of legitimation and subversion. He cites a text from the Ethics of the Fathers (well-known to traditional audiences, since it was read in sections weekly every summer) to illuminate the discontinuities between rabbinic tradition and current practice, thus opening a space for legitimated reform. The subversion comes in the reasoning and the logic Wolfssohn ascribes to the rabbis: he presents them as completely in agreement with the tenets of late eighteenth-century pedagogical theory, similar to Mendelssohn's presentation of the rabbis as followers of Wolffian and Leibnitzian metaphysics.

This strategy of traditional legitimation combined with subversion and "rehabilitation" applies not only to the motives for issuing such a primer, but to the actual contents of the book as well. *Avtalyon* employs selections from the Bible, adapted in simpler language,[25] as set texts in order to introduce the Hebrew language to the young reader.[26] Wolfssohn's decision to use classical texts helps to legitimate his project to traditionalist audiences, but his selection criteria reveal his Enlightenment sensibilities: he claims in his introduction to include only "those things which an enlightened teacher would give to his students in order to provide them with ethical teachings, to fear God, and to do what is good and righteous in his eyes."[27]

To emphasize the importance of universal moral lessons over particularistic history, however, Wolfssohn prefaces his retelling of Biblical history with a set of moral guidelines. These guidelines are generally

25. Wolfssohn does, however, use more complex language to make his ideological points. For example, despite his desire to make the adoption of Biblical Hebrew grammar and vocabulary as easy as possible, he uses the rare word *khermesh* (sickle), which appears only twice in the Bible (Deut. 16:9 and 23:6), because he wants to introduce the children at a young age to the idea of agriculture. See *Avtalyon* 7a.

26. Strauss (89) notes that Wolfssohn was probably the first writer to adapt the Biblical stories for children.

27. *Avtalyon* 4b.

adapted from Biblical passages, but are placed in a non-Biblical, generally hortatory framework. Wolfssohn accentuates the universal moral lessons that can be drawn from the Bible, those in accord with Enlightenment tenets, over particularistic approaches, while simultaneously affirming traditionalist principles sufficiently to avoid strong opposition.

For example, Wolfssohn proclaims his fidelity to Jewish dogma early in the work ("Come children and listen to me! The Lord our God the Lord is One and there is no other beside Him"),[28] but then writes: "And what does the Lord your God ask from men? Simply to know him, and to understand his works, and to do justice and charity. And so said Solomon: Do righteousness and charity, which are more pleasing to God than a burnt-offering."[29] Wolfssohn again stresses the universalist aspects of Judaism when, after discussing the importance of honoring one's father and mother and honoring one's teacher,[30] he stresses the value of being good to one's neighbor, including one's Christian neighbor, "for do not all have one Father, and did not one God create all of them . . . "[31] Though Wolfssohn never presents himself in *Avtalyon* as an opponent of the traditional Jewish law, he clearly views the universal aspects of Judaism as more important than its particularistic ones.[32]

Wolfssohn also shares the Enlightenment emphasis on reason: his early discussion of the Creation story, located in his preface, not his subsequent retelling of Biblical history, concludes with the summation that "God gave into his being the soul of life *to know good and evil, to make plans and to achieve desires*: and therefore his fear was upon all of the beasts and animals of the earth."[33] Later in the preface, Wolfssohn reiterates the importance of wisdom, writing that "one should

28. *Avtalyon* 7b.

29. *Avtalyon* 8a.

30. *Avtalyon* 8a–9a.

31. *Avtalyon* 9b.

32. Earlier, he notes the importance of observing the commandments, but, in classically Mendelssohnian fashion, grounds such ceremonial observance on God's omniscience, which is beyond human apprehension; see *Avtalyon* 7b–8a.

33. *Avtalyon* 6b–7a, emphasis mine.

buy wisdom and knowledge with all of one's possessions, for wisdom is better than pure gold, and knowledge is more choice-worthy than glory and great wealth."[34]

After these and other general warnings,[35] the majority of the book consists of Wolfssohn's retelling of Jewish history, from the story of Adam and Eve to the destruction of the first Temple and the Babylonian exile.[36] *Avtalyon*'s account seems to be entirely based on the Biblical account of Jewish history; notably, Wolfssohn even follows the traditional schema of Biblical chronology, citing the "ten generations" between Adam and Noah and from Seth to Abraham.[37] Strauss's claim that Wolfssohn "does not . . . keep the language of the original" is certainly true, but her assertion that he "combin[es] them with fragments from Midrash and Agadah" seems to be unfounded, at least narratively and thematically speaking.[38] In fact, the stories follow the Biblical account very closely. Considering the problematic nature of aggadic material in the Prussian milieu discussed in the previous two chapters, such a strategy seems eminently sensible.

Wolfssohn does, however, occasionally interject subtle editorial comment. In discussing Joseph's elevation to viceroy status, he accounts for Joseph's elevation in that "the Lord filled him with wisdom and understanding surpassing all other men."[39] In the analogous Biblical passage, Genesis 41:39, it is *Pharaoh* who makes such a claim about Joseph; the narrator of the Bible does not, preferring merely to state that "God was with him."[40] Again, we see that wisdom and understanding are the keys to winning favor with the absolutist authority—a useful metaphor for the maskilic view of the current situation.

---

34. *Avtalyon* 10a.

35. These include warnings against the dangers of bad company (10b), against forgetting the poor (11a), against taking revenge on people who treat one badly (11a-11b), against answering someone quickly before hearing their question out (11b–12a), and even an exhortation to wear white and well-made clothes and to take care of them (12a).

36. *Avtalyon* 12b–32b.

37. *Avtalyon* 12b–13a.

38. Strauss 79.

39. *Avtalyon* 16a.

40. See Genesis 39:5, 23.

Wolfssohn not only emphasizes some episodes, but deemphasizes others: in his retelling of the Exodus, the Ten Plagues are downplayed—only the last plague is mentioned—since the Jews want to be perceived neither as hostile to external authority nor as prone to leaving their country of residence.[41] Similarly, episodes that put Jewish progenitors in a less than moral light, such as the stories of Judah and Tamar or David and Bathsheba, are notably absent, though Wolfssohn may have simply deemed such stories unsuitable for children. Finally, *Avtalyon* ends with a section retelling certain Biblical anecdotes insufficiently important to be featured in the historical account but which have easily elicited moral lessons,[42] as well as a number of ethical parables.[43] The inclusion of these last sections particularly illuminates Wolfssohn's desire to link traditional texts with modern moral genres in much the same fashion as in Mendelssohn's *Kohelet Musar*.

Avtalyon was remarkably successful; by 1814, it was in a fourth expanded printing.[44] Wolfssohn's pedagogical contributions were not limited to textbook writing, though: Wolfssohn and Bril also headed the modern "Königlecher Wilhelmschule," founded in Breslau in 1791. The school's educational approach was based on new German pedagogical methods, and its emphasis on modern learning and its, at best, ambivalence toward the Talmud provoked great hostility in the general Jewish community.[45] Hebrew teachers at the school were required to teach the language "according to a rational method . . . not in the manner of Polish Jews" and had to be "free from silly Talmudic and rabbinic ideas."[46] It was as performance pieces for his school's students

41. *Avtalyon* 19b. See the discussion of the analogous theme in *Jerusalem* in Chapter Four.

42. *Avtalyon* 33a–34b. The stories include Gideon's father tricking the hostile villagers (Judges 6:28–32), David's pretense of insanity to escape Akhish, king of Gat (1 Samuel 21:13–16), and Solomon's ruling to divide the baby sought by two mothers (1 Kings 3:16–28).

43. *Avtalyon* 34b–37a.

44. See Dov Rafel, *Bibliografia shel sifrei limud yehudiim (1488–1918)* (Tel Aviv: Tel Aviv University, 1995), 51 (Hebrew section).

45. Reyzen 28; Miron "Volfson" 7–8. On the new German schools founded by maskilim, see Strauss 24–31.

46. Cited in Strauss 52. The anti-*Ostjude* bias here is notable as well.

that Wolfssohn wrote his two other main belletristic works—his two plays. The first, *Laykhtzin un fremelay*, was first published in 1796, and the second, *Dovid der baziger fun golyes* ("David the Victor over Goliath"), appeared in 1802. Both, as we will see in the next section, were designed to replace the traditional Purim plays of the late Middle Ages and early modern period.[47]

Wolfssohn's literary activity in Hebrew and Yiddish essentially concluded around the turn of the century. He continued to publish subsequently, but in German, and it is in these works that he turned further toward the radicalism so generally ascribed to him. This shift may be due to considerations of audience (at this point, he is writing for non-Jews and assimilated Jews who could already read German), considerations of time and demography, or a combination of these.[48] In 1804 Wolfssohn published *Jeschurun*, a German language apologia for Judaism that also articulated a modern Jewish philosophy.[49] Certainly, there is radicalism here: in the book, Wolfssohn sketched the "ideal image of a rational religion, which, 'purged of all ceremonies and customs,' would become the purpose and final goal of religious history . . . Wolfssohn and his radical associates believed the highest stage of the Jewish historical continuum was a faith purified by reason. They did not wish to see this as a total break with tradition but interpreted it as keeping with the Jews' new status."[50]

47. Wolfssohn also wrote an earlier play on the question of early burial. Sadly, the play is no longer extant. See Y. Shatsky, "Der kamf kegn purim-shpiln in praysn," *YIVO-Bleter* 15 (1940), 30–38. On early burial, see Chapter Four, esp. n. 30.

48. On Wolfssohn's radicalism, see Isaac Eisenstein-Barzilay, "National and Anti-National Trends in the Berlin Haskalah," *JSS* 21:3 (1959), 165–192, 168–169. Note, however, Eisenstein-Barzilay's overdeterminative ascription of radical or conservative tendencies to maskilim based on their language of composition; see 167 and Isaac Eisenstein-Barzilay, "The Treatment of the Jewish Religion in the Literature of the Berlin Haskalah," *PAAJR* 24 (1955), 39–68, 40–41. See Pelli *Age* 53, 58–59 for a critique of Barzilay and a more conservative view of Wolfssohn based on textual analysis; for a similar critique, see also Lowenstein *Berlin* 96–97.

49. *Jeschurun* (Breslau: 1804). On *Jeschurun* and the circumstances surrounding its publication, see Strauss 180–220, 262, and Miron "Volfson" 8–9.

50. *GJH* 1:352.

Though Wolfssohn certainly did wish to reform certain aspects of contemporary Jewish practice,[51] his discussion of reform is less radical than often supposed and reflects his respect for and influence by Mendelssohn. Wolfssohn's sense of the historical development of Jewish law, his "altogether positive view of the Talmud and normative rabbinic Judaism" despite his objections to the contemporary manner of its teaching, his praise of the medieval Biblical exegetes, and his statements on the (judicious) benefits of the aggada, the importance of religious law, and the observance of (Pentateuchal) religious festivals are all essentially Mendelssohnian.[52] Wolfssohn mentions Mendelssohn early in *Jeschurun*,[53] comparing him to the idealized Joseph figure seen earlier in *Avtalyon*; later in the book, Wolfssohn describes Mendelssohn as the epitome of the new type of enlightened Jew.[54] Wolfssohn's reforms echo Mendelssohn's; in fact, he approvingly cites Mendelssohn's approach in *Jerusalem* to questions of Jewish law.[55] Following Mendelssohn, he notes the importance of serving the state even when this leads to conflict with ceremonial law,[56] and that the state needs to help Jews change to become *warhaft gebildeten und aufgeklarten Juden*.[57] However, this is certainly far from an overtly antinomian approach to Judaism.

Wolfssohn's similarities to Mendelssohn can also be seen in his approach to classical texts in *Jeschurun*. Like Mendelssohn, Wolfssohn is dedicated in his work to presenting a contextualized view of the Jewish rabbinic tradition, opposing figures like Eisenmenger and Grattenauer, who distort rabbinic texts for anti-Semitic purposes.[58] Arguing that "rabbinic Judaism" has to be understood as not simply the Tal-

---

51. See *Jeschurun* 105–121.

52. See Strauss 256–260.

53. *Jeschurun* 24–26.

54. *Jeschurun* 115.

55. *Jeschurun* 116, 119.

56. *Jeschurun* 120–121; see the discussion of Mendelssohn's approach to military service on the Sabbath discussed in Chapter Four.

57. *Jeschurun* 114.

58. See Chapter Three; Wolfssohn explicitly mentions these figures in *Jeschurun* 18–19.

mud, but the entire corpus of rabbinic law as well,[59] Wolfssohn cites numerous passages from the *Shulkhan Arukh*, the code of normative Jewish law, in Hebrew and in German, in order to illustrate that anti-Semitic charges, such as those alleging that the *Kol Nidrei* service on Yom Kippur allows Jews to break their contracts with non-Jews, are completely without foundation.[60] Wolfssohn uses a similar process to prove that Jews are as forbidden to cheat non-Jews in business as they are other Jews.[61]

Wolfssohn's polemic and apologetic efforts also include his insistence, repeated again and again in later maskilic sources, that a differentiation must be made between the Talmud's discussion of pagans and Christians.[62] Finally, Wolfssohn spends numerous pages elucidating principles of Biblical grammar and examples of Biblical vocabulary to prove that non-Jewish claims about maltreatment at Jewish hands are unfounded.[63] Though this work was published twenty years after *Jerusalem*, Wolfssohn's strategy remains similar to Mendelssohn's. We will similarly see Wolfssohn attempt to walk the Mendelssohnian path, under the changed circumstances of the 1790s, in his implicit treatment of the Haskala's future in *Laykhtzin un fremelay*.

Aside from *Jeschurun*, Wolfssohn also wrote a work of exegetical criticism on Habbakuk in German in 1806;[64] subsequently, he wrote very little until his death in 1835. Despite his literary inactivity, he remained revered by members of the new generation of German Jewish

59. *Jeschurun* 73–84, esp. 82–83. In this section, Wolfssohn also downplays the importance of the aggada (78–79).

60. Wolfssohn's attack on the non-Jewish claims appears in *Jeschurun* 55–63; he returns to the subject of oaths in general in *Jeschurun* 91–99, and then to Yom Kippur and the release of oaths in the *Kol Nidrei* service in particular on 99–102. In these sections, he cites the *Shulkhan Arukh* (*Yore Dea* 228:1, 3, 210:3, 211:2, 4, 225:14, 230:1, and 239:1).

61. *Jeschurun* 85–90. In this section, Wolfssohn cites the *Shulkhan Arukh* (*Khoshen Hamishpat* 228:6, 231:1, 348:12, 356:1, 358:5, 359:1, 7, 8, and 369:2).

62. *Jeschurun* 70–71. See the discussion of this topic in Joseph Perl's *Megale Temirin* in Chapter Seven.

63. *Jeschurun* 30–51.

64. See Strauss 221–228.

intellectuals, the founders of the *Wissenschaft des Judentums*, and was invited to join the *Verein* in 1822.[65]

Wolfssohn's New Theater and Writing in Yiddish

By 1797, it was clear that the original maskilic projects needed some modification. *Hameasef*, the flagship work of the Berlin Haskala, was continually losing support, with only 120 subscribers then remaining.[66] This trend reflected the increasing complexity of the linguistic dynamics of German society. A 1797 essay by the maskil Isaac Euchel appearing in *Hameasef* shows that the maskilim of the 1790s understood that any attempt at reaching a mass audience of German Jewry by writing in Hebrew was doomed to failure.[67]

Euchel's essay concerns the composition of maskilic essays intended to influence a Jewish audience. He writes that such essays should be written in German in Hebrew characters, reasoning that those who could read a Hebrew essay encouraging affiliation with the Haskala would have no need of doing so, having clearly already adopted the maskilic tenet of Hebrew language revival; conversely, those who would need to read the essay could not understand Hebrew.[68] The essay acknowledges that since Mendelssohn's death, the possibility of developing a mass Hebrew-speaking population in Germany had vanished.

The non-Jewish community and its reactions also play a role in Euchel's considerations, however. The fact that these essays appear in Hebrew characters, writes Euchel, allows Jewish writers freer expression, assured that (almost) no non-Jew could understand them. Cul-

65. Strauss 65. See also Reyzen 29 and Miron "Volfson" 9.

66. Khone Shmeruk, *Sifrut yidish: prakim letoldoteha* (Tel-Aviv: Porter Institute, Tel-Aviv University, 1978), 157n18. Even at its height, though, its circulation was hardly massive: during the years 1785 to 1788, *Hameasef* had 295 subscribers who ordered 318 copies. Feiner "'Mendelssohn's Disciples'" 138.

67. The essay appears in *Hameasef* 7:361–391. On Euchel, see Pelli *Age* 190–230, *Sugot vesugyot* 291–309, and Shmuel Feiner, "Yitzkhak Aykhl—Ha'yazam' shel tenuat hahaskala begermania," *Zion* 52 (1987), 427–469, esp. 456–462. See also Shmeruk *Prakim* 156–7.

68. *Hameasef* 7:361–362.

tural works such as Wolfssohn's plays, then, were required to function within the cultural and linguistic milieu described by Euchel's essay: they could not have been written in Hebrew, since they would have then failed to fulfill their didactic function. Writing them in German, however, would have alerted non-Jewish readers to internal Jewish criticism, not to mention that some Jewish readers would have been unable to read the Latin lettering.[69] Wolfssohn's decision, then, to take a Hebrew play he wrote,[70] transpose it into a more accessible form,[71]

69. Shmeruk estimates that, generally speaking, German Jews gained the ability to read Latin lettering in the 1830s; Shmeruk *Prakim* 152–4. Similarly, it seems that Yiddish remained a living language, as opposed to German, in Western Europe until the 1830s. See Shmeruk *Prakim* 154n13 and Weinberg 234–235 for discussion.

70. A Hebrew manuscript has been discovered, though not in Wolfssohn's hand, implying that Wolfssohn wrote a Hebrew version of the play before the published German/Yiddish version; see Bernard Weinryb, "An Unknown Hebrew Play of the German Haskalah," *PAAJR* 24 (1955), 165–170, text (Hebrew section) 1–37. Weinryb's claim that the Hebrew version preceded the published version seems sound. However, his conclusions, that Wolfssohn would have preferred to publish the play in Hebrew, but was prevented from doing so by various circumstances relating to the play's radicalism and *Hameasef*'s straitened circumstances, seem less warranted. After all, Wolfssohn was able to publish the equally radical and significantly longer *Sikha beeretz hakhayim* in 1797, when the journal was in even direr financial straits. Rather, I believe that Wolfssohn realized the play's dramatic potential, in contradistinction to *Sikha beeretz hakhayim*, and thus chose to transform it into a likely candidate for his project to replace the older Purim plays; see Jeremy Dauber, "The City, Sacred and Profane: Between Hebrew and Yiddish in the Fiction of the Early Jewish Enlightenment," in *Urban Diaspora: The City in Jewish History*, forthcoming. The Hebrew version has also been reprinted in a modern edition: Aaron Wolfssohn, *Kalut dat* (see note 1 *supra*).

71. I use the word "transpose" intentionally: the multivocality and greater linguistic flexibility (expressed, among other ways, in differing usages of classical textual material) in *Laykhtzin un fremelay*, and the resulting change in our perceptions of its characters means, in effect, that it is a different play from its earlier Hebrew counterpart, and therefore allows (and, perhaps, demands) a different analysis. The following analysis, then, refers only to the Yiddish/German play; for a fully developed interpretation of the Hebrew play, see Miron "Volfson" 16–55. For a sustained comparison between the two works, as well as historical and textual arguments for elucidating real ideological and thematic transformation between the two versions, see Dauber, "The City," *passim*.

and then to publish it in Hebrew characters becomes clearer in this light.[72]

But in what language is *Laykhtzin un fremelay* written? *Laykhtzin un fremelay* is often referred to as the first modern Yiddish play, and literary historians as distinguished as Zalman Reyzen have discussed the conundrum of a maskil as ardent as Wolfssohn writing in Yiddish, given the well-known maskilic antipathy toward the language.[73] Wolfssohn himself was certainly no ardent Yiddishist; in fact, he was one of the founders of the *Gesellschaft der Freunde*, a society whose correspondence took place entirely in German.[74] As a result of these attitudes by Wolfssohn's circle, and by Wolfssohn himself, a great deal of scholarly confusion has emerged about the langauge of Wolfssohn's play and its relationship to his Enlightenment goals.

Reyzen's solution, that "Wolfssohn did not write his comedy because he was a Haskala-fighter, but in spite of it," makes much of the fact that no mention is made of the play in Wolfssohn's other works or in *Hameasef*.[75] Reyzen's approach, however, is belied by Wolfssohn's statements in his introduction to the play, which indicate that he did indeed intend it as a means through which to disseminate maskilic ideals; he hoped to replace the current "corrupt" and "retrogressive" Purim plays with ones more in keeping with the image of Jewry the maskilim wished to project, as we see in more detail below.

72. These comments refer to the published, rather than performed, version of the play: in the latter, a wider range of individuals, including non-Jews, would of course be able to understand the German, regardless of the orthography of the playscript. A contemporary non-Jewish reviewer's comments on the printed version of *Laykhtzin un fremelay* in the *Schlessiche Provinzialblätter*, who presumably could read Hebrew characters, lends credence to the notion that the play would be of interest to a general audience, explicitly suggesting such at the end of his review. The (German-language) anonymous review is reprinted in full in Yaakov Shatsky's "Vegn Arn Hale-Volfsons pyesn (naye materyaln)," in Yaakov Shatsky, ed., *Arkhiv-geshikhte fun yidishn teatr un drame* (New York: YIVO, 1933), 147–150, 147–148.

73. See Chapter Four.

74. See Strauss 44–45. For more on the *Gesellschaft der Freunde*, one of the Jewish institutions that developed at the turn of the nineteenth century to mirror bourgeois German societal institutions, see Sorkin *Transformation* 116–117.

75. Reyzen 30.

A somewhat more convincing explanation is provided by Strauss, who argues that Wolfssohn, in using Yiddish, is engaging in exactly the same activity as later maskilim do; he writes in Yiddish because it is the language of the people. Writing in their language allows him to "reach their hearts and minds, to imbue them with the ideas of the Enlightenment by means of his play. Thus he was able to reach an audience still knowledgeable about tradition with a non-traditional message."[76] While this position is undoubtedly correct with regard to the position of the later maskilim, as clearly shown by Miron,[77] the case of the German maskilim of the 1790s may be somewhat more complex.

This is not a Yiddish play; it is a play with Yiddish in it.[78] This is a crucial distinction. Most of Wolfssohn's most important points—the points that most clearly and obviously articulate Enlightenment principles—are made in German (albeit a German written in Hebrew letters), though, as we will see, the play's true message results from a complex interaction between the statements of the German- and Yiddish-speaking characters. Any reader who could have understood the Yiddish of Reb Yoysefkhe and Reb Henokh but not the German of Markus would have failed to fully grasp the play's positive program— the very positive program about which Wolfssohn cared so much.[79] This play was designed for an audience who understood Yiddish, certainly, but who were also precariously balanced between that language and German, trying to decide in which language to conduct their daily life activities. Within the next few decades, of course, the decision would be made, and it had much to do with general cultural shifts in German Jewish history and little to do with the literary efforts of the maskilim. But that is a subject beyond the scope of this chapter.

76. Strauss 145. See also Strauss 242; a similar view is expressed in Michael "Hahaskala" 293.

77. See Miron *Traveler* 4.

78. See Steven M. Lowenstein, "The Yiddish Written Word in Nineteenth Century Germany," in Lowenstein *Mechanics* 183–199, 188–189, and Miron "Volfson" 28–29.

79. More accurately, one might refer to the language of Markus as "Standard High German," since "High German" includes non-standard vernaculars, possibly even Western Yiddish. I am grateful to Ben Sadock for this suggestion.

Wolfssohn's dramatic development was also tied to the maskilic plans for a refined and reformed Jewish theater. Jewish theater did exist in the late medieval and early modern period, but was delimited to the time around the holiday of Purim, the Jewish equivalent of Carnival, where various restrictions and cultural boundaries, like the general bias against drama, were inverted or removed.[80] Aside from these *Purim-shpiln*, there was really no Jewish theater to speak of in wide circulation in Wolfssohn's day, and certainly very little maskilic drama. A few proto-maskilic plays had previously been published in Hebrew, primarily in Renaissance and early modern Italy, like the allegorical plays of Moshe Chayim Luzzatto and the Biblical dramas of David Franco Mendes and Yosef Haefrati. These works were few and far between, however, and were designed more as literary pieces than drama.[81]

However, in the years leading up to the Enlightenment, significant changes took place in traditional Jewish drama. For example, one of the classic Purim plays of the early modern period, the *Akhashveyroysh-shpil*, had been updated and revised (most notably in a 1780 Amsterdam edition) in a manner highly influential on developing maskilic dramatic norms.[82] New versions of the *Akhashveyroysh-shpil* reveal striking similarities to Wolfssohn's new play. First, and most notably, there are linguistic shifts between the serious characters, who speak Standard High German, and the stock comic characters, most notably Mordechai, who speak Yiddish.[83] Also, the play, which traditionally

80. See Khone Shmeruk, ed., *Makhazot mikraiim beyidish, 1697–1750* (Jerusalem: Israel Academy of Sciences and Humanities, 1979), 20–44.

81. Nonetheless, the traditionalist manner in which they dealt with the portrayal of their Biblical subjects, including their long introductions indicating their unwillingness to diverge from the traditionalist point of view and their unwillingness at moments of dramatic crisis to present their heroes as differing from their traditional images, made them a paradigm for later maskilim struggling to relate to the earlier canonical body of Jewish literature. See Ben-Ami Feingold, "Makhazaei hahaskala vehamikra," *Teuda* 7 (1991), 429–449, and Miron "Volfson" 25–26.

82. On the variants of the *Akhashveyroysh-shpil*, see Yitzkhak Shiper, *Geshikhte fun yidisher teater-kunst un drame fun di eltste tsaytn biz 1750* (Warsaw: Kultur-Lige, 1923–28) 3:262–293.

83. See Shmeruk *Makhazot* 45–72, esp. 49–53, 71–72. For examples of some of the earlier versions, see Shmeruk *Makhazot* 155–532; for examples of Mordechai speaking prose Yiddish and using anachronisms, see 164–166, 180, 219, 221, 226.

functioned as the basis for slapstick and other comic improvisation in much the same manner as in the *commedia dell'arte*, is treated as a more serious drama and shortened to give it more professional possibilities. Though the *Akheshveyroysh-shpil* is not a maskilic play, it indicates the direction toward which writers like Wolfssohn and Euchel would turn,[84] the first steps toward a movement in Jewish dramatic literature in which current issues are discussed, not framed in the canonical-mythical past or an allegorical limbo, but in a contemporary realistic setting.

Wolfssohn had always been particularly interested in the Book of Esther; as mentioned earlier, he contributed the translation and commentary to Esther in the maskilic Bible translation project begun by Mendelssohn.[85] In his commentary, Wolfssohn discusses the authorship and dating of the book, attempting to connect it to both the history of the kings of Persia and to other parts of the Bible by linking the figure of Mordechai in the Book of Esther to the Mordechai mentioned in the Books of Ezra and Nehemiah and with the Petakhia mentioned in connection with the Temple.[86]

Wolfssohn's comments on this issue reflect his ambivalent position between traditionalism and reform: he does not deny these links, since he lacks convincing external evidence to the contrary, but he is surprised at them.[87] In his commentary, Wolfssohn also rehabilitates the character of Mordechai from his role as the obscenity-spouting, improvising, stock comic character of the early modern Purim play,

84. See Aviezer 165.

85. The translation was fairly popular by maskilic standards: it had 384 subscribers. In comparison, as mentioned above, *Hameasef* had 295 subscribers from 1785 to 1788. Feiner "'Mendelssohn's Disciples'" 140–141.

86. Wolfssohn *Megilat ester*, Introduction, esp. 1a, 3b, 4b, 6–9. See *Mishna Shekalim* 5:1, *BT Megila* 13b, and *BT Menakhot* 68b. Intriguingly, the narrator of Joseph Perl's *Megale Temirin*, the primary satirical text of the Galician Haskala, is named Ovadia ben Petakhia—perhaps Perl also wishes to link his character to the same debate over the rehabilitation of the Mordechai figure. Mordechai's name appears more obviously in *Megale Temirin* as well, of course; the main maskilic character's name is Mordechai Gold (see Miron "Volfson" 16). Finally, the name Mordechai also appears in the parodies of Rabbi Nachman's tales, where the maskilic figure is also named Mordechai.

87. Wolfssohn *Megilat ester* 4b; see also his commentary to Esther 2:5–6.

presenting him as a proto-maskil to be emulated by the Jewish polity: he defends the character of Mordechai against Talmudic criticism[88] and proudly mentions his knowledge of languages[89] and proximity to the absolutist authority[90]—two prime maskilic goals. Wolfssohn's modern rehabilitations, interestingly, are based solely on a traditionalist understanding of the text. Without midrashic interpretation, the plain text of Esther warrants neither of these portrayals of Mordechai. In other words, Wolfssohn is interested in the book in terms of its frame of interpretation and its contextualized position in Jewish life. To Wolfssohn, one of the book's most important functions was the basic story of the holiday of Purim; it could thus serve as a wedge for efforts to reform the mass of "retrogressive" Jewish customs that surrounded that holiday.

Wolfssohn's play *Laykhtzin un fremelay* marks the culmination of his interests in Esther and Purim: it is his effort to create a Purim play suitable for maskilic readers and performers. In his introduction to the play, he explains his opposition to the current traditional Purim-play: "On the days of Purim . . . youths arise and joke in front of us with filthiness and frivolity . . . which, upon hearing it, sickens the soul of any listening enlightener."[91] Wolfssohn's first edition of the play (the play was published in two editions during his lifetime—an amazingly popular response for such a work) includes a translation of the German comedy *Di Shtoltse Vashti* ("The Proud Vashti") by Friedrich Gotter. Wolfssohn intended these two plays to indicate the direction of future Jewish drama, replacing both Harlequins and Jewish life cycle

---

88. *BT Megila* 16b interprets Esther 10:3, which states that Mordechai was "accepted by most of his brothers," to mean that some of the Sanhedrin criticized Mordechai for giving up the study of Torah to serve the absolutist authority. Of course, Wolfssohn could hardly agree with this position, and reinterprets the passage (see his commentary *ad loc*) to place Mordechai in a highly favorable light. See also Wolfssohn's commentary to Esther 2:10 and 3:2.

89. *BT Megila* 13b; see Wolfssohn on Esther 2:22. See also Khone Shmeruk, "Hashem hamashmauti Mordekhai Markus—gilgulo hasifruti shel ideal khevrati," *Tarbiz* 29 (1959–1960), 76–98, 90.

90. On Mordechai's success as an aide to the non-Jewish authorities, see Wolfssohn on Esther 10:2 and 10:3.

91. See Miron "Volfson" 12–16, citation from 13.

activities carried out in Yiddish.[92] His later 1802 play, *Dovid der baziger fun golyes,* written in German in Hebrew characters, was intended to fulfill the same purpose.[93] Besides the desire to remove retrogressive elements from the traditional Purim play, Wolfssohn's presentation of these new plays as Purim plays allowed them to be less confrontational and more easily palatable to traditional audiences, many of whom were "still influenced to a large extent by the traditional view advocated by the rabbis for many years, namely that theater is a sinful pastime." As such, "Wolfssohn found it easier to publish his play as a Purim play, the only time of the year when theater was not only permitted but even . . . a religious duty."[94]

Wolfssohn's play, published around Purim of 1796,[95] is often confused with a very similar play of Isaac Euchel's, *Reb Henokh oder vos tut men damit* ("Reb Henokh, or, What are you going to do about it").[96] The confusion is hardly surprising. Both plays were published within three years of each other in the same maskilic circle. Both feature characters with the same names, particularly the befuddled paterfamilias Reb Henokh and the maskilic hero-figure Markus. Both take place in the same setting, an urban town in the north of Prussia—almost certainly Berlin in both cases—during the last decade of the eighteenth century. Both plays "showed Jews in the round of their daily lives, in

---

92. Shmeruk *Prakim* 163–164. In a standard strategy of Jewish cultural and dramatic adaptation, Wolfssohn adapts Gotter's play by removing certain overtly anti-Jewish elements. See Shmeruk *Prakim* 149–151.

93. Shmeruk "Hashem" 78–79. Unlike *Laykhtzin un fremelay*, this play, set in Biblical times, has no stock characters speaking in improper diction. Everyone speaks German—the current maskilic analogue to elevated Biblical language. See also Strauss 170–178.

94. Strauss 149. For a selection of classical Jewish sources on the theatrical tradition, see Sh. Ernst, "Tekstn un kveln tsu der geshikhte fun teyatr, farveylungn un maskeradn bay yidn," in Shatsky *Arkhiv* 5–37.

95. See Strauss 136 on the editions of *Laykhtzin un fremelay*. See also Michael "Hahaskala" 293–294.

96. On Euchel's play, see the discussions in Meyer *Origins* 118–119; Aviezer 166–170; and Gilman 110–114. See Shmeruk *Prakim* 157n17 for a detailed discussion of versions of *Reb Henokh*. On the meaning and the antecedents of the phrase *vos tut men damit,* see Dov Sadan, *A vort bashteyt* (Tel Aviv: Y.L. Peretz Farlag, 1975), 194–201.

the framework of the family of the rising middle class, within the stratum that provided the Haskala with its socioeconomic basis."[97]

The plot of *Laykhtzin un fremelay*, in many ways a Judaization of Moliere's "Tartuffe,"[98] is essentially quite simple, and falls into the contemporarily popular pattern of the *Sächsiche Typenkomödie*. Importantly for our analysis, this genre of comedy featured the importance of dramatic language as a vehicle for the moral of the play, and a favorite topos of this kind of comedy is the "ridiculousness and absurdity of all technical terminology."[99] Wolfssohn's use of dramatic language as moral vehicle has already been dealt with at length; his adoption and development of "technical terminology" will become clear in our analysis of his usage of classical Jewish texts.

A quick plot summary may be in order. Briefly, Reb Henokh, deeply influenced by the Polish rabbi and Hasid Reb Yoysefkhe and his constant perversions and misinterpretations of Jewish tradition, has decided to marry off his daughter Yetkhen—and thus give his new-made fortune—to Reb Yoysefkhe, despite the warnings given him by his solid and sensible wife, Teltse, and her enlightened brother Markus. When Reb Yosefkhe reveals her father's intent to Yetkhen, she becomes so enraged and terrified that she runs away from home with an ardent admirer, a non-Jew named von Schnapps (who is never seen).[100] Von Schnapps betrays her trust, however, and places her in a

97. *GJH* 1:319.

98. See Bernard Weinryb, "Aaron Wolfssohn's Dramatic Writings in Their Historical Setting," *JQR* 48 (1957–1958), 35–50, 47. Weinryb notes that "Tartuffe" was translated into German many times (1721, 1748, 1752, 1768, 1784) and was performed by a troupe of French actors before Frederick the Great in Berlin. The first critic to notice the resemblance seems to have been the contemporary German reviewer mentioned in note 71, who refers to the play as "ein jüdischer Tartuffe." See Shatsky 147.

99. For more on this genre, see Strauss 162–167, particularly 165, where the play is compared to a Johann Elias Schlegel comedy in which Latinisms serve the same function as Wolfssohn's Hebraisms. On contemporary German theater, see W.H. Bruford, *Theatre, Drama, and Audience in Goethe's Germany* (London: Routledge and Kegan Paul, Ltd., 1950), 163–202, particularly the discussion of the "prose domestic drama" on 193.

100. Note that the German word *schnappen* means "to snatch or kidnap." I am grateful to Dr. Dov-Ber Kerler for this suggestion.

brothel. She is saved from a fate worse than death by the timely inter-vention of Markus, whose actions cause Reb Henokh to reevaluate his position and arrange a marriage between his daughter and Markus. His reevaluation is aided by the fact that Reb Yoysefkhe, the suppos-edly pure and holy Reb Yoysefkhe, is revealed as a regular visitor to the brothel, having even offered to pawn his phylacteries to help pay the large bill he has run up.[101]

The play, in many ways, does indeed function as a modern Purim play, an updated version of the Book of Esther. Like the Book of Es-ther, *Laykhtzin un fremelay* features a hypocrite who has wormed his way into the good graces of the ruling authority finally unmasked due to the efforts of the main hero and heroine.[102] Like the Book of Es-ther, *Laykhtzin un fremelay* mixes comic elements with dramatic mo-ments. Like the Book of Esther, *Laykhtzin un fremelay* deals with the future of the Jewish people in a society seemingly capable of seesaw-ing dramatically between total tolerance and absolute hostility. Finally, in both cases a seemingly simple positive ending leads, upon further reflection, to deeper ambivalence about the future.

Laykhtzin un fremelay: A Theoretical and Textual Introduction

In our previous analyses of authors' textual usage, citations were di-rectly used in a polemic context: quotations or terminology were mar-shaled by the author (or, in rare cases, a persona serving as a direct manifestation of the author, as in certain sections of Mendelssohn's *Kohelet Musar*), and aimed directly at the audience. With *Laykhtzin un fremelay,* a crucial step is taken in the development of this strategy, and

101. On the patronage of prostitutes by Jews in the period, see Shohat 166 and Hertz 76: "Dance halls were often attached to bordellos. Male visitors could re-tire to a back room, order a bowl of punch and some wine, and a wink would suffice to bring them a woman of their choice. . . . " A similar scene occurs in Wolfssohn's play.

102. Significantly, in both texts the unmasking occurs at a place ostensibly de-signed for entertainment and pleasure: a feast or wine party in the Bible, and a bordello (where punch is regularly served) in *Laykhtzin un fremelay*.

concomitantly with the development of Jewish literature as a whole. In this *familien gemelde*, fashioned after similar pieces on the German stage, full-fledged characters with separate personalities appear, and the author's polemical result emerges from the dramatic or comedic result of the characters' interaction, rather than from a single polemical speech (though at times, certain ponderous monologues delivered by Markus, the main enlightened character, might suggest the contrary).

As mentioned above, there was little Yiddish theater to speak of outside the tradition of itinerant and ephemeral Purim plays. While *Laykhtzin un fremelay* might, in certain circumstances, have been performed, we can certainly suppose it was just as easily intended to be read. This is particularly true given the contemporary intelligentsia's cultural institutions, like the salon culture with its emphasis on reading aloud. As an ideologue, then, Wolfssohn had to depend as greatly on his language as on his staging.[103] The characters' usage of classical texts is only one of many possible ways to analyze Wolfssohn's use of language in the play; it is, however, a technique that strongly illuminates Wolfssohn's polemical and ideological goals, as we shall see.

Wolfssohn, a follower of Mendelssohn, was deeply imbued with his spirit. As discussed in the previous chapter, Mendelssohn mounted a vigorous defense of the classical Jewish canon in the face of its polemical misreading or misinterpretation by non-Jews for theological or anti-Semitic purposes. Efforts were made to subordinate the—for lack of a better phrase—eccentricities of traditional Jewish hermeneutics to a universalist rationalist framework. Recontextualizing and rehabilitating Talmudic passages and figures, Mendelssohn presented normative Judaism as adhering to an externally determined social ideal.

Wolfssohn, on the other hand, uses the same strategy of citing texts in a different manner. Though he too is concerned with external perceptions of Judaism, a greater comfort with non-Jewish society resulting from changed conditions allows him to switch focus from non-Jewish misreadings and misinterpretations to an internal critique

103. This should not, however, be taken as slighting Wolfssohn's abilities as a dramatist; in fact, his play is eminently stageable, and contains some powerfully dramatic scenes, like the encounter between Reb Yoysefkhe and Yetkhen in her room.

of Jewish (and specifically Eastern European Jewish) perceived misinterpretations and perversions of canonical texts. Wolfssohn has Jewish characters misuse texts in clearly perverse and unethical ways, locating the necessity for textual reform (and thus ethical reform) in a subset of the Jewish polity rather than throwing the blame on external factors. Eastern European Jews in general and Hasidim in particular are implicated in Wolfssohn's Prussian eyes. Within a year of the publication of *Laykhtzin un fremelay*, Wolfssohn's 1797 *Sikha beeretz hakhayim*, discussed briefly earlier, contains a much fuller critique of the *Ostjuden's* misinterpretation and perversion of classical rabbinic and rational Judaism (for in the maskilic eye, the two were identical).

Why does Wolfssohn feel free to express these misquotations so freely, in contrast to Mendelssohn's circumspection? Importantly, Mendelssohn did not deny the accretion of false and dangerous interpretive traditions within Jewish history. Had there been no such traditions, there would be no need of rehabilitation. In his writing, however, Mendelssohn felt no need to give non-Jews further polemical ammunition by providing examples of Jewish misinterpretation, and every need to provide examples of what a correct Jewish citative and interpretive framework would look like. The more radical Wolfssohn feels less need for such circumspection.

Wolfssohn has created characters whose command and usage of language—particularly the presence or absence of Hebraisms and references to classical Jewish texts—raises a whole series of satirical and critical comments about the successes, failures, and possibilities of the Enlightenment at a critical period. Since, as we have said, the strength of Wolfssohn's argument is based on the interaction of the characters, and the characters' usage of texts is our most important consideration, the discussion focuses on the characters individually.

The Characters

The literary historian Khone Shmeruk identifies three typologies in the Haskala plays of Wolfssohn and Euchel: (1) the maskilic hero; (2) the old traditionalists, who are also the hypocrites; and (3) the new generation, who are young, foolish, and too in love with current styles and modes of life to realize the dangers of adopting them too whole-heartedly.[104] A similar typology can also be used to divide the characters, not only by generation, but also by theme. In light of Wolfssohn's satirical and polemical goals, the characters can be divided into: (1) representatives of a worrisome future; (2) models of a perverted and corrupted past; and (3) a snapshot of the present crisis. These divisions can be seen clearly by viewing the characters through their usage of classical Jewish texts.

The Ambivalent Future of Absence: Markus and Yetkhen

This play, along with Euchel's *Reb Henokh oder vos tut men damit*, marks the beginning of a standard topos in maskilic literature and particularly maskilic drama: the use of the name Markus or Mordechai for the maskilic hero. The character of Markus in Euchel's play may be modeled after the Berlin maskil Markus Herz, who served as a maskilic ideal for both his contemporaries and for later generations.[105] While this may be so, the usage of the name Markus can be seen primarily as Wolfssohn's rehabilitation of the Mordechai character who figured so prominently in the traditional Purim plays.[106] We have already seen Wolfssohn's interest in rehabilitating the Purim play in

104. Shmeruk *Prakim* 164; see also Miron "Volfson" 17–18. Wolfssohn's contemporary Sabattia Wolff similarly divided the Jews of his period into four classes, the learned and pious traditionalists, the unlearned traditionalists, the enlightened, and the unlearned imitators of the enlightened. See *GJH* 2:103–104.

105. See Shmeruk "Hashem" 77 and Gilman 118–119. In his article, Shmeruk notes the appearance of Markus-Mordechai in a number of plays, including, among others, *Laykhtzin un fremelay*, *Reb Henokh*, Abraham Goldfaden's *Di kishefmakherin*, and Shloyme Ettinger's *Serkele*. Shmeruk suggests, however, that the success of the name Markus-Mordechai in Eastern Europe has more to do with the rehabilitation of the traditional Purim plays than with homage to a particular figure, since Markus Herz would have been virtually unknown there.

106. See Shmeruk *Prakim* 166; *Makhazot* 45–53; and Miron "Volfson" 14–15. Wolfssohn's exchange of letters with David Theodor in 1790 (printed in *Hameasef* 6:249–253, 279–284), indicates that he was indeed interested in the changing and the Germanizing of Jewish names as well as what he perceived to be a lowering of the language of German as spoken by Jews. See Shmeruk "Hashem" 86.

general and the character of Mordechai in particular, treating him as a maskil, a man of the Persian world. The character of Markus in the play is portrayed in much the same way. The Biblical Mordechai was said to have been steeped in worldly knowledge and knew seventy languages. Filtered through the Haskala, Markus is an intimate of non-Jews, has studied to become a doctor, and knows the one important language—German—very well indeed. In fact, he knows it to the absence of all else.[107]

From Markus's first entrance, when he interrupts an argument between Reb Henokh and his wife, Teltse, the reader realizes that Markus speaks differently from all the characters who have previously appeared. For example, though there are numerous expressions of shock, dissatisfaction, and surprise that normally call upon the Hebraic component of the Yiddish lexicon, expressions frequently used by the other characters, Markus uses none of them, preferring to use Germanic expressions like *Got bevahre* and *um himls viln*.[108] This first appearance is a portent for the future: throughout the entire play, Markus does not use a single word belonging to the Hebraic or Semitic component of Yiddish, much less cite or refer to a classical text from the Jewish canon.

It is generally difficult to argue from absence, but the maskilic insistence on purity of language makes this particular absence very significant, particularly in light of the Hebraisms and texts studding the other characters' conversations. Markus represents the maskilic dream of the fully integrated German Jew—so much so that in many ways he appears foreign to the family drama, an external observer. He seems to have no link whatsoever to the traditional past, focusing entirely on the future. Significantly, when Reb Henokh and Teltse want to bemoan their fate after Yetkhen has run away, Markus tells them: "There's no way to change what happens in the past, and what happens in the future is up to each of us."[109]

107. On the historical development of secular-language education among eighteenth-century German Jews, see Shohat 58–63.

108. Reyzen 40–41. All page references are taken from the edition published in Reyzen 37–68, which (excepting a few minor typographical errors) is identical to the Breslau 1796 edition.

109. Reyzen 58.

Wolfssohn's ambivalence about the future of the Haskala is amply displayed here. As a character, Markus does not come off well. Aside from his lack of empathy and his alienation from all the other characters, he feels stiff and one-dimensional when compared to more subtly drawn characters like Reb Henokh or even Reb Yoysefkhe.[110] Wolfssohn is developing an argument about the future of the Haskala throughout the play, looking for the proper balance between assimilation and particularism. This balanced solution may be seen in light of an appropriate and balanced usage of classical Jewish texts. While Markus's insistence on rational and moral behavior and his burning desire to root out hypocrisy are valued by Reb Henokh and within the play, it is not at all clear that, in the end, Markus represents the optimal solution, with his almost antiseptic absence of any and all Jewish identifying characteristics, such as texts. He may well, in pursuing the right path, have gone too far along it.

Yetkhen is quite similar: her speech is also free of Hebraisms in general and traditional and classical references in particular. Rather, she constantly makes reference to the accoutrements of eighteenth-century bourgeois German culture: the books from the lending library she reads, the operas she listens to, the theater she attends, the klavier she plays.[111] But she, too, hardly appears in the most positive light: she is petulant, demanding, and uses fake refinement to cover snobbery and ill-temper. Yetkhen, of course, more clearly represents Shmeruk's category of the "foolish new generation" discussed above, as opposed to Markus; though linguistic similarities between Yetkhen and Markus exist, they differ substantially in terms of wisdom and moral sensibility. Nonetheless, it seems that the future of German Jewry that Wolfssohn suggests cannot lie only with these acculturated figures who are, at play's end, united by the playwright.

110. See Miron's comments on Markus's language in the Hebrew play in "Volfson" 43–44.

111. On the cultivation of musical instruments and art by the parvenu elites, see Shohat 36–42; the rise of libraries and reading in German of contemporary Jews, see *GJH* 2:201; and the theater, see *GJH* 2:203. See also Miron "Volfson" 19–21, 40–41.

The Past Perverse: Reb Yoysefkhe

The character of Reb Yoysefkhe, the corrupting element at the heart of Reb Henokh's family, is based on the common occurrence of an *Ostjude* acting as tutor to a Jewish bourgeois family.[112] There are many things not to like about Wolfssohn's character of Reb Yoysefkhe. For one thing, contemporary readers cannot help but feel uncomfortable at the internal adoption of contemporary anti-Semitic terminology, of Wolfssohn's usage of the sexualized and animalized imagery used to describe the *Mauscheln*, the stock Jewish theater characters, to refer to Reb Yoysefkhe. (In fact, the non-Jewish owner of the bordello explicitly refers to him as a "Mauschel.")[113] From the first serpentlike description of his onstage entrance ("he creeps and crawls"),[114] to his sudden outbursts of rage and violence when he is refused by Yetkhen, to the goatlike description of his sexual desire ("the Moyshe-goat is twenty times wilder for the ladies"),[115] we are introduced to the bestial nature of this *poylisher*, this raging id of the East. He represents the atavistic specter of what these salon Jews had left behind, the nightmare doppelgänger of the refined, correct Jew. This Jewish self-hatred is a disturbing feature of the Haskala that unfortunately cannot be dealt with at length here.[116]

Reb Yoysefkhe is not merely an example of perverted moral and social behavior, though, but of perverted textual behavior as well: he takes the rabbinic tradition and twists it to serve his morally depraved purposes. He does so in three distinct ways. First, he correctly cites

112. See Shohat 135.

113. Reyzen 64.

114. Reyzen 43.

115. Reyzen 64. It may also be possible to link this sexualization of Reb Yoysefkhe's character to the Hamanic archetype he represents: though Ahasuerus's assumption that Haman, fallen on Esther's couch in presumed supplication for his life, has in fact attempted to ravish the queen (Esther 7:8) says more about his own ignorance than Haman's lust, the connection between Haman and an unchecked erotic drive, possibly leading to his destruction, is established nonetheless.

116. See, however, Gilman, *Jewish Self-Hatred*, where the phenomenon is discussed at length.

statements in their original and appropriate context, but delivers them in an ironic manner, indicating he disagrees with the sentiment expressed therein. Second, he uses terminology and quotations believable enough in themselves but indicating a problematic tradition. And finally and most importantly, he actively misinterprets citations, reflecting his fidelity to no tradition or hermeneutic but his own cause.

Reb Yoysefkhe's first citations from classical texts take place at the very beginning of his first encounter with Reb Henokh. It is a textual tour de force; Reb Yoysefkhe uses these texts to sow so much confusion that he takes a clear-cut situation of his guilt (Reb Henokh discovers him *in flagrante delicto* with the maid) and turns it into a ringing endorsement of his own moral worth.

At first, Reb Yoysefkhe's citations are merely ironic: he begins with a citation from the *Hagada, borukh hamokoym borukh hu* ("Blessed is the Holy One, blessed is He").[117] Though Reb Yoysefkhe thanks the God who delivered Israel from slavery for delivering him from his current situation, he hardly believes his own sentiments: in fact, Reb Henokh's appearance is a far cry from deliverance. Reb Yoysefkhe immediately continues with a citation from Psalms, *ki hitsalta nafshi mimoves es ragli midekhi* ("For You have saved my soul from death . . . and my feet from stumbling"), generally familiar to the average Jewish reader from the full recitation of Hallel, the extra prayer of praise.[118] Of course, praising intervention is the last thing on Reb Yoysefkhe's mind right now. In these cases, the texts are used correctly, in the sense that they function similarly to the way they do within the classical tradition, but ironically, hardly reflecting the speaker's actual sentiment. At the same time, such textual usage allows Reb Yoysefkhe to perpetuate his pose as a holy and religious man.

Reb Yosefkhe then launches into a mosaic of phrases that locate his penitential approach in a medium he knows to be efficacious as far as Reb Henokh is concerned: the classical textual tradition. Thus he be-

117. Though the most common reference is to the Passover *Hagada*, the citation also appears in *Tana Debe Eliyahu*, Chapter 1. Reyzen 44. The phrase as a whole is absent from Yiddish dictionaries, though *borukh hu* can be found in Perferkovitsh 37; Shteynberg 52; and Spivak and Yehoyesh 42.

118. Psalms 116:8 (omitting the middle clause). Reyzen 44.

gins by quoting the Biblical cry for the frailty and humanity of the individual, *ma enoysh ki tizkereynu* ("What is man that You are mindful
of him"), whose penitential resonances are heightened by the fact that
the phrase also appears in the High Holiday service.[119] Reb Yoysefkhe,
in recounting the details of his "fall," then begins to cite not merely
liturgical and Biblical texts, but rabbinic sayings and concepts, and
does so in a way that begins to blur the line between simple irony and
more dangerous types of interpretation.

He begins with the rabbinic dictum *aveyre goyreres aveyre* ("Sin begets sin"),[120] which seems appropriate, and then cites the Talmudic
quotation *im pogo bekho menuvol zeh moshkheyhu leveys hamedresh* ("If
this disgusting person grabs you, drag him to the house of study"),[121]
a phrase not without its ironic component. He also uses the phrase
hirhurin deaveyre koshim meaveyre ("That which surrounds sin is harsher
than sin").[122] All of these rabbinic texts are cited ironically, in much the
same way that the Biblical and liturgical texts were used in the first
flush of discovery.

A deeper irony, one based not merely on the text itself but its context within the Jewish tradition, comes significantly later in the discussion, where, after Reb Henokh offers to marry Yetkhen to Reb
Yoysefkhe, the latter piously intones, *mehashem yoytse hadovor* ("The
matter has emerged from God").[123] On one level, the quotation is
simply ironic, since the marriage proposal has clearly emerged as a result not of Divine decree, but rather Reb Yoysefkhe's machinations.
On the other hand, a closer look at the text's provenance indicates the

119. Psalms 8:5. Reyzen 44.

120. *Mishna Avot* 4:2. Reyzen 44. Though this is a phrase in the Yiddish lexicon (see Perferkovitsh 214; Weinreich 1:224), its location in a stream of textual citations by Reb Yoysefkhe, a Talmud instructor whose position in the household
is based on his mastery of and familiarity with texts, calls attention to the phrase's
textual origins. This is true of many of Reb Yoysefkhe's citations, particularly since
Wolfssohn is clearly developing an argument concerning the hypocritical fashion
in which this Hasid hides his immoral behavior behind such texts.

121. *BT Suka* 52b. *BT Kidushin* 30b. Reyzen 44.

122. *BT Yoma* 29a. Reyzen 45. See also Perferkovitsh 64.

123. Genesis 24:50. Reyzen 46.

appropriateness of Reb Yoysefkhe's choice of phrase: the verse is spoken by Laban, known both within the Bible and within the broader sphere of Jewish interpretation as the paradigmatic trickster and hypocrite. Reb Yoysefkhe is well aware of his own machinations and his place in a long line of hypocrites.

Beyond irony, though, Reb Yoysefkhe also begins to adopt the kabbalistic and mystical terminology associated by Wolfssohn and other contemporaries with the *Ostjuden* in general and the Hasidim in particular and believed by them to be so inimical to the construction of a modern Jewish identity. First, Reb Yoysefkhe uses the mystical phrasing *yikhed hashem yishmereynu veyotsileynu* ("May the Unity of God preserve us and save us"),[124] a phrase placing him firmly within the kabbalistic camp. He later blames his behavior on the mystical impediments to unity and perfection, saying that *der sam mit ale zayne klipes hot an akhize gekrign* ("The evil impulse with all of its husks possessed me"),[125] as well as citing the evil impulse ("my evil impulse has triumphed over me") and speaking of ritual bathing. The resonances of Sabbateanism and the connection made and implied between antinomianism, eroticization, and kabbala are also very strong here: Reb Yoysefkhe's comments and behavior remind the reader of the notion popularized by Sabbatai Zevi that, to reach the highest levels of morality, one must first wade through the deepest levels of immorality.[126] These arguments connecting Hasidism with Sabbateanism and immorality are repeated and expanded by later maskilim like Joseph Perl, as we will see.

But where Reb Yoysefkhe moves from irony—or identification with a problematic tradition—to outright perversion and misinterpretation is with his insistence on sharing a private audience with Yetkhen before the marriage is announced, presumably for nefarious purposes. He justifies this, of course, through the citation of a Talmudic law: *oser leodom lekadeysh isho ad sheyirenoh* ("A man is prohibited from marrying a

124. Reyzen 46.

125. Reyzen 44. On Hebraisms in Yiddish stemming from kabbalistic sources, see Weinreich 1:229.

126. For a detailed discussion of this aspect of Sabbateanism, see Gershom Scholem, *Major Trends in Jewish Mysticism* (New York: Schocken, 1974), 315–324.

woman until he sees her").[127] When he is asked by Reb Henokh, quite reasonably, how he could not have seen her, given that they eat at the same table daily, he replies that his behavior is governed by the Biblical verse *ma esboynen al bsule* ("I made a covenant with mine eyes; *how then should I look upon a maid?*")[128] Reb Yoysefkhe presents himself as a second Job, unwilling to engage in worldly behavior when there is thought of serving God. Clearly, though, Job is hardly the actual paradigm for Reb Yoysefkhe's behavior.

This argument convinces Reb Henokh—until he realizes that Reb Yoysefkhe's behavior would transgress the general standard of *yikhud*, the prohibition against an unmarried man and a woman being alone together. When Reb Henokh raises this objection, Reb Yoysefkhe responds with, of course, the citation of what is presented as an overmastering text: *ikh vil aykh zogn, dos kon men zoy keyn yikhed nisht heysn, vorem? s'iz leshem mitsve, un shlukhey mitsve eynem nizokin* ("I'll tell you something—this can in no way be called *yikhud*. Why? Because this is for the sake of a commandment, and *shlukhei mitzve eynam nizokin*—no harm can come to someone fulfilling a commandment.")[129] While the statement is indeed based on a rabbinic dictum, the perversion of normative rabbinic texts and contexts has never been clearer: *shlukhei mitzva* (messengers to perform a commandment) is a *terminus technicus*, referring to a very specific set of situations—not one of which can conceivably be applied here.[130] At the time, seeing the bride before marriage and conducting marital arrangements without using a marriage broker was considered immoral. At best, this was seen as a sign of the new radicalism, and was certainly not legitimated by tradition.[131]

127. *BT Kidushin* 41a. Reyzen 46.

128. Job 31:1. Reyzen 47.

129. See *BT Pesakhim* 8a-b, *Kidushin* 39b, *Hulin* 142b. Reyzen 47. The latter phrase may be part of the Yiddish lexicon (see Perferkovitsh 280); but in this case it seems that Reb Yoysefkhe is "deciding *halakha*" (that is, determining whether as a legal matter he may be permitted to seclude himself with Yetkhen) based on his knowledge of Talmud. As such, the phrase is, at the very least, reminiscent of its textual origins, and possibly a direct reference to them.

130. For a discussion of the concept of *shlukhey mitzve eynam nizokin*, see sources cited in the footnote above.

131. See Shohat 164–165.

The most powerful symbol of Reb Yoysefkhe's perverse linguistic behavior, though, is his ability to change it altogether.[132] Every other character in the play has one mode of discourse that remains constant throughout the play: for example, we have seen that Markus and Yetkhen's language remains as free of Hebraisms at the end of the play as it is at the beginning. Reb Yoysefkhe, however, consciously controls his discourse: when he speaks to Reb Henokh, as we have seen, his speech is full of Hebraisms and consciously ironic allusions to classical texts. However, when speaking to Yetkhen, whom he knows prefers a more rarefied, less Hebraic language, or Sheyndl, the maid after whom he chases and who knows his true nature, his speech becomes almost free of Hebraisms; he slips into them only in cases of surprise or anger. This phenomenon becomes particularly interesting in the scene where Reb Yoysefkhe reveals his intentions to Yetkhen, since Wolfssohn makes use of the technique of the aside. As a result, Reb Yoysefkhe's statements to Yetkhen are Germanic (or, at least, non-Hebraic), but his asides are filled with Hebraisms and quotes such as *kol haskholes kashes* ("all beginnings are difficult"),[133] *moyre derekh* ("instructor"),[134] and *meshumedeste* ("female apostate").[135]

Reb Yoysefkhe is the antithesis of the emphasis on linguistic fidelity decreed by the Prussian maskilim. He obeys no rules but his own, the rules that will give him the greatest advantage, and so is singled out for opprobrium. On the other hand, the power and influence his linguistic flexibility allows him contains an important message for later generations of maskilim: the advantages of speaking to the people you hope to influence in their own language are great indeed. Opposed by the countervailing linguistic ideology that shunned Yiddish, and more importantly, the demographic fact that much of the audience could understand the "pure" language supported by the maskilim, there was little need to transform this issue into a practical matter in Wolfssohn's

132. Compare Miron "Volfson" 45–47.

133. The phrase is originally from *Mekhilte derabi Yishmael, Masekhta Debakhodesh,* 2 but has entered the standard Yiddish lexicon; see Perferkovitsh 66. Reyzen 51.

134. See Perferkovitsh 150; Shteynberg 150; Spivak and Yehoyesh 148. Reyzen 51.

135. See Perferkovitsh 185; Shteynberg 183; Spivak and Yehoyesh 175. Reyzen 51.

milieu. Later generations of maskilim, lacking such a demographic advantage, would throw this ideological principle into question.

In illustrating Reb Yoysefkhe's perversion of texts, though, Wolfssohn, through a negative paradigm, suggests the hope of a return to proper standards of textual interpretation, standards in accordance with "normative" Judaism as refracted through a maskilic lens. The possibilities and the conditions of this return can be seen in the last character to be discussed.

Reb Henokh: The Traditional Jew at the Crossroads

Reb Henokh, the paterfamilias, is the focal point around which the play revolves.[136] This is certainly true from a dramatic perspective; all of the play's action is conditioned by his decisions. It is he who decides to betroth Yetkhen to Reb Yoysefkhe; it is he who threatens Yetkhen when she refuses the betrothal, causing her to flee the house into the clutches of von Schnapps; it is he, presumably, who hired Reb Yoysefkhe and brought him into the house in the first place, though this takes place before the play actually begins.

More important, however, is Reb Henokh's role as an ideological fulcrum: he is the Everyman, the archetype of the Jew whose heart needs to be won over by the forces of the Enlightenment, but has so far resisted its arguments. He is the dramatization of the real obstacle to the success of the Haskala: the general public. During the play, we trace his movement from immersion in a corrupted and problematic situation to articulation of a position in line with Enlightenment ideology. For Wolfssohn, Reb Henokh's transformation echoes the desired conversion of the entire traditionalist Prussian Jewish community.

Echoing Mendelssohnian doctrine, Wolfssohn shows that Reb Henokh's transformation constitutes neither the abandonment of Judaism nor the abandonment of Jewish texts. Rather, Wolfssohn hopes for a general understanding of the possibilities of perverse misinterpretation of Jewish texts or the misapplication of a dangerous and flawed hermeneutic to them, followed by a decisive rejection of

136. See Miron "Volfson" 30–38.

those types of interpretation. With that recognition and rejection, Reb Henokh and the Jewish community he represents can instead adopt a more universalistic, rationalist interpretation of texts and Judaism as a whole. In short, Reb Henokh exemplifies maskilic educational theory, the almost Platonic notion that the adult man is no longer a *tabula rasa*, but has been inculcated with a series of incorrect opinions and beliefs. The task of the Enlightenment is to show these individuals the error of their ways and to replace them with "real truths" as defined by the Enlightenment.

This process is illustrated throughout the play by Reb Henokh's citation of texts from the canon.[137] From the very beginning of the play, Wolfssohn clearly takes pains to present Reb Henokh as an Everyman, textually speaking. Reb Henokh is a traditionalist: the opening of the very first scene has him bent over the Talmud. However, Wolfssohn provides a universal, abstract feel to the scene by using Talmudic language without markers to locate what Reb Henokh is learning: "*Nu vayter—fregt der makshen bemay ka mifligi—vurdn krign zi zikh? Rabi Eliezer soyver* . . . (Nu, further—so then he asks *bemay ka mifligi*, what are they arguing about? So Rebbe Eliezer maintains . . .)"[138] On one level, Reb Henokh seems to be somewhat conversant with Jewish

137. Compare Miron's comments on the (quite different) effect of Reb Henokh's textual usage in the Hebrew version of the play in "Volfson" 37–38.

138. Reyzen 38. The Aramaic phrase *bemay ka mifligi*, whose meaning might have been unfamiliar to the general public, is translated into Yiddish. On the other hand, *Rabi Eliezer soyver*, and much of the general Talmudic language which simply indicates the traditionalist mindset, such as the phrase *pshite* ("it is obvious") and a reference to the Talmudic commentator the Maharsha, as well as the later usage of the phrases *mistome* ("probably") and *bishlome* ("if you want"; see Reyzen 56) is not. See Weinreich 1:229–230 for a discussion of Talmudic phrases that have entered the Yiddish vocabulary; notably, *bemay ka mifligi* is absent. A possible reason for translating the phrase is the potentially universalist message subversively hidden here: the phrase, translated as "What are they arguing about," could be referring on some level to Wolfssohn's view of the irrelevance and meaninglessness of the arguments between traditionalists and maskilim, since, in his Mendelssohnian view, the two had a great deal in common. On *mistome,* see Golomb 243; Perferkovitsh 172; Shteynberg 170; and Spivak and Yehoyesh 164. On *bishlome*, see Perferkovitsh 38 and Spivak and Yehoyesh 44.

texts on his own: when he has problems understanding the phrase, he is able to go beyond Rashi and Tosfot to look at the more difficult traditional commentator the Maharsha.[139] On the other hand, Reb Henokh is willing to violently reject these texts as well: in the very next line, when he cannot understand the text, he suggests that the Talmud is incorrect. Reb Henokh's vagueness in his study of Talmud and his vacillation between depths of textual understanding and textual rejection show him as a man adrift, a traditionalist in search of a firm tradition.[140]

Nonetheless, as the play continues, we see that Reb Henokh has indeed fallen sway to the influence of a foreign hermeneutic: the mystical,

139. On the Maharsha, see "Edels, Samuel Eliezer ben Judah Halevi," in *EJ* 6:363–364. Though the Maharsha was certainly a traditionalist commentator whose novellae would have appeared in every edition of the printed Talmud, his rational approach to explaining aggadic material and his hatred of certain forms of meaningless *pilpul* would have made him appealing to Wolfssohn. This could be a subtle hint at the existence of useful aids to proper study within the canonical tradition, and it is only the intervention of people like Reb Yoysefkhe who prevent proper understanding of Jewish texts.

140. This is not to say that every citation of Reb Henokh's is used to make some grand thematic point. At times citations are used simply to locate Reb Henokh in his particular milieu. For example, the fact that Reb Henokh uses the phrase "*b'khayey royshi mosek midvash*" ("By my life, as sweet as honey," Reyzen 38) to express his joy at understanding the Maharsha's comment does not mean he is referring to the passage in Judges 14:18. The saying is a common one among a certain type of Jew of the period (see Perferkovitsh 189 and Spivak and Yehoyesh 179); the fact that Reb Henokh uses it anthropologically locates him in that subgroup. (An analogous source, *hametukim kidvash venofet tsufim* ("as sweet as honey or the honeycomb"), which more closely hews to the emotional sensibility of the expression, can be found in Psalms 19:11 and is used to similar effect in Perl's *Megale Temirin*; see Chapter Seven.) This anthropological approach is also seen in Reb Henokh's reference to the traditionalist worldview, even when he does not actually quote a canonical text. For example, asking Reb Yoysefkhe why he has not yet married, he says, *ir zayt dokh bevaday iber ben yud khes shonim.* ("You're certainly at least eighteen," Reyzen 45.) Reb Henokh is clearly referring to the saying in the *Ethics of the Fathers* that *ben shmone esreh lekhupa* ("Eighteen years old is time for marriage," *Ethics of the Fathers* 5:24), indicating that Reb Henokh's world is still shaped by the rhythms and flows of traditional society. Ironically, a similar technique was used by the anti-Semites to put stock phrases in the mouths of the *Mauscheln*.

kabbalistic, and implicitly Hasidic approach of Reb Yoysefkhe. Reb Henokh swears by the *oysyes hakdoyshim* ("holy letters"),[141] and refers to his son's absence from his learning as *a mayse shin tes* ("an act of the Evil One").[142] These phrases, which appear in the first scene, already suggest that Reb Henokh has been influenced into holding onto a more mystical or superstitious view of the world than the rationalistic Haskala might desire.

Reb Yoysefkhe's influence over Reb Henokh can be seen even more clearly in the final phrases Reb Henokh quotes at the end of the first scene. The first, *kol beisho ervo* ("The voice of a woman is like her nakedness"),[143] is a well-known and controversial Talmudic phrase, even entering the Yiddish lexicon, though Reb Henokh himself calls attention to his usage of the phrase as a citation, following it with the comment *zogn undzer khakhomim* ("say our Sages").[144] In the salon culture of late eighteenth-century Berlin, ruled by strong, vivacious, and gregarious women, the notion that a woman should be neither seen nor heard would not have had made great inroads in enlightened circles. Reb Henokh's traditionalist conception of this issue seems to be at least partially due to the eroticization of "normalized" (by Enlightenment standards) male-female relations in Reb Yoysefkhe's eyes.[145] If there is any

141. Reyzen 38. This phrase appears in early Hasidic teachings, some of which were later collected into works like the *Sefer Degel Makhaneh Efrayim* (the phrase appears in *Parshat Tetzaveh*) and the *Sefer Kedushat Levi* (the phrase appears in *Parshat Vayetzei, Parshat Pekudei*). Whether or not Wolfssohn intended us to believe that Reb Henokh himself was familiar with similar teachings or collections is unclear, but unlikely. However, it is eminently possible that Reb Yoysefkhe would have known of such teachings, since he is characterized as a Hasid.

142. Reyzen 38.

143. *BT Kidushin* 70a; Reyzen 40.

144. See Perferkovitsh 251.

145. Interestingly enough, the sexualized phrase used early in the play by Reb Yoysefkhe to refer to himself—*tipe srukhe* or "stinking drop (of semen)"—which characterized him as a man prone to moral depravity, is repeated by Reb Henokh in charging his own daughter with obstinacy in refusing to submit to his will and marry the man of his choice. See Reyzen 44, 53. The Freudian implications here, though fairly clear, will not be elaborated upon: suffice it to say that the undercurrent of erotic tension and sublimation spreads through the play in many dimensions.

doubt that Reb Yoysefkhe has been whispering in Henokh's ear, the last quotation, *leoylem yisa odem es bisoy letalmid khokhem* ("A man should always marry his daughter to a scholar"), provides ample indication.[146] The ambiguous phrase *talmid khokhem* has moral and ethical connotations in addition to intellectual ones; the fact that Reb Yoysefkhe has convinced Reb Henokh he fits this textual category testifies to the former's influence in shaping the terms of discussion.

In fact, many of Reb Henokh's quotations and citations seem to have been provided to him directly by Reb Yoysefkhe for purposes of self-defense or justification: for example, when Reb Henokh catches Reb Yoysefkhe with his maid, the latter's explanation, discussed earlier, where he blames his actions on the evil impulse, is justified by Reb Henokh through the citation of a text: *kol hagodoyl mekhaveyroy yitsro godoyl* ("Anyone who is greater than his fellow man, his evil impulse is also greater").[147] One would hardly be surprised to learn that this Talmudic lesson also came from Reb Yoysefkhe. Wolfssohn stresses the danger of improper interpretation of these texts: when mistaught, the classical Jewish canon becomes the excuse for immoral and improper behavior. Even if the average person would not engage in that behavior himself, the texts, as taught, require him to condone it.

Wolfssohn implies that a reference point must be developed *external to the system of interpretation itself* from which to judge the value of these texts and their interpretations. Reb Henokh is not wrong, for example, for suggesting that Reb Yoysefkhe not be alone with his daughter; his failure lies in his inability to recognize from an external set of principles that Reb Yoysefkhe's interpretation of these texts *cannot* be correct. This is an individualistic approach, in the sense that it allows a limited break with tradition in the form of rejecting particularly objectionable interpretation, and yet there is communal continuity on the plane of a higher, moral consensus that can be construed as universal.

In other words, the search for a suitable hermeneutic for Reb Henokh is, at its very core, the Mendelssohnian search for a universalist interpretation of the classical Jewish canon—hardly surprising,

146. *BT Pesakhim* 49a–49b. Reyzen 40.
147. *BT Suka* 52a. Reyzen 45.

considering the close affinities between Wolfssohn and Mendelssohn. Reb Henokh even expresses a Judaized version of Mendelssohn's Leibnitzian philosophy: at the beginning of Act Three, after Yetkhen has disappeared, Reb Henokh remarks that *kol ma deoveyd rakhmono letav oveyd* ("Everything that the Merciful One has done, He has done for the best")[148] and *gam zu letoyve* ("This too is for the best")[149]—that this must be the result of Divine plan. Though challenged by his wife, who plays Voltaire to Henokh's Leibnitz, the play's ending shows that Henokh is actually correct—were it not for Yetkhen's flight and subsequent kidnapping by von Schnapps, Reb Yoysefkhe would never have been unmasked, Markus would never have been truly appreciated, and Henokh would never have learned his lesson.[150]

Reb Henokh's final statement in the play is crucial, indicating his growth and development in textual terms. For the first time, Reb Henokh is able to take a text from the classical canon and shape it, interpreting it to fit contemporary historical circumstances while at the same time cherishing it as rabbinic wisdom: exactly the position of the Mendelssohnian-influenced maskilim. He says to Markus: *rov bonim holkhim akher akhey hoeym, zogn undzere khakhomim, nu azoy meg zi in emes hoylekh akher akhey hoeym zayn . . . (lekhelend) farshteyt ir mikh?* ("Most children follow their mother's brothers, say our sages. Well, I hope she'll truly follow her mother's brother as well . . . *(laughing)* do you get me?") In this case, Henokh has taken a passage from tradi-

148. *BT Berakhot* 60a. Reyzen 56.

149. *BT Taanit* 21a. Reyzen 56. This was also a standard Yiddish phrase; see Perferkovitsh 46; Shteynberg 64; and Spivak and Yehoyesh 53.

150. In fact, the entire play can be seen as an extended metaphor of the historical development of the Jewish people: the daughter of the people is forced into exile and, in almost kabbalistic fashion, is forced to spend time in the most degraded and impure areas (in this case, the Gentile whorehouse), before redemption and reunion with the father. In this reading, it is not Henokh who symbolizes the Jewish people, but Yetkhen, and the play becomes a polemic not about the necessity for the acculturation of the older traditionalist generation, but a cautionary tale concerning the overacculturation of the younger generation. (A similar reading can be suggested where Yetkhen, instead of representing the Jewish people, represents the *shekhina*, the Divine presence, itself.)

tional sources[151] and interpreted it himself to support the Haskala, allowing Markus to marry his daughter Yetkhen. And it is this decision and change in Reb Henokh's character that seems to be the real victory in the play.

This transformation is also reflected in the transformation of Reb Henokh from a man of unreasonable emotion to one who has learned the importance of reason and the necessity of its application even in the most trying situations. At the beginning of the play, Henokh throws a fit over the fact that his son (whom we never see) has taken a few hours off from his studies in order to attend a friend's party. By the end of the play, he has been able to reach a state of something resembling equanimity mere moments after he discovers that the man he wished to betroth to his daughter is a regular visitor to the local bordello.

In fact, the question of fathers, sons, and daughters raised here may suggest one final point: the question of the tutoring of Reb Henokh's son, the other generational link to the future. The question of the son's education is the burning question of the play's opening, but then disappears from the stage completely.[152] The son himself never appears onstage at all—like all the best symbols of future promise and potential, he is imagined, never realized. The absence of the explicit treatment of the question, though, does not mean it is not answered. Though it is possible to suggest that Wolfssohn simply forgot about this theme in the excitement of the marriage plot—it would not be the first time that a dramatist left threads dangling—a better answer seems to be available. As the play opens, the son is about to fall into Reb

151. Calqued on BT *Bava Batra* 110a. A late nineteenth-century commentator, Rabbi Tsadok of Lublin, links this statement to what Jacob believed about Laban, who was his mother's brother (see *Sefer Kometz Hamincha* 1:114). Wolfssohn could not have known this later commentary, obviously; however, he may have arrived at the same connotation on his own—which would have made the thematic connection between this story and the story of one of the great Biblical hypocrites, Laban, even stronger (though in this case, of course, the connection is inverted). We have seen a quotation from Laban earlier in the play, referring to Yetkhen's proposed marriage to Reb Yoysefkhe, and now a reference to Laban is used to indicate Yetkhen's proposed marriage to Markus. The parallelism is somewhat pleasing.

152. See Miron "Volfson" 23–24, 50–51.

Yoysefkhe's clutches, where presumably he would have learned the (mis)interpretations and overly mystical approach of the *Ostjude* rabbi. Clearly, the progress of the play indicates that this is no longer an option. But it is not so clear that the boy will be taught by Markus either. After all, Reb Henokh wanted a traditionalist education for his son, and, it seems, might well still want one, were that education to be properly provided. Markus does not seem to be the one to provide it to him, for all his enlightened principles. Another aspect of Henokh's citative behavior intrigues: though the passage he cites at the play's end clearly suggests, with its reference to "most sons," a parallel with Henokh's own son, Henokh's interpretation of that passage clearly and consciously breaks that parallelism to transform Markus's charge from male to female. Markus may end up with Reb Henokh's daughter, but Reb Henokh's son may be another matter altogether. Perhaps the newly educated Reb Henokh, who has learned to put things in perspective, will teach him himself.

Conclusion

The 1790s marked a time of greater radicalism in the maskilic community; their hopes buoyed by the French Revolution and greater non-Jewish social acceptance, writers were willing to take a more radical set of steps to ask for emancipation. One of their main strategies—to further separate themselves from the unemancipated and unemancipatable *Ostjuden* by attacking their Judaism and their corruption of Jewish texts—can be clearly seen in Wolfssohn's work, particularly his play. This development marks the real beginning of the Haskala as a satirical, critical movement, a characterization that certainly applies throughout the rest of its history.

At the same time, these maskilim had not completely moved away from traditionalism; the shadow of Mendelssohn was still strong. Circumstances in the 1790s gave rise to ambivalence about full participation in non-Jewish society, and an examination of Wolfssohn's work, particularly his usage of classical texts, reveals strong Mendelssohnian links and real questions about the future of the Jewish Enlightenment.

Part Three   Galicia

Six   Joseph Perl: Between Hebrew and Yiddish

Introduction

The preceding chapters have focused on the Haskala's beginnings in Prussia, examining its traditionalist roots with a study of Moses Mendelssohn, and its increasing radicalization after the French Revolution through an analysis of Aaron Halle Wolfssohn's work. As I have argued, though the two writers' works react to different issues and provide different perspectives, they generally operated within the same political and social background and dealt with a roughly identical audience. Examining the development of the Galician Haskala yields new literary as well as geopolitical territory. Galicia's political and social conditions differ significantly from Prussia's, creating a different set of maskilic problems and challenges. The work of Joseph Perl, the Galician educator, polemicist, and satirist, provides a perfect lens through which to observe these differing conditions and the changing literature that emerges to reflect them.

General background information concerning the Galician Haskala was given in the third chapter; this chapter, and the one that follows, accordingly provide relevant biographical information on Perl, and analyze Perl's work itself, emphasizing his usage of classical Jewish texts. Additionally, the two chapters examine the development of Perl's Hebrew and Yiddish style and show how his citation of the classical canon is both predicated on Hasidic strategies of textual usage and subversively employed to promote the Haskala's ideological agenda.

Analysis of Perl's usage of these intertexts reveals that it is difficult to maintain a monolithic view of his stylistic choices; instead, he must be viewed as an ideologue who subordinated literary style to polemical purposes. This subordination was not without its cost, though: Perl displayed real ambivalence in balancing polemical success and adherence to the Berlin Haskala's linguistic orthodoxy, and it is this struggle between these values that will hopefully explain his complex attitude toward the employment of Yiddish for literary purposes.

Perl: A Brief Biography

Joseph Perl was born on November 10, 1773, the only son of a wealthy man, a businessman and *misnaged* whose family had interests in wine, lumber, and manufactured goods.[1] He received a traditional education and became known as a child prodigy, engaging in Talmudic discussions with learned rabbis by the time of his bar mitzvah. Even at this early age, however, hints of the future maskil appear: Perl wrote in a letter that his parents wanted him to be a rabbi, and so he engaged in Talmud study, but he often hid German books under his Hebrew ones.[2] Perl was married at 14, and spent several years continuing to learn at his father's table in the traditional manner—knowing little of Western culture, or even much of the Bible or Hebrew grammar.

By the early 1790s, Perl was traveling extensively for the family business, and in the process met numerous Hasidic rabbis, becoming extremely attracted to Hasidism. This attraction may have given his later vitriolic attacks a more personal coloring; it is certainly where he gained the familiarity with Hasidic texts and doctrines on which he drew in his later satirical work. One critic even suggests that he may have met Rabbi Jacob Isaac Halevi Horowitz ("the Seer of Lublin"),

---

1. For more on Perl's biography, see Vaynlez, "Yoysef Perl" vii–lxx. See also Dov Taylor's valuable "Introduction," in Joseph Perl's *Revealer of Secrets: The First Hebrew Novel* (Boulder, CO: Westview Press, 1997), xix–lxxv, to the best of my knowledge the sole sustained treatment of any aspect of Perl's life and work in English.

2. Perl's letter is reprinted in Yisroel Vaynlez, "Fun Yoysef Perls arkhiv," *Historishe shriftn* 1 (1929), 809–814, 811–813. See also Friedman "Yoysef Perl" 131–133 for more early biographical information.

Rabbi Nachman of Bratslav, and Rabbi Levi Yitzchok of Berditchev, though no concrete evidence exists for such meetings.[3] Perl met many maskilim on these travels as well, and for three years, between 1801 and 1803, was tutored by Bernard Gunzburg of Brody, who taught him German, French, Latin, history, mathematics, and natural sciences. Through Gunzburg and his business travels, Perl became acquainted with all of the prominent Galician maskilim and became a staunch maskil himself.

The Perl family's wealth increased during the Napoleonic wars in the nineteenth century's first decade, the family business in Tarnopol employing hundreds of people.[4] Perl used his family's wealth for the classic maskilic goal of educational reform: in 1813, Perl became the founder and director of a Jewish school in Tarnopol that taught general studies in the morning and Jewish studies in the afternoon. Originally called the "Israelitische Freischule," the name was changed to the "Deutsch-Israelitische Hauptschule" after official recognition and accreditation by the Austrian government in 1819, at which point it had 118 students and its own building.[5] Perl personally supervised the school for thirty years, developing a full curriculum for Jewish youth from ages 7 to 14, which included Hebrew, Polish, and German language instruction and privileged Bible study over Talmud study.[6] Perl, out of a combination of real religious feeling and ideological canniness, did not remove Talmud study completely, though, and still insisted on its importance as a, though not the, subject of Jewish study. This careful balance might have been one of the reasons the school

3. Silberschlag 129. Klausner (2:281) suggests that the period of Perl's turn toward Hasidism takes place between 1795 and 1800.

4. See Vaynlez "Yoysef Perl" xii. Tarnopol, an important trade center, fell under Russian hegemony between 1809 and 1815.

5. See Vaynlez "Yoysef Perl" xii–xxiii for more details. It is worth noting that Perl's pedagogic activity was at its peak at exactly the same time that he was writing his most important literary works—he was indeed proceeding on all fronts. See Friedman "Yoysef Perl" 146–152, 164–168.

6. For full details of the curriculum see Friedman "Yoysef Perl" 152–157 and Vaynlez "Yoysef Perl" xvii–xx.

would subsequently become the model for all the modern Jewish schools in Galicia and Eastern Europe.[7]

Perl even donated his own annual salary of 600 gulden to the purchase of books for the school library, and presented the school building and the adjacent synagogue as gifts to the Tarnopol Jewish community. In his will, he left half of his fortune and his eight-thousand-item library to the school, as well as 6,000 gulden for the education of artisans.[8] In addition to all of this, he succeeded in obtaining subventions for his school from Tarnopol and adjacent communities, and for his efforts was awarded medals by the Russian government in 1815 and the Austrian government in 1821.[9] Perhaps one sign of Perl's significance as a pedagogue is the fact that, in light of his modernizing pedagogical efforts, he was the first Eastern European Jew to be recognized as an honorary member of the *Gesellschaft für Kultur und Wissenschaft*.[10]

Perl did not limit his efforts to pedagogy, however; he was also active in political and literary forums. In 1815, a ritual ban of excommunication was pronounced by the traditional community against the maskilim of Lemberg, Eastern Galicia's major city, pauperizing one of the major maskilic figures there, Shlomo Yehuda Rapaport, and causing another, Isaac Erter, to flee to Brody. What happened next, though, must have taught the maskilim a valuable lesson: by exerting political pressure on the local governmental authorities, they persuaded them to force the rabbi to publicly revoke the ban.[11] This unqualified maskilic victory almost certainly provides the impetus for the stream of memoranda Perl submitted to the Russian and Austrian governments between 1816 and 1838.[12]

7. Klausner 2:289.

8. On Perl's will, see Klausner 2:293.

9. Silberschlag 130n68. See also Klausner 2:284–287.

10. Klausner 2:289.

11. Viner 1:44; Zinberg, 9:52–56.

12. Besides Perl's polemical and literary work, the ban inspired other writers as well, notably the author of the anonymous play *Di Genarte Velt* ("The False World"), the first modern Yiddish play written entirely in Yiddish (Wolfssohn's and Euchel's plays, as noted in Chapter Five, both contain German in Hebrew characters). On *Di Genarte Velt*, see Viner 1:50–63; Zinberg 8:216; and Khone Shmeruk, "Nusakh bilti yadua shel hakomediya haanonimit 'Di Genarte Velt',"

Many of these memoranda request permission to publish his own or others' work, ranging from an unsuccessful request in 1816 to publish his German anti-Hasidic work *Über das Wesen der Sekte Chassidim* ("On the Nature of the Hasidic Sect"),[13] to the successful 1819 publication of *Megale Temirin* ("The Revealer of Secrets"), to an unsuccessful attempt to republish Israel Loebl's 1798 anti-Hasidic tract *Sefer Vikuakh* ("The Book of Polemic") in 1826,[14] to the 1829 attempt to publish another of his own Hebrew works, *Sefer Katit Lamaor* ("The Book of Preparedness for Lighting"), attacking Hasidic charity practices.[15] Perl's great wealth and government connections gave him the arrogance and willingness to continue his polemical activities at times when other maskilim, more dependent on the traditionalist system for their livelihood, might have backed down.[16]

In later years, Perl submitted memoranda to the government calling for more direct and repressive governmental action, sometimes even against particular individuals—a rare phenomenon even in the

---

Kiryat Sefer 54 (1979), 802–816. See also Werses "Hakhasidut" 95 for examples of other Hebrew and Yiddish works in Perl's circle.

13. The work was originally anonymous, and was first identified as Perl's by Simon Dubnow; see Simon Dubnow, "Der ershter kamf fun haskole kegn khsides," *YIVO-Bleter* 1 (1930), 4–8. The book has appeared in a critical edition: Joseph Perl, *Über das Wesen der Sekte Chassidim*, ed. A. Rubinstein (Jerusalem: Israel Academy of Sciences and Humanities, 1977).

14. Israel Loebl, *Sefer Vikuakh* (Warsaw: 1798). This book is Klausner's candidate for the identity of the mysterious *bukh* at the heart of *Megale Temirin*; see Klausner 2:299–300. As we will see later, however, the *bukh* is almost certainly Perl's own German-language *Über das Wesen der Sekte Chassidim*. For a subtle reference to the book in Perl's work, see Perl's *Maasiyot veigrot mitsadikim umeanshei shlomeinu*, Khone Shmeruk and Shmuel Werses, eds. (Jerusalem: Israel Academy of Sciences and Humanities, 1969, hereafter *S/W*), 173 and footnote *ad loc.* On the republication controversy, see Mahler *Hasidism* 85–89.

15. The title phrase is taken from Leviticus 24:2. For more on Perl's later polemical pieces, see Shmuel Werses, "Khibur satiri lo noda shel Yosef Perl," *Hasifrut* 1 (1968), 206–217, esp. 209. See also Mahler *Hasidism* 127–129. On *Sefer Katit Lamaor* and its accusations against the Hasidim, see Werses *Haskala veshabtaut* 106–108.

16. For an instructive comparison in this regard between Perl and Shlomo Yehuda Rapaport, see Vaynlez "Yoysef Perl" xxxi–xxxii.

heyday of maskilic activity.[17] Memoranda written in 1827 and 1838 attacked particular Hasidic rebbes by name, while a different 1838 memorandum suggested that the government "censor Jewish libraries, close traditional Jewish schools, and prohibit meetings in Jewish ritual baths."[18] Many of these memoranda were intended to be secret, for obvious reasons, but Perl's authorship became generally known, and it is said that Hasidim danced on Perl's fresh grave immediately after his burial.[19] Perl died on Oct. 1, 1839—the festive holiday of Simkhat Torah. The date would hardly have been viewed as a coincidence by the Hasidim.

It says much about Perl's self-perception and the image he projected to his contemporaries that despite the tremendous amount of writing on Perl's gravestone, no mention is made of his literary activity. Rather, the inscription focuses on his pedagogical efforts; the poem engraved on the headstone can be translated:

> This small amount of writing is far too faint praise/his deeds alone will commemorate his days. Go and look at his mighty actions/his house of worship, the school of his benefactions. There children learn, no more or less/Torah and ethical righteousness. To provide their aid was his only drive/In them, in death he stays alive.[20]

Even in death, then, Perl the writer remained secretive.

17. On this stage of Perl's polemical career, see Avraham Rubinstein, "Hahaskala vehakhasidut: peiluto shel Yosef Perl," *Bar Ilan Annual*, 1974, 166–178, 176, and Mahler *Hasidism* 76–103, 121–148. See also Raphael Mahler, "Milkhamto shel Yosef Perl bekhasidut leor mismakhim," in Immanuel Etkes, ed., *Hadat vehakhayim: tnuat hahaskala hayehudit bemizrakh eyropa* (Jerusalem: Zalman Shazar, 1993), 64–88.

18. Taylor "Introduction" xxvi. See also Klausner 2:288–289 and Mahler *Hasidism* 134–140 on the 1838 memorandum. Interestingly, Mahler (*Hasidism* 96) cites a Galician governor's comment that one of Perl's memoranda contained "'numerous grammatical errors'" and adds, "One may conclude from this that the man who devoted his life to the germanization of Galician Jewry did not, it seems, write correct German!"

19. See Mahler *Hasidism* 148.

20. The engraving is cited in Vaynlez "Yoysef Perl" lxx.

Perl's Literary Work: Details and Jewish Influences

As we have said, Galician maskilic literature was fundamentally shaped by the conflict with Hasidism, and Perl, a disillusioned Hasid himself, was certainly no exception. Within several years of the return of Austrian hegemony to Galicia, Perl had written his most influential and most interesting works.

First, there were the Hebrew almanacs he wrote in Tarnopol annually between 1813 and 1815. While the almanacs posed as traditional works, their subversive methodology is clear: to take just one example, their expanded chronologies spread general knowledge and identified readers more closely with their own countries.[21] Mahler writes that the almanac's "introduction is filled with citations concerning fear of the Lord so that the simple reader hardly notices that the new Haskala notions have been interwoven in the text."[22] Perl claims to retell Talmudic stories within the almanac in a "lucid and fluent style," translating Aramaic portions of the stories into Hebrew.[23] Not coincidentally, all the stories Perl cites support maskilic ideological positions, and in a fairly straightforward manner.[24]

Immediately after composing the almanacs, Perl wrote the German-language *Über das Wesen der Sekte Chassidim* (1816), which uses quotations from Hasidic works to implicate them in a variety of crimes,[25] and, at approximately the same time, a set of unpublished parodies of the tales of Rabbi Nachman of Bratslav (1816?) and his masterwork,

21. See the extensive excerpts from the almanacs reprinted and discussed in Mahler *Hasidism* 149–168.

22. Mahler 152.

23. Mahler 152, see example on 153.

24. See the examples from *BT Kidushin* 32b, *BT Berakhot* 10a, and *BT Taanit* 20b cited by Mahler (154–168), who identifies and discusses the various sources cited in each article of the almanacs.

25. See, as well as the sources in note 13 *supra*, Rubinstein's series of articles on *Über das Wesen der Sekte Chassidim*, "Al mahut kat khasidim," *Kiryat Sefer* 38 (1964), 263–272; 415–424; 39 (1965), 117–136, as well as Reuven Michael, *Haketiva hahistorit hayehudit: meharenesans ad haet hakhadasha* (Jerusalem: Mosad Bialik, 1993), 126–129.

Megale Temirin (published 1819, composed 1816–1818), the epistolary novel purporting to be a collection of authentic Hasidic letters compiled by a faithful Hasid. It is these works that serve as the basis for the discussion in the next two chapters.

Perl's other major work, which will not be considered in this book, is his second novel, *Bokhen Tsaddik* ("The Test of the Righteous"), in many ways a sequel to *Megale Temirin*. Besides dating from a significantly later period (it was published in 1838), *Bokhen Tsaddik* is generally considered to be a lesser literary success as well—its style is inconsistent, and its plot is weak. This judgment was reflected in contemporary readers' choices: it went through only one printing, as opposed to *Megale Temirin*'s four. In *Bokhen Tsaddik*, Perl attacks Galician Jewry for not resisting the power of the rabbis, and locates the salvation of the Jewish people in agricultural productivization.[26] Perl's final, no longer extant writings— his Yiddish translation of *Tom Jones* and his fragmentary historical novel *Antignos*—are discussed briefly in the section on Perl's attitude toward Yiddish.[27]

While Perl continued throughout his life to send requests, memoranda, and ideas to the government, his belletristic efforts are, without exception, intended for an entirely Jewish audience.[28] Perl could be fairly sure that his Hebrew and Yiddish works were to be read by Jews and Jews alone, in contrast to the Prussian maskilim discussed earlier, where the dynamics of Christian Hebraism created the perception that many were at least theoretically addressing an audience of Christian enlighteners.

The years from 1815 to 1817, in particular, represent what may be the zenith of maskilic and Hasidic literary and stylistic development in

26. See Zinberg 9:89–90, esp. notes 1–2. For a plot summary and discussion of *Bokhen Tsaddik*, see Klausner 2:308–313.

27. See *infra*.

28. Perl also wrote most of a chapter on Hasidism that appeared in Peter Beer's 1823 German-language book on sectarianism in Judaism, in which he uses Hasidic texts to support his severe criticism much as he does in *Über das Wesen der Sekte Chassidim* and *Megale Temirin*. Some scholars have, in the past, believed Beer's book to be the "*bukh*" of *Megale Temirin*, but as *Megale Temirin* was published years earlier, this could hardly be the case. See Rubinstein "Al mahut" 271.

Galicia. The incredible ferment then taking place in Jewish literature contained a number of important trends and figures that would influence Perl ideologically and formalistically.

First, there was the example of the maskilim who had preceded Perl, primarily Prussian maskilim, many of whom hewed more directly to the style of Hebrew literature previously discussed—the Biblicism of *melitsa*, where every sentence is a mosaic of Biblical quotations, sometimes thematically allusive, sometimes used merely from a general love of Biblical language. As noted in previous chapters, *melitsa* was not quite as straitjacketed and Prussian maskilim were not quite so Biblicistic as earlier scholars suggested; nonetheless, the general theme and approach was there. Perl's proclaimed linguistic preference as far as Hebrew was concerned was indeed a more classically maskilic Hebrew; he uses the word *tsakhut* (purity), a favored term of the Prussian Haskala, in an 1815 essay.[29]

However, another strand of maskilic thought came from the north as well; a minority one, to be sure, in the face of this linguistic and ideological orthodoxy of *melitsa*, but one that would have an important effect on Perl and, in addition to satiric circumstances, required him to write in a different type of Hebrew altogether, as we will see. This approach was exemplified by the maskil Mendl Lefin, a transitional figure between the Prussian and the Galician Haskala and a close friend of Perl's.[30] By 1808, Lefin had left his hometown of Satanow, moved to Berlin and spent time with Mendelssohn and his circle, and then moved to Galicia, living first in Brody and then Perl's home town of Tarnopol.[31] Lefin's task there, in the words of his major

29. See Werses "Khibur" 216–217.

30. On Lefin, see Klausner 1:199–225; Yisroel Vaynlez, "Mendl-Lefin Satanover (biografishe shtudiye afn smakh fun hantshriftlikhe materyaln)," *YIVO-Bleter* 2 (1931), 334–357, and, more recently, Nancy Beth Sinkoff, "Tradition and Transition: Mendel Lefin of Satanów and the Beginnings of the Jewish Enlightenment in Europe, 1749–1826" (Ph.D. dissertation, Columbia University, 1996), an expanded and revised version of which, *Out of the Shtetl: Making Jews Modern in the Polish Borderlands* (Providence: Brown Judaic Studies, 2004), is currently in press.

31. Klausner 1:211–12, especially 212n2, and Sinkoff 29–34. See also Shmuel Werses, "Iyunim bemivne shel 'Megale Temirin' ve'Bokhen Tsaddik'," *Tarbiz* 31 (1962), 377–411, 384–385, and Shmeruk *Prakim* 181–182.

expositor, was "to interpret and reformulate [the German model of Haskala] to suit the needs of the society in which he lived."[32]

In doing so, Lefin produced several works that were to have major influence on Perl. In 1792, he published a French essay ("Essai d'un plan de réforme ayant pour l'objet d'éclairer la Nation Juive en Pologne et de redresser par là ses moeurs") in which he suggested that the Hasidic community was a threat to the spread of Enlightenment and was best dealt with through the publication and dissemination of satirical materials lampooning Hasidic thought and practice.[33] Lefin himself, practicing what he preached, seems to have written several such pieces; sadly, these works are no longer extant.[34] At least one of them, a book called *Sefer Makhkimat Peti* ("Book of the Enlightening of the Foolish"), seems to have been an epistolary novel purportedly written by Hasidim—probably the most direct inspiration for Perl's masterwork, *Megale Temirin*, which has an identical form.[35] Lefin also wrote in Yiddish: *Der Ershter Khosid* ("The First Hasid") seems to have concerned the Baal Shem Tov, but is also no longer extant.[36] This quasi-historical sounding title may have inspired Perl's historicist attacks on the founder of Hasidism, which are discussed in more detail in the next chapter on *Megale Temirin*.

Lefin's other important influential work for Perl was his Yiddish Bible translation.[37] Influenced by his contact while in Berlin with

32. Sinkoff xii–xiii.

33. For a detailed analysis of this essay, see Rubinstein "Peiluto" 168–171; Roland Goetschel, "L'hostilité du monde hassidique à la révolution française," in Hadas-Lebel and Oliel-Grausz 267–283, esp. 267–271; and Sinkoff 71–89, esp. 78–81. See also N.H. Gelber, "Mendl-Lefin Satanover vehatzaotav letikun orakh khayim shel yehudei polin bifnei haseym hagadol (1788–1792)," in Bernard Lander, ed. *The Abraham Weiss Jubilee Volume* (New York: Shulsinger Bros., 1964), 271–306.

34. On Lefin's anti-Hasidic efforts more generally, see Sinkoff 113–169.

35. For one of the few extant pieces of documentary evidence on this epistolary piece—Perl's notes from his Tarnopol library—see Shmuel Werses, "Beikvotav shel hakhibur 'Makhkimat Peti' heavud," in Werses *Megamot* 319–337, where the notes are reprinted with critical apparatus.

36. Viner 1:38–42; Werses "Hakhasidut" 94–95; "Iyunim" 385; Klausner 1:205; Zinberg 8:220.

37. On Lefin's translation, see Khone Shmeruk, "Vegn etlekhe printsipn fun mendl lefins mishley-iberzetzung," *Di yidishe shprakh* 24 (1964), 33–52, as well as

Moses Mendelssohn's circle, who were engaged in producing a German Bible translation,[38] as well as by the success of the Hasidic movement, whose linguistic base was in Yiddish,[39] Lefin decided that the Yiddish-speaking masses of Eastern Europe would benefit from a new translation of the Bible into Yiddish—that is, the modern Yiddish of contemporary Eastern European life, rather than the increasingly outdated, but still widely used, older Yiddish translations and paraphrases, written in a stylized literary Western Yiddish.[40] This translation would also, as much as possible, attempt to incorporate the aims and ideals of the Haskala, particularly by the removal of non-literalist material whose implications disagreed with maskilic agendas. Lefin translated Psalms, Proverbs, Job, Lamentations, and Ecclesiastes into Yiddish, but the only translation published at the time was Proverbs, printed in 1814 with Perl's financial assistance.[41] Lefin's choice of which Biblical books to translate was hardly coincidental. His choice of Psalms, written in a poetic style appealing to contemporary Western European literary mores, and Ecclesiastes and Proverbs, both typical examples of wisdom literature, reflect earlier maskilic taste and judgment.[42] The Galician maskilim, in presenting and emphasizing the same selections from the classical Jewish canon as the Prussian

---

the expanded Hebrew version, "Al ekronot akhadim shel targum Mishlei leMendel Lefin," in Khone Shmeruk, *Sifrut yidish bePolin: mekhkarim veiyunim historiim* (Jerusalem: Magnes Press, 1981), 165–183. See also Zinberg 8:200 and Klausner 1:212–213. Lefin also retranslated Maimonides' *Guide to the Perplexed* into Hebrew, though not all of it was published. Klausner 1:219–223.

38. See Sinkoff 219.

39. At the time, however, their writings were almost entirely in Hebrew. See Khayim Liberman, "Tsu der frage vegn der batsiyung fun khsides tsu yidish," in his *Ohel Rokhl* (Empire Press: New York, 1980), 2:1–11, 1–3. See also the discussion of *Shivkhei HaBesht* (hereafter *SB*) in the next chapter.

40. On the relation between Lefin's and earlier Yiddish translations, such as the *Magishey Minkhe*, see Shmeruk "Vegn etlekhe" 36–39.

41. Lefin's translation of Ecclesiastes was subsequently published in 1873 and reprinted in 1930. Selections of some of the other translations appear in Simkha Katz, "Targumei tanakh meet Menakhem Mendel Lefin misatanov," *Kiryat Sefer* 16 (1939–1940), 114–133.

42. On the maskilic attraction to wisdom literature, see Sinkoff 220–221 and the discussion of Mendelssohn's usage of Psalms in Chapter Four *supra*.

maskilim, once more reveal the continuities between the early and transitional Haskala.

Lefin's Yiddish, as well as his more relaxed Hebrew style, incorporated later strata of mishnaic Hebrew, Yiddish vocabulary and syntax, and Slavicisms. In doing so, Lefin may have been influenced by his fellow townsman Isaac Satanow, a maskil well known for his satirical writings.[43] When the two met in Berlin in the 1780s, Satanow advised Lefin to eschew *melitsa* and to utilize mishnaic material.[44] Additionally, Lefin, having seen Mendelssohn's Bible translation aimed at German readers, tried to create an analogous translation that would have a similar effect on Eastern European Jews, particularly Podolian Jews—in other words, that would present them with a text they could actually read. The translation is therefore written in a Podolian dialect of Yiddish, avoiding contemporary Germanisms, maintaining Hebraisms, and using Slavicisms to create synonyms and explain metaphors. Lefin's Biblical translations exemplified the approach that governed his writing and would later influence much of Perl's: the maskil's task is to disseminate the ideology of the Haskala by the most efficient means possible, regardless of whether those means contradict other cherished maskilic principles, such as the maskilic aversion to (at least the public usage of) Yiddish.[45]

This approach was difficult for many maskilim to accept. Most of their positions on Yiddish were taken from that of the Berlin Haskala and were just as inflexible, despite the fact that the relationship between Yiddish and Polish in Galicia was significantly different from the relationship between *Hochdeutsch* and Yiddish in Prussia. Nonetheless, characterizations of Yiddish by Galician maskilim included

43. On Isaac Satanow, see Altmann *MMBS* 352–354 and *GJH* 1:322–323.

44. On the similarities and differences between Lefin's and Satanow's usage of mishnaic Hebrew, see Joseph Klausner, "Hishtalsheluto shel signon-hamishna besifrut haivrit hakhadasha," in *Kitvei Prof. Yosef Klausner: Beaiot shel sifrut umada* (Tel Aviv: Masada 1956), 118–146.

45. See Shmeruk *Prakim* 182–187 and Sinkoff 215–216. For more on Lefin's Hebrew style, see *S/W* "Introduction" 50–51. Lefin produced other nonfiction Hebrew works, such as the popular medical book *Refuot Haam* ("Medicines of the Nation"), which incorporated the same flexible style. See Shmeruk *Prakim* 190, 194.

phrases such as "a torn, ragged, and corrupt language."[46] Lefin's translation sparked a war in the maskilic community, with letters and pamphlets flying back and forth between various maskilic figures.[47] Though
Lefin did have some vocal defenders—most notably Yaakov Shmuel
Bik—Bik's arguments had little effect on the climate of public opinion
within the maskilic community: in fact, until the first appearance of
the journal *Kol Mevaser* ("The Voice of the Herald") in 1864, the only
maskilic material published in Yiddish in Eastern Europe is Moyshe
Markuze's *Eyzer Yisroel* ("Aid to Israel"),[48] Lefin's Bible translation,
and the previously mentioned *Di Genarte Velt*.

Perl's complicated, ambiguous, and ambivalent role in the debate
allows us to take a closer look at his attitude toward the Yiddish language in general and writing in Yiddish in particular.[49] At the time
of Lefin's 1814 translation of Proverbs, Perl owned the one maskilic
printing press in Eastern Europe, founded in Tarnopol in 1812, and the
translation would have to have been printed with his knowledge and
presumably his approval.[50] Though some evidence exists indicating

46. Mahler *Hasidism* 39.

47. See Sinkoff 222–243 and Klausner 1:213–219 for a description of the polemic and the arguments that ensued, as well as a biographical sketch of the main
public objector, Tuvia Feder. For more on the conflict, see also Joshua A. Fishman, *Language and Ethnicity in Minority Sociolinguistic Perspective* (Philadelphia:
Multilingual Matters Ltd., 1989) 70–82; Shmuel Werses, "Bein shnei olamot:
Yaakov Shmuel Bik bein haskala lekhasidut—iyun mekhudash," in Werses *Megamot* 110–159, esp. 116–119, and "Hanusakh hamekori habilti yadua shel igeret
Yaakov Shmuel Bik el Tuvia Feder," in Werses *Megamot* 338–355. See also Khone
Shmeruk, *Prokim fun der yidisher literatur-geshikhte* (Tel Aviv: Farlag Y.L. Peretz,
1988) 265–269, and Pelli *Sugot vesugyot* 73–89.

48. Markuze himself may not even have been a maskil; on Markuze and his
work, see Shmeruk *Prakim* 187–197.

49. Compare Werses "Yad" 22–26 for a more general overview of the issue.

50. See Vaynlez "Yoysef Perl" xxv. All other Galician Jewish printing presses
were controlled by the traditionalists, who were naturally hostile to maskilic
efforts. On printing in Eastern Europe in general, see Shmeruk *Prakim* 176–179
and Khayim Liberman, "Legende un emes vegn khsidishe drukerayen," in *Ohel
Rokhl* 2:17–160. On censorship of Hebrew and Yiddish books in Galicia, including the maskilic attempt (by Herz Homberg) to ban various Jewish books, see
Mahler *Hasidism* 106–110.

his approval and even financial support of the translation's printing, the indications are not entirely one-sided. Shmeruk writes: "It seems that Joseph Perl, who was an influential force at the Tarnopol printing press where Lefin's Proverbs was printed, was opposed to its publication, and only the Russian governor of the province, 'in his love for the translator in his understanding of the internal needs of the nation,' removed this obstacle for the printing of the book."[51]

Perl's ambiguous attitude toward the printing of the translation is hardly illuminated by the fact that he takes no public position during the subsequent debate. His only public statement on the language question comes from his comments in a lecture he delivered in Yiddish in the Tarnopol synagogue in 1838, decades after the Lefin controversy. A communal crisis had developed over the appointment of the maskil Shlomo Yehuda Rapaport as the head of the Tarnopol synagogue, and Perl felt it necessary to address the congregation in a manner that would allow no possibilities for misinterpretation. It is only necessity that drove him to do so, he said, and in his speech he seems to parrot the party line of the conservative imitators of the Prussian Haskala, referring to Yiddish as a "vulgar" language and preferring the "gentle" language of German.[52]

51. Shmeruk *Prakim* 187n60.

52. Cited in Zelig Kalmanovitsh, "Yoysef Perl's yidishe ksovim: literarisher un shprokhiker analiz," in Perl *Yidishe ksovim* lxxi–cvii, lxxx. Large sections of the (extremely long) speech are printed in Vaynlez "Yoysef Perl" l, lviii–lxv. See also Shmuel Werses, "Tsvishn dray shprakhn: vegn Yoysef Perls yidishe ksovim in likht fun naye materyaln," *Di Goldene Keyt* 89 (1976), 150–177, 156. On Rapaport's appointment as the head of the Tarnopol synagogue, see Vaynlez "Yoysef Perl" lv–lviii, lxv–lxvi and Mahler *Hasidism* 140–141. The speech itself bears similarities to a traditional speech, with "no fewer than 56 citations brought from the Bible and the Talmud, not including different midrashim and other old books" (Vaynlez "Yoysef Perl" lvii). Even in this mediated form between his polemical essays and his polemical literature, Perl's tendency to cloak his ideas in traditionalist clothing is evident—a tendency apparent throughout his work. Perl's 1838 synagogal address in Yiddish is based on an earlier draft he wrote in Hebrew, and in fact, it seems that all of Perl's Yiddish work (with the exception of *Antignos*) conforms to a linguistic hierarchy where the Yiddish text is a later version, albeit often an expanded and developed one, of an earlier Hebrew text. For more on this linguistic hierarchy in Perl's work, see Werses "Tsvishn" 162.

Perl, however, did write in Yiddish. This chapter and the next discuss two of his Yiddish works in detail, his parodies of the *Tales* of Rabbi Nachman of Bratslav and his Yiddish translation of his own Hebrew *Megale Temirin*. Besides these works, Perl also translated Fielding's *Tom Jones* into Yiddish[53] and wrote at least sections of *Antignos*, a historical novel set in the time of the Second Temple.[54] Perl's introductions to these works suggest he wrote them for the same reasons he spoke Yiddish in the Tarnopol synagogue: perceived necessity. In his parody of the *Tales* and *Megale Temirin*, as we will see, that necessity stemmed from his perceived need to combat Hasidism and his realization that such combat could only be carried out in Yiddish; in the latter two cases, the necessity was more positive and programmatic—to provide the Eastern European Jewish reading public with what the maskilim regarded as proper and edificatory reading material, material which would hopefully replace the retrogressive storybooks currently popular. Perl's introduction to *Antignos* encapsulates this attitude: "The Polish general community has, sadly nothing to read . . . particularly when a Sabbath or a festival comes around, what should a Polish *prostak* do . . . they will sit at home, and they read, they read the *mayse-bikhlekh* [storybooks], which are senseless, stupid, and partially filled with foolishness and coarse talk to boot."[55]

Perl's need to write in Yiddish, then, mirrors his support of Lefin's translation; it is based on a perception of Yiddish's necessity, rather than true approval. However, when it came time to take the definitive step of becoming publicly identified with even a utilitarian approach to the language, Perl balked. He was unable to make the final break with the Galician Haskala's more conservative wing, even if intellectually he

53. For more on Perl's translation of *Tom Jones*, particularly its Judaicization, employing traditional acronyms and Talmudic texts, see Werses "Tsvishn" 170–176, as well as Shmuel Werses, "Yosef Perl kemetargem leyidish shel 'Tom Dzhons' leFilding," in his *Milashon el lashon: yetsirot vegilguleihen besifruteinu* (Magnes Press: Hebrew University, Jerusalem 1996), 383–405.

54. Vaynlez (liv) describes *Antignos* as the "translation of an English novel of the time of the destruction of the Second Temple," of which only part survives. However, Kalmanovitsh and later scholars believe that *Antignos* was actually an original composition; see Kalmanovitsh lxxxin20. See also Werses "Tsvishn" 169–170.

55. Cited in Shmeruk *Prokim* 288.

tended to agree with Lefin's approach. In the case of Lefin's translation, he refused to support it publicly and may even have tried to stop its printing; in the case of his own literary work, he withheld it from publication and, more significantly, from the circulation in manuscript among maskilim which was the common practice with the few contemporary maskilic Yiddish works.[56] Perl, it seems, was unwilling to risk the opposition and disapproval of his valued maskilic circle by contravening established maskilic dogma, as Lefin had. As such, he kept his rebellion a secret.

Tellingly, there are no contemporary accounts whatsoever of Perl as a Yiddish writer; the first indications that he wrote in Yiddish come from researchers in his Tarnopol library a century later, immediately before the Second World War. In fact, Perl kept his Yiddish writing such a secret that the scholarly community seriously doubted for decades whether Perl actually wrote the Yiddish version of *Megale Temirin*.[57] It is possible to suggest that Perl's unwillingness to publish or even circulate his Yiddish work comes from his love of secrecy. However, such an argument is unconvincing in and of itself. Perl's

56. See Werses "Tsvishn" 153. Examples of works that did circulate include Lefin's *Der Ershter Khosid*, the work of Yisroel Aksenfeld, the anonymous play *Teater fun Khasidim* ("Theater of Hasidim"), and the play *Gedules Reb Volf* ("The Greatness of Rabbi Wolf"). The last of these was erroneously attributed to Perl in the 1937 publication of his Yiddish writings; the real author was later shown to be Chayim Malaga. See Simkha Katz, "Naye materyaln fun dem Perl-arkhiv: Yoysef Perl's hakdome tsu zayn 'Megale Tmirin' in yidish," *YIVO-Bleter* 13 (1938), 557–576, 561–565. Shmeruk's summation, that "we have actually no knowledge concerning the influence of the Yiddish maskilic work on the general public which constituted its potential readership," is well worth keeping in mind. Shmeruk *Prokim* 291.

57. On the question of authorship of the Yiddish *Megale Temirin*, see Kalmanovitsh lxxx–lxxxi and Werses "Tsvishn" 154; a more recent expression of scholarly skepticism concerning Perl's writing in Yiddish can be found in A.M. Haberman, "Haim katav Yosef Perl khiburim beyidish," in his *Kvutsei yakhad* (Jerusalem: Rubin Mass, 1980), 143–149. See the next chapter on *Megale Temirin* and see also Shmuel Werses, "Milashon el lashon: semamanei hanusakh beyidish shel 'Megale Temirin' shel Yosef Perl," *Khulyot* 3 (1996), 59–108, 61, where he conclusively determines Perl's authorship by comparing the Yiddish version of *Megale Temirin* (which we do not have in an autograph version) and the pseudo-*Tales* of Rabbi Nachman written in Yiddish (which we do).

love of secrecy certainly helped to dictate the anonymous form and mystificatory elements of *Megale Temirin*, for example, but he still published the book and clearly was not unhappy to be generally recognized as its author.

Indeed, Perl's authorship of *Megale Temirin* was an open secret among the maskilic community, and later in life, he openly admitted his authorship, writing in a letter to the Galician journal *Kerem Khemed*,

> and you should not think that the fact that I did not reveal my name in [my] writing was because of my fear of the wrath and the fury that would be poured upon me by some of our fellow Jews; God forbid such a thing should be thought . . . even if a thousand hostile writings were to be issued against me, I would not fear them . . . as for the reason that led me to hide my name (*lehastir et shmi*), I cannot reveal that to you (*legalot etkhem*) at this time, but I hope, God willing, that in the near future I will be able to explain to you my reasons in the matter.[58]

To the best of our knowledge, Perl never explicitly did so, but, when viewed from an ideological perspective, his reasons for secrecy seem fairly obvious. As far as Perl's airy claims of thick-skinned reaction to all hostility, while Perl may have cherished the opposition of the Hasidic world as proof of his maskilic *bona fides*, he might well have been leerier of the opprobrium of his fellow maskilim, which would explain his continuing ambivalence about publishing in Yiddish.

Thus, though Perl is undoubtedly a Yiddish writer, he is at best ambivalent about the expression of Yiddish in a public forum.[59] This ambivalence has a tragic character, since he perceives the necessity for publication of maskilic Yiddish works but is unwilling or unable to do anything to address that need. It is true, then, that Perl's Yiddish work had no influence on the later development of modern Yiddish literature and the Haskala. However, the work still repays careful analysis for two reasons. Firstly, Perl is an important figure in the history of modern Jewish literature, and knowledge of his Yiddish work provides a more complete view of his oeuvre. More importantly, though

58. *Kerem Khemed* 2 (1836): 36–37. See also Taylor "Introduction" xxviii.

59. Shmeruk's phraseology of *maskilishe bushe* (maskilic shame) to describe Perl's attitude seems to me to be perfectly apt. See Shmeruk *Prokim* 272.

the Yiddish work was not published, it remains a snapshot of what a highly effective ideologue of the Galician Haskala *believed* would be effective in the *kulturkampf* of his day, particularly against the perceived ravages of Hasidism.

As such, Perl's Yiddish work can provide essential information about his perceptions of and expectations from the Yiddish-reading audience of the time: what did they know and believe, and how could ideologues like Perl turn that knowledge and belief to their own advantage? This book chooses to approach that question by focusing on Perl's usage of classical texts, directly comparing the Yiddish texts with their Hebrew analogues, allowing the reader to see how Perl structured his work differently to appeal to the knowledge and understanding of two discrete audiences. Additionally, examining the different usages of classical texts throws the differences between the Galician and Prussian milieus into even sharper relief. There are many other complementary approaches, each demanding further study.

Hasidic Literature and Perl's Hasidic Parodies

Both of Perl's major Yiddish works, the pseudo-Hasidic *Tales* of Rabbi Nachman of Bratslav and the Yiddish version of *Megale Temirin*, are written in direct response to Hasidic texts, the *Tales* of Reb Nachman of Bratslav and the *Shivkhei HaBesht* ("Tales in Praise of the Baal Shem Tov") respectively, though other Hasidic books influence each of these works.

Tales of various Hasidic leaders, particularly the movement's founders, had circulated among the faithful for decades before the printing of the first Hasidic book. These tales were often a mixture of adventure story (*mayse*) and homiletic teaching, and were generally transmitted in Yiddish, whether at fairs, at festive religious meals, or on the road. The tales were instrumental in the emergence of Hasidism as an integral part of typical Eastern European Jewish life.[60] Since the 1780s,

---

60. See Gedaliah Nigal, "New Light on the Hasidic Tale and Its Sources," in Rapoport-Albert *Hasidism Reappraised* 345–353; idem., *Hasiporet hakhasidit: toldoteha venos'eha* (Jerusalem: Marcus Press, 1981), esp. 13–22, 57–83; Yoav Elshteyn,

books of homilies and teachings of Hasidic masters had been printed, like the *Toldot Yaakov Yosef* by Rabbi Jacob Joseph of Polnoye. These earliest books, though, were not based on those Hasidic tales, but were instead dedicated to the articulation of early Hasidic philosophy, generally through homiletic means. These Hasidic leaders' teachings (known as *droshes* or *khasidishe toyre*), though almost always first orally delivered in Yiddish, were always printed in Hebrew, thus preserving the linguistic hierarchy of Hebrew over Yiddish, despite the fact that "the movement generally had a positive and warm relationship to Yiddish."[61]

It was not until the years 1815 and 1816 that the two books of Hasidic literature that would fundamentally transform Hebrew and Yiddish literature were to emerge. The books appeared roughly simultaneously, both were highly influential, and yet it is the differences between the two works—particularly the linguistic and stylistic ones—that are important to our study of Perl.[62] These collections, the *Sipurei Maasiyot*

Haekstaza vehasipur hakhasidi (Ramat Gan: Bar-Ilan, 1998), 23–35; and Joseph Dan, *Hasipur hakhasidi* (Jerusalem: Keter Publishing House, 1975), esp. 4–57. The tales are placed in broader ethnographical perspective in Barbara Kirshenblatt-Gimblett, "The Concept and Varieties of Narrative Performance in East European Jewish Culture," in Richard Bauman and Joel Sherzer, eds., *Explorations in the Ethnography of Speaking* (Cambridge: Cambridge University Press, 1989), 283–308; see esp. 290–293. For a particularly tendentious elucidation of this approach, see Meyer Viner, who praises the Yiddish literature of the period in general, and Hasidic literature in particular, for being particularly attuned to the needs of the people and "transmitting their voice." In contrast, Viner condemns early modern Hebrew literature of the first half of the nineteenth century as dry, intellectual, and unrealistic. Full of *melitsa*, it is unconnected to "the organic life of the people"; the only exception is Perl's (Hebrew) *Megale Temirin*, presumably because it mimics the "authentic" voice of Hasidism. See Viner 1:16–17.

61. See Shmeruk *Prokim* 212–213.

62. Despite their importance and influence (and their effect on Perl), these were two of only three Hasidic works to appear in Yiddish at all until the 1860s. On the third work, *Seyfer Poykeyakh Ivrim*, ("The Book of the Opener of the Eyes of the Blind," published 1814), see Shmeruk *Prokim* 213 and Liberman "Batsiyung" 2. The author's approach is the Hasidic mirror image of the attitude developed (though not implemented) by Perl: he insists on writing in Yiddish so that his ethical message will be understood, since it would be a "difficulty" for the general public to read a work written in Hebrew.

(the *Tales*) of Rabbi Nachman of Bratslav and the *Shivkhei HaBesht* ("Tales in Praise of the Baal Shem Tov"), "embody a radical expansion and refinement of literary sensibility in the Jewish world," to quote Arnold Band, and can be seen as a new beginning point in modern Jewish literature.[63] Certainly they mark the beginning of a new phase in Perl's literary activity.

Rabbi Nachman's *Sipurei Maasiyot* and Perl's Parodic *Tales and Letters*

Rabbi Nachman of Bratslav (1772–1810), born a year before Perl, was the great-grandson of the Baal Shem Tov and one of the most important Hasidic leaders of his time. While a full biographical treatment of Rabbi Nachman is beyond the scope of this book, suffice it to say that his claims of messianism, coupled with the zealous fidelity of his followers, made him a perfect example of the type of Hasidic rabbi despised by Perl.[64] Of concern here, however, is his literary work. Near

63. Arnold J. Band, "The Function of the Enigmatic in Two Hasidic Tales," in Joseph Dan and Frank Talmadge, eds., *Studies in Jewish Mysticism* (Cambridge, MA: AJS, 1978), 185–210, 185. Band himself (199) links these tales, stylistically if not historically, to the work of the Haskala.

64. The standard biography on Rabbi Nachman of Bratslav is Arthur Green, *Tormented Master: A Life of Rabbi Nachman of Bratslav* (University, Alabama: University of Alabama Press, 1979). Other biographical sketches of Rabbi Nachman, along with some psychobiography and Freudian analysis drawn from his own statements and works, can be found in Shmuel Niger, "R[eb] Nakhman Bratslaver un zayne sipurey-mayses," in Niger *Bleter-geshikhte* 111–177, 124–137, and Arnold J. Band, "Introduction," in Nahman of Bratslav, *The Tales*, ed. and trans. Arnold J. Band (New York: Paulist Press, 1978), 9–25. For a particularly perceptive essay on Rabbi Nachman and his tales, see Roskies *Bridge* 20–55. Interestingly, modern research has indicated that Rabbi Nachman's personal relations with maskilim in the city of Uman were significantly warmer than might be expected; in fact, the first place Rabbi Nachman lived when he moved to Uman near the end of his life was with a maskil. See Khayim Liberman, "R[eb] Nakhman Bratslaver un di umaner maskilim," in *Ohel Rokhl* 2:161–197, esp. 164–165, 175–177, as well as Mendel Piekarz, *Khasidut bratslav: prakim bekhayei mekhollela uviketaveha* (Mossad Bialik: Jerusalem, 1995), 27–31 and Green *Tormented Master* 250–259. On Rabbi Nachman's re-

the end of his life, in 1806, he said, according to his scribe and amanuensis, Natan Sternhartz, *ikh vel shoyn onheybn mayses dertseyln* ("Now I will begin to tell stories"), and he began to deliver the tales that assured him a place in modern Jewish literature.[65]

Roskies phrases it particularly well: "Reb Nachman's discovery of a new symbolic language came after he had mastered all the traditional forms of Jewish self-expression: the languages of prayer and song; of biblical, rabbinic, and kabbalistic exegesis; of ethical exhortation."[66] The *Tales* are different from all of these genres, and yet seem fundamentally continuous with them. Rabbi Nachman seems to have told these stories on the same occasions that he delivered his more straightforward homiletic interpretations and teachings (his *toyre*), thus stressing the essential lack of difference between the two.[67]

The *Tales* were originally told in Yiddish, and then translated into the still higher-status Hebrew by Natan Sternhartz. However, at the behest of Rabbi Nachman, almost all editions of the book published by Bratslav Hasidim, including the first 1815/1816 Ostrog edition that Perl would have seen, appeared in a bilingual format, the Hebrew printed above the Yiddish.[68] This bilingual format reflected the fact

---

lationship with the other Hasidic figures of the time, see Ada Rapoport-Albert, "Hasidism After 1772: Structural Continuity and Change," in *Hasidism Reappraised* 76–140, 113–119.

65. For a dating of the tales, see Band "Introduction" 44. "The Tale of the Loss of the Princess," the tale Perl "completes" and parodies, is the first of Rabbi Nachman's tales, told in the summer of 1806. Niger also stresses the improvisational nature of the stories, their function as responses to certain events, and discusses in greater detail Natan's role and the circulation of the tales in manuscript; see Niger 143–154. On Natan, see also Green *Tormented Master* 7–8, 148–149.

66. Roskies *Bridge* 26.

67. See Shmeruk *Prokim* 244.

68. See Piekarz 184–190 for a discussion of various editions of the text. This book does not discuss the complex issue of which version was first written down: at best, this is an open question. See Piekarz 160–184 for an overview of the whole discussion and the critical issues involved; he ends with the assumption that the tales, despite being delivered in Yiddish, were first written down in Hebrew. Natan Sternhartz cites Rabbi Nachman's statement regarding the bilingual nature of the *Tales* in his introduction to the first edition; the introduction is reprinted in *S/W* 92–95.

that the Hasidic movement considered the Yiddish language a positive good rather than a necessary evil. As mentioned earlier, Hasidism did much to legitimize the Yiddish language as a spiritual language appropriate for prayers and religious sentiment, at times even preferable to Hebrew, though in no way depriving Hebrew of its linguistic pride of place.[69] Rabbi Nachman was unquestionably one of the Hasidic figures most responsible for this sanctification of Yiddish: he himself admired the *tkhines*, the Yiddish prayers traditionally recited by women, and even urged his disciples to pray in Yiddish.[70] As a result, it is not surprising to find that Rabbi Nachman's Yiddish version of the *Tales*, when printed, appeared in an Eastern Yiddish based primarily on and structurally close to a modern southeastern Yiddish dialect.[71]

The Hebrew translations of the Yiddish *Tales* were often mocked by maskilim for their "corrupt" style of Hebrew. However, as in the controversy surrounding Lefin's Bible translation, what the maskilim considered "corrupt" was often a more flexible and naturalistic idiom.[72] With Lefin, that idiom was primarily, though not solely, achieved through the incorporation of later strata of Hebrew, particularly though not solely mishnaic Hebrew, into the text. With Rabbi Nachman's translators, linguistic flexibility stems primarily from the attempt to render the Hebrew as similar to Rabbi Nachman's Yiddish as possible, meaning that Yiddish syntax and sentence structure is often transferred into the Hebrew text, sometimes successfully, sometimes not.

The tales themselves are highly symbolic and allegorical, mixing superficially external folk motifs[73] and certain realistic elements with traditional Jewish symbolism, mysticism, and *musar* genres for powerful

69. See Niger 114–122.

70. Zinberg 8:134. On Nachman's appreciation for the *Eyn Yankev*, see Green *Tormented Master* 30.

71. I am grateful to Dr. Dov-Ber Kerler for his comments on this issue.

72. See *S/W* "Introduction" 52–53 for more maskilic comments on Rabbi Nachman's style. See also Cohen "Hateknika" 154–155.

73. The positive attitude toward non-Jewish stories implied by this usage of folk motifs will have important implications for maskilic writers as well. See Shmeruk *Prokim* 250 for a discussion of this characteristic of Hasidic narrative, traceable back to Beshtian Hasidism. See also Roskies *Bridge* 26–33 and Elshteyn 39–63.

literary effect.[74] Rabbi Nachman, who viewed storytelling as a holy act through which man could help achieve the reunification of the God-head, believed a spark of holiness to exist in every story, Jewish and non-Jewish alike.[75] As a result, he often kept the frame of a non-Jewish story and imbued it with Jewish content—though the reader may often be forgiven for failing to find the story's connection to Judaism.

This may be because Rabbi Nachman's strong esoteric leanings, stemming from his alienation and elitist tendencies in general and his mystical tendencies in particular, led to a belief that the true meanings of these stories, possessing mystical power, should not be explained to the uninitiated. At the beginning of his first story, "The Tale of the Loss of the Princess," Rabbi Nachman appends an introduction about secrets, citing the Zohar concerning the necessity of unveiling them and the danger in doing so. He writes elsewhere that many things must be kept secret in order to be most efficacious; at the same time "one is forced, at times, to reveal some sort of hint, so that they will know that there are secret things within [the stories]."[76] This idea that Rabbi Nachman's stories contain secret meanings lying just out of sight explains why commentaries were added to the *Tales* as early as the book's first editions. The commentaries, while often linking particular stories to sets of Biblical passages, figures, or mystical symbols,

74. Previous approaches to the *Tales* include Niger's (165–177), which divides them into two categories: "realistic" and "symbolic," and Viner's (1:36–38), which acknowledges Nachman's mastery of narrative structure, but asserts that his tales can never reach the heights of literature. Viner gives two reasons for his judgment: first, despite the occasional absorption of a western tactic or theme, the stories are fundamentally traditional and Hasidic, and thus cling to the outmoded feudal order, preventing them from achieving the status of great literature; and secondly, the tales are overinterpreted by the followers, who take realistic elements and give them highly symbolic meanings. Neither Niger's binary nor Viner's Marxist approach is entirely determinative; for directions toward a more nuanced approach, see also Green *Tormented Master* 337–371 and Ora Wiskind-Elper, *Tradition and Fantasy in the Tales of Reb Nahman of Bratslav* (Albany: SUNY Press, 1998), esp. 11–23, 33–39, 62–65.

75. For more on Rabbi Nachman's philosophy of storytelling's essential holiness, see *Likutei Moharan* 60 (Mohilev: 1809); Band "Introduction" 29–39; and Dan *Hasipur hakhasidi* 4–57.

76. See *Sikhot Haran* 151 (Jerusalem: Kedem, 1944).

also hint at hidden depths neither explained by the master (as a result of his unwillingness to do so) nor by the commentator (as a result of his lack of ability to penetrate the deep, miraculous wisdom of the divinely inspired storyteller).[77]

Because of these various linguistic and literary considerations, the stories are free from the resonance of classical Jewish texts—almost eerily free, particularly when compared to the textually laden work of the Prussian maskilim.[78] Rabbi Nachman's countervailing example is, stylistically speaking, highly influential to Perl as a potential alternative to the Prussian Haskala's *melitsa*. Additionally, Nachman's conception of a complex layering of openness and secrecy would have been highly attractive to someone as obsessed with secrets as Perl. And more generally, Bratslav theories of garbing truth in narrative clothes and achieving ultimate goals through telling tales can notably also be secularized and applied to the maskilic narrative process.[79]

The main reason Perl had to take these stories seriously, though, was their popular appeal; Rabbi Nachman's *Tales* were fantastically popular in Eastern Europe.[80] Perl, the ardent maskil and despiser of

77. This commentary tradition may therefore help illuminate the question of the *Tales'* potential didactic function. Joseph Dan ("Preface" xv) writes that "if there was any didactic purpose to the stories, they should be regarded as an attempt which had failed completely." I believe that the existence of a commentary tradition, both written and oral, side by side with the tales as they existed in Eastern European life, allowed such a didactic function to exist. These tales were not told in a vacuum; they were told, explained, and scrutinized by tellers, listeners, and readers explicitly to find the messages they "knew" to be there. The lessons that these audiences elicited and their relationship to any possible didactic motives of Rabbi Nachman is, of course, another matter.

78. As we will see in the next chapter, the *Tales* even differ in this respect from other contemporary Hasidic works, particularly the *Shivkhei HaBesht*. See Roskies *Bridge* 30 and Joseph Dan, "Preface," in Nachman of Bratslav *Tales* xiii–xix, xvi.

79. See also Green *Tormented Master* 223–224.

80. Rubinstein notes, however, (*Peiluto* 174) that this popular appeal was limited to the *Tales*: many of Rabbi Nachman's other books (including those from which Perl would cite throughout his work) had a select and small circle of readers. In fact, it was certainly possible that Perl's intended Hasidic audience might have first encountered Rabbi Nachman's theoretical literature in Perl's work—where, of course, it had been recontextualized and shaped to fit Perl's maskilic

Hasidism as only a disillusioned follower can be, viewed the book's success as both a horror and an opportunity.[81] Perl seems to have pictured Hasidim as well-meaning but credulous individuals taken in by and swept up in a movement created by the Hasidic rebbes, actively malicious and evil people. He felt it his job to liberate those individuals using any and all weapons at his disposal, including turning their own credulity against them. If the Hasidic tale in general and Rabbi Nachman's *Tales* in particular could be highly successful at propagating Hasidic positions, the same medium could be used to propagate maskilic positions through Perl's composition of a parodic version of the *Tales* with a maskilic slant. In writing the parody, Perl would be following his friend and teacher Lefin's directive, and would hopefully appeal to the traditional audience eager to buy another book of Rabbi Nachman's stories but who would never buy a maskilic work.[82]

To convince the audience that this was an actual work of Rabbi Nachman, however, Perl had to produce a work sufficiently similar to the well-known book not to arouse suspicion, as well as provide a plausible reason for the publication of more stories. After all, Rabbi Nachman had died several years before, and Natan Sternharz, in his introduction to the *Tales*, had not indicated more stories were forthcoming. Perl, learning that Rabbi Nachman had delivered the tales orally and left no posthumous manuscripts, and reading Natan's complaint in his introduction to the *Tales* about defective copies of the

---

purposes. Even the *Tales* were not as familiar to Galician readers as they would have been in other parts of Eastern Europe; because of a Galician ban on the importation of Russian books, these works needed to be smuggled in illegally. Nonetheless, they were important enough to arouse Perl's concern and, significantly, to indicate a direction in which Galician maskilic literary activity could evolve. See also Liberman "Batsiyung" 3–5.

81. Perl seems to have discovered the *Tales* subsequent to his discovery of the *Shivkhei HaBesht*, since the former is not mentioned in his *Über das Wesen der Sekte Chassidim*; see S/W "Introduction" 31. However, it seems clear that, finding the literary form of the *Tales* more suitable for subversion than that of the hagiographic genre, he was immediately drawn to it, writing the parodic tales between the completion of his German essay (Fall 1816) and the completion of the draft of *Megale Temirin* (July 1818). See S/W "Introduction" 32.

82. See S/W "Introduction" 36–41.

Tales appearing by different hands, conceived of an audacious plan to remove this obstacle.

In 1807, Rabbi Nachman, who had contracted tuberculosis, had traveled from his home in the Pale of Settlement in Russia to Lvov in Galicia to see a doctor and stayed there for about eight months.[83] Perl uses this real event as the takeoff point for his fictional parody. His parodic stories are framed by an exchange of letters between a Hasid in Lvov who claims to possess stories told by Rabbi Nachman during his stay there, and a Bratslav Hasid in the Pale of Settlement, who in turn relays the Lvov letters and included stories to Natan himself. In a particularly bold move, Perl creates a letter purportedly from Natan, who himself expresses his approval of the new works.[84]

Perl knew he would need to write in Yiddish, that maskilic bane, in order to convince the world he had "discovered" a new set of texts by Rabbi Nachman, since the stories were originally delivered in Yiddish, and no Bratslav Hasid would have abandoned the holy rabbi's original spoken words. Perl's actual attitude to Yiddish, as we have seen, is ambivalent at best—but if the new work were to be published, it would have to appear in the bilingual format and style of the *Tales*, with a Yiddishized, non-Biblicistic, less textually resonant Hebrew over a contemporary Yiddish.[85]

The rest of this chapter is dedicated to an analysis of one aspect of the resulting parodies, Perl's *Tales and Letters*: Perl's usage of classical Jewish texts within the work in order to fulfill his maskilic goals. As we have said, mimetic considerations forced Perl to limit the number of texts cited to conform to Rabbi Nachman's Hebrew and Yiddish prose

83. See *S/W* "Introduction" 16–18 and Green *Tormented Master* 238–241.

84. See *S/W* "Introduction" 20 on the dangers of imitating an actual historical personage.

85. It is difficult to be definitive about this text, however, collected and printed as Perl's *Maasiyot veigrot* (*Tales and Letters*; see note 14 *supra* for bibliographic details), since it was only discovered in fragments at various times and places, and it is clear that we have only an unfinished draft of the Hebrew text, and what may or may not be a finished draft of the Yiddish text. See *S/W* "Introduction" 11–14, 76 on textual details. On the necessity of linguistic mimesis to satire, see Kurzweil "Al Hasatira" 73.

models; *Megale Temirin*, discussed in the next chapter, is significantly more allusive. Nevertheless, enough citations exist in the various sections of the text to make this approach a powerfully illustrative one.

Perl's parodic text consists of three distinct parts: (1) the frame letters of the Hasidim, which provide the background to the "new" tales of Rabbi Nachman; (2) Perl's completion of a tale left unfinished by Rabbi Nachman, "The Tale of the Lost Princess"; and (3) a related story entirely of Perl's invention, "The Tale of the Lost Prince." The analysis, and the rest of the chapter, are accordingly divided into three corresponding sections.

Perl's Tales and Letters: The Frame Letters

The frame letters between the Hasidim, which provide the exposition and background legitimizing Perl's parodic efforts, also are clear precursors of Perl's epistolary masterpiece *Megale Temirin*. The letters are in Hebrew, the language in which the Hasidim would have written to one another. Biblical phrases and quotations, as well as selections from Rabbi Nachman's work, appear in these letters, though the letters are hardly the Biblicistic mosaics of the earlier Haskala: the citations appear only occasionally, resonant ornaments in a generally non-resonant setting.

In the first letter,[86] for example, intertexts appear from several different strata of Jewish tradition. There are liturgical texts, such as the phrase *elef alfei alafim verivevei revavot* ("thousands of thousands of thousands, tens and tens of thousands") from the Sabbath prayer *Nishmat kol khai*, and the syntactically similar *pil'ei pil'ei plaim* ("wondrous wonder of wonders").[87] There are two phrases of Talmudic provenance, *khaval al deavdin velo mishtakekhin* ("Woe to those who have

86. Reprinted in *S/W* 91–92.

87. All translations in this section are mine unless otherwise noted; note also that though the transliteration here follows the general standard of the *Encyclopaedia Judaica*, these texts were conceived and pronounced in Eastern Ashkenazic Hebrew.

been lost and are no longer present")[88] and *leyadayim mesuavot* ("loath-some hands").[89] And there is one quotation from the Bible, *devar yekar mipaz umipninim* ("a matter dearer than pure gold and rubies").[90] However, these intertexts, the only ones appearing in the entire letter, seem to be used merely as the occasion for a felicitous turn of phrase, rather than as a reference to the source's context as a comment on underlying thematic issues. The texts could also be used for purely anthropological and mimetic purposes: their function is to ape the Hasidic epistolary style so precisely, textual catchphrases and all, that readers would be convinced of their authenticity.

The second letter[91] contains similar usages of Biblical phraseology, such as *uma lanu lavo akhar hamelekh* ("and how can we follow after the king")[92] and *meet hashem hayta hadavar* ("the matter is from God").[93] A more significant intertextual development in the second letter is the discussion concerning Rabbi Natan, which involves a parody of Ha-sidic interpretive methods—a theme increasingly important to Perl in his later work, as we will see in the next chapter. First, Perl has the Hasid remark that Natan is a great name, because, firstly it is palin-dromic (*ntn*), and, secondly, that the last two letters spell *tn* ("give"), a reference to the Biblical passage *ten lekhakham veyakhkem* ("Give to the wise man, and he will become wiser").[94] So far, merely an inter-esting nomenclatural play, though Perl may be castigating the Hasidic practice of offering gifts to the zaddikim in return for their blessings, in which case "*tn*" becomes a symbol of greed and venality.

The Hasid continues, however, to serve as a forum for Perl's mock-ery of the pervasiveness of Kabbala—and its misunderstanding and misapplication—among the Hasidim.[95] The Hasid claims that Rabbi

88. *BT Sanhedrin* 26a.

89. *Mishna Khala* 2:2, *BT Khagiga* 20b, *BT Shabat* 145a.

90. Calqued on Proverbs 3:15 and Proverbs 8:19.

91. Reprinted in *S/W* 95–97.

92. Calqued on Esther 4:11.

93. Calqued on Jeremiah 26:1.

94. Proverbs 9:9.

95. On Perl's attack on Hasidism's embrace of Kabala in *Über das Wesen der Sekte Chassidim,* and the erotic and immoral significance he attaches to it, see Rubinstein "Al mahut" 126–128.

Natan is a *gilgul* (reincarnation) of Natan the Biblical prophet,[96] and that he has been created to serve as a counterweight to Natan of Gaza, the polemicist of Sabbatai Zevi:

> *veyadua shebekhol hadevarim asa hashem yitbarakh ze leumat ze velakhen*
> *neged natan haazati bara et natan han'l, vehu gilgul minatan hanavi,*
> *vegam yesh lo khelek minatan haazati letakana mah shekilkela beet hazot,*
> *veal yedey shenatan haazati gila devarim misitra akhra, hu yegale devarim*
> *misitra dikedusha, lenatan haazati haya azut dikelipa, lakhen yesh lo azut*
> *dikedusha*

And it is known that in all things, the Holy One, Blessed be He, created one thing to correspond to another; and therefore corresponding to Natan of Gaza, he created the above mentioned Natan [Sternhartz], and he is metempsychosed from Natan the prophet, and he also has within himself a part of Natan of Gaza, in order to rectify what he has corrupted at this present time. Because Natan of Gaza has revealed matters from the Other Side, he will reveal things from the Side of Holiness; Natan of Gaza had the audacity of the husk, therefore he [Natan Sternhartz] has the audacity of holiness.[97]

This sentence, filled with kabbalistic terminology, also cleverly links the Hasidic movement to Sabbateanism—the epitome of mysticism and antinomian sentiment run rampant, even claiming, with a straight face, that Natan Sternhartz is in some sense the spiritual successor to the Sabbatean second in command! It is also notable that, at least in draft, Perl feels the need to write an explanatory footnote concerning Natan of Gaza's identity, but allows the reference to Natan the prophet to stand without explication, indicating fairly precisely Perl's particular expectations about what his Hebrew-reading audience did or did not know.[98]

96. On the belief in reincarnation among Hasidism, see Nigal *Hasiporet hakhasidit* 185–203.

97. Perl cites the concept of *azut dikedusha* (the audacity of holiness) from Rabbi Nachman's theoretical work *Likutei Moharan*, though he fails to give a source; Shmeruk and Werses (*S/W* 97) note Perl's later usage of the term in *Bokhen Tsaddik* (38), where he refers to *Likutei Moharan* 41a. For more on *azut dikedusha*, see Green *Tormented Master* 108. On Nathan of Gaza, Sabbateanism, and the Hasidic tale, see Dan *Hasipur* 21–34.

98. This question of audience knowledge, and particularly the differing knowledge of Hebrew- and Yiddish-speaking audiences, has been discussed in previous

The linkage of Hasidic textual and onomastic interpretive schemas to antinomian and even heretical interpretive frameworks is also hinted at in the letter's reference to Rabbi Nachman. The primary allusion to Rabbi Nachman's work is the use of the phrase *tora rakhava . . . meod* ("truly broad learning/Torah"),[99] which seems, superficially, to praise Rabbi Nachman's skill in transmitting and interpreting the actual Torah.[100] However, on a deeper level, the words are twisted: Perl may mean that Rabbi Nachman's interpretations of the Torah are overly wide, extremely broad and incredibly inclusive, allowing interpretations which are, to Perl's eyes, erroneous and even immoral and dangerous. Perl's view of the failure of the Hasidic hermeneutic is further developed throughout the stories and reaches its apex in *Megale Temirin*.

The third letter[101] has very few citations from the classical Jewish canon; still, the letter continues to refer to the superstition and mysticism Perl believes to be present in Hasidism. The phrase *roa mazal* ("bad fate"/"bad astrological fortune"), accompanied by the acronym *shin mem* in parenthesis, standing for *shlim mazelnik* (lit. "the person of bad fortune," referring to the personification of the Evil Impulse),[102] testifies to the irrationalism in the movement Perl wanted so badly to eradicate.

The fourth letter,[103] purportedly written by Natan Sternharz, is strewn with phrases from his own introductions to Rabbi Nachman's works—not merely to the *Tales*, but to the *Likutei Moharan* and the *Likutei Moharan Tanina* as well. Perl ranged far and wide to get as broad a sample of Natan's style as possible in order to make his imita-

---

chapters; it is taken up more directly in the discussion of *Megale Temirin*, where the opportunity exists to directly compare Hebrew and Yiddish versions of the same text, and where both texts feature extensive treatment of classical Jewish intertexts.

99. The phrase is taken from *Kitsur Likutei Moharan* 59a (Mohilev: 1811); see *S/W* 96. Perl also uses it in *Megale Temirin*, Letter 84.

100. Of course, the phrase also refers to the word *toyre* in the Hasidic sense, as in "the teachings of a Zaddik."

101. Reprinted in *S/W* 97–98.

102. See *S/W* 98 and *Likutei Moharan Tanina* 3a (Mohilev: 1809).

103. Reprinted in *S/W* 99–100.

tion that much more convincing. The letter attributed to Natan also includes a wide selection of Biblical and Talmudic references. The very first sentence, dating Natan's receipt of one of the letters by referring to the weekly Torah portion, begins the intertextual motif. Dating by means of the Torah portion was a traditional method in Jewish Eastern Europe, and doing so places the reader into a context and a world shaped by resonant, "Jewish" time. However, none of the earlier or later letters are dated, and the choice of Torah portion to date this one, the portion of *Vayigash*, can hardly be coincidental. The portion (Genesis 44:18–47:27) deals with the second half of the Joseph story, where he reveals himself to his brothers. Perl, a secretive author and latter-day Joseph himself, has chosen a portion that concerns the long-term moral benefits of deception, as well as, quite literally, the revealing of secrets.

This letter marks Perl's most audacious references to his maskilic agenda; hiding behind the sheer amount of quotation and Natan's historicity, he uses some of his most daring, resonant, and barbed references yet. Certainly the Biblical *umaskil al davar yaskil* ("and he who approaches a matter wisely will become wise")[104] and *maskil kaet yidom* ("and one who is wise will for the moment be silent")[105] must be read with a double meaning: superficially they refer to any wise person, the equivalent of the modern phrase "a word to the wise," but on a deeper level, these phrases are Perl's in-joke, his wink to maskilic readers that real wisdom is in maskilic hands. The phrase *etsati uvakashati* ("my advice and my request"),[106] with its implication of the deception Esther perpetrates on both Haman and Ahasuerus, is similarly used here: Perl (in the guise of Natan) asks the Hasidim to provide the "lost stories" of Rabbi Nachman, knowing that these stories will provide a blow to the Hasidic power structure, just as Esther asks Ahasuerus to allow her to invite him and Haman to a banquet, knowing Haman's acceptance will ensure his unmasking and subsequent downfall.

104. Calqued on Proverbs 16:20; original is *maskil al davar yimtsa tov* ("One who approaches a matter wisely will find goodness").

105. Calqued on Amos 5:13; original is *umaskil baet hahi yidom* ("And one who is wise will be silent at that time").

106. Calqued on Esther 5:7; original is *sheelati ubakashati* ("my question and my request").

The Book of Esther is a powerful reference point and touchstone in all of Perl's work. First, of course, there were obvious populist and polemical benefits of using a text highly familiar to the general public, associated as it was with the most joyous festival of the Jewish year. Beyond that, though, the book contains themes familiar and attractive to maskilim: the unmasking of hypocrisy, the defeat of a strong group by a weaker one, and the use of clever deception, to name just three. This letter contains several references to Esther hinting at these ideas. For example, the phrase *veet yekar tiferet gdulato* ("and the honor of the glory of his majesty")[107] is used ostensibly to refer to the glory of Rabbi Nachman, but the reference to Ahasuerus, often considered a fool, seems parodically to undercut the phrase's majesty.

Bearing more directly on Perl's themes in the work, the notion of *venahafokh hu* ("And the order of things will be reversed")[108] is expressed in a series of uses of the same phrase, in a flexible mosaic of Hebrew phrases:

> *velakhen tire shezot hi sakana yoter misakanat nefashot im khas veshalom ehye atsel badavar, velo ekhtov ot ekhad karaui o sheehefokh et haseder khas veshalom al tiftakh peh vekhu[lei]*[109] *ehefokh haolam letohu vavohu.*

> And you will see, therefore, that there is a danger greater than danger to life and limb, if, God forbid, I will delay in this matter or write one letter improperly or reverse the order, God forbid, not to tempt fate, or I will revert the world to formlessness and void.[110]

This notion can obviously be applied to Perl's parodic reversal and subversion of the literary order. Some of these phrases appear in Natan's writings; their juxtaposition, and the additional nuances they thus provide to the learned reader, though, are all Perl's doing.[111]

---

107. Esther 1:4.

108. Esther 9:1.

109. *BT Berakhot* 19a.

110. The last phrase is taken from the liturgy of the High Holy Days, from the section of the Ten Martyrs.

111. Other Biblicistic phrases also appear in the letter: *kegakhalei esh boarim kelapidim* ("like fiery coals burning like torches," Ezekiel 1:13), *akhazuni tsel pakhad* ("the shadow of fear has seized me," calqued on Isaiah 33:14).

Perl makes his maskilic project clearer and clearer as these letters continue. After reprinting Rabbi Nachman's first (unfinished) tale, "The Tale of the Loss of the Prince," Perl has the Hasid from Lvov react:[112]

veamarti ze hayom asa hashem nagila venismekha vo,[113] *ki mi asher lo einayim lir'ot veoznayim lishmoa*,[114] *yavin veyaskil*.[115]

And I said: "This is the day that the Lord has made, let us rejoice and exult in it," for "whoever has eyes to see and ears to hear" "will understand and become enlightened.")

Perl practically says explicitly, in other words, that after reading Rabbi Nachman's words, including Perl's parodic words placed in Rabbi Nachman's mouth, anyone with any sense at all will "see the light" and become a maskil. Also, many of the Biblicisms used in this setting to refer to Rabbi Nachman's stories — *mimekor mayim khayim nav'u* ("they have flowed from a source of living water")[116] and *leshon zahav* ("a golden tongue")[117] — are phrases typically used to describe classic maskilic *melitsa*. These phrases are, of course, used ironically: in maskilic eyes, these stories are hardly worthy of these adulatory characterizations.

The final two frame letters[118] follow the presentation of Perl's parodic tales, and attempt to contribute to the air of authenticity surrounding the entire project by describing a fictional acceptance of the tales within the Hasidic community. The first of these letters follows the previously outlined general format: an occasional use of Biblicistic phrases with even more occasional references to Jewish events or stories. In the final letter, a Hasid encloses the outlines of tales Rabbi Nachman was "supposed" to have told, and asks if the Galician maskilim have the full stories corresponding to these outlines; obviously, this is Perl's effort to legitimize production of future parodic tales. These outlines are even more resonant and allusive than the other frame

112. Letter reprinted in *S/W* 109–111.
113. Psalms 118:24; from the Hallel prayer in the liturgy.
114. Ezekiel 12:2.
115. Possibly calqued on Isaiah 41:20.
116. Jeremiah 2:13.
117. Joshua 7:21; used here in a different context.
118. Reprinted in *S/W* 223–225.

letters; they essentially consist of fragments from particular Biblical passages, notably from Genesis and Isaiah.[119] This approach stems from the previously mentioned Bratslav belief that most of Rabbi Nachman's tales are, among other things, commentaries on specific Biblical texts. As we will see in the next two sections, Perl uses this belief to make powerful parodic points.

Perl's *Tales and Letters*: The "Completion" of "The Tale of the Loss of the Princess"

The frame letters, of course, are merely a device to prepare the reader for what follows: Perl's "completion" of the first tale of Rabbi Nachman's and Perl's own parodic tale.[120] We lack the final versions of these two tales, and we have only Perl's own story in the bilingual version; his completion of "The Tale of the Lost Princess" exists only in Hebrew. Nonetheless, we can see that Perl obediently follows Rabbi Nachman's own work in breaking sharply from the traditional maskilic style of *melitsa*, but, ideologically speaking, expresses standard maskilic positions.

Rabbi Nachman's first tale, "The Tale of the Loss of the Princess," has been widely interpreted as an allegory for the exile of the *shekhina*, the Divine Presence, from the Divine Unity, as well as the exile of Israel from the Divine Presence, and the quest to bring about the messianic era through the unification of the Divine Godhead, which can be achieved by human efforts to achieve ethical perfection.[121] The fact that the story does not end—we are assured of the princess's eventual salvation, but left unaware of the circumstances of that deliverance—is thus intentional; according to this reading, only Divine redemption can bring about this union and end the story. Perl, however, ends the

---

119. Citations include Genesis 32:4, 47:29, and Isaiah 7:3.

120. Perl's "completion" is reprinted in *S/W* 111–117; for his own tale, see *S/W* 117–222.

121. For one such analysis, see Shmeruk *Prokim* 251–255, and his comments there on the Hasidic (and general Jewish) tendency toward allegory when dealing with provocative or challenging canonical material. For other readings of the tale, see Roskies *Bridge* 33–36; *S/W* "Introduction" 21–27; and Dan *Hasipur* 132–141.

story with the wise servant of the king using his rational faculty to triumph over obstacles and rescue the princess, thus turning the story into a vehicle for the Enlightenment notion that perfection is within the grasp of human endeavor.

Befitting a parody of Rabbi Nachman's stories, very little of Perl's own Hebrew text contains resonant intertexts from Biblical or Talmudic sources. There are several exceptions, of course: the occasional Aramaicism or Hebraism which seems to be used for solely linguistic purposes, but seems not to comment thematically on the story, or a final traditional formulation included precisely to give the impression that the story is the traditional work it purports to be.

There are a few notable exceptions, however, where an intertext with important thematic and polemical meaning appears. The first example occurs in the coda at the end of Perl's completion of "The Tale of the Loss of the Princess." In the coda, Perl plays with the Bratslav belief that the tales can be seen as an extended commentary to, or explication of, a given Biblical text. For example, at the end of "The Tale of the Cripple," a note is appended from the earliest traditional version of the *Tales* that *sod hamaase merumaz bekapitl alef shebatehilim* ("the secret behind the tale is hinted at in the first chapter of Psalms").[122] Perl uses the idea of commenting on a traditional text to neatly set up a situation where the Hasidim appear to have been so carried away by their own hermeneutical cleverness that they subvert their own agenda; they are so eager to fit these stories into a traditional framework they ignore the fact that their interpretation, properly explicated, calls for their own destruction.

Perl appends a long coda to his conclusion of the tale where the story is interpreted in terms of two particular chapters of Psalms, with Rabbi Nachman's original story alluding to Psalm 148 and Perl's addition referring to Psalm 104.[123] Both of these Psalms appear in the regular liturgy (the former recited in the daily morning prayer, the latter

122. Cited in *S/W* 116. Another example: "The Tale of the King Who Decreed Conversion" can be read as a running commentary on Psalm 2. Rabbi Nachman memorized the book of Psalms at an early age, and the book clearly remained influential throughout his life. Roskies *Bridge* 39.

123. Perl seems to have originated this interpretation of the story as a commentary on Psalm 148. However, the parallels between the story and the Psalm are certainly telling.

said every Sabbath), so Perl could assume his audience's familiarity with the texts, allowing the satirical interpretation he develops to be understood more widely.

These "commentary" texts, however, at first seem somewhat banal, as they apparently merely illuminate one-to-one correspondences with the story, asserting that certain elements in the story mirror certain elements in the psalm. For example, the mountains, trees, armies, and other objects appearing in the story are all present, according to the commentary, because they serve as narrative analogues to the identical objects mentioned in Psalm 148. In fact, Bratslav Hasidim would have said that, on some level, the story *was* Psalm 148—simply revealed in a different manner.[124] Perhaps Perl does this to show the paucity of actual textual inspiration of the Bratslav stories. Rather than a deep story full of mythic resonances and deep insights into the Jewish condition, in Perl's eyes the story stands revealed as a mechanical rendering of a psalm into a fairy story for the faithful.

However, Perl's reading of the story as an extended commentary on Psalm 148 may also be seen as a reinterpretation of the tale in accordance with his own ideological aims. Perl hopes to change the story from an allegory about Jewish particularism, and Jews' self-designation as the prime actors in achieving Divine perfection and unity, into an allegory about Jews learning from Gentiles and overcoming the excesses and errors of particularism to achieve human and social perfection. It is no wonder, then, that Perl chooses explicitly to cite Psalm 148, a psalm focusing prominently and explicitly on the universal, which reads in part: *haleluhu kol tsvaav . . . malkhei erets vekhol leumim, sarim vekhol shoftei arets, bakhurim vegam betulot, zekenim im nearim. Yehalelu et shem hashem* ("Praise Him, *all* of his hosts . . . kings of the earth and *all* nations, princes and *all* judges of the earth, young men and maidens, old and young, let them praise the name of the Lord.")[125] Perl, in typically maskilic fashion, wishes to stress a universalist approach, hoping to achieve his dreamed-of goal of social integration and acceptance between Jews and non-Jews.

124. The analogues are given precisely by Perl at the end of his "completion" of the story on *S/W* 116–117.

125. Psalms 148:2, 11–13.

At first, Perl's decision to base the two parts of the story on two different psalmic prooftexts seems confusing and polemically counterproductive. If his goal is to perpetuate the illusion that they stemmed from the same writer, he should try to blend the source materials of the two together. There must be a good reason for his citation of the second text, a reason that becomes quite clear as Perl's cleverly deconstructive explication of his own addition to the story unfolds. Perl may well have constructed the conclusion of the tale around the latter Psalm, it fits so neatly—but his reason for doing so becomes clear only at the very end of his explanation, where, as elements from the story continue to correspond to parts of the Psalm, the story's final section is connected to Psalm 104's final passage.

The final section of Perl's "completion" describes a group of people who, through the acquisition of a magic piece of paper, are able to open any doors. They use the magic paper to create a society, portrayed ironically as a wonderful community, but which seems repressive at best. A prominently mentioned aspect of the "ideal society" is, ironically, its tax collectors.[126] The king's tax collectors would call out the phrase *shitla meg lashezt mahir* when they wanted to use their magic to enter people's houses and take their money.[127] The phrase is explained by a simple cypher, where *alef* stands for *lamed,* *bet* stands for *mem,* and so on throughout the Hebrew alphabet. Decoding reveals that the phrase called out is actually the name *Yisroel ben Eliezer Besht*—the Baal Shem Tov, the founder of the Hasidic movement— and that the officers of this repressive society are Hasidim in disguise.

It is these figures, then, these disguised Hasidim, who become the subjects of the final passage of Psalm 104: *yitamu khataim min haaretz ureshaim od einam* ("May the sins be removed from the earth, and let the wicked be no more").[128] The original text, of course, was not vocalized, and thus could read *khotim* (sinners) as easily as *khataim* (sins), perhaps more easily because of the syntactic parallelism with *reshaim* in

126. In this sense, the end of the story once more parallels the Book of Esther, whose last passages describe the taxes levied by Ahasuerus on his provinces. See Esther 10:1.

127. *S/W* 116.

128. Psalms 104:35.

the second clause; as Perl well knew, this (mis)reading was famously enshrined within Talmudic tradition, in a conversation between Rabbi Meir and his wife Beruriah.[129] Perl has used the interpretive schema of Bratslav Hasidism to neatly tighten the noose around its expositors—this Hasidic story has now been interpreted as containing a deeper meaning praying for its own destruction!

Perl's Parodic Tale: "The Tale of the Loss of the Prince"

Perl's story, "The Tale of the Loss of the Prince," is far longer than any of Rabbi Nachman's, and, as befitting a polemical piece, the heroes and villains, the lessons taught, and the story's symbolism are much clearer. Suffice it to say that the story features a poor man in a forest who seems to be a simple man but has actually been teaching Enlightened material to his students all along. The character is even named Markus, that maskilic standard.[130] Since the story is intended to mimic the style of Rabbi Nachman's tales, Perl wrote both Yiddish and Hebrew versions of the story, both of which are extant.

The story's extant versions indicate that its Yiddish version, far more complete than the Hebrew version, was almost certainly written second—a reversal of the creation process of the *Tales*, but similar to Perl's creative process in writing his later *Megale Temirin*, and, indeed, almost all of Perl's Yiddish work, including his 1838 synagogal address.[131] With only one or two exceptions, all the Hebraisms appearing in the Yiddish text of Perl's own parodic tale are words already part of the Yiddish lexicon, and often merely kabbalistic and theological/philosophical terminology, not quotations or phrases.[132]

129. See *BT Berakhot* 10a.
130. See *S/W* 193.
131. See *S/W* "Introduction" 27n23 and Werses "Tsvishn" 162. Claims by earlier literary critics that Perl wrote the Yiddish version of *Megale Temirin* before the Hebrew one have been dismissed in the light of historical and linguistic evidence. For one statement of this earlier position, see Viner 1:9–23, especially 1:14.
132. For a related discussion, see Jeremy Dauber, "Some Notes on Hebraisms in the Yiddish 'Megale Temirin,'" *Zutot* 1:1 (Fall 2001), 180–185.

A few Biblicisms exist: for example, the authorial use of the phrase *vayekhredu meod vayikzu mehasheina verau shehu khalom* ("And they became very frightened, and they awoke from their slumber and saw that it was a dream");[133] the head robber's usage of the phrase *shishim giborim takhat yadi* ("sixty men under my hand");[134] or the usage of the Estherian *ketov lev* ("when [the man's] heart was joyous").[135] Certain of the phrases seem to be used in a more directed fashion, like the phrase *kinat sofrim tarbe khakhma* ("with the zealousness of scribes, wisdom will increase"),[136] where Perl suggests a connection between zealousness and wisdom, implying the necessity for ardent polemics (and polemicists) to spread true wisdom, the wisdom of the Haskala. Perl calls the students who gather together to learn modern material *mitasfim* ("those who are gathered"), a name highly similar to the *Measfim* ("the Gatherers") who founded the influential Prussian maskilic journal *Hameasef*; the phrase is another wink by Perl at those in the know.

One interesting reference Perl employs in his story is the suggestion of the use of immersion in the Dead Sea to remove an enchantment, which, as Werses and Shmeruk point out, has roots in Talmudic references.[137] However, this reference provides a perfect example of the difficulties involved in determining intent and source in questions of intertextuality. Werses and Shmeruk suggest that Perl's inspiration comes from a phrase of Rabbi Nachman's: *veein takana lehaben melekh ki im sheyashlikhu hamekhashef sheasa hakishuf lemayim* ("And there was no salvation for the prince unless the enchanter who put the spell on him throws him into the water").[138]

133. Calqued on Genesis 41:7.

134. Calqued on Song of Songs 3:7.

135. Esther 1:10. See *S/W* 178.

136. *S/W* 188; *BT Bava Batra* 21a.

137. *S/W* 123. See *BT Temura* 4b: *Hamafrish maot lekhataat veneevdu vehikriv khataat takhteihen veakhar kakh nimtseu hamaot yelkhu leyam hamelakh* ("One who sets aside coins to buy a sin-offering, and the coins became lost, and he sacrificed a sin-offering [bought with other coins] in their place, and then the coins were found afterwards, he should take them to the Dead Sea"). See also *BT Bekhorot* 53b, *maot veklei matekhot yolikh leyam hamelakh* ("Money and metal vessels should be taken to the Dead Sea").

138. *Sipurei Maasiyot* (Jerusalem: 1985) 57.

Knowing Perl's love of using Rabbi Nachman's sources to increase the mimetic effect on the reader, this is certainly a reasonable hypothesis; however, other cultural forces may also be operating here, since Rabbi Nachman's phrase, which does not mention the Dead Sea in particular, does not necessarily resonate in the classical Jewish canon. Instead, it may well partake of the general folkloric motif of the power of water to disrupt evil magic. If this text is indeed based on a statement by Rabbi Nachman, it is Perl who "reattaches" it to traditional Jewish categories and texts. Perl's need to restore or retextualize this phrase may once again suggest his concern that Hasidism is alienating itself from normative Judaism, in this case by partaking of non-Jewish superstitions.

The two most important intertexts in Perl's story, however, appear only in the fuller Yiddish version. The story features a zaddik who is supposed to help the king's messengers recover the lost prince, but ends up being a hypocrite, an evil enchanter, and even partially responsible for the prince's kidnapping. This figure clearly represents the Baal Shem Tov; in Perl's original drafts of the Hebrew story, the word Dishpol appears, well known in anti-Hasidic literature as the *gematria* (numerological equivalent) of the Baal Shem Tov's hometown, Miezdybocz.[139] Additionally, textual references from *Shivkhei HaBesht* further corroborating the identification are woven into both the story's Hebrew and Yiddish versions.[140]

On one occasion, the protomaskil speaks about his reasons for opposing the magician/tzaddik, the Beshtian figure. Magic was, of course, representative of the kind of superstition that angered maskilim the most. In the earlier, less developed Hebrew version, he merely states his reason as *ki kishuf hu bevadai ra meod* ("because magic is certainly very bad"). However, in the longer Yiddish version, possibly stemming from Perl's need to legitimate his position to a more devoutly Hasidic, and perhaps more superstitious, audience, he writes: *hob ikh amol gezogt az di toyre hot ongeshribn mekhasheyfo loy sekhaye iz es min*

139. The town of Dishpol and its rebbe figure prominently in Perl's later *Megale Temirin*. Ironically, the figure of the evil enchanter is used in Rabbi Nachman's work to refer to the maskil; see Green *Tormented Master* 109.

140. See notes in *S/W* 168–70 for more details.

hastam a shlekhte zakh ("I once said that it is written in the Torah 'Thou shalt not suffer a witch to live' [Exodus 22:17]—[magic] must be a terrible thing.")[141] Perl has subtly, but distinctly, linked Beshtian Hasidism with the violation of a Biblical commandment—enough to give even ardent supporters pause.

The final reference to a classical text is hidden within the text of an amulet.[142] The amulet, written in a cryptographic script called "angel script" (*malokhim ktav*), explicitly cites Isaiah 43:2, a passage concerning the immunity of the reader (or, in this case, bearer) from harm.[143] The subversiveness of citing the passage becomes clear upon the discovery that the name in the amulet's center is not of God, but rather of the Baal Shem Tov:[144] it is his merit, rather than God's, that serves as the protective agency, thus detheurgizing and profaning the Biblical passage. Perl, using classical texts, again illustrates how Hasidism leads to immoral and sinful conclusions.

There are hardly any other references at all within the Yiddish version to classical texts in a story the length of a short novel.[145] This, as

141. *S/W* 169. Perhaps the Hebrew audience would have been subtly reminded of the commandment by the word *kishuf*, and thus did not need the full textual citation.

142. On amulets through Jewish history and particularly in Hasidism, see Gedaliah Nigal, *Magic, Mysticism, and Hasidism* (London: Jason Aronson Inc., 1994), 123–124.

143. The verse reads: *Ki taavor bamayim itkha ani uvanaharot lo yishtefukha ki telekh bamo esh lo tekhave ulehava lo tevaer bekha* ("If you should pass through water, I will be with you; rivers will not engulf you; if you should walk through fire you will not be burned, and flame will not scorch you"). For a usage of this phrase in Rabbi Nachman's own writing and its links to both travel and to a particularly ideologically difficult statement by Rabbi Nachman (a statement to the effect that he was able to see the Patriarchs whenever he wanted), see Natan Sternhartz, *Khayei Moharan* (Jerusalem: 1976) 5:19. Perhaps Perl meant to refer to this; if so, it was very oblique, since no reference is made in his manuscript to the Hasidic text.

144. See *S/W* 216 for text of the amulet; explanation is on *S/W* 231–232.

145. A possible exception is the usage of the phrase *adoyni hameylekh* ("my master, the king") in the Yiddish version (*S/W* 203), where the analogous Hebrew phrase is only *adoni*. But this seems so minor as to be almost insignificant. The phrase is used again later (*S/W* 208), but we lack the Hebrew version of the story at this point. Another possible exception is the use of the phrase *yom hahu* ("that

previously mentioned, stems from Perl's attempts to achieve mimesis.[146] Still, even the judicious usage of classical texts seen here seems to illustrate his point quite clearly. In reading the story, one is struck by how skillfully Perl has internalized the superficial stylistic aspects of Rabbi Nachman's work without managing to uncover and use its depths. Though his usage of Hebraisms in the Yiddish and a less resonant, flexible idiomatic Hebrew is eerily similar to Rabbi Nachman's, his story sounds little like the Hasidic master's: it lacks the universality, the grandeur, the moral tone. Perhaps Perl sensed this and this is why

---

day"), the eschatological phrase in the *Aleinu* prayer, to refer to the condition of a world free of Hasidim in the future, at the very end of the story (*S/W* 222; original passage from Zechariah 14:9). For other literary comparisons between the Hebrew and Yiddish versions of Perl's tale, such as the expansion or deletion of details, the greater traditionalism in the Yiddish version, the greater emotional range and intensification in the Yiddish, and the addition of dialogue, see *S/W* "Introduction" 77–86.

146. For the sake of impersonation, Perl manages to include many of Rabbi Nachman's major and minor thematic topoi, such as the childless king (S/W 119; from the beginning of "The Tale of the King and the Emperor" (*Sipurei Maasiyot* 12)); the turn to magic when doctors fail (*S/W* 120; seen in "The Tale of the Prince Who Was Made from Precious Stones" (*Sipurei Maasiyot* 57)); the loss of the travellers' way in the forest (*S/W* 131; from "Tale of a Cripple" (*Sipurei Maasiyot* 30)); the destruction of all of the robbers at each others' hands (*S/W* 144; from "Tale of a Cripple" (*Sipurei Maasiyot* 34–35)); note here Shmeruk and Werses' comments about Perl's copying so directly from Rabbi Nachman that he left in a detail of the story that makes no sense in his own story, though it is deleted from the later Yiddish version) and the use of magical or wondrous musical instruments and songs (*S/W* 198; from "Tale of the King's Son and the Maidservant's Son That Were Switched" (*Sipurei Maasiyot* 158)). He also borrows the phrase *peti yaamin lekhol davar* ("A fool will believe anything," Proverbs 14:15), adding the word *sheker* ("false"), using the fairly common contemporary acronymic device of *notarikon* in order to provide the resulting word *fildsh* (see *S/W* 190–191 and note there the reference to *Likutei Moharan Tlitai* 17b and *Sikhot Haran* 103). He also uses certain topoi from *Shivkhei HaBesht* (Hebrew version: Kopust: 1814, critical edition edited by Avraham Rubinstein (Jerusalem: Reuven Mass, 1991); Yiddish version: Korets: 1816, reprinted Jerusalem: 1965) such as invaders despoiling a city (*SB* 1:1 (Rubinstein 39); *S/W* 119), the dream of a feast with mute servants (*SB* 1:4–2:1 (Rubinstein 42–43); *S/W* 131), and the revelation of the common individual as a great man (*SB* 3:4–4:1 (Rubinstein 55); *S/W* 153).

he never published it; a more likely reason is his ambivalence toward Yiddish, even if, as was certainly the case here, its usage was legitimated for polemical purposes. Perl left behind no explanation.

Nonetheless, Perl's discovery of the strategy of parodying Hasidic texts, particularly through the epistolary medium, was clearly the essential step in creating the most important satirical text of the Galician Haskala—*Megale Temirin*.

Seven Joseph Perl: *Megale Temirin*

Introduction: The Shivkhei HaBesht

Perl's parodies of Rabbi Nachman's *Tales* remained unpublished during his lifetime. The second Hasidic book Perl parodied yielded better results for him, however, both in terms of publication success and literary quality: his efforts to parody one of Hasidic literature's seminal texts resulted in one of the most important and influential maskilic works of the nineteenth century. Comparing Perl's published Hebrew masterpiece, *Megale Temirin*, with its then-unknown Yiddish counterpart can substantially illuminate Perl's assumptions about his differentiated audiences, as well as further explicate his general usage of classical Jewish texts for polemic purposes.

Shivkhei HaBesht ("Tales in Praise of the Baal Shem Tov") was first published in Hebrew in Kopust in 1814, then in Yiddish, in response to popular demand, a year later.[1] As the name implies, the book con-

1. The first Yiddish translation of *Shivkhey HaBesht* appears as early as 1815 in Ostrog; this translation, however, is almost certainly based on a different manuscript than the later 1816 Warsaw and 1817 Zolkiev editions of the Yiddish *Shivkhey HaBesht*. See Shmeruk *Prokim* 240–241. For a more detailed discussion of the differing Hebrew and Yiddish versions of *Shivkhey HaBesht*, see Shmeruk, 119n2, 127n21, 128n25 and the sources cited therein, particularly the work of A. Yaari, and Dan Ben-Amos and Jerome Mintz, ed. and trans., *In Praise of the Ba'al Shem Tov: The Earliest Collection of Legends About the Founder of Hasidism* (Northvale, NJ: Jason Aronson Inc., 1993), xvi; Karl Erich Grözinger, "The Source Value of the Basic Rescensions of *Shivhei HaBesht*," in Rapaport-Albert *Hasidism Reappraised* 354–363; Moshe Rosman, *Founder of Hasidism: A Quest for the Historical Ba'al Shem Tov* (Berkeley: University of Calfornia Press, 1996), 147, 260n68; and idem., "Letoldotav shel makor histori," *Zion* 58 (1993), 175–214, esp. 180–183.

sists of a series of stories that purport to describe the birth, life, deeds, teachings, and death of the founder of Hasidism.[2] The largely hagiographic work contains a strong polemical component: a number of stories, for example, concerning doubters who meet the Baal Shem Tov and subsequently become his disciples are obviously intended to diffuse and disarm contemporary readers' analogous doubts and criticisms about the Besht's disciples. The book also contains a homiletic component: several stories offer an interpretation of a Biblical verse, often concretized through narrative events in the tale. This combination of story and text may well have accounted for the book's enormous popularity.

Much scholarly debate surrounds the book's formation and the authenticity of certain of its "realistic" details: after all, the book was first published almost half a century after the death of its primary subject,[3] as opposed to Rabbi Nachman's *Tales*, published less than a decade after the teller's death and even appearing in an edition containing the author's (partial) imprimatur. Clearly, no such approbation is possible with the *Shivkhei HaBesht*.[4] The tales within the book almost certainly circulated orally in Yiddish for some time before the decision to publish them in Hebrew, thus canonizing and legitimating them, was

2. The standard work on the Baal Shem Tov's life is now Moshe Rosman, *Founder of Hasidism*; see particularly 13–26, on the reevaluation of the social status of the *baalei shem* in general, and 159–170 on archival information yielding new information about the Besht's status in the Miedzyboz community. For more material on the Baal Shem Tov's biography and philosophy, see the sources cited in Ben-Amos and Mintz, and Zinberg 8:33–64. On the book's structure, see Shmeruk *Prokim* 214–215.

3. On the historicity of the *Shivkhei HaBesht*, see Rosman *Founder* 143–155 and the sources cited there.

4. For an attempted partial authentication of *Shivkhei HaBesht* based on a long-held Bratslav Hasidic tradition, see Shmeruk *Prokim* 224. Scholarly research has illustrated some of these stories' definitive origins in other times and contexts, with details changed to fit eighteenth- and nineteenth-century Eastern European contexts; see Rosman *Founder* 144–146, 149–150. On one such series of stories, featuring Rabbi Adam Baal Shem, see Khone Shmeruk, "Hasipurim shel Reb Adam Baal Shem vegilguleihem benuskhaot sefer *Shivkhei HaBesht*," in Shmeruk *Sifrut* 119–146.

made.[5] As we will see, these questions of historical authenticity, supported by the existence of various versions of the text, provided grist for Perl's parodic mill.[6]

Linguistically and textually speaking, the Hebrew version of *Shivkhei HaBesht* combines Hebrew words with Yiddish syntactic structures and "is sprinkled with phrases from the Bible, Talmud, and Zohar, usually without any indication of the source or even that they are quotations."[7] The reader of the *Shivkhei HaBesht* is nonetheless far more aware of the book's participation in an intertextual tradition than a reader of Rabbi Nachman's *Tales*. Perl's parody, as we will see, echoes this intertextual approach and itself includes quotations from a wide variety of sources; unlike its subject, though, it will draw attention to many of its quotations, particularly those from Hasidic sources.

As Perl was well aware, *Shivkhei HaBesht* enjoyed great success:[8] in his *Über das Wesen der Sekte Chassidim*, he mentions its five reprintings in two years, and characters in his novels, less restrained than their author was in his political work, marvel at its sales of six, then ten, thousand copies.[9] For Perl, obsessed with the success and failure of his

5. See Shmeruk *Prokim* 217–219, 242, particularly Rabbi Nachman's statement about tales concerning the Baal Shem Tov told in the 1780s and the 1790s. Shmeruk attributes the long delay between circulation and publication to Hasidic ambivalence concerning the publishing of narrative (as opposed to philosophic or exegetical) material. This opposition was even expressed by Rabbi Nachman, who asserted that not every reader would be capable of understanding the hagiographic tales properly, that is, of putting aside the tales' miraculous aspects and focusing on the real spiritual issues contained within. The amount of exegetical material contained in the ostensibly narrative *Shivkhei HaBesht* would strongly seem to confirm this hypothesis.

6. For a critical Hasidic response to *Shivkhei HaBesht*, anticipating this maskilic response, see Shmeruk *Prokim* 234–235 and Viner 1:31–33.

7. Ben-Amos and Mintz xvii–xviii.

8. On *Shivkhei HaBesht*'s popularity, see Liberman "Batsiyung" 5, 9–10, who considers the book's appeal that of a contemporary *Mayse-Bukh*.

9. *Über* 77–78; the former sales figure can be found in *Megale Temirin* (Vienna: Anton Strauss, 1819), Letter 78; the latter in *Bokhen Tsaddik* (Prague: M.J. Landau, 1838), 24.

books and his own goals, such success was a terrifying symptom of the ever-growing power of Hasidism and demanded a response.[10] That response was to differ strongly from that of his pseudo-Hasidic tales, both formalistically and stylistically.

Formal and Historical Details: The Making of *Megale Temirin*

Perl's early parody of Rabbi Nachman's stories aimed for formalistic mimesis, but his *Megale Temirin* does not: insofar as it attacks and parodies *Shivkhei HaBesht*, it does so on very different structural grounds. To show how this is so necessitates a brief review of the book's meta-narrative structure.

Purportedly, *Megale Temirin* is written, or, perhaps, compiled, by a faithful Hasid named Ovadia ben Petakhia.[11] In the book's prologue, Ovadia explains that through miraculous means he has gained the

10. At times, Perl grudgingly admires the Hasidic success, as one polemicist might praise a more successful competitor. For an example, see the selection from Letter 76 of *Megale Temirin* cited in Werses "Iyunim" 395. Perl was not the only figure to attack the *Shivkhei HaBesht*. Documentation exists to the effect that Nachman Krochmal, the noted philosopher of the Galician Haskala, may have given his approval to a parody of the *Shivkhei HaBesht* by Shimshon Bloch Halevi known as *Shivkhei Aleksi*. See Simkha Katz, "Igrot maskilim bignutam shel khasidim," *Mosnayim* 10:2–3 (1940), 266–276.

11. All the names in *Megale Temirin*, of both people and places, have numerological, symbolic, or anagrammatic significance. At the time of the book's publication, keys were passed around in manuscript, revealing the various secrets hidden within. See Shmeruk *Prokim* 290–291; Khone Shmeruk, "Dvarim kehavayatam udvarim shebadimyon be'Megale Temirin' shel Yosef Perl," *Zion* 21 (1956), 92–99; Avraham Rubinstein, "Midrash hashemot shel Yosef Perl," *Tarbiz* 43 (1974), 205–216; and Simkha Katz, "Hosafot lireshimat dfusei Tarnopol," *Kiryat Sefer* 15 (1938), 515–516. The findings up to now have been admirably summarized in Taylor's "Excursus 2: Deciphering the Names," 253–262, and are only briefly touched on here. Shmeruk also notes that the Hasidim, who lacked the key, were often at least partially unaware of Perl's intended satire, though their hostile reaction quite clearly reveals their apprehension of Perl's general intent. In his introduction to *Megale Temirin*, Perl has Ovadia note that the Hasidic names in the book are actually codes

power of invisibility, and he has used that power to gather a collection of actual letters exchanged between Hasidim—naturally, all for Hasidism's greater glory.[12] The book's ironic effect stems from the very different picture the letters provide, Ovadia's editorial attempts to justify the material he has gathered through logical explanation, and, most importantly, through carefully barbed and recontextualized citation (in footnotes) of works written by Hasidim themselves.

One of Perl's most important sources for the structure and design of *Megale Temirin* is his own previous work. In 1816, as mentioned previously, Perl wrote *Über Das Wesen der Sekte Chassidim*, in which he cited Hasidic texts in order to characterize Hasidism as a "lecherous, fanatic, retrogressive movement."[13] This aspect of the book is so important that it appears in the book's subtitle: *aus ihren eigenem Werken gezogen* ("on the basis of their own books"). Perl's work is grounded

---

for other names, though Ovadia's reason for changing the names is presumably different from Perl's:

> For since I knew that due to their great humility they would not agree to inform the world of those deeds which they do in secret, I have therefore copied all of the letters and the stories in the actual language as they appear in the letters that I have in my possession, and I have only made this change, that I did not write down some of the names of people and cities as they appear in my letters, for I said that it might not have been the will of these righteous *tsadikim* to have themselves and their deeds made famous in the world . . . and as a result I hid (*nistarti*) their names and their cities' names, and I wrote them in the hidden language of numerology (*lashon nistar gematria*) and so forth, and the wise/enlightened one will understand (*vehamaskil yavin*). (*Megale Temirin*, Introduction.)

12. Ovadia is also the narrator of Perl's next book, *Bokhen Tsaddik* (see Chapter Six, esp. n. 26). Though Ovadia remains credulous throughout *Megale Temirin*, in *Bokhen Tsaddik*, he, like so many other characters in maskilic literature, becomes an ardent convert to the Haskala. For more on Ovadia and his double role as knowing editor and credulous character, simultaneously disengaged and engaged, see Werses "Iyunim" 396–400, as well as Shmuel Werses, "Shitot hasatira shel Yosef Perl," in his *Sipur veshorsho* (Ramat Gan: Massada, 1971), 9–45, 29–34.

13. Silberschlag 130. On the book's references to various Hasidic works, many of which would later also be cited in *Megale Temirin*, see Rubinstein "Al mahut" 118, 267–269 and Mahler 110–114.

on the assumption that quotation—the usage of textual material—is the most effective means for the assault on Hasidism. Perl's strategy in this light differed from that of most other maskilim, whose critiques of Hasidism generally stemmed from Hasidic life, not Hasidic texts.[14] However, as Perl almost certainly knew, this strategy had worked, at least temporarily, once before. In 1800, Avigdor ben Khayim sent a memorandum filled with quotations from Hasidic texts to the St. Petersburg authorities, which led to the subsequent arrest of the Habad rebbe Shneur Zalman of Lyady.[15] This claim resonates throughout Perl's work and is an important aspect of *Megale Temirin*; notably, one of the most frequently cited books in *Über das Wesen der Sekte Chassidim* is the *Shivkhei HaBesht*.[16]

Perl issued the work anonymously, unwilling to be viewed an informer within the Jewish community; this began a pattern of anonymity that continues through his parodic *Tales* and culminates in *Megale Temirin*. Perl was seemingly often unwilling to face up to the social and political consequences of his literary stances.[17] The book was submitted to the Austrian authorities in 1816 for approval for publication, and rejected. Perl, who like many Austrian maskilim was convinced of the absolutist regime's absolute goodness and its intent and ability to bring about Jewish emancipation, had felt that once the authorities were apprised of Hasidic philosophy and ideology, to say nothing of its practices, they would waste no time in stamping it out root and branch.[18] The government's failure to do so, exemplified by their rejection of Perl's book, compounded by their official reasoning—that their policy of toleration meant they could not privilege any

14. See Werses "Hakhasidut" 101. See also Rubinstein "Peiluto" 171–173, who suggests that *Über das Wesen der Sekte Chassidim* is Perl's way of applying Lefin's directives concerning satire, designed for internal communal use, in an external context.

15. See Zinberg 8:102.

16. On the book's references to the various Hebrew and Yiddish editions of *Shivkhei HaBesht*, see Rubinstein "Al mahut" 264.

17. See discussion in Chapter Six and Taylor "Introduction" xxviii.

18. Perl's attitude toward the government is amply illustrated in its appearance as a *deus ex machina* in *Megale Temirin*; see Kalmanovitsh lxxxv.

particular group or subgroup in the kingdom—must have been particularly crushing for Perl.[19]

Perl seems to have turned that disappointment into a burst of literary creativity, writing *Megale Temirin* almost immediately.[20] The book's title, usually translated as "The Revealer of Secrets," is itself an intertext, describing Joseph's role as a dream interpreter to Pharaoh in Egypt;[21] the suggested image of an elite figure using rationalist wisdom to influence the absolutist authority would certainly have appealed to Perl, and a titular reference to a Biblical figure with the same name as the maskilic author is, as Rubinstein notes, a fairly common maskilic strategy.[22]

The new book itself, revolving around Hasidic efforts to retrieve a Galician German-language *bukh* that has turned the rulers of Eastern Europe against Hasidism, is a fictional adoption of Perl's previous plans; in *Megale Temirin*, the vast majority of the mysterious *bukh*'s readers are non-Jews, in accord with Perl's belief that the battle for Galician Jewish emancipation would be fought and won as much in the non-Jewish sphere as the Jewish one, if not more so.[23] The relationship to Perl's earlier efforts becomes eminently clear when the

19. On the government's refusal to issue the work, see Rubinstein "Al mahut" 270–271.

20. On dating *Megale Temirin* and its relationship to a shorter, no longer extant possible draft called *Megale Sod*, see Shmeruk "Devarim" 98; Rubinstein "Al Mahut" 422–424; and Vaynlez "Yoysef Perl" xxviii.

21. See Genesis 41:46, and *Targum Onkelos ad loc*, who uses a similar phrase to translate the Biblical *tsafnat paaneakh*. Interestingly, this Biblical phrase was the title of another semi-maskilic book published in 1817 by Khaykl Horowitz, a free adaptation and reworking into modern Eastern Yiddish of the German *Kolumbus oder die Entdeckung von Westindien* by J.H. Campe (1798). On Horowitz and his work, see Shmuel Niger, *Dertseylers un romanistn* (New York: CYCO Bikher Farlag, 1946), 25–26; Menashe Unger, "Khaykl Horovitses yikhes-briv," *Filologishe shriftn* 3 (1929), 83–88, 605–606, esp. 84, 605; Kalmanovitsh lxxxixn23; and Jean Baumgarten, "Émancipation et langue yiddish chez les écrivains de la Haskalah," in Hadas-Lebel and Oliel-Grausz 285–298, 285.

22. See also Rubinstein "Midrash hashemot" 206–207 and Taylor 254–255, who notes the Zoharic resonances of the phrase (I:32a), as well as its similarity to several passages from Daniel (2:18, 28, 47) also cited in *SB*.

23. See Rubinstein "Peiluto" 167–168 and Rubinstein "Al mahut" 117. On the book as symbol in nineteenth-century maskilic literature, see Ben-Ami Feingold, "Hasefer vehasifrut kenose besiporet hamaskilit," *Teuda* 5 (1986), 85–100.

bukh turns out to be Perl's *Über das Wesen der Sekte Chassidim*.[24] *Megale Temirin* is Perl's wish-fulfillment fantasy, a fantasy created in the wake of his realization that the government would vary the pace and level of emancipation only as it suited its own purposes, and not for (as Perl perceived it) Jewish communal benefit.[25]

Perl took the idea of quotation from his *Über das Wesen der Sekte Chassidim*; the novel's epistolary structure further developed the form he had used for the frame letters in his parodic *Tales and Letters*. Both those letters and this epistolary novel, though, were almost certainly influenced by French and German rationalist and satiric traditions, themselves often featuring epistolary forms and a combined writer/editor interacting with his reading audience.[26] The epistolary writers and novels that were most likely direct influences include Wieland and Jean Paul, Montesquieu's *Lettres Persanes* and the Marquis d'Argens's *Lettres Juives*;[27] earlier claims that Perl's model was Ulrich von Hutten's 1515 book *Epistolae Obscurorum Virorum* seem to be unfounded, despite the similarities between the corrupt Hebrew of Perl's Hasidim and the corrupt Latin of von Hutten's monks.[28]

There were numerous Jewish influences as well. As mentioned earlier, the work of Mendl Lefin, particularly *Sefer Makhkimat Peti*, was

24. For an overview of the debate over the identification of the *bukh* at the heart of *Megale Temirin*, see Rubinstein "Al mahut" 415–422. Another veiled reference to *Über das Wesen der Sekte Chassidim* may appear in Perl's pseudo-Hasidic tales; a reference is made to a book written about the deeds of the thieves in the story, and the thieves, as discussed earlier, symbolize the Hasidim. See *S/W* 205.

25. A strange episode from Perl's life mirrored his work: Perl himself spent some time searching for a German-language book, this one written by a would-be Jewish messiah, Karl Seyfart. The Austrian authorities wanted Perl to read it and determine if it was harmful to the community. See Klausner 2:290–292. Had this not happened decades after *Megale Temirin*'s publication, one would be tempted to cite this as a major influence on the novel's plot.

26. This relationship was noted as early as 1839 by S.Y. Rapaport in his review of *Bokhen Tsaddik*; see Shmuel Werses "Iyunim" 377ff, particularly n. 4.

27. See Werses "Iyunim" 379 on Galician maskilic familiarity with the *Lettres Juives*.

28. For a statement of this claim, see Nathan Gordon, "Joseph Perl's Megalleh Temirin," *HUCA* (1904), 235–242, 235; for the final word on this bibliographical controversy see Werses "Iyunim" 378.

both strategically and stylistically central to Perl's approach;[29] in fact, Lefin's name actually appears in *Megale Temirin*, numerologically disguised, as the writer of the rabbinical approbation.[30] Another influence was almost certainly the series of twenty anonymous anti-Hasidic letters from around 1814 found in Perl's library in Tarnopol. Written by a traditionalist author, they attempt, by citing classical Talmudic and halakhic sources, to convince the Hasidim that they have left normative rabbinic Judaism.[31]

Perl had also almost certainly seen Isaac Euchel's epistolary collection *Igrot Meshulam ben Uria HaEshtemoi* ("The Letters of Meshulam, the son of Uria the Eshtemite"), originally published in *Hameasef* in 1790.[32] This series of letters, written from the perspective of an innocent outsider, lampooned German Jews not yet subscribing to Enlightenment tenets.[33] Perl was probably also influenced by epistolary traditions popular among Jews in both Eastern and Western Europe, particularly among Hasidim.[34] Perl's awareness of the epistolary form's popularity and his resulting usage of it is illuminated by his later comment in *Bokhen Tsaddik*: "For this reason the author chose to write his book in an epistolary manner, because he knew the ways of our countrymen, that if they see some sort of long article they do not want to take

29. See Chapter Six and Werses "Shitot" 17–18.

30. See Rubinstein "Midrash hashemot" 212.

31. The twenty letters were found in Perl's library in Tarnopol. The text of these letters has been edited and presented in a critical edition by Shmuel Werses, in "Igrot vikuakh genuzot al mahut hakhasidut," *Mekhkerei yerushalayim bemakhshevet yisrael* 13 (1996), 447–493.

32. *Hameasef* 6:38–50, 80–85, 171–176, 245–249.

33. See Werses "Shitot" 11; Michael "Hahaskala" 284–288; and Moshe Pelli, "The Beginning of the Epistolary Genre in Hebrew Enlightenment Literature in Germany: The Alleged Affinity Between Lettres Persanes and 'Igrot Meshulam'," *LBIYB* 24 (1979), 83–103, revised and expanded in *Sugot vesugyot* 28–47.

34. On the Hasidic epistolary tradition, see Taylor "Introduction" xlii; the discussion of the *brivnshteler* (collections of model letters popular in Eastern Europe) in Yudl Mark, "Tsu der geshikhte fun der yidisher literatur-shprakh," in Moshe Shtarkman, ed., *Shloyme Bikel yoyvel-bukh* (New York: Farlag "Matones," 1967), 121–143, 129–132; and the (modern) collection of letters by Hasidic masters, beginning with the Besht, *Sefer Khakhmei Yisrael Besht: Kitvei kodesh mikol*

it at all, only short articles, and they particularly read those like let-ters."[35] As an ideologue, Perl chose a format he knew would appeal to his audience, despite its formalistic difference from the work he was parodying. Additionally, the eighteenth-century justifications for the epistolary form—its allowance for the insertion of philosophical di-gressions, its built-in structure, its possibilities for ironic juxtaposition and numerous perspectives on the same subject, and, most of all, its claim on the audience for truth and believability—must have appealed strongly to Perl.[36]

Perl's use of the epistolary form was influenced by both internal and external sources. Similarly, the voluminous apparatus of footnotes that is one of the most important features of *Megale Temirin* has both Jewish and non-Jewish precursors. Perl's use of extensive and often misleading quotations in footnotes stems from his own earlier work, the Jewish tradition of textual legitimation, and the influence of Wieland, Jean Paul, and D'Argens, who themselves borrowed from Rabelais, Swift, and Sterne. Wieland, for example, also falsely ascribed his own work to other authorities, and his work featured long and narratologically complex introductions. Wieland even regularly uses

---

raboteinuhakedoshim khokhmei yisrael (New York: Ner Tamid Press, 1924). See also Dov Rafel, "Al sifrut haigronut," *Mekhkerei yerushalayim besifrut ivrit* 13 (1992), 119–135.

35. *Bokhen Tsaddik* 31. This said, Perl was probably only partially satisfied with *Megale Temirin*'s reception even among the maskilim, presumably his most faith-ful audience. As Kalmanovitsh remarks (lxxv), "It became a book that everyone talked about, but very few people had the patience to read it through to the end." Perhaps the book's epistolary format encouraged people to read it more selec-tively. See also Werses "Iyunim" 403. In *Bokhen Tsaddik*, characters discuss the success of *Megale Temirin*, and comparing its sales figures to those of Hasidic books, consider it a failure. Only once failure is acknowledged on those terms does Perl change strategies, saying that if his message reaches one person in a thousand, then he has achieved his goal. Werses "Hakhasidut" 94–95. Finally, de-spite its influence, Perl lost money on *Megale Temirin*. Klausner 2:306.

36. See Werses "Iyunim" 378–379 and the writings of Montesquieu cited there. For more discussion on the epistolary genre's benefits for Perl, see Werses "Iyunim" 388.

opponents' quotes against them in order to articulate Enlightenment ideology.[37]

The main purpose of Perl's footnotes is pseudo-apologetic: while purporting to explain Hasidic behavior and philosophy, they actually inextricably connect Hasidic action to the movement's theoretical doctrines. Through selective or over-quotation, the Hasidic texts damn themselves. Additionally, the voluminous footnote apparatus gives the book the appearance of both a scholarly and traditional work.[38] Perl's genius in designing the Hebrew *Megale Temirin* was thus expressed in form as well as content. The Hebrew version bears substantial similarities to a typical Hasidic holy book, a *sefer*, containing a rabbinical approbation, a set of acknowledgments, and a prologue. The footnotes are printed in the "Rashi script," which is standard for additions, references, and commentary often printed on the margins of traditional books,[39] and the method of abbreviated citation is as cramped and insular as any traditionalist might wish for.[40] Perl's efforts at liter-

37. For more on Wieland as the "most important representative of German rationalism" and his effect on the Galician maskilim, particularly through his German translation of Lucian's satires, see Werses "Iyunim" 380–384. Perl almost certainly took his chosen anagram for the city of Brody, "Abderi," from Wieland's work, where it serves as the name of a town known for its foolishness. See also Werses "Shitot" 10–16. For more on Jean Paul, who used footnotes similarly and turned the introduction into an art form, see Werses "Iyunim" 381–382.

38. On the footnotes in *Megale Temirin*, see Werses "Iyunim" 389–394, and "Shitot" 21–28. Footnotes, however, were not particularly common in contemporary Hasidic works; this style owes as much to the developing spirit of *Wissenschaft* among certain Jewish groups as it does to the material it parodies. I am grateful to Dov-Ber Kerler for this suggestion.

39. Additionally, such "Rashi script" was used as *the* font for certain works of specialized rabbinic literature. Perl's choice of "square letters" for the main body of the text may thus be an intentional departure, if he intended the book to pose as one of these works. This is Kalmanovitsh's assumption (lxxi).

40. On the more standard maskilic typography, which was noticeably different with its square Hebrew typeface, expansive layout, small size, and modern punctuation, see Roskies *Bridge* 58. All these comments refer only to the Hebrew version of *Megale Temirin*. Because the Yiddish text remained unpublished in Perl's lifetime, we have little idea how the published version of that text might

ary disguise seem to have met with some success; a fairly common story cited in the secondary literature is that for a time, the Hasidim actually believed *Megale Temirin* to be a Hasidic book.[41]

Megale Temirin: The Anti-*Shivkhei HaBesht*

As previously discussed, Perl wrote *Megale Temirin* in response to the threat he perceived in *Shivkhei HaBesht*'s success. Though various Hasidic texts are cited or referred to throughout *Megale Temirin*, the *Shivkhei HaBesht* is by far the most heavily quoted of all the texts, sometimes explicitly cited,[42] sometimes merely alluded to.[43] Though this essay focuses primarily on the usage of classical Jewish texts, not Hasidic texts, a brief discussion of Perl's treatment of texts from *Shivkhei HaBesht* and how that treatment differs between the Hebrew and Yiddish versions of *Megale Temirin* can serve both as a paradigm and an introduction to the larger discussion.

Perl's book itself indicates the *Shivkhei HaBesht*'s almost universal influence: all the characters in *Megale Temirin* interact based on the mutual assumption that everyone has read the book and will act based on an understanding and appreciation of its content.[44] In fact, characters' desires and behavior are often directly conditioned by the *Shivkhei HaBesht*, such as when a Hasid provides a list of relics he hopes to acquire

---

have looked. The Yiddish version does contain footnote numbers but lacks footnotes, a discrepancy that is discussed later in greater detail.

41. See Lachover 2:14 and Viner 1:46. This may have been a rumor spread by the maskilic community, however; Perl's authorship was public knowledge by 1824 at the latest. See Taylor "Introduction" xxxviii.

42. See, for one of many examples, the citation of *SB* 36:4 (Rubinstein 315) in Letter 60.

43. On one such theme of *Shivkhei HaBesht* alluded to in *Megale Temirin*, that of papers hidden in a rock, see Shmeruk *Sifrut* 133n32.

44. See Werses "Iyunim" 406–408. In fact, the universes of the two books overlap: a number of character names in *Megale Temirin* are taken from the *Shivkhei HaBesht*, though the characters in the former are not necessarily identical to those in the latter. See Werses "Shitot" 36–37.

drawn from various stories in the *Shivkhei HaBesht*. The ridiculousness of the list, Perl hopes, may lead readers to similar conclusions about the book from which the list was culled.[45]

Indeed, while references to *Shivkhei HaBesht* may be ostensibly designed to elicit a sympathetic response from the Hasidic or traditionalist reader, Perl is actually satirizing the public's respect for the book. That respect is so exaggerated, Perl suggests, that it is little more than outright superstition and idolatry: in fact, one character treats the *Shivkhei HaBesht* as a form of amulet, suggesting that the mere recitation of a passage from it will assure another character a comfortable living.[46] In fact, adoration of the book, its stories, and its main character has even reached heretical proportions, as Perl neatly shows in Letter 77, where stories from the *Shivkhei HaBesht* are compared, episode by episode, to stories about Elijah the Prophet. The letter quotes liberally from both the *Shivkhei HaBesht* and the Elijah narrative in 1 and 2 Kings; in all the stories cited, the Besht always emerges superior to Elijah, no matter how violently logic and tradition are tortured to provide such an outcome.[47] In Perl's view, the Hasidim, for the sake of their movement, are willing to de-emphasize and even overturn elements of the traditional canon—a charge that is examined in detail later in the chapter.

All these examples are part of Perl's plan to create not merely an anti-Hasidic book in general, but an anti-hagiography in particular.[48] Perl attempts to produce this anti-hagiography in two ways: by attempting to sketch a historical portrait of the Besht sharply at odds

45. For the lists, see Letters 64 and 67. The citations to *SB* are "helpfully" provided by Perl in the Hebrew version, though not the Yiddish version.

46. This suggestion appears in Letter 47 and is referred to in Letters 48 and 49; in a footnote, Perl cites the source as *SB* 28:3.

47. Citations are provided in the Hebrew but not the Yiddish version; the Biblical texts are translated almost entirely and directly into Yiddish, since Perl wanted to ensure the reader received the full and sustained comparison of the Biblical and Hasidic texts. I discuss Perl's style of translation and his conceptions of differing levels of audience knowledge in greater detail *infra*.

48. On this dynamic, see Ada Rapoport-Albert, "Hagiography with Footnotes: Edifying Tales and the Writing of History in Hasidism," *History and Theory* 27 (1987), 119–159, 130–131. See also Dan *Hasipur* 129–131.

with the saint portrayed in later hagiographic material, and by attacking the historicity of the *Shivkhei HaBesht* itself.

Perl takes aim at the historical figure of the Besht by claiming that the *Shivkhei HaBesht* is an attempt to whitewash a figure that was at best marginal among his contemporaries and at worst morally opprobrious. In the same letter discussed earlier, one of the more progressive characters writes:

> Indeed, our rabbi, the Light, the Rov, the Great Light, Our Teacher Rabbi Elijah, told me and my companions that he had known the Besht well. He told us that in his generation he [the Besht] was like the rest of the wonder-workers and he wasn't even learned but was even more of an insolent man and a swindler than the other wonder-workers of his generation.[49]

Perl is using a staple of "proper" historiographical technique—eyewitness testimony—to counter the pseudo-history of Hasidic hagiography. Even this "historical" account, however, bears traces of literary playfulness: in reasonably citing one of the individuals considered a great opponent to Hasidism, Rabbi Elijah of Vilna (better known as the Vilna Gaon), Perl has also summoned a second Elijah in the letter, a contemporary Elijah to support the prophet under siege by the pro-*Shivkhei HaBesht* characters.

Perl also calls attention to the artificial, hagiographic nature of the *Shivkhei HaBesht* by inventing stories concerning the Besht that he claims were omitted from the book because they cast the Besht in an unfavorable light.[50] Though Perl's attacks on the historical figure of the Besht date back to *Über das Wesen der Sekte Chassidim*, where he writes extensively on the historical figure of the Besht and his "invention," as Perl phrases it, of a philosophy and system of action foreign to Judaism,[51] these attacks reach their apex in *Megale Temirin*.

49. Letter 77, translation Taylor's.

50. For one example, see Letter 57. On the maskilic attack on the historicity of the *Shivkhei HaBesht* in particular and the Hasidic tale as an historical source in general, see Taylor "Introduction" xxxviii–xli; Werses "Iyunim" 402; "Shitot" 34–35; "Hakhasidut" 96–98; and Rubinstein "Al mahut" 119, 130.

51. See *Über* 70–78, esp. 77–78, and Rubinstein "Al mahut" 266–267. Conversely, recent research on Hasidism has emphasized continuities between early

Perl attacks the historicity of *Shivkhei HaBesht* in two different ways. First, he makes much of the book's late issuance. For example, in Letter 77, one character says: "And why didn't they publish the book *Shivkhei HaBesht* while the Besht and his generation were still alive? Why did they wait until the whole generation who knew and saw his deeds and acts had died?"[52] More importantly, Perl calls attention to the fact that several different editions of the book were published, and that changes occur in various motifs between these different versions of the *Shivkhei HaBesht*, particularly between the Hebrew and the Yiddish versions. These changes are a bonanza for Perl: seeking to cast doubt on the material's veracity, he can claim that the discrepancies between the versions imply a less than certain origin of the book's stories.[53]

A section of Perl's Yiddish translation serves to indicate the suspicion cast upon the book as a result:

> "Fine, upon my word," says the arendar, "but what you're telling me here about the Besht, now that was something else. He had the writings of Adam Balshem, and with them he could do whatever he wanted."
>
> "You see, this here already isn't true," says the householder.
>
> "What are you saying isn't true?!" the arendar screamed.
>
> "Just don't scream," the householder replies. "What you're saying—'Rabbi Adam was a balshem'—isn't true."
>
> "Who are you telling this isn't true?!" the villager screams again. "What I read with my own eyes, no one can deny!"
>
> "I know," says the householder, "you read it in the Yiddish Praises of the Besht. Don't get so upset. You must know that the Yiddish Praises of the Besht is only a translation from the Hebrew."
>
> "Indeed," says the arendar, "you're not telling me anything new. I read it right on the title page!"
>
> "Well," says the householder, "you may believe me that in Hebrew it doesn't say anything that Rabbi Adam was a balshem. It was only

Hasidism and normative Judaism. See Moshe J. Rosman, "Social Conflicts in Miedzyboz," in Rapoport-Albert *Hasidism Reappraised* 51–62, 52, 57–59.

52. All translations from the Hebrew and Yiddish *Megale Temirin* are mine unless otherwise noted.

53. On one of the more blatant differences between the versions of *Shivkhei HaBesht*, see Shmeruk *Sifrut* 126–129; see also Rosman *Founder* 155, 264n68.

the one who translated Praises of the Besht who added it on his own."

"What does that mean 'added on his own'?" says the villager. "How can he add something on his own? How does somebody who translates add something of his own?"

"Well, believe me," says the householder, "this wasn't all he did. He added lots of things out of his own head, and lots of things he didn't even include . . . And if it comes to that, I'll show you stories in the Yiddish that don't appear at all in the Hebrew, and many more—maybe ninety—things that are in Hebrew but not in Yiddish, and there are some here that he didn't write at all as they are in Hebrew."[54]

Besides casting doubt on the *Shivkhei HaBesht*'s authenticity, Perl also subtly establishes the primacy of the Hebrew version of the text, perhaps to persuade Yiddish readers to value the *Megale Temirin*'s Hebrew version, even as their lack of Hebrew reading ability "forced" them to read it in Yiddish.[55] In making these points, Perl therefore implicitly attacks the entire traditional educational system, predicated on the assumption that Yiddish meanings/translations cognized by cheder schoolboys or *Tsene-rene* readers are indeed the "intended meaning" of the actual Hebrew or *loshn-koydesh* canonical text. In his introduction, then, Perl alerts the readers to a certain discrepancy with respect to one of their most cherished books, hoping in doing so to alert them to the dangers of a new and different antinomian way of reading—namely, the Hasidic approach.[56]

Perl's introduction thus indicates his recognition—and his desire to spread that recognition to the less literarily conscious Eastern European Jews—that translation is not the yielding of identical material into a more familiar language, and that the "gaps" between nominally identical material in different languages may be significant indeed. Of

54. Translation of Perl's Yiddish introduction taken from Taylor 266–267. The Yiddish introduction does not appear in Perl's collected Yiddish writings; for the Yiddish text, see Katz "Naye materyaln" 557–576.

55. Perl's view of the "primacy" of the Hebrew *Megale Temirin* is discussed in more detail *infra*.

56. An analogous attack on Hasidic oral interpretation is discussed *infra*.

course, gaps can exist in both directions; for example, Perl was certainly aware of, though chooses not to discuss, the oral (Yiddish) sources of the *Shivkhei HaBesht* and must have been conscious of the changes necessary to transform them into their first (Hebrew) printed version. As we will see, Perl's awareness and manipulation of these gaps has important consequences for the differences between the Hebrew and Yiddish versions of his work.

Textual Citation in *Megale Temirin*

Both the Hebrew and Yiddish versions of *Megale Temirin* imitate Hasidic writing in general and the *Shivkhei HaBesht* in particular, especially those sections of the novel purportedly written by Hasidim and not maskilim. As shown later in the chapter, the book is multivocal, moving back and forth between Hasidic and maskilic characters, and the quality of grammatical Hebrew and the levels of textual resonance shift as the writers do.[57] Most of the linguistic and stylistic aspects of this comparison are beyond the scope of this discussion; as in earlier chapters, I limit my focus to Perl's usage of classical Jewish texts.

Textually speaking, *Shivkhei HaBesht* lies between the two standards of Hebrew referentiality discussed in previous chapters. While containing far more quotations and Biblically resonant phrases than Rabbi Nachman's *Tales*, its language is still primarily the "Hasidic" style of Yiddishized and more flexible Hebrew,[58] much freer linguistically than Prussian *melitsa*. *Megale Temirin*, modeled on *Shivkhei HaBesht*, provides the happy stylistic medium Perl had begun to discover in composing his pseudo-Hasidic parodies' frame letters: sufficient resonance and intertextuality to express his traditional maskilic love for

57. See Kalmanovitsh lxxv. Klausner (2:303–304) gives three characteristics of *Megale Temirin* style: (1) blatant grammatical errors; (2) "awful jargonisms" (by which he means the usage of Yiddish syntactic structures and the Hebraicized versions of Yiddish expressions); (3) usage of foreign words. As discussed in the previous chapter, however, one critic's "jargonisms" is another's evidence of linguistic creativity and flexibility; see Kalmanovitsh lxxiv-lxxv.

58. On this term, see Klausner 2:303–306 and Liberman "R[eb] Nakhman" 186–187; compare Kalmanovitsh xcviii–c.

classical Hebrew and to make subtle polemical points, and yet enough flexibility to make the Hebrew more readable and popular. In the Hebrew of Perl's *Megale Temirin*, a complex interplay of various strata of language, of resonance and nonresonance, of Biblicism and secularism, emerges that had yet to appear in any earlier modern Hebrew literature. This final synthesis of Perl's work becomes the stylistic starting point for the later *nusakh Mendele*, which in turn subsequently influenced writers like Bialik and Agnon.[59] Perl, then, was clearly deeply influenced by the very movement he excoriated: he journeys into the Hasidic heart of darkness and does not emerge unscathed. Perl owes at least a partial debt to Hasidism for the many developments in his Hebrew style, to say nothing of his at least partial adoption of Yiddish as a literary language.

Hebrew and Yiddish Versions of *Megale Temirin*

Perl's Yiddish translation of *Megale Temirin* remained unpublished.[60] He may have written the Yiddish version for his own pleasure. Alternatively (and, to my mind, more persuasively) he may have intended it for publication and, at the last minute, decided the personal cost would outweigh the gain of the cause; a calligraphic copy of the Yiddish version in Perl's secretary's hand exists, suggesting Perl viewed the manuscript as ready for publication. Unlike in his parodic *Tales*, Perl's use of Yiddish here is not a matter of structural necessity. It stems, if anything, from ideological necessity: Perl would reach a far greater reading audience writing in Yiddish. As one character remarks

59. Kalmanovitsh (lxxix) notes the sharp differences between this and previous parodies. Earlier parodies discussed secular topics in the elevated language of canonical texts like the liturgy or the Talmud. *Megale Temirin*, however, attempts a more natural Hebrew idiom, to the extent that such existed.

60. Viner (1:45) posits a printed version of the Yiddish *Megale Temirin*, arguing that it no longer exists because the Hasidim bought up and destroyed all copies. Though Perl may have intended to follow the historical path of the *Shivkhei HaBesht*, releasing *Megale Temirin* first in Hebrew and then Yiddish, it seems highly unlikely that he actually did so, considering the lack of any extant record of any such Yiddish publication.

in Perl's introduction to the Yiddish version: "But Yiddish chapbooks, upon my word, we common folk buy as many as we can. Hebrew books are bought by people who don't understand them, but we unfortunates read all the Yiddish chapbooks and have ourselves a real pleasure with them."[61]

A good ideologue like Perl is acutely aware of his audience's knowledge and the capability to understand and interpret references and allusions of any sort, textual or otherwise. When the maskilim wrote in Hebrew, however, they were often more concerned with the preservation of maskilic aesthetic and linguistic principles than maximizing polemic power. The low subscription numbers of *Hameasef*, for example, illustrate that this seminal maskilic journal could not be credibly regarded as an instrument of mass influence.[62] Anything written by a maskil in Yiddish, though, was by definition subordinating the Haskala's aesthetic and literary ideals to the goal of mass appeal.[63]

As a result, Yiddish writings, especially in comparison with Hebrew ones, may serve as guidelines to the *Zeitgeist* of the Eastern European traditional audience Perl was attempting to convince of his own maskilic positions. Our examination of the usage of classical texts in *Megale Temirin*, then, follows two intertwined paths. First, it attempts to examine Perl's usage of these texts in general. Second, in investigating the differing usage of particular texts from one language to the next, it hopes to begin to outline a general picture of audience knowledge, at least as Perl perceived that knowledge.

One major difference between the versions immediately strikes the reader. As mentioned above, Perl's Hebrew version of *Megale Temirin* cites Hasidic texts in frequent and copious footnotes. These footnotes are one of the book's most powerful means of parodying Hasidic doctrine and action. The Yiddish version of *Megale Temirin*, however, lacks these footnotes. On rare occasions, Perl integrates ideas from the

---

61. Translation from Taylor 271.

62. See Alter *Modern* 11.

63. Or, of course, simply acknowledging the aesthetic drive to express themselves in their mother tongue. See Kalmanovitsh lxxxi.

missing Hebrew footnotes into the text of his Yiddish version,[64] but
these are the exceptions that prove the rule.[65]

Perl gives one explanation for this exclusion of a vital portion of the
book in his Yiddish prologue:

> But I must also say this, that a very few things in all—maybe two
> or three from the book itself and something from the Hebrew Pro-
> logue—aren't translated because in Yiddish they can't be expressed.
> In the Hebrew version, there are many footnotes that appear beneath
> [the text]. These too aren't in the Yiddish version because they can't
> be translated into Yiddish. Such things appear in those [Hebrew]
> books that, were they in Yiddish, people would stuff their ears so as
> not to hear them, while the Hebrew-reading public is already used to
> hearing them, because people say them and no one can make sense of
> them anyway. For example, lots of Jews study Zohar and don't know
> what it says there, or they recite *Targum*, *Yoytsres* and *sikhes*, and have
> no idea what they mean. And what's more, if the public knows they'll
> see a footnote here from the *Praises of the Besht* or from *The Tales* and
> won't find this footnote in the Yiddish version of those books, they
> shouldn't be at all surprised because they read here that the Yiddish
> translation of those books isn't accurate and the footnotes from the
> Hebrew version are left out.[66]

Perl's explanation for the lack of footnotes seems sensible. As mentioned above, Hebrew and Yiddish versions of Hasidic texts like the

64. See, for example, Letter 3, immediately preceding footnote 2, and Letter 5,
where an explicit mention of the *Noam Elimelekh* appears in the Yiddish text when
the book's name only appears in a footnote in the Hebrew text.

65. This difference also highlights another important distinction between the
versions: Ovadia's increased unobtrusiveness in the Yiddish version. Since the Hasidic letters are purportedly composed without knowledge of the invisible editor,
without footnotes, his editorial presence shrinks dramatically. On the other hand,
Perl is (at least playfully) more open about his authorship in the Yiddish version. In
both versions of the novel, the Zaliner rebbe's wife is obsessed with jewelry. Perl decides to give the rebbetzin a special affinity for pearls, the Yiddish for which is *perl*,
thus calling attention to his status as author lurking within the text. In the Hebrew
version, however, Perl uses the Hebrew word for pearls, *margaliot*, rendering the
authorial presence less obtrusive. See Letter 80 and 103 for two examples.

66. *Megale Temirin*, Yiddish prologue. Translation from Taylor 273.

Shivkhei HaBesht do differ, sometimes markedly. In *Megale Temirin*, for example, one Hasidic rabbi bemoans the omission of certain stories from a Hasidic printer's Yiddish translation of the Kopust edition of *Shivkhei HaBesht*.[67] Perl, the ideologue, was thus at least partially telling the truth here: he was unwilling to provide his Hasidic opponents with any counter-polemical defenses, claiming Perl got his sources wrong because the Hasidim could not find his citations in their versions.

Perl's description of the Hebrew and Yiddish versions of *Megale Temrin* in this passage is also truthful, by and large: with only two exceptions, the prologue and the citation of classical Jewish texts, almost no narrative differences exist between the two versions.[68] The high degree of similarity between the versions makes these few differences all the more jarring and important, and thus provides the focus for the rest of this chapter.

However, Perl's account fails to explain one phenomenon that has puzzled critics for decades: the preservation of the footnote numbers in the Yiddish version. Perl has already explained the reason for the omission of the footnotes to his audience; the numbers should be omitted as well![69] The numbers' appearance in the calligraphic copy, however, particularly given the changes already made to that version to incorporate other information from the footnotes, implies that they were considered an essential part of the Yiddish version. One possible explanation for maintaining the numbers may illuminate Perl's view of the relationship between the Hebrew and Yiddish versions of *Megale Temirin*.[70]

---

67. Letter 60. See Zeev Gries, "The Hasidic Managing Editor as an Agent of Culture," in Rapoport-Albert *Hasidism Reappraised* 141–155, esp. 151. In Letter 26, the *Shivkhei HaBesht* is simultaneously pictured in both its Hebrew and Yiddish versions, the Hebrew for the man and the Yiddish for his wife. The gender dynamics of Hebrew and Yiddish literature have been briefly discussed in Chapter Two, esp. note 33.

68. Numerous stylistic differences exist, however, that are briefly discussed *infra*.

69. Kalmanovitsh (lxxiin2) discusses the question but does not propose a solution.

70. Of course, these conclusions are necessarily tentative, given that no printed version of the Yiddish *Megale Temirin* exists.

Perl preserved the footnote numbers because *he wanted his Yiddish readers to feel they were missing something*. Despite Perl's efforts to create a Yiddish version of *Megale Temirin* that succeeded independently, he still viewed Yiddish, as we have seen, as a necessary evil at best. This work's ultimate purpose, like all of Perl's other work, was for readers to eventually emancipate themselves from *having* to read *Megale Temirin* in Yiddish. These footnote numbers tantalize the reader with the suggestion that a certain component of the literary experience will be withheld from them until they learn Hebrew. Indeed, the reference to the footnotes in the Yiddish introduction—the claim that the footnotes themselves are not included because they "can't be translated into Yiddish"—can be viewed as a challenge to the Yiddish reader to learn Hebrew in order to read and understand the "complete" *Megale Temirin*. This is true regardless of whether these Yiddish readers are viewed as dupes, reading this as an actual Hasidic book, or proto-maskilim who sympathize with the maskilic cause but have yet to learn Hebrew sufficiently well to read *Megale Temirin* in the Hebrew original.

This approach, in which a Yiddish book is presented as a first step to a Hebrew book and from the latter to a full participation in the Haskala, is asserted even more explicitly later in *Megale Temirin*. In Letter 109, after reading the heretical *bukh* at the novel's center, a maskil turned Hasid compares it (unfavorably) with a long list of heretical books. Despite these books' obvious incomprehensibility to the Yiddish reader, Perl prints the list in full in the Yiddish version. Similarly, Isaac Loebl's anti-Hasidic *Sefer Vikuakh* is explicitly mentioned in Letters 17 and 52 in the Yiddish text only; in the Hebrew, books in general are referred to. Perl does this essentially to provide these readers a definite goal to work toward and a reading list for once their education is complete—an excellent ideological strategy.

However, the paragraph cited above from Perl's Yiddish introduction discusses not merely form, but readership; Perl's characterization of his audience, while partially satiric, is crucial to an understanding of his work. On the simplest level, Perl identifies two distinct audiences for his work: individuals who can read and understand Hebrew texts, and those who, due to a lack of full Hebrew literacy, only read

Yiddish.[71] The former audience, presumably those who might be perusing the Hebrew *Megale Temirin*, can be further subdivided into two audiences, as Perl also suggests: readers whose familiarity with classical Jewish sources allows them a contextual and subversive understanding of their textual usage in Perl's novel, and those who read and recognize the texts without really understanding what they *mean*.

As suggested in previous chapters, maskilic Hebrew works may well have primarily been written for a small group of insiders with excellent textual skills; as a result, these works use classical texts subtly and cleverly, though doing so may admittedly leave less informed readers attempting to understand deeper meanings in the texts confused and ignorant of the works' polemic goals. This dichotomy is also suggested implicitly in Perl's characterization of his Hebrew audience. However, when writing in Yiddish, the maskilim have sacrificed certain maskilic aesthetic and linguistic principles for ideological appeal; thus, their textual usage is also highly polemic and directed to achieve that appeal. As ideologues, they wrote with the understanding that a portion of the Yiddish-reading audience would have only limited textual knowledge, and they therefore could not manipulate classical texts too esoterically and still maintain their polemic effectiveness.

A vivid illustration of this dynamic is provided through the novel's multiple voices—the writers of the letters that constitute the book. Most of the characters, the uneducated Hasidim whose ignorance Perl specifically mocks, can hardly be expected to be self-conscious, ironic, deep users of classical texts. Accordingly, texts quoted and referred to in their letters appear uncomplicatedly, unselfconsciously, and rarely. On the other hand, the maskilic characters, whose full Hebrew literacy enabled them to understand and use classical texts with ease, write letters that use these texts easily, frequently, and playfully. But the maskilic letters, befitting Perl's image of the maskilim as an embattled minority, are few and far between.

71. On audience differentiation, see Chapter Two, esp. notes 24, 33, and 34 and the articles cited there, as well as Shaul Stampfer, "Heder Study, Knowledge of Torah, and the Maintenance of Social Stratification in East European Jewish Society," *Studies in Jewish Education* 3 (1988), 271–289, esp. 277–280.

The Battle of the Books: Dueling Canons

Perl uses classical sources in both the Hebrew and Yiddish *Megale Temirin* to attack Hasidism by portraying it as an antinomian movement. The antinomian critique of Hasidism hardly originates with Perl. It can be seen as early as Solomon Maimon's comments on Hasidism:

> The fact that this sect spread so rapidly, and that the new doctrine met with so much approbation, may be very easily explained. The natural inclination to idleness and a life of speculation on the part of the majority, who from birth are destined to study, the dryness and unfruitfulness of rabbinical studies, the great burden of the ceremonial law which the new doctrine promised to lighten, the tendency to fanaticism and the love of the marvellous, which are nourished by this doctrine—these are sufficient to make this phenomenon intelligible.[72]

However, just as Perl unusually attacked Hasidic text rather than Hasidic life, his antinomian critique of the movement was particularly textual: Hasidism, Perl charges, attempts to deemphasize or ignore the traditional Jewish canon and set up a new canon of Hasidic texts in its place. This was a particularly grave charge at a time when the Eastern European Jewish community was still recovering from divisions caused by Sabbateanism and responding to Frankist attacks.[73]

Perl's interest in this critique is already evident in *Über das Wesen der Sekte Chassidim*, where the already discussed phrase "from *their* own books" both creates and disparages a Hasidic canon. By the time

72. Maimon 17, emphasis mine. See Rivka Schatz-Uffenheimer, *Hasidism as Mysticism: Quietistic Elements in Eighteenth Century Hasidic Thought* (Princeton: Princeton University Press, 1993), 111–143, for a more objective view of the Hasidic approach to Jewish law.

73. Tarnopol maskilim believed Sabbatean books to circulate among Hasidim and that the "R[eb] Adam" cited in the *Shivkhei HaBesht* was a pseudonym for the Sabbatean leader Reb Heshl Tsoref. On this controversy, see Shmeruk *Sifrut* 137–139 and the sources cited there, and Werses *Haskala veshabtaut* 99–124, especially 103–106 on Lefin's charges of Sabbateanism. Several oblique accusations of Sabbateanism appear in *Megale Temirin*, as we will see.

Perl composes *Megale Temirin,* the idea of two canons is fully formulated: the traditional canon of Bible, Talmud, and Midrash,[74] and the "new canon" of recently published Hasidic books. The dozens of citations of Hasidic texts in footnotes throughout the Hebrew version are ample evidence for the existence of this second canon, a canon that Perl charges the Hasidim value at the expense of the first.

For example, in Letter 34, the rebbe at a Hasidic ceremony quotes a formula from the Karaite prayer book, *barukh hamakom shekervani leavodato yitbarakh barukh hu* ("Blessed be God who has brought me close to His service, may He be blessed; blessed is He").[75] The Koliner Rav, in Letter 76, says the Hasidim believe that "their Zaddikim's words are more important than the Torah of Moses."[76] The Zaddik's words are claimed to be more important than the *maase merkava,* the ultimate secrets of metaphysics (Letter 83), and that "every single Zaddik in our generation is greater than the forefathers, than Moses our Teacher, and than God" (Letter 78). Other illustrations abound, often through the use of classical texts. For example, Perl uses the Biblical description of the manna, *tsapikhit bidevash* ("Like wafers made with honey")[77] to describe the food at the rebbe's table, and, in the same letter, puts Moses' words from the episode of the manna, *ad kama meantem lishmoa bekol devari* ("How long have you refused to heed my words"),[78] in the rebbe's mouth to complain about the Hasidim. In all cases, the Hasidim are seen to place themselves above or in the place of canonical figures.

74. This canon, as we have seen, has itself undergone certain interpretive and rationalist changes, or, at the very least, shifts of emphasis, under the aegis of the Haskala. See Chapter Three.

75. Letter 34. See Taylor "Notes" 325–326. It is unclear that Perl or the Hasidim were familiar with the phrase in that context, however.

76. In the Hebrew version of the text, this statement is cited from the *Midot miMoharan* 51:60 in Perl's footnote; the statement, though not the citation, appears in the Yiddish as well.

77. Exodus 16:31. Letter 60. This phrase also appears in the Yiddish. Perferkovitsh (123–124) claims the phrase existed in idiomatic Yiddish as early as the late nineteenth century; however, it is possible that the phrase was a less familiar and more resonant one in Perl's day.

78. Exodus 16:28. This phrase does not appear in the Yiddish version.

To Perl, though, the Hasidim do not merely ignore the first canon; they pervert it, twisting its teachings to support their own heretical and corrupt ideology. Perl himself states this charge clearly in *Bokhen Tsaddik*:

> And behold, the Torah and the words of our sages, may their memory be remembered for a blessing, have already been uprooted from their plain meanings, and there is no passage from the Torah, the Prophets, or the Writings, nor any statement from our sages that they are not able to turn to their own intentions as they desire, as we have seen in *Megale Temirin*.[79]

This hermeneutical, as opposed to canonical, critique is foreshadowed by Maimon's polemic statements:

> I observed that their ingenious exegesis was at bottom false, and, in addition to that, was limited strictly to their own extravagant principles, such as the doctrine of self-annihilation . . . by means of correspondence and spies and a certain knowledge of men, by physiognomy and skillful questions, the superiors were able indirectly to elicit secrets, so that they succeeded with these simple men in obtaining the reputation of inspired prophets.[80]

In *Über Das Wesen der Sekte Chassidim*, Perl had excoriated the Hasidim for, among other crimes, misrepresenting and misinterpreting texts from the classical Jewish canon. He took issue with their often mysticist and esotericist interpretive schemas, complaining that they do not interpret according to the *peshat*, the text's literal meaning.[81] In *Megale Temirin*, Perl combines Maimon's critique with his own to cleverly present himself and the Haskala as the guardians of both the traditional Jewish canon and its traditional interpretation, and thus of traditional Judaism. Throughout *Megale Temirin*, maskilim are presented as actually engaged in study, in contrast to the Hasidim, as we will see. Perl manages simultaneously to present the Hasidim as waging a canonical war and as textually ignorant—a neat bit of polemic twisting on his part.

79. *Bokhen Tsaddik* III. Compare Kurzweil's discussion on 55–85.
80. Maimon 20.
81. See *Über* 113 and David Tamar, "'Kat hakhasidim beeinei Yosef Perl," *Haaretz*, 18 November 1977.

It is only fair to note that while accusing the Hasidim of doing violence to the rabbinic canon's plain meaning, Perl does analogous violence to the Hasidic canon. Though Perl correctly quotes and identifies all of his citations, he certainly edits and decontextualizes them for
his own polemical purposes.[82] And, as we have seen in previous chapters, maskilim also engaged in interpretation and representation of the
classical Jewish canon. Natan Sternhartz's comments about maskilim
are instructive in this regard: "and they wrestle with the entire Torah,
and even more so with the Oral Law, from the words of the Talmud
and the Agadah . . . and it is impossible to argue and to take issue with
them . . . because they pervert the words of the living God and they
find topsy-turvy interpretations of foolishness and nonsense that will
certainly, God forbid, attract school children to these terrible and confused paths . . . "[83]

Regardless, *Megale Temirin* is Perl's opportunity to critique the
Hasidim unanswered, and he does so throughout the book. A first
straightforward example appears in Letter 43, where a Hasid questions the traditional custom of reciting Psalms to effect recovery from
illness. He does so not in the name of modern medical principles,
however, but rather because one should instead recite from the Bible
of the Hasidic canon, the *Shivkhei HaBesht*, instead: *ukvar katav li
khaverai Reb Gedalia meAklev shekol haomro tfilato eino khozeret reikam
kemo tehilim* ("And my friend, Reb Gedalye from Aklev, already wrote
me that anyone who recites (from *Shivkhei HaBesht*), his prayers don't
go unanswered, like with Psalms.") Perl portrays the Hasid as sufficiently impudent to place the new Hasidic book on the same level as a
book of the Bible.

Conversely, Perl presents the maskilim as guardians of the traditional canon. One Hasid disparagingly describes the books surround-

---

82. See Rubinstein "Al mahut" 120, 124–125 and Mahler 43, 48–49, for examples of such disingenuous interpretations by Perl and other maskilim on messianic
issues.

83. *Likutei Halakhot*, (*Hilkhot Pesakh*, law 7), cited in Liberman "R[eb] Nakhman" 185. Note, however, Liberman's sketch of friendly personal relationships between Sternhartz and the maskilim of Uman; see Liberman "R[eb] Nakhman"
173–175.

ing Moyshe Fishls, a maskil: "He just sits in the old house of study, and doesn't have anything there other than a couple of old tractates of the Talmud, the four volumes of the *Shulkhan Arukh*, a *Khovot Halevavot*, and a couple of other such books."[84] The *Shulkhan Arukh* is a standard code of Jewish law, first printed in Venice in 1565; the *Khovot Halevavot* is one of the most important works of medieval Jewish ethics, dating from the late eleventh century, and particularly, though not exclusively, beloved by maskilim. In one sentence, Perl both presents the maskilim as guardians of traditional Jewish law and traditional Jewish morality, and simultaneously condemns the Hasidim for antinomian and morally corrupt tendencies, exemplified by their attacks on these books. In Letter 136, Perl even illustrates one character's "return" from the erroneous path of Hasidism to the "proper" path of the Haskala by having him learn Talmud with commentaries daily.

The existence of two opposing canons, however, is most clearly stated in Letter 15. A prince, having read the mysterious *bukh*, accuses Hasidic leaders of encouraging Hasidim in their books to cheat non-Jews. When one Hasid protests that these comments refer only to ancient idolaters, the prince replies:

> I know . . . that that's what you scoundrels tell us. There's a notice right at the beginning of the *Seyfer HaMides*[85] *like in all the other Jewish books*, but I know perfectly well that *in the Talmud and in other Jewish books* when the word *akum* appears it means only the nations which existed long ago who served idols. I even know *that it says in the Talmud* that Jews should pray for the welfare of the government. *But in your books*, whenever it says (and here he looked once again in the *bukh* and said) *akum, umes, noykhri*, or *goy*, it means us[86] . . . Tell

84. Letter 26. On Torah study in Hasidism, see Schatz-Uffenheimer 310ff.

85. Presumably the *Midot miMoharan* (1810–11), no longer extant, referred to in Perl's appendix. For an extant example of such a notice, see the title page to the 1809 *Likutei Moharan*.

86. For a discussion concerning the reference of "idolaters" to "peoples of classical antiquity," not contemporaries, see *GJH* 1:161 and the discussion of Wolfssohn's *Jeschurun* in Chapter Five. Perl's personal reaction, unsurprisingly near-identical to the prince's, can be found in his *Über das Wesen der Sekte Chassidim*; see *Über* 47, 141 and Rubinstein "Al mahut" 125.

me, I ask of you, why did Rabbi Nachman, in his *Kitsur Likutey Moharan* write that it's a commandment for the tzadik to bribe the *akum*? Does he also mean that the Zaddik should give a bribe to those people who served idols eighteen hundred years ago?[87]

In an elegant paragraph, Perl simultaneously presents the traditional canon he defends as supportive of absolutist authority while Hasidic books are presented as false to both normative interpretations and to the government. Better yet, all this appears in the mouth of the irreproachable (to the Haskala) non-Jewish absolutist authority.

For that matter, the *bukh* itself, Perl's own *Über das Wesen der Sekte Chassidim*, provides another example of the maskilic usage of the traditional canon: in Letter 109, it is described as *umakhzik meod im harabanim veim hagmara* ("strongly support[ing] the rabbis and the Talmud"). Similarly, in Letter 69, when another maskil, Mikhl Kahane, writes a book he claims will reveal the Hasidim to be idol worshippers, a long footnote in the Hebrew version states that the book brings many proofs from the Talmud and the commentators. While the Hasidim look to their own Hasidic rabbis for authority, Perl suggests, the maskilim look to Jewish tradition.

Perl's attack on Hasidic interpretive approaches is also seen in Letter 61, in which a Hasidic rebbe's novellae are described as *vos zenen nokh gor keyn pashtes nisht* (lit. "making no literal sense"). This sentence is a perfect example of the novel's subversive quality; the line is actually written by a Hasid, who *means* to say that the novellae are deep and esoteric, as opposed to simple and straightforward. To the enlightened reader, however, the line simply suggests that the Hasidim

87. Letter 15, Yiddish version, translation and emphasis mine. Note that Taylor's translation, good as it usually is, has erred here (the Hebrew and Yiddish versions are essentially identical): Taylor's translation groups the "other Jewish books" and the Hasidic books together, whereas the prince (and, of course, Perl) clearly means to distinguish the two groups as separate categories, one capable of harmonious reconciliation with the non-Jewish state, the other antithetical to such synthesis. This phenomenon also occurs elsewhere; a discussion of the Hasidic *Toldot Yaakov Yosef* in Letter 54 is also prefaced by the phrase "our books" in both the Hebrew and the Yiddish, and in the Yiddish version, the words *di sforim* ("the books") are also occasionally used to mean Hasidic books. See Letter 141.

are incapable of offering interpretations according to the text's straight-forward and literal meaning. To Perl, the Hasidim have even redefined the very definition of *peshat*, corrupting it into something different and confusing. In Letter 71, referring to a new convert to Hasidism, the Hebrew version says *veyihyeh amud haolam behitkarvuto letorat haemet bivkhinat peshat* ("And he will be a pillar of the world in his ap-proach to the true Torah from a literal perspective"), and the Yid-dish—which can be read here complementarily—says *tsu der emeser toyre nokh undzer shteyger* ("to the true Torah according to our man-ner"). Obviously, the Hasidic definition of *peshat* here differs from the maskilic definition.

Perl attempts not only to provide a negative image of Hasidic in-terpretation, but a positive image of maskilic interpretation. In the Yiddish version of Letter 60, a Hasidic rabbi delivers a sermon against the maskilim, characterizing them as "[l]earners . . . who believe only in the Talmud, the legal authorities, the Tosafists, and in other such commentators, who explain everything in a literal way, and when they come to a place where you can't understand things in the literal way, they say: there must be some sort of a secret here, and what does that matter to us? We don't need to know any secrets." The maskilim, then, are identified in *Megale Temirin* not only with the traditional canon, but also with a literalist and rationalistic approach to interpreting those canonical works in order to preserve and re-present traditional Judaism—the same approach we have seen the maskilim adopt in pre-vious chapters.[88] Perl's playfulness here is also apparent; though the phrase "We don't need to know any secrets" clearly refers to the mask-ilic rejection of mystical or esoterical interpretations, Perl is certainly the sort of individual for whom secrets are crucial.

The context of the rabbi's charge only deepens the satire: the rebbe presents the maskilim as part of an age-long chain of Hasidic detrac-tors: *in itlekhen dor shteyt men af undz oyf* ("In every generation they rise against us"; the Hebrew version, *bekhol dor vador*, is a parodic refer-ence to the phrase in the Passover Hagada). Of course, to the histori-cally minded maskil, the rebbe's claim is absurd: the newly established

88. See, particularly, Chapter Four.

movement of Hasidism could hardly make honest claim to such entrenched status, and, indeed, this statement can be seen as another
satirical thrust at the Hasidic movement's attempts to give itself canonical status by creating works such as the *Shivkhei HaBesht*.

Perl's presentation of the maskilic viewpoint is further developed in
the same sermon, as the rabbi continues: "And they bring themselves
proofs from the Talmud. For example, they ask, 'Is the present generation better?,'[89] and the saying of the Midrash that the Divine Presence
did not rest on Moses in Egypt because he was outside the Holy
Land[90]—they only interpret these statements literally." Perl has this
Hasidic rebbe praise the maskilim with faint damnations. On the
other hand, the Hasidim provide interpretations of the Bible that have
nothing to do with their actual literal or rational explications. To Perl,
the Bible is meaningless for the Hasidim: a floating signifier for them
to remake in their corrupt and superstitious image.[91]

The paragraph cited above features another difference between the
Hebrew and Yiddish versions, significant for our further discussion of
Megale Temirin. In the Yiddish version above, the Hasidic rabbi speaks
of an unspecified "place where you can't understand things in a literal
way." In the Hebrew version, he gives an example of such a place:
ukeshehem magiim leeize plia kemo haagadot shel raba bar bar khana . . .
("And when they come to some miracle like the legends of Raba bar
bar Khana").[92] In omitting the detail from the later Yiddish version,
Perl must have presumed either that the specificity would have been

---

89. Citation from *BT Yevamot* 39b and *BT Khulin* 93b. In these Talmudic passages, the phrase questions the *moral* superiority of the later generations. The Yiddish version, *azoyne mentshn kenen keyn ruekh hakoydesh hobn* ("such people cannot
possess the Holy Spirit"), however, implies Perl is discussing *spiritual* superiority,
and thus the Hebrew passage may refer to a different discussion on this topic in
BT Yoma 9b, which uses similar though not identical language.

90. See *Tankhuma Bo* 5. The Yiddish version explains that Moses here is just an
example; the Divine Presence never rests on anyone outside the Holy Land. For a
fuller discussion of this complex issue, see *Encylopaedia Judaica*, *q.v.* "Shekhina."

91. As previously seen, maskilim opposed such mystical or anti-rationalist interpretations even when not provided by Hasidim. However, for Perl at least, little
distinction is made between the interpretations themselves and their expositors.

92. See *BT Bava Batra* 73a–74a for the collection of legends related by this late
third-century scholar, many of which strain credulity if taken literally.

lost on the less educated Yiddish-speaking audience, or, perhaps, that the audience's greater traditionalism would have meant that their strong belief in these legends made it too dangerous to directly satirize the topic.

As we will see, this brief episode encapsulates the two main factors in Perl's changing usage of citations between the Hebrew and Yiddish versions: a sense of the Yiddish audience's greater traditionalism, and an understanding of their lesser textual familiarity. These criteria function in almost every substantive difference between the two versions' citations of classical texts.

A final example of Perl's process of translating these citations from one language to another ends this section, as well as completing our presentation of Perl's antinomian critique.

One of the most important premises of Jewish jurisprudence is the concept of the constantly declining chain of tradition. In the Hebrew version, Perl has a Hasid cite the seminal text discussing the matter in its original Talmudic language, quoting from a maskil: *vekaasher tzivikhei kamaei, im harishonim bnei adam anu kakhamorim vekhu[lei] veanu ad kama vekama* ("And as our ancestors said, if our forefathers were human beings, we are like donkeys, etc., and how much more so are we").[93] However, the Hasid adds an editorial comment: "That's how he spoke to me. I started shuddering he shouldn't lead me astray too, God forbid!"[94] For Perl's Hasid, this highly normative statement is ultimately heretical with its implication that Hasidic leaders and their works are inferior to earlier rabbinic works.[95]

93. Letter 26; quote is from *BT Shabat* 112b. The full quote reads: "If our forefathers were like sons of angels, then we are human beings, and if our forefathers were human beings, then we are like donkeys, and not like the donkeys of R[abbi] Yosi of Yokeret [following textual emendation] and R[abbi] Pinkhas ben Yair, but actual donkeys." It seems clear why Perl omitted the last section; tales about donkeys who were able to calculate the amount of money placed on their backs (*BT Taanit* 24a) and who refused to eat produce when it was not tithed (*BT Khulin* 7a-b), respectively, might have made it difficult to marshal this text as a bastion of maskilic support.

94. Translation Taylor's.

95. For a more objective analysis of the Hasidic view of this doctrine, see Louis Jacobs, "Hasidism and the Dogma of the Decline of the Generations," in Rapoport-Albert *Hasidism Reappraised* 208–213.

Perl clearly believed his Yiddish readers would have been unfamiliar with the Talmudic text, at least in its actual language, though they may well have been aware of the general concept. However, Perl felt the point was of great ideological importance, and as a result translated the idea into Yiddish, though the new version lacks the conciseness of the original: *undzere kadmoynim hobn shoyn lang gezogt, di shpetere kenen zikh nisht glaykhn tsu di frierdike. Zey hobn shoyn af zikh gezogt, az di frier-dike zenen geven vi di malokhim, zenen zey vi mentshn; un az di frierdike zenen geven mentshn, zenen zey nor vi ayzlen* ("Our ancestors have long said that the later generations cannot be compared to the earlier ones. They have already said concerning this, that if the early ones were like the angels, then they are like people; and if the early ones were people, then they were like donkeys").

In this case, the lack of conciseness owes as much to stylistic considerations as to help the audience to understand the polemical point. However, we will see later cases where Perl feels translation to be unnecessary, where he adds details not in the original version, or where he omits the text altogether; in these cases, Perl's most important consideration seems to be ensuring that powerful ideological points made in the Hebrew version through usage of classical texts do not get lost in the Yiddish version due to the Yiddish readership's lesser familiarity with those texts. Secondarily, Perl was careful in the Yiddish version not to damage his polemical cause by offending Yiddish readers' more traditionalist sensibilities.

In summary, the maskilim are constantly identified as the bearers of an old classical tradition, as opposed to the new textual and ideological revolution of the Hasidim. Hasidism must be eliminated to return to a model of reasonable Judaism that mixes fidelity to tradition with a set of logical principles. Perl's particularly virulent attack on Hasidic antinomianism is understandable in light of the early Haskala's attempt to synthesize its tenets with a genuine commitment to traditional Judaism. It cannot be stressed too strongly that Perl himself, like many of the first-generation maskilim throughout Europe, was a traditional Jew, one who taught Talmud in his school and fired a teacher when it was rumored that smoke emerged from his chimney on the Sabbath.[96] Like Mendelssohn's, his traditionalism seems to have been a matter of honest belief, rather than an instrumental tactic to preserve status as a communal leader, which may be why some of the more heretical maskilim disliked him. A portrait of Perl, hung in his school in Tarnopol, illustrates the contradictions of his life: while wearing the two medals given to him by the Russian and Austrian governments for his work in spreading Enlightenment, he still has the beard and sidecurls of the traditional Jew.[97]

Perl's "antinomian" approach bears within it its own dangers, however. Perl believed in the sanctity of the traditional Jewish book, and believed Hasidic misinterpretation to be destroying that sanctity. Perl engaged in this battle on behalf of rabbinism and what he believed to be an interpretive schema faithful to a proper understanding of rabbinic Judaism. However, once faith in one system of interpretation has been weakened, the satirist's arrows, in some sense, cannot be controlled, and all ideologies, all systems of interpretation, are rendered equally suspect.[98] In saving rabbinism from the evils of Hasidism, Perl has introduced forces such as modern literary and historical criticism into the system and, in doing so, has deeply and dangerously undermined rabbinism as well. It is as unsurprising that Perl himself was a traditionalist as it is that some of his successors were not.

The Texts Themselves

Referentiality and Transferability

As I have briefly suggested, the best test of whether or not Perl translates or transfers materials from the Hebrew to the Yiddish is how strongly it supports Perl's ideological arguments, even if the material seems awkward in the Yiddish version because of the Hebraic nature of certain wordplay or assumptions of the Yiddish-speaking audience's ignorance. In such cases, Perl nonetheless makes great efforts to render

96. Klausner 2:282, 287.

97. His beard appears to be trimmed, however. The picture is reprinted as the frontispiece to *Yoysef Perl's yidishe ksovim*.

98. See Kurzweil 74–79.

the material intelligible to the Yiddish reader. Parts of the Hebrew narrative, however, which are felicitous, thematic, clever, or graceful are not necessarily translated if they do not "work" in the Yiddish version. This results from Perl's genuine sensibilities as a Yiddish stylist: if the material does not serve an ideological purpose, then Perl prefers to use a flexible and natural Yiddish idiom over an awkward Biblicistic phrase.

The remainder of the chapter is divided into two main sections. The first section focuses on canonical material not transferred from the Hebrew to the Yiddish version; the second on material appearing in both versions. Within these sections, discussion of the texts are divided into thematic categories. Hopefully, these divisions will lead to a greater understanding both of Perl's textual strategies and of his perceptions of his two audiences.

Non-Transferred Material

Felicitous phrasing: a critical introduction

Notwithstanding his ultimate ideological aims, Perl put great effort into producing a Yiddish version of *Megale Temirin* of high literary quality and excellent contemporary style. Important scholarly work has been done on the stylistic aspects of the Yiddish version and on the stylistic differences between the *Megale Temirin's* Hebrew and Yiddish versions. Though these studies focus primarily on the versions' differing linguistic attributes rather than their respective places in intellectual history and the clues they give to understanding their various audiences, the conclusions they reach are significant and worth briefly reviewing here, as they implicitly focus on one type of material derived from classical texts *not* transferred from the Hebrew to the Yiddish version of the novel.

Shmuel Werses suggests that though *Megale Temirin* was originally written in Hebrew and only subsequently translated into Yiddish, Perl's process of Hebrew composition included producing a mental template of the book in Yiddish that he simultaneously translated into Hebrew. Subsequently, Perl translated the Hebrew *Megale Temirin* back into Yiddish for the second version.[99] Werses bases this thesis on

99. Werses "Shitot" 80.

Zelig Kalmanovitsh's 1937 introduction to Perl's Yiddish writings, which advances the notion of a spoken Hebrew based on Yiddish syntax and cognition; Kalmanovitch coins the term *folklorishe hebreyish* ("folkloric Hebrew") to describe it. Werses follows Kalmanovitsh's approach in a number of his comments on comparative stylistics of the Hebrew and Yiddish versions, noting the Yiddish text's greater emotional intensity compared to the Hebrew, boasting increased superlatives, and emphasizing greater levels of action and motion.[100] The Yiddish removes the sense of emotional distance created by the Hebrew, which, framed in a generally unspoken language, was unable to transcend that cognitive gap and allow full identification with the material.[101] Perl also expands passages and uses more dialogues in the Yiddish version in order to create a more realistic sensibility.[102]

Werses' and Kalmanovitsh's claims seem essentially correct and explain many of the changes in phraseology between the Hebrew and the Yiddish versions—as long as the effect Perl hoped to achieve was stylistic, not ideological. Numerous cases seem to exist where Perl sought an interesting and euphonious version of a fundamentally Yiddish phrase while constructing his Hebrew work, and a particular Biblical phrase sounded felicitous—the remnants of the love of *melitsa* common to all early maskilic writers. In the Yiddish version, he simply returned to the Yiddish phrase in his "mental template," since his

100. This is evident, for example, in passages ecstatically praising the rebbe. Kalmanovitsh gives five strategies of translation: (1) simple translation, illustrating how the Hebrew is built on the Yiddish basis; (2) the "overformation of a Yiddish style"—using the richer Yiddish to expand and intensify, particularly ironic effects; (3) stylistically strengthening sentiment expressed in the Hebrew; (4) explanatory (*ayntaytshndike*) translation, where Kalmanovitsh discusses only the expansion of the Yiddish as a translation to Biblical passages cited (this will be discussed in much greater detail *infra*); (5) changing and reversing sentence order. See Kalmanovitsh xcix–cvii for these categories and examples. Werses "Milashon" 65–68.

101. See Werses "Milashon" 62–65.

102. Werses "Milashon" 79. Of course, satirical points based on the "corrupt" Hebrew of the Hasidim were removed in the Yiddish version. Werses "Milashon" 62. Kalmanovitsh also ventures into dialectology, though simultaneously noting Perl's movement toward a more modern "literary" or "standard" Yiddish. See Kalmanovitsh lxxxix–xciii, xcviii.

considerations in employing the original textual citation were stylistic, not ideological, ones.[103]

For example, though the phrase *bar enosh* ("son of man") is a Biblical text (Daniel 7:13), it seems to appear in the Hebrew text only because Perl needed a good way to translate the Yiddish *a mentsh* ("a man"). Similarly, in Letter 3, the Hebrew *ad lev hashamayim* (lit. "to the heart of heaven") is used to indicate the amount of heresy present in a set of questions a group of non-Jewish officials who have read the *bukh* ask a Hasid. An overzealous exegete, noting that the phrase comes from Deuteronomy 4:11, where Moses recapitulates the past forty years' history, might think Perl is parodying the Sinaitic revelation. This seems unlikely; rather, Perl probably wanted a Hebrew verse that gave the sense of the idiomatic Yiddish *biz unter dem himl*, and found this one.[104] A third example is the Yiddish phrase *gezunt un shtark* ("strong and healthy"), which is the translation of the Hebrew phrase *bari ulam* ("and their body is sound").[105] The esotericism of the Hebrew phrase and the commonness of the Yiddish phrase suggest that the former was sought out as a Hebraic analogue to the latter. In all these cases, needless to say, the classical texts are not maintained in the Yiddish version.

Further proof of Werses's and Kalmanovitsh's thesis is that certain common Yiddish phrases are usually analogous to certain Biblical verse fragments, though the verses themselves seem to have little if any additional ideological or polemical function. One of the most prominent examples is the Yiddish *hot mikh a tsiternish ongekhapt* ("trembling seized me"), which appears several times and is the analogue of the phrase *ak-*

103. On the Yiddishized Hebrew of the Hebrew version of *Megale Temirin*, see Kalmanovitsh xcix–c.

104. This is the analogous phrase in the Yiddish translation. Other, more idiomatic Yiddish phrases include *biz in himl arayn* and *[loybn emetsn] in himl arayn*. For that matter, the phrase *ad lev hashamayim* itself seems to have been extant in idiomatic Yiddish (see Perferkovitsh 215; Weinreich 3:233; Golomb 286; Spivak and Yehoyesh 201; Shteynberg 210). Why these phrases were not used is a mystery; perhaps they were less familiar or Perl simply preferred them less. I am grateful to Dr. Dov-Ber Kerler for this suggestion.

105. Letter 57; Psalms 73:4. See also Letter 131, where it is translated as *gezunt gevorn* (lit. "became healthy"; i.e., "recuperated").

hazuni reada, a close equivalent to Psalms 48:7—the Psalm recited by traditional Jews every Monday.[106] We would not wish to hold Perl to a foolish consistency, however; in Letter 54, the phrase *akhazuni reada* is translated in the Yiddish as *hot unter mir ongehoybn hent un fis tsu tsitern* ("I began to tremble from head to foot"), and in Letter 26, the Yiddish phrase appears in the Hebrew as *palatsut akhazatani* ("shuddering seized me"), a calque from Job 21:6.[107] This "inconsistency" results from Perl's activity as writer and literary stylist; he translates creatively and idiomatically according to stylistic sensitivity in either language.

Werses, following his style-based approach, claims that many Talmudic passages used descriptively in Hebrew are changed into more idiomatic and realistic ones in Yiddish.[108] This formulation is correct, but requires a change in emphasis: it is precisely and only those Biblical and Talmudic passages used for merely felicitous, not for polemical, purposes that are changed, since Perl is always concerned about his Yiddish audience's knowledge level.[109] Werses notes that Perl fills in certain narrative gaps in the Yiddish version, not expecting his Yiddish reader to be able or willing to do so.[110] Werses's work, however, can be built upon to address the more complex issue of the *cognitive* gaps in the various readerships raised by esoteric and complex allusions.

Felicitous phrasing and multivocality

This phenomenon of "felicitous phrasing" is particularly evident, perhaps unsurprisingly, in maskilic letters. Perl has subtly drawn his characters to speak in different ways befitting their backgrounds, and

106. Though a closer—though still not identical—version of this phrase appears in Isaiah 33:14, I believe the verse from Psalms is more resonant because of its prominent appearance in the liturgy. See Letters 1, 35, 58, 94.

107. For the verbal form *akhazatani*, however, see Psalms 119:53.

108. Werses "Milashon" 69–70, 76–77.

109. The Talmudic example Werses cites, an Aramaic quote from *BT Shabat* 10a, is a prime example of Talmudic language used for purely literary purposes. See Letter 40.

110. Werses "Milashon" 73–74. Though Werses does write ("Milashon" 70) that Perl excised or shortened certain passages because Yiddish readers might be unfamiliar with them, he seems to view this as a minor aspect of the translation, and does not relate it to the general maskilic polemical project.

maskilim are, of course, more enamored with classical texts and use them more frequently for the purposes of graceful expression in their writing than their Hasidic counterparts do.

The maskil Reb Moyshe Fishls, in his first letter (Letter 7), writing of his good fortune in being able to study Torah for ten years in his father-in-law's house, refers to Psalms 27:4, *rak shivti beveit hashem veyehi ratson sheyihye kol yemei khayai* ("May I simply be able to reside in the house of God, and may it be His will that I remain there all the days of my life.") The passage is a well-known part of the liturgy, recited throughout the month preceding Rosh Hashana, and gracefully expresses a noble sentiment. It is possible that Perl intends the reader to take advantage of the phrase's context for thematic reasons—to hint, for example, that the forthcoming period in Moyshe Fishls's life will be a critical one of penitence and judgment—but the phrase is more likely employed simply to illustrate Moyshe Fishls's familiarity with the Bible. It is hardly a surprise, then, that the phrase is eliminated in the Yiddish version, replaced with the simple *un zits nor in besmedresh* ("And simply sit in the house of study").

This strategy is not entirely limited to maskilic writers, however: the Hasidic respondent to Reb Moyshe's letter, in Letter 13, uses the same strategy of felicitous citation. Punning on Moyshe's name, the writer, tweaking him for his tardiness in responding, parodies Israel's complaints about another Moses immediately before constructing the Golden Calf: *hinei ze Moshe haish lo yadati me haya lo* ("And this person Moses, I don't know what's become of him").[111] Perl may intend to remind the readers of contextual circumstances, hinting, for example, that Moyshe's maskilic actions will be misunderstood by ungrateful and misguided Hasidim, as are those of the Biblical Moses. However, it is far more likely that Perl is simply illustrating the writer's playfulness in finding a Biblical phrase that, when misapplied, speaks perfectly to the situation. Since the phrase has little if any polemic value, it is hardly surprising that it vanishes in the Yiddish version, which simply reads *zeyer a lange tsayt iz shoyn avek, az ikh hob fun dir nisht gehert un hob nisht gevust vos mit dir tut zikh* ("A great deal of time has

---

111. Reference is to Exodus 32:1.

passed in which I haven't heard from you and haven't known what's going on with you").

Perl seems to apply the criterion of polemic value even when the Biblical citations seem integral to the letter's construction; regardless of their stylistic centrality, if they are not ideologically significant, they are not transferred. Letter 68 may be the most Biblicistic letter of the entire novel, containing references to Proverbs 19:24; Ecclesiastes 1:9; 1 Kings 11:4; 2 Samuel 14:19; Isaiah 14:5 and 41:10; Job 28:17, 28:19, and 41:21; Jeremiah 23:24; and Ethics of the Fathers 1:6. All these citations seem to be used for stylistic purposes. Not a single one appears in the Yiddish.[112] Letter 63, the letter of the Koliner Rov to the Hasidim, contains references to the Psalms, Exodus, and Ruth. As befitting citations used for stylistic purposes, they occur most frequently at the letter's highly stylized beginning.[113] Unsurprisingly, they too are absent from the Yiddish version.

While most of the felicitous citations employed by Perl (and his characters) are Biblical, numerous Talmudic phrases are similarly cited and are transferred or not transferred based on identical criteria. In Letter 1, a Hasid wishes to "push away melancholy with both hands"; the reference to *BT Sanhedrin* 107b disappears in the Yiddish. Similarly, in Letter 14, one Hasid "never leaves the side of another." The phrase used, *lo zaza yado miyado*, calqued on *BT Ketuvot* 27b, seems merely expressive, and is thus replaced by the idiomatic and nonallusive Yiddish phrase *un zol im nisht optretn af eyn oygnblik* ("and would not separate from him for the [duration of a] blink of an eye"). In Letter 43, a Hasid uses the Talmudic phrase *ulai ukhal lavo lesof daato* ("perhaps I may discover what he intends"), taken from *BT Menakhot* 4a; the Yiddish *un vel gevor vern vos in im tut zikh* ("and I'll find out what's up with him") makes no such reference.

These last examples particularly illustrate the problem with examining the phenomenon of felicitous phrasing: simply because a Hebrew phrase is identifiable with a phrase in the rabbinic canon does not mean

112. See Letters 76 and 118 for similar phenomena.

113. References are to Exodus 25:37, Psalms 119:14, 120:3, Ruth 1:17, and Genesis 24:50.

its usage intentionally and intertextually refers to that canonical phrase. In fact, the phrase may have become part of the general lexicon and is thus used non-referentially, even among classically minded maskilim. The rest of this chapter accordingly focuses on intertexts that seem particularly selected by Perl for thematic or polemical effect, not merely for linguistic felicity.

In-jokes

In the Hebrew version of *Megale Temirin*, Perl often employs classical canonical references that can be understood to possess polemical effect. According to our previously established criteria, Perl should transfer these polemical references to the Yiddish version. However, he occasionally does not do so, necessitating a slight modification of our criteria: despite a passage's ideological effect, Perl will not transfer the reference if it (1) is tangential to the passage's narrative or general satirical thrust; (2) is sufficiently subtle that it would take a great deal of explanation; or (3) relies on not only the recognition, but the contextual understanding of a particular Hebrew phrase not in the general lexicon of the average Yiddish speaker.

An example of this can be seen in the first sentence of the first letter, which, in Yiddish, reads *nekhtn nokh mayrev hob ikh mikh bam rebn zol lebn farzoymt un hob tsugehert zayne tsuker-zise verter* ("Yesterday after evening prayers I stayed by the rebbe, he should live long, and listened to his sugar-sweet words"). In the Hebrew version, Perl uses the Biblical phrase *hametukim kidvash venofet tsufim* ("as sweet as honey or the honeycomb").[114] That Biblical phrase would have at least sounded familiar to most Jews; not only was the recitation of Psalms common among traditional Jews, but Psalms 19 formed part of the Sabbath morning liturgy and would have been recited weekly by most of the book's readers, regardless of which version they were reading. However, the latter part of the verse, at the very least, was not a part of the *loshn-koydesh* component of Yiddish,[115] and the possibility existed that

114. Psalms 19:11.

115. On the first part of the verse, see Chapter Five. See Weinreich's note (3:233) on the surprisingly small number of stock Yiddish phrases actually drawn from Psalms despite its frequent recitation among traditional Jews.

the Yiddish audience would fail to understand the words' meaning.

More to the point, though, the citation's real import was far more complex and subtle. Perl's ideal Hebrew audience, an audience of educated Jews or of maskilim, would remember that in Psalms, the subject of the phrase was God's laws, and might find the Hasid's use of the same phrase to refer to the rebbe's speech ironic, at the very least. That textually knowledgeable audience might also remember the phrase's appearance in the *Shivkhei HaBesht,* in a story where the Hasidic rebbe Nachman of Kosov tells a group of worshippers who object to his differing from their liturgical custom, "Who says that the fathers and forefathers are in paradise?"[116] For Perl, Nachman of Kosov's comment, and the story as a whole, perfectly illustrate Hasidic arrogance and antinomianism; it also exemplifies the unintended internal subversion Perl hoped to echo in his own work, since the actual story in *Shivkhei HaBesht* itself militates against Hasidism.[117] In short, the very first intertext, when explicated, bears within it Perl's strategic and satirical goals for the entire book.

However, much of the Yiddish-speaking audience would presumably have been unable to follow these subtleties. Perl therefore chooses to use an idiomatic and colorful Yiddish phrase rather than a Hebrew one whose import would be largely lost on his reading audience. The ideological point here is not sufficiently pressing for Perl to take the great pains that would be necessary to stress it.

In the Hebrew version of the same letter, Perl has a Hasid refer to Hasidim by the Biblical phrase *anshei shlomeinu,* a name the Hasidim used for themselves.[118] For the educated maskilic reader, though, the name is deeply ironic because the chapter of Psalms from which the Hasidim have drawn their name begins with the phrase *ashrei maskil* ("Happy is the maskil")![119] However, Perl may have believed this

116. *SB* 16:4 (Rubinstein 181–182).

117. In the story, Nachman is only rehabilitated through a *deus ex machina* — the arrival of another rebbe who strongly defends his actions.

118. The phrase, taken from Psalms 41:10, appears at least as early as Natan Sternhartz's introduction to the first edition of *Sipurei Maasiot* (*S/W* 93).

119. On one translator's sensitivity to other old Hebrew words that gained a clearly new connotation (such as *tsadik* and *khasid*), see Shmeruk's comments on Mendl Lefin's translation of Ecclesiastes and Proverbs in *Sifrut* 180–183.

contextual connection to be beyond the capacity of the Yiddish readership, and so the reference accordingly disappears in the Yiddish version.

Biblical materials

Introduction. On numerous occasions in *Megale Temirin*, the book's
general satirical thrust is heightened through Perl's suggestion and
parody of a Biblical archetype or narrative. This often takes place quite
subtly in the Hebrew version, since there the use of a single carefully
chosen word can be sufficient to throw the entire narrative episode
into new parodic relief for the educated reader familiar with not only
the Biblical narrative, but also with the interpretive material from the
Jewish exegetical tradition surrounding it. In many cases, though,
these Biblical images are merely icing on the satirical cake, and an extensive effort to explain them would detract from the story's narrative
thrust. When this is the case, the words or phrases in question are
omitted in the Yiddish version. However, in cases where the reference
affects the general thrust of the story or makes a larger thematic point,
it is indeed transferred, as we will see. Perl often incorporates one explicit Hebrew reference near the beginning of the novel in the Yiddish
version to alert Yiddish readers to a general archetype or narrative analogue employed, but the subsequent, subtler references from the Hebrew version remain untransferred.

In Letter 8, one Hasid tells another of his interception of a potentially incriminating letter. The second Hasid's reaction is described in
the Hebrew version as *vayipol al tsavari venashak oti elef peamim* ("And
he fell upon my neck and kissed me a thousand times"). The phrasing
clearly refers to Genesis 33:4, when Esau warmly greets Jacob after
years apart. A prominent strain in Jewish exegesis, however, interprets
these actions of Esau's as hypocritical masks for attempted assault—a
useful archetype for Perl's Hasidim, who are at base false and hypocritical.[120] Educated readers and maskilim would certainly have been
aware of this image; at the very least, they would have recognized the
reference to Esau, which was certainly uncomplimentary.

The Yiddish reader, however, may have been less familiar with the
story; the passage itself only is read once a year in synagogue, and the

---

120. See, for example, Genesis Rabbah 78:9.

exegetical reading does not appear in the *Tsene rene*.[121] Perl may have felt the reference too obscure for certain identification without further explanation for his Yiddish readership, and too tangential to the narrative to warrant further explanation. The Yiddish, therefore, merely reads *iz er mir arum gefaln arum dem haldz, un hot mikh ongehoybn tsu kushn on an ek* ("he fell around my neck, and began to kiss me endlessly"). While this may suggest some of the Biblical story's resonances, they are much harder to find.

Similarly, in Letter 16, a Hasid declares his obligation to cast himself into a *kivshan haesh*, a fiery furnace, for his rebbe. The phrase refers to either (or both) the Biblical story of Khanania, Mishael, and Azaria,[122] or the midrashic story about Abraham and Nimrod.[123] In both cases, the encounters with the fiery furnace stemmed from a refusal to accept any form of external human autonomy, only Divine word or rule; here, however, the antinomian rebbe has taken over the Divine role. The Yiddish version, *in fayer arayntsuvarfn* ("to throw myself into the fire"), unlike some of the other examples given, maintains a general sense of the issue, perhaps because the image is so striking and unique; nonetheless, it lacks the Hebraism's concrete Biblical resonances.[124] In changing the phrase, however, Perl has substituted a richly idiomatic Yiddish phrase for a Hebrew phrase that would have been awkward in transference and, crucially, not ideologically necessary.

Sexualized Material. One of the critiques appearing throughout *Megale Temirin* is Perl's accusation of the Hasidim as deviant and corrupt; the maskilic community frequently charged the Hasidim with engaging in deviant sexual practices.[125] Though Perl does not actually accuse the Hasidim of homosexuality, he frequently disparagingly suggests the eroticization of the Hasid-Zaddik relationship in the book.

---

121. Yaakov b. Yitzchak Ashkenazi, *Tsene rene* (Amsterdam: 1736); see 35b.

122. See Daniel 3:1–31; the phrase used there is in Aramaic, however.

123. See Genesis Rabbah 38:13.

124. Notably, this episode does appear in the *Tsene rene* in similar language; see 10a and Dov-Ber Kerler, "The Eighteenth Century Origins of Modern Literary Yiddish," (D.Phil. thesis, University of Oxford, 1988), 176–207, 497–507, for a comparative discussion of this episode in several versions of the *Tsene rene*.

125. For a maskilic accusation of Hasidic homosexual practices, see Isaac Ber Levinson's letter reprinted in Katz "Igrot" 270; for an accusation of Hasidic murder

He does so not through direct statements, but subtle hints and references. Many of these hints are provided by judicious usage of Biblical texts.

In Letter 26, a Hasid decides not to swear to a maskil about the truth of a miracle story about his rebbe, giving his reason as *pen ehye lavuz* ("because I may become contemptible"); he realizes the maskil is skeptical, and believes the maskil's doubt will lead to future skepticism. The Biblical phrase used here comes from Judah's statement referring to revelations of his sexual indiscretions.[126] The phrase may be Perl's subtle mockery of the eroticization of the Zaddik-Hasid relationship: the Hasid is afraid that his beloved's impotence will be generally revealed. The reference is sufficiently subtle, though, and its explanation would be so extensive and necessarily coarse that it is unsurprising that the Yiddish analogue, *dervayl vel ikh bay im durkh di shvues nokh mevuse vern* ("because I may come to be further ashamed through the oath"), lacks any such resonance.

A more widespread and powerful method Perl uses to critique and eroticize the Hasid-Zaddik relationship is to present it as a blasphemous parody of the Song of Songs. In traditional Judaism, the book is generally interpreted allegorically as a description of the relationship between Israel and God; by using phrases and motifs from the book, Perl can both allude to its eroticism and critique both the Hasidim for worshipping their leaders as if they were God, and the Zaddikim for agreeing to be worshipped as divine. Indeed, Perl parodically twists one of the major themes of the Song of Songs—the protagonist's search for the vanished lover—when, at the end of the novel, the rebbe/lover has fled, and the Hasidim, abandoned, tell tales of their lover's accomplishments to a slightly dubious audience. For Perl, this is a powerful polemical mechanism, and the book of the Song of Songs

and rape, see Levinson's letter reprinted in Katz "Igrot" 271. Perl also mentioned such practices in his 1838 memorandum; see Mahler *Hasidim* 138. See also David Biale, "Eros and Enlightenment: Love Against Marriage in the East European Jewish Enlightenment," *Polin* 1 (1986), 49–67, 61. For a scholarly view on Hasidism and erotic imagery and symbolism, see Moshe Idel, *Hasidism: Between Ecstasy and Magic* (Albany: SUNY Press, 1995), 133–140.

126. Genesis 38:23. Judah has not yet paid a temple prostitute what he owes her.

was fairly well known among traditional Jews, who customarily recited it every Sabbath eve.[127] As a result, some early references appearing in the Hebrew version are transferred into the Yiddish; once Perl has made the point, however, subsequent subtle references fall by the wayside.

Perl refers to the Song of Songs as early as Letter 4, when one Hasid informs another that his love-sickness (*kholat ahava*) for his rebbe is stronger than it is for women. This reference to Song of Songs 2:5 is particularly important to Perl, as it clearly demonstrates the eroticization of the Hasid-Zaddik relationship. Since Perl wants every reader to understand this, and feels they have the ability to do so, he maintains the reference. It is helpful for Perl that both components of the Hebrew expression *kholat ahava*, though not the phrase itself, are part of the Semitic component of Yiddish.[128] Once the archetype has been established, however, other equally pointed references may fall by the wayside. For example, though a rebbe describes one of his favorite Hasidim with the phrase *et sheahava nafshi* ("who my soul loves"),[129] a perfect example of this eroticized relationship, the language only appears in the Hebrew version. Perl can afford to let such references go untranslated because the Yiddish readership has been given the mechanism to interpret the entire book as, in some way, related to the Song of Songs. Further proofs might be desirable, but are not polemically necessary.

Esther. Another obvious Biblical model for Perl to employ was that favorite of maskilic authors, the Book of Esther, with its parodic feel, its subversion of the internal order, and its familiarity and popularity among traditional Jews.[130] As early as Letter 4, Perl makes the archetype explicit: a Hasid reminds a woman of her communal obligations by referring to Esther's willingness to sacrifice herself to Ahasuerus for

127. The book was also recited every Passover as part of the liturgy.

128. See, for example, Perferkovitsh 77 for the Yiddish *kholas*, though this word's exact provenance in Yiddish is unclear, and Perferkovitsh 3 and Golomb 22–23 for *ahava*. I am grateful to Dr. Dov-Ber Kerler for this suggestion.

129. Song of Songs 1:7, 3:2–4. Letter 126.

130. On Purim and its appeal to the maskilim, see Chapter Five.

the communal good. The sexual and erotic parallels to Esther's situation are completely intentional. Though the *reference* to Esther, reminding readers of a familiar archetype to be borne out through the novel, is maintained in the Yiddish, no effort is made to transfer the *language* of the Hebrew, reminiscent of Esther 4:11, into the Yiddish.[131]

This model holds for most of the references to Esther in *Megale Temirin*: many of the thematic similarities are transferred, but the textual ones are not. The Hebrew phrase at the end of Letter 4, *revakh vehatsala yaamod lanu mimakom akher* ("relief and deliverance will come to us from another source"), refers to Esther 4:14. Though this notion is still thematically suggested in the Yiddish version, the Yiddish language of the passage, *mir zoln geholfn vern durkh epes andersh* ("we will be helped some other way"), bears no textual resonances. Other citations from Esther include, in Letter 114, the phrase *katov beeineikhem* ("as is fitting in your eyes")[132] in describing the attempt to marry the rebbe's less than virtuous son to a wealthy merchant's daughter. Here, too, the parodic language does not transfer to the Yiddish.

At times the omission seems to take place primarily because explaining a complicated reference to Esther would simply take too long. At the end of Letter 23, there is a long discursus where the rebbe uses numerology and numerous Hebrew wordplays to prove conclusively that the Book of Esther contains hidden messages militating against Mordechai, the name of *Megale Temirin*'s heroic maskil. (Since the Book of Esther's hero, or at least one of them, is named Mordechai, this notion seems fairly ludicrous, which is, of course, Perl's intention.) The material is so complex, the puns, number crunching, and wordplay so fast and furious, there seems to be no way for the Yiddish language, much less the Yiddish reader, to keep up. Perl therefore cuts the entire section, with little hint it ever existed. His drastic editing extends to changing the next letter as well to expunge reference to the previous letter's efforts.

Perl's use of the Book of Esther may also subtly reinforce his antinomian critique, since, in Jewish tradition, Esther marks the second giving

131. This is true despite the fact that certain whole expressions from Esther (though not the ones under discussion) are considered part of the Yiddish lexicon. For a by no means complete list, see Weinreich 3:234.

132. Esther 8:8.

of the law.[133] The antinomian Hasidim are thus unflatteringly juxta-posed with the Jews of Esther's time that once more took upon them-selves the law's burden. Since this critique is based on a fairly esoteric Talmudic statement, it is unsurprising that nothing is made of it in the Yiddish version. A similar antinomian critique is suggested through a reference to Sinaitic themes, reminiscent of the first giving of the law. Describing a Zaddik's miracle, the phrase *lo naase velo nishma* (lit. "we will not do and will not hear") is used, clearly referring to the Sinaitic acceptance of Divine law.[134] Though the phrase itself is easily recogniz-able to even the least learned reader,[135] Perl's use of the phrase for paro-dic critique, predicated on its Talmudic explication, is significantly more subtle, and therefore it also does not appear in the Yiddish.

Transferred Material

Perl takes pains to ensure that material constituting strong ideological criticism of Hasidism is transferred to the Yiddish version. In doing so, however, he takes into account the difference in knowledge be-tween his Hebrew and Yiddish reading audiences, and his efforts to explicate or more clearly present certain important ideological cri-tiques tell us much about his perception of these audiences' differing levels of knowledge. Secondarily, Perl's transference of *Megale Temirin* into Yiddish also allows him to parody Hasidic styles of oral interpre-tation, naturally conducted in Yiddish. This parodic goal allows Perl to incorporate a slightly larger stratum of material from the Hebrew version, as we will see.

Knowledge and ignorance

In Letter 104, during an interchange between a maskil and a rebbe, the rebbe accuses the maskil of lacking *tselem elokim* ("the image of God").[136] The maskil's retort employs the verse *umoraakhem vekhitk-hem yihye al kol khayat haarets* ("and the fear of you and the dread of

---

133. See *BT Shabat* 88a, explaining Esther 9:27.
134. See *BT Shabat* 88a, explaining Exodus 24:7. Letter 13.
135. See Perferkovitsh 202.
136. Genesis 1:27.

you will be on every creature of the earth")[137] to indicate the rebbe's willingness to attach himself to sinners simply because they provide him with money. This is a powerful and yet fairly straightforward critique of Hasidic venality, which simultaneously buttresses the notion of a correct maskilic usage of text in contrast to the Hasidic misuse of the same canon. Perl accordingly maintains the episode in the Yiddish version; however, his audiences' differing knowledge levels necessitated linguistic and narrative manipulation.

In the Hebrew *Megale Temirin*, the language of the episode is fairly sparse; in the Yiddish, unsurprisingly, Perl provides a longer explication—but only for the latter passage. Apparently, since Yiddish readers were sufficiently familiar with not only the phrase *tselem elokim*,[138] but also the rabbinic or midrashic connotations vital for understanding Perl's satirical thrust, such as the universalist and humanist approaches suggested in the rabbinic treatments of the related topic of *imitatio Dei*,[139] it was unnecessary for Perl to explain them in Yiddish. On the other hand, the readers were not sufficiently comfortable with Hebrew to understand the latter passage, particularly the word *khitkhem*, which has no analogue in the *loshn-koydesh* component of Yiddish.

With enough of these examples, one may begin to develop a sense of Perl's perceptions of the level of Hebraic and classical knowledge of his Yiddish-speaking audience. Several more examples follow.

In Letter 114, the rebbe, at the signing of the contract betrothing his son to a rich man's daughter, interprets Genesis 6:2, "And the sons of Elohim saw the daughters of the land, that they were good, and took wives from whom they chose," in a typically hubristic and antinomian fashion, presenting members of the Zaddik's dynasty as divine figures, able to do as they please with the lesser Jews. The passage appears untranslated in the Yiddish, and is immediately followed by its parodic interpretation. Perl clearly supposes the verse's Hebrew to be sufficiently simple for the Yiddish reader to understand the distance between the passage's actual literal meaning and its Hasidic interpretation.

137. Genesis 9:2.
138. See Golomb 318; Perferkovitsh 236; Spivak and Yehoyesh 227.
139. See *Sifra* 19:2 and *BT Sota* 14a for examples.

Such an example indicates Perl's clear belief that the Yiddish reader had some knowledge of Hebrew beyond the recognition of *loshn-koydesh* components of Yiddish in their original contexts. However, he was acutely aware of his Yiddish reader's inability to grasp the sort of wordplay in which the maskil delighted and which elegantly exposed Hasidic ignorance and irrationalism. Though at times Perl would still engage in wordplay in his Yiddish version, he was aware of the necessity for careful explanation.

In Letter 19, a Hasid explains his rebbe's curious dictum concerning *pidyoynes*, monetary gifts sent to the rebbe in return for his intervention in the Heavenly spheres on the supplicant's behalf. The rebbe refuses to accept silver coins; only gold will do. In Hebrew, the explanation reads:

> *od amar rabeinu shemakhmat hamatbea kesef ba lesakana atsuma, ki af al pi yesh shekesef hu rakhamim, akh it kesef veit kesef, it kesef bivkhinat kosef vezehu rakhamim, veit kesef bivkhinat nahama dikesifin.*

And our rabbi also said that because the coin was silver he had come to great danger, because even though silver (*kesef*) is mercy, there's silver and there's silver. There's silver in the sense of "yearning" (*kosef*), and that's mercy, and there's silver in the sense of beggar's bread (*nahama dikesifin*).

The pun is handled curtly and there are numerous Aramaicisms in the explanation—a fairly complex joke for readers.

The Yiddish version is more expansive, and the only Aramaic is included because otherwise the pun would quite literally fall apart:

> *haynt hot mir der rebe, zol hundert yor lebn, nokh gezogt, az durkh dem zilber gelt, vos du host geshikt, iz er geven in a groyser sakone, vorn khotshe zilber izt* [sic.] *rakhmim, zenen ober farhandn tsveyerlay taytshn fun dem vort kesef. Eyn kesef izt* [sic.] *fun dem shteyger glistn (in loshn-hakoydesh heyst koysef glistn), dos izt* [sic.] *rakhmim. Es iz ober vider farhandn kesef vos batayt shemen, azoy zogt men nehome diksifin, dos iz taytsh broyt vos men est mit bushe, hayne betelbrod* [sic.].

Today the rabbi, may he live a hundred years, also said that through the silver money you sent he was put into a great danger, since even though silver is mercy, there are two different meanings of the word *kesef.* One *kesef* is in the sense of yearning (and in Hebrew yearning is called *koysef*), this is mercy. But there is also another *kesef* which means shame, as in the phrase *nekhame dikesifin*, which is bread that people eat with shame, beggar's bread.

Though some of the greater expansiveness is natural, a necessary consequence of the translation of material into a different style and register, the previous example's lack of translation shows that Perl had located the average Yiddish reader's level of Hebrew comprehension somewhere between these two extremes.[140]

The Yiddish reader's familiarity with classical and canonical characters and themes, however, is more easily determinable than their level of Hebrew language understanding. In Letter 76, for example, Perl uses the curious phrase *veilmalei nagduhu vekhulei* ("and had they been lashed, etc."). The phrase cites *BT Ketuvot* 33b, which comments on the Biblical story of Khanania, Mishael, and Azaria, thrown into a fiery furnace by Nebuchadnezzar rather than betray their faith and miraculously saved. The Talmud suggests that had they been lashed instead of thrown into the furnace, the pain would have been unbearable and they would have turned to idol worship. In the novel, a maskil uses the phrase to justify keeping his opposition to Hasidism secret—clearly an idea resonant to the subversive and secretive Perl. Simultaneously, the maskil (and by extension, Perl) casts himself as a hero braving the dangerous environment of Hasidism for the true faith.

Perl's expectations of his Hebrew readers are clearly high: they are required to recognize the reference and derive its relationship to the narrative from these three brief words. In contrast, the Yiddish readers are given a great deal more information: "The Talmud says: Khanania, Mishael, and Azaria were thrown into a burning oven because they would not worship idols; if they had been beaten, however, they would

140. For an almost identical example, see the rebbe's teaching in Letter 62, particularly the example of the *ofanim*. There, again, the maintenance of the teaching in the Yiddish version can be attributed to the inclusion of antinomian themes, such as the breaking of the tablets, among other numerous references to Exodus. See also Letter 71 where the Baal Shem Tov's daughter's name, Odel, is explained as an acronym of the Biblical passage *eish dat lamo* ("lightning flashing at them," Deuteronomy 33:2), and the passage is left untranslated in the Yiddish.

have served the idols to avoid punishment." All the information Perl expects his Hebrew readers to know is provided for the Yiddish readers, including even the three figures' identity.

A slightly more complex example occurs in Letter 16, where the rebbe refers to Freyde, a Hasidic woman who attempts to seduce a local noble for the rebbe's benefit, as the reincarnation of Yael, the wife of Khever the Kenite. In the Hebrew version, the Hasid attending him immediately asks if the noble is also a reincarnation of Sisera, illustrating the absurdity of the mystical belief in reincarnation in general and the Hasidic version of it in particular.[141] Perl clearly believes his Hebrew audience to be sufficiently familiar with the events described in Judges 4, where Yael seduces and then kills Sisera, the Philistine general, to follow the Hasid's leap of choplogic. In the Yiddish version, however, Perl adds the parenthetical phrase *vos hot Sisre'n geharget* ("who killed Sisera") to his description of Yael, indicating the Yiddish audience's general familiarity with the story (since no other details are added, such as that Sisera was a Philistine, that the story dates from the period of the Judges, or that the Judge Deborah was involved) but acknowledging the necessity to jog the Yiddish audience's memory a bit. Perl inserts a similar parenthetical reminder in the Yiddish version of Letter 103, which also discusses Freyde and Yael.

A similar example stems from Perl's presumption not of his Yiddish audience's *textual* ignorance, but of their *legal* ignorance. In Letter 57, a Hasid tells stories about the Baal Shem Tov not included in the *Shivkhei HaBesht*; one story describes his ignominious ejection from the synagogue after making a blessing over a Torah scroll containing a ritual imperfection. The Hebrew version assumes the readers understand why this action is risible; the Yiddish version, however, provides more clarity, when the ejectors comment: *a besht zol nisht derkenen, az dos seyfer iz posl un zol makhn a brokhe levatole* ("How does a Baal Shem Tov not recognize that the scroll is ritually imperfect and he is thus making a blessing in vain?"). The Yiddish readers need extra information that the Hebrew readers, presumably more familiar with details of Jewish law, seemingly find unnecessary.

141. See Chapter Six, n. 96.

This is not to say that Perl believes the Yiddish readers to be total naïfs. As we have seen, he credits them with knowledge of the Hebrew language transcending the *loshn-koydesh* components of Yiddish, and certain oblique references presume significant knowledge on their part. For example, several apodictic references in the Yiddish to "the incense which helps with the plague"[142] refer to Numbers 17:11–13, where Aaron and the priests use incense to stop a plague in the Israelites' camp. Perhaps the concept was more recognizable than its lack of Biblical prominence would suggest due to the ubiquity of plague in Eastern Europe; alternatively, the passage was read annually, and "incense" appeared in the liturgy on a weekly basis. Nonetheless, it is fair to say that in leaving the passage unexplained, Perl certainly assumes a certain degree of Biblical knowledge.

Perl also believed Yiddish readers to be familiar with certain Talmudic dicta, though almost certainly not through Talmud study.[143] For example, the idea that saving one Jewish life was equivalent to saving the entire world, though appearing in *BT Sanhedrin* 37a, is alluded to in both the Hebrew and Yiddish versions. Perl's sense that the classical formulation of this ethical idea was fairly common in Eastern Europe explains why he felt no need to expand upon it in the Yiddish.[144]

A more intricate example illustrating the Yiddish audience's complex levels of knowledge appears slightly later in the novel. The maskil Moyshe Fishls explains his dedication to teaching a student who is neither brilliant or rich by referring to the famous Talmudic statement in *BT Sanhedrin* 19b: "He who teaches a boy Torah, it is as if he were his son." Perl here reiterates his polemical point and presents the maskilim as guardians of the traditional canon and opponents to Ha-

---

142. Letter 19 and Letter 26; in the latter, Aaron and Moses are mentioned in both the Hebrew and Yiddish.

143. For a general discussion, see Weinreich 1:222–227.

144. Letter 9. It appears more explicitly in both versions in letter 76. The expression could be used in terms of "ransoming captives" (*pidyon shvuyim*), which in Hasidic circles meant saving someone from financial catastrophe. See Letter 49 and Taylor 328.

sidic greed and ignorance.[145] This statement, seemingly both important and (in its broad outlines, at least) familiar, appears in both Hebrew and Yiddish versions; however, the Hebrew letter names the
particular Mishna they are studying, *BT Bava Metzia* 9b's "If he were
riding a donkey," and the Yiddish does not. Somewhat slyly and cru-
elly, Perl may be suggesting the act of reviewing and reviewing with a
dumb student, trying to force the knowledge into his head, is very
similar to the act of "riding a donkey," perhaps a manifestation of the
intellectual elitism shown by Perl and other maskilim. Though a subtle in-joke is lost in translation by omitting this detail, Perl realizes the
Yiddish audience will not understand it, or, possibly, will take offense
at it, and it is not worth the expansion needed to explain it.

Even a seeming exception to these criteria can help us further understand Perl's literary and polemical strategies. In Letter 104, a Hasid
uses ignorance and superstition, not science, to explain the efficacy of
a lightning rod. The Hasid claims that the lightning rod works because of the merit of the four Biblical mothers, saying:

> *vezot makhmat shehabarzel mesugal legaresh haklipot kayadua, sheotiot
> barzel rashei tevot Bilha Rakhel Zilpa Lea, venimtsa hu davar pashut
> uvarur meod.*

And this is because, as is known, iron is able to drive away the husks,
as the letters of iron (*barzel*) are an acronym for Bilhah, Rachel, Zil-
pah, and Leah, and it turns out to be a very clear matter.

However, the Yiddish version adds details that it is virtually certain
the Yiddish audience knew:

> *makhmes ayzn iz mesugl far klipes. Vorn ayzn heyst af loshn hakoydesh
> barzel un barzel vert geshribn beyz, reysh, zayen, lamed. Di beyz makht
> Bilho, di reysh Rokhl, di zayen Zilpo, un di lamed Leye, azoy hobn geheysn
> di arba imoes. Meyle is dokh gor a poshes.*

Because iron is capable of driving away the husks, since iron, in
Hebrew, is called *barzel*, and *barzel* is written *beyz, reysh, zayen, lamed*;

---

145. Letter 26. A satirical trope in *Megale Temirin* is the idea of Hasidic seduc-
tion of the young, particularly of the young rich. See Werses "Hakhasidut" 103–
104 and Rubinstein "Al mahut" 129.

the *beyz* stands for *Bilho*, the *reysh*—*Rokhl*, the *zayen*—*Zilpo*, and the *lamed*—*Leye*, and these are the four mothers. It's simple.

Though these factual details were hardly necessary from Perl's perspective as an ideologue, we must remember that the words in question are spoken by a Hasidic character, and Perl includes the full details in his voice to mock the character's pedantry and stupidity at length. As a result, in order to understand Perl's use of these texts, one must explore the *narrative* circumstances of the citation in conjunction with its polemical and cognitive circumstances.[146]

This last point is also echoed in Perl's dictum about his various audiences, cited earlier in the chapter, when he wrote that their *claims* of knowledge may differ substantially from what they actually *know*. In the same letter, for example, a Hasid, explaining the wisdom of the Zaddikim, quotes the Zohar to explain why the Zaddik of Lublin referred to a woman by the title "Reb" Tomorl,[147] but in both the Hebrew and Yiddish versions, the context indicates that the speaker does not understand the text he is citing, confusing the woman's name Tamar with the symbolic image of the date tree (*tamar*). It is hard to find a more straightforward portrayal of Hasidic ignorance in the entire novel. Perl, as the author, makes different points from his characters; this must be kept in mind during any serious reading of *Megale Temirin*.

Transference and translation: a critique of interpretation

In Letter 68, sent by one maskil to another, almost all of the felicitous Biblical phrasings that characterize the Hebrew version are re-

146. This passage begs an interesting narratological question: the Yiddish passage implies that this letter's writer spoke Yiddish to his audience, and thus needed to frame his ideas in Yiddish. Conversely, in the Hebrew version, a very different conversation seems to have taken place. The universe of the novel has seemingly changed between the Hebrew and the Yiddish versions; the medium of translation has somehow affected the actual narrative itself, and audiences within the novel have also changed to reflect changing audiences outside the novel. (Alternatively, of course, the changes could have been the work of Ovadia.)

147. For another example of a "female Zaddik," see the discussion in Ada Rapoport-Albert, "On Women in Hasidism, S. A. Horodecky, and the Maid of Ludmir Tradition," in Rapoport-Albert and Zipperstein 495–525, esp. 495–500.

moved in the Yiddish translation, as we have seen earlier. However, on one occasion, referring to a Hasid, the maskil explicitly cites a passage from Psalms used by the Talmud to refer to the heretic and antinomian figure Elisha ben Abuya: "What right have you to tell of My laws?"[148] Unlike all other citations in the letter, the passage is actually retained in the Yiddish, chapter and verse: *af im iz der posek in tilim (kapitl nun posek tes zayin) gezogt gevorn: vos host du shmisn mit mayn toyre?* ("The passage from Psalms (chapter 50, verse 16) was said about him: what have you said about My laws?")[149] Perl maintains the passage, even taking pains to add in the source, because of its strong ideological point; the passage on its own terms can be used to illustrate Hasidic antinomian tendencies, even if Yiddish readers are unaware of the passage's even more damning Talmudic explication.

Particularly interesting, however, is the formula Perl uses, reminiscent of the *taytsh* tradition.[150] Perl appeals to the pedagogical methods and formulae through which most male Yiddish speakers with elementary education would have acquired much of their familiarity with classical Jewish texts. Perl, however, uses these methods to mock corrupt and perverted Hasidic interpretation, particularly oral interpretation. In doing so, the ability to use Yiddish, the language in which oral interpretations were delivered, merely improves the parody; simultaneously, though, Perl needed to remain aware of the varying levels of audience knowledge discussed earlier. We see both considerations at work in our discussion of Perl's attack on Hasidic interpretation.

To mock the Hasidic style of interpretation effectively, Perl needed to include examples of that interpretation. Perl surrounds many of the Hasidic ceremonies with Hasidic exegesis and scriptural interpretation, often in an oral context. In doing so, Perl intends to illustrate

148. Psalms 50:16. The reference to Elisha ben Abuya comes from *BT Khagiga* 15b. The passage is also used to refer to Doeg the Edomite; see *BT Sanhedrin* 106b.

149. Compare Letter 78, where a Biblical verse retained in the Yiddish is prefaced by the phrase *hot der navi gezogt* ("the prophet said") though here the citation (Isaiah 6:10) is not provided.

150. On *taytsh*, see Benjamin Harshav, *The Meaning of Yiddish* (Berkeley: University of California Press, 1990), 14–15; Shmeruk *Prokim* 171–179, and Shlomo Noble, *Khumesh-taytch* (New York: YIVO, 1943).

that just as the interpretations surrounding the ceremony are absurd or morally corrupt, the ceremony (at least as practiced by the Hasidim) is equally so.

One ceremony appearing several times in the novel is the *pidyen*, a particularistically Hasidic ceremony, mentioned briefly above.[151] In the first *pidyen* the rebbe, alluding to the gold coins he receives from the supplicant, cites a Biblical phrase referring to gold, *vezahav haaretz tov* ("and the gold of the land is good").[152] Perl's Yiddish version calls attention to the quoted nature of the passage and its role as formula in the ceremony: *hob ikh dem enteres farbesert in dem shteyger fun dem posek vos er zogt: un dos gold fun dem dozign land iz gut* ("I improved it in the manner of the passage which says: and the gold from that land is good").[153] This entire procedure pokes fun at the rebbe's lust for money and his willingness to profane holy texts, Hasidic interpretations of those texts, and the liturgical or ceremonial usage of those texts and interpretations for the sake of acquisitiveness. All this would be made clear to Yiddish readers only if the passage were both understandable and clearly demarcated as a holy text used in an oral ceremonial context.

Perl refers to the oral *taytsh* tradition explicitly in the next few sentences when the rebbe makes a second *pidyen*. Perl writes: *vetsaak od khai khai yodekha uveamira zot naasa hapidyon* ("And he cried out, 'the living, the living shall praise Thee,' and with this utterance the *pidyen* was made"). In the Yiddish, though, the levels of authorial intrusion and multireferentiality proliferate: *un dernokh hot er geshrign "khay khay yoydekha" (dos iz taytsh: di lebedike, di lebedike, veln dikh loybn)* ("And afterwards he cried out, 'khay khay yoydekha' (this means: the

151. On the ceremony of the *pidyen* and its role in Hasidic society, see Khaviva Fedye, "Lehitpatkhuto shel hadegem hakhevrati-dati-kalkali bakhasidut: hapidyon, hakhavura vehaaliya laregel," in Menakhem Ben-Sasson, ed., *Dat vekalkala* (Jerusalem: Zalman Shazar, 1995), 311–374, 329–338; on the maskilic critique of such economic behavior, see Israel Bartal, "Lean halakh tseror hakesef? Habikoret hamaskilit al hebeteha hakalkaliyim shel hakhasidut," in Ben-Sasson 375–385. See also Nigal *Hasiporet hakhasidit* 92–95, 166–167.

152. Reference is to Genesis 2:12. Letter 19.

153. See Fedye "Lehitpatkhuto" 331 and Aaron Wertheim, "Traditions and Customs in Hasidism," in Hundert *Essential Papers* 363–398, 380.

living, the living will praise You)").[154] Perl maintains this passage in Hebrew, though Yiddish readers may have understood it only through the translation; in doing so, he once more accentuates the oral and ceremonial nature of the Hasidic textual misuse.

A prime example of the retention of a Hebrew phrase and its explication in Yiddish, a process allowing Perl to mock the irrationalities of Hasidic oral and textual interpretation, appears in Letter 84 when a Hasid repeats one of his rebbe's teachings, his *toyre*, to a maskil. The *toyre* consists of the citation and exegesis of three Biblical passages that on their face seem to be perfectly self-explanatory: Numbers 25:14 ("Zimri, son of Salu, prince of the house of Simeon"), Deuteronomy 17:11 ("According to the voice of the Torah which will instruct you"), and Numbers 7:9 ("And he did not give it to the children of Kehat, because the service of the holy things belonged to them; they carried it upon their shoulders.").[155] The rebbe, though, derides them as requiring explication: in the Yiddish version, each Hasidic teaching is prefaced by a phrase analogous to *di verter hobn gor keyn perush nisht* ("the words simply have no explanation"). The rebbe then provides a series of explanations deriving loosely from Hebrew wordplays that lead to lessons crudely supportive of the Zaddik or Hasidism. The first passage, apparently a simple genealogical statement, is actually revealed as a commandment to drag obstreperous opponents to the Zaddik's house. The second, seeming to refer to the Torah as a pedagogical instrument, is revealed as a commandment to financially support the Zaddik. And the third, which seems to be a historical statement about a certain family, seems to be interpreted as allowing the Zaddik to commit sins, once again reminding the readers of Hasidic antinomian tendencies and potential links with Sabbateanism or Frankism.[156]

The Yiddish translations of these wordplays presume at least some familiarity on the readers' part with the Hebrew grammar and root system, presumably the same type of familiarity gained through exposure

154. The passage (Isaiah 38:19) is located among several passages concerning Hezekiah and his critical illness. This is certainly not coincidental.

155. The Yiddish translation is explicitly given for the first and last passage. The middle passage is not explained.

156. The wordplays are developed in Letter 84, Yiddish version.

to traditional oral interpretation and the *Tsene rene*. Perl maintains the teachings at length in the Yiddish version, however, and in doing so does not merely provide a strong ideological critique of Hasidic interpretive practices, but also calls the entire system of traditional oral interpretation into question. The Zaddikim and Hasidim are unable or unwilling to understand the plain sense of the passage, and so pervert them, Perl argues, for their own ends. The reader is thus challenged to learn Hebrew and the Bible, presumably in the rationalist, literalist manner so beloved by the maskilim, to prevent such textual corruption, whether by Hasidim or anyone else.

Conclusion

The Galician Haskala differs from its Prussian counterpart in significant ways; one of the most important of those differences is its need to deal directly with the powerful Hasidic movement. It is perhaps unsurprising, then, that the strategies of textual usage developed by Joseph Perl, Galicia's most important maskil, are fundamentally conditioned by the usage of classical texts in Hasidic works. Perl's parodic style demands a certain mimesis of Hasidic textual usage, but uses the texts to further parody styles of Hasidic interpretation and to spread the notion of Hasidic antinomianism. The form in which these attacks occur, however—the prose satire—is new and will remain influential in modern Jewish literature.

At the same time, the Galician Haskala is responsible for another development: the growth of maskilic material in Yiddish. Though Perl's attitude toward Yiddish seems at best ambivalent, the success of Yiddish writings in the Hasidic world rendered it necessary for maskilim to begin to consider using the language as well. In doing so, Perl had to consider how to make his satirical points to a Yiddish readership, bearing in mind their lesser familiarity with the classical texts often used as the basis for that satire in previous maskilic works. The solutions he developed point the way to the development of the full-fledged Yiddish literature that begins to flourish several decades later in the Pale of Settlement and as such constitute a crucial transition point in the history of modern Jewish literature.

Part Four   Coda

Conclusion and Further Directions for Study

Despite a brief preface in Elizabethan England and a quick excursus into the thickets of literary theory, the story this book tells began in Berlin in the 1780s, where hopes for full Jewish participation in the Enlightenment began to flourish in a way they never had before. Flush with possibility, unwilling to rock the boat, the new maskilim attempted to prove to non-Jewish society—and to themselves as well—that their tradition, when properly defined and presented, was as good as any (and perhaps better than most) according to Enlightenment tenets. This period, exemplified by its towering figure Moses Mendelssohn, was accordingly marked by a cautious and conservative use of classical texts in order to achieve a rehabilitation of Jewish tradition, particularly the then-demonized rabbinic texts.

After Mendelssohn's death and the outbreak of the French Revolution, the Haskala took a more radical turn. Maskilim, willing to be more active and outspoken in their demands for rights, developed a more satirical and critical style, even overtly attacking other Jewish interpretive styles, particularly those of the *Ostjuden*. Simultaneously, real continuities existed between this group, exemplified by Aaron Halle-Wolfssohn, and the Mendelssohnian conservatism of the 1780s, and these continuities led to the expression of real ambivalence about the future of the Haskala. All these issues are revealed through a study of Wolfssohn's work, particularly of the types of classical texts used by various characters in his seminal play *Laykhtzin un fremelay*.

Finally, this study's shift to the Galician Haskala in the early nineteenth century illuminates a very different set of circumstances: located in a massive Hasidic center, local maskilim needed to develop a set of polemical strategies, including textual ones, which responded to that movement. One crucial strategy was the use of the Yiddish language, which raised questions about textual allusion in Yiddish language works aimed at Yiddish-speaking readers. Comparing Joseph Perl's Hebrew and Yiddish works accordingly allows us to study maskilic strategies of audience differentiation and targeted allusiveness.

This book, therefore, consists not only of individual studies of aspects of three maskilic authors' works and how those authors' usage of classical texts offered a lens through which to examine the changing nature of the Haskala: it should also be seen as a further refinement and development of a particular technique, the study of textual allusion by scholars to yield more detailed and nuanced understanding of literary texts in general and maskilic work in particular. These readings and theoretical comments hopefully constitute some progress in this regard: however, further refinement is both possible and necessary. In this book's second chapter, I suggested certain chronological, geographical, ideological, textual, and cultural axes along which interpretive subcommunities can be constituted; these axes, expanded and discussed, may provide concrete directions for further study.

First and perhaps most obviously, the chronological axis: this book does not even begin to cover the most active period of maskilic activity in Eastern Europe. Research needs to be done on how the usage of classical texts manifests itself in later nineteenth century Hebrew and Yiddish writers' works, particularly as audiences for maskilic efforts grew. Allusion to classical Jewish texts outlasted the Haskala as well, of course, and later Yiddish authors like Sholem Aleichem and Itzik Manger, with their text-citing Tevyes and their updated Purim ballads, can be fruitfully seen as later links in this literary chain. Sholem Aleichem conducted correspondence with Simon Dubnow in "the language of Megale Temirin";[1] Manger was from Perl's Galicia.[2] Real connections and continuities are possible. In the same vein, this

1. See David Assaf, "'Ahuvi rei, hamagid midubno': mikhtevei bedikhot besignon 'megale temirin' shehekhelifu beineihem Shalom Aleichem veShimon Dubno," *Chulyot* 5 (Winter 1999), 61–107.
2. I am indebted to Ruth Wisse for this insight.

work generally focused on the "first generations" of maskilic activity in a given region: fruitful work can be done on the changing nature of the Haskala in a given region by focusing on the changing usage of classical text between generations. Such an effort was undertaken in distinguishing between Mendelssohn and Wolfssohn's textual usages, but it can, of course, be expanded further.

Second, the geographical axis, by which I mean not only the differences between Galicia and the Pale of Settlement, but also within regions already discussed. This essay focuses on the urban centers of Prussia and the work of a maskil in a major Galician city: however, research has shown that modernization rates in rural communities differed drastically from urban centers.[3] Texts written for or by maskilim in these areas may differ in their classical textual usage from those in urban centers. This approach also clearly calls for studies of classical textual usage in other geographical regions. David Ruderman's recent studies of the Haskala in England, which focus on the similarities and differences between Enlightenment movements in London and Berlin, may serve as a starting point for one such analysis.[4] Additionally, local custom might well shift and refocus particular textual interpretation, not merely legally but hermeneutically.[5]

Third, the ideological axis: though this book focuses on *maskilic* activity in the periods under discussion, fruitful work can be done comparing maskilic textual usage to works produced by members of what might be called the "Counter-Haskala": traditionalist responses to textual and polemical challenges posed by the maskilim. As Edward Breuer has taken pains to note, the gap between rabbis and the more

3. *GJH* 1: 53, 82, 191–193, 375 and *GJH* 2:90–91. See also Paula E. Hyman, "Traditionalism and Village Jews in 19th Century Western and Central Europe: Local Persistence and Urban Nostalgia," in Jack Wertheimer, ed. *The Uses of Tradition: Jewish Continuity in the Modern Era* (New York: Jewish Theological Seminary, distributed by Harvard University Press, 1992), 191–201.

4. See David Ruderman, "Haim hayta 'haskala' beanglia—iyun mekhadash," *Zion* 62:2 (1997), 109–131, and, more recently, *Jewish Enlightenment in an English Key: Anglo-Jewry's Construction of Modern Jewish Thought* (Princeton, NJ: Princeton University Press, 2000), esp. 7–8, 10–15, 21–56, 276–286.

5. For a parallel account, see Halbertal 93n4.

traditionalist maskilim is significantly narrower than often suggested by historians and critics, and a comparative study between rabbinical statements and maskilic works would be useful.[6]

Fourth, what might be called the textual axis: in all probability, many of the less educated members of the Hebrew and especially the Yiddish reading audience encountered their knowledge of classical Jewish themes and topoi not merely or primarily through the classical texts themselves, either in their original or later liturgical frameworks, but through designated "textual intermediaries" such as the *Tsene-rene*, *tkhines*, morality literature, traditional literature like the *Mayse Bukh* (which billed itself as the "Yiddish Talmud"), and the *Eyn Yankev*, as well as through the complex oral traditions of folk religion.[7] Work needs to be done on the maskilic usage of the textual tradition as they appear and are mediated in these forms, not merely in their original settings; a paradigm for this approach can be found in the work of Yaakov Elbaum who, in his masterful history of the intellectual and cultural production of sixteenth-century Jewish Poland, emphasizes the necessity of including the ethical and intellectual works of pre-modern Yiddish literature in any study of the period.[8]

Finally, there is the cultural axis: this book has intentionally focused on maskilic usage/reusage/misusage of the classical Jewish canon. As has been briefly noted in passing, though, such usage was clearly only one aspect of their work, albeit a significant one, and should be balanced, for a full understanding of the maskilic project, with their importation of texts, themes, and genres from the classical Western

6. See Edward Breuer "Between Haskalah and Orthodoxy" 260–261, 271, as well as Edward Breuer, "Reading the Silences: Rabbinic and Maskilic Cultures in the Early Nineteenth Century," unpublished paper presented February 1998 at the Conference in Honor and Memory of Professor Isidore Twersky, esp. 1, 11. See also Ruderman *Jewish Thought* 339–340.

7. See Weissler 83 and Katz *Tradition* 166. The maskilim were well aware of this phenomenon: Herz Homberg created a maskilic version of the *Tsene-rene* that was never published. See Shmeruk *Perakim* 152–153, esp. 153n11, and Chava Turniaski, "Nusakh hamaskili shel Tsena ureena," *Hasifrut* 2 (1971), 835–841.

8. See his *Petikhut vehistagrut: hayetsira harukhanit-hasifrutit bePolin ubeartsot Ashkenaz beshilhei hamea hashesh-esre* (Jerusalem: Magnes Press, 1990), esp. 67–71.

canon,[9] to say nothing of comparative approaches viewing the movement as a whole in light of similar contemporary movements in the non-Jewish world.[10] Perspective must also be kept by remembering that the Haskala was by no means the only important force in the modernization of European Jewry.[11]

In Antonio's warning to Bassanio, Shakespeare tells his readers something students of the Haskala know: Jews who cite Scripture possess a certain power and pose a certain danger. Historians can and should speculate on the effect of maskilic polemic activity. But for students of maskilic literature in particular and Jewish literature in general, the power and danger of Antonio's devils is unquestioned and majestic.

---

9. For one version of this process, see Uzi Shavit, "Model hahashpaa hakfula: leyikhuda shel situatsia sifrutit-historit ulehashlikuteha hamekhkariut-parshaniut," in Shavit *Baalot* 37–75, esp. 41. Robert Bonfil (151–154) has developed a provocative model of the process in his discussion of Jewish innovation and borrowing in Renaissance Italy. For an excellent monograph on maskilic borrowing from German culture, see Chayim Shoham, *Betsel haskalat berlin* (Tel Aviv: Publication of the Porter Institute for Poetics and Semiotics, 1996), who invokes the dialogic model, portraying the maskilim in a state of duality, familiar with and between two worlds (16–17).

10. Such an approach has recently been adopted by David Sorkin in his *Berlin Haskalah and German Religious Thought*; for his methodological assumptions, see 1–4.

11. See the important essay by Jonathan Frankel, "Assimilation and the Jews in Nineteeth Century Europe: Towards a New Historiography?" in Jonathan Frankel and Steven J. Zipperstein, eds. *Assimilation and Community: The Jews in Nineteenth Century Europe* (Cambridge: Cambridge University Press, 1992), 1–37, esp. 18–20.

Bibliography

Abarbanel, Isaac. *Commentary on the Torah.* (Hanau: 1710).

Abramsky, Chimen. "The Crisis of Authority Within European Jewry in the Eighteenth Century." In Stein and Loewe, 13–28.

——. "La révolution française dans les sources hébraïques." In Hadas-Lebel and Oliel-Grausz, 229–236.

Abramson, Glenda, and Tudor Parfitt, eds. *Jewish Education and Learning.* (Reading, Berkshire: Harwood Academic Publishers, 1994).

Albrecht, Michael, Eva J. Engel, and Norbert Hinske, eds. *Moses Mendelssohn und die Kreise seiner Wirksamkeit.* (Tübingen: Max Niemayer Verlag, 1994).

Alexander, Gerhard. "Die Einfluß von Hermann Samuel Reimarus auf Moses Mendelssohn." In Katz and Rengstorf, 17–24.

Alter, Robert, ed. *Modern Hebrew Literature.* (West Orange, NJ: Behrman House, Inc., 1975).

Altmann, Alexander, ed. *Between East and West: Essays Dedicated to the Memory of Bela Horovitz.* (London: Horovitz Publishing Co., 1958).

——. *Moses Mendelssohn: A Biographical Study.* (Philadelphia: Jewish Publication Society, 1973).

——. *Essays in Jewish Intellectual History.* (Hanover, NH: University Press of New England, 1981).

——. "Mendelssohn on Excommunication: The Ecclesiastical Law Background." In Altmann *Essays* 170–189.

——. "Moses Mendelssohn's Proofs for the Existence of God." In Altmann *Essays* 119–141.

——. "The New Style of Preaching in Nineteenth Century Germany." In Altmann *Essays* 190–245.

——. "The Philosophical Roots of Mendelssohn's Plea for Emancipation." In Altmann *Essays* 154–169.

——. "Introduction." In Mendelssohn *Jerusalem* 3–29.

——. "Moses Mendelssohn as the Archetypal German Jew." In Reinharz and Schatzberg, 17–31.

Aptroot, Marion. "Blitz un vitsenhoyzn: naye penimer fun an alter makhloykes." *Oksforder yidish* 1 (1990), 3–38.

Arendt, Hannah. *Rahel Varnhagen: The Life of a Jewess*. Ed. Liliane Weissberg (Baltimore: Johns Hopkins University Press, 1997).

Arkush, Allan. "The Contribution of Alexander Altmann to the Study of Moses Mendelssohn." *Leo Baeck Institute Year Book* 34 (1989), 415–420.

——. *Moses Mendelssohn and the Enlightenment*. (Albany: State University of New York Press, 1994).

——. Review of David Sorkin's *Moses Mendelssohn and the Religious Enlightenment*. *Modern Judaism* 17 (1997), 179–185.

——. "The Questionable Judaism of Moses Mendelssohn." *New German Critique* 77 (Spring–Summer 1999), 29–44.

Aschheim, Steven E. *Brothers and Strangers: The East European Jew in German and German Jewish Consciousness, 1800–1923*. (Madison: University of Wisconsin Press, 1982).

Ashkenazi, Yaakov b. Yitzchak. *Tsene rene*. (Amsterdam: 1736).

Assaf, David. "'Ahuvi rei, hamagid midubno': mikhtevei bedikhot besignon 'megale temirin' shehekhelifu beineihem Shalom Aleichem veShimon Dubno." *Chulyot* 5 (Winter 1999), 61–107.

Auden, W.H. "Brothers & Others." In Wheeler, 59–78.

Aviezer, Shmuel. *Hamakhaze vehateatron haivri vehayidi: kerakh aleph: mereshitam vead sof hamea hayud tet*. (Jerusalem: Reuven Mass, 1996).

Awerbuch, Marianne and Stefi Jersch-Wenzel, eds. *Bild und Selbstbild der Juden Berlins zwischen Aufklärung und Romantik*. (Berlin: Colloqium Verlag, 1992).

Awerbuch, Marianne. "Moses Mendelssohns Judentum." In Awerbuch and Jersch-Wenzel, 21–41.

Babylonian Talmud. Ed. Dr. I. Epstein. (London: Soncino Press, 1935).

Band, Arnold J. "The Function of the Enigmatic in Two Hasidic Tales." In Dan and Talmadge, 185–210.

——. "Introduction." In Nachman of Bratslav *Tales* 9–48.

——. "The Beginnings of Modern Hebrew Literature: Perspectives on 'Modernity'." *AJSReview* 13:1–2 (1988), 1–26.

Bar-El, Yehudit. "Hapoema haivrit mereshita: hapoetika shel hazhanr." *Kongres olami lemakhshevet yisrael* 10C2 (1990), 129–136.

Barber, C. L. "The Merchants and the Jew of Venice: Wealth's Communion and an Intruder." In Barnet, 11–32.

Barnet, Sylvan, ed. *Twentieth Century Interpretations of the Merchant of Venice*. (Prentice Hall: Englewood Cliffs, NJ: 1970).

Bartal, Israel. "'The Heavenly City of Germany' and Absolutism a la Mode d'Autriche: The Rise of the Haskala in Galicia." In Katz *Emancipation* 33–42.

——. "The Imprint of Haskala Literature on the Historiography of Hasidism." In Rapaport-Albert *Hasidism Reappraised* 367–375.

——. "Lean halakh tseror hakesef? Habikoret hamaskilit al hebeteha hakalkaliim shel hakhasidut." In Ben-Sasson, 375–385.

Baumgarten, Jean. "Émancipation et langue yiddish chez les écrivains de la Haskalah." In Hadas-Lebel and Oliel-Grausz, 285–298.

Baumgarten, Jean, Rachel Ertel, Itzhok Naborski, and Annette Wievorkia, eds. *Mille ans de cultures ashkénases.* (Paris: Liana Levi, 1994).

Bechtel, Delphine. "La Haskalah berlinoise." In Baumgarten, Ertel, Naborski, and Wievorkia, 354–357.

Beck, Wolfgang, ed. *Die Juden in der europäischen Geschichte.* (Munich: Verlag C.H. Beck, 1992).

Ben-Amos, Dan, and Jerome Mintz, ed. and trans. *In Praise of the Ba'al Shem Tov: The Earliest Collection of Legends About the Founder of Hasidism.* (Northvale, NJ: Jason Aronson Inc., 1993).

——. "Introduction." In Ben-Amos and Mintz, xxi–xxx.

Ben-Porat, Ziva. "The Poetics of Literary Allusion." *PTL: A Journal for Descriptive Poetics and Theory of Literature* 1 (1976), 105–128.

——. "Hakore, hatekst, veharemiza hasifrutit." *Hasifrut* 26 (1978), 1–25.

Ben-Sasson, Menakhem, ed. *Dat vekalkala.* (Jerusalem: Zalman Shazar, 1995).

Benbassa, Esther, ed. *Mémoires Juives D'Espagne et du Portugal.* (Paris: Centre Nationale du Livre, 1996).

Benston, Alice N. "Portia, the Law, and the Tripartite Structure of *The Merchant of Venice.*" In Wheeler, 163–194.

Berger, Michael S. *Rabbinic Authority.* (New York: Oxford University Press, 1998).

Biale, David. "Eros and Enlightenment: Love Against Marriage in the East European Jewish Enlightenment." *Polin* 1 (1986), 49–67.

——. *Power and Powerlessness in Jewish History.* (New York: Schocken Books, 1986).

Bonfil, Robert. *Jewish Life in Renaissance Italy.* (Berkeley: University of California Press, 1994).

Borokhov, Ber. *Shprakh-forshung un literatur-geshikhte.* (Tel Aviv: Y.L. Peretz Farlag, 1966).

——. "Di bibliotek funem yidishn filolog." In Borokhov, 76–136.

Boyarin, Jonathan, and Daniel Boyarin, eds. *Jews and Other Differences: The New Jewish Cultural Studies.* (Minneapolis: University of Minnesota Press, 1997).

Bradford, Richard, ed. *Introducing Literary Studies.* (London: Prentice Hall, 1996),

Brawer, Avraham. *Galitsia veyehudeha: mekhkarim betoldot galitsia bemea hashmona esre.* (Jerusalem: Mossad Bialik, 1956).

Brenner, Michael. Review of David Sorkin's *Moses Mendelssohn and the Religious Enlightenment. Journal of Jewish Studies* 48:1 (1997), 178–180.

Breuer, Edward. "Hahaskala vehamikra: iyun bikhtavav hakedumim shel Moshe Mendelson." *Zion* 59:4 (1994), 445–463.

——. "Of Miracles and Events Past: Mendelssohn on History." *Jewish History* 9:2 (1995), 27–52.

——. "Between Haskalah and Orthodoxy: The Writings of R. Jacob Zvi Meklenburg." *Hebrew Union College Annual* 66 (1996), 259–287.

——. *The Limits of Enlightenment: Jews, Germans, and the Eighteenth-Century Study of Scripture.* (Cambridge, MA: Harvard University Press, 1996).

——. "Rabbinic Law and Spirituality in Mendelssohn's Jerusalem." *Jewish Quarterly Review* 86:3–4 (1996), 299–321.

——. "(Re)Creating Traditions of Language and Texts: The Haskalah and Cultural Continuity." *Modern Judaism* 16:2 (1996), 161–183.

——. "Reading the Silences: Rabbinic and Maskilic Cultures in the Early Nineteenth Century." Unpublished paper presented February 1998 at the Conference in Honor and Memory of Professor Isidore Twersky.

Breuer, Mordechai. "Hashpaa sfardit beashkenaz besof yemei-habeinayim uvereishit haet hakhadasha." *Peamim* 57 (1994), 17–28.

Brown, John Russell. "Love's Wealth and the Judgment of *The Merchant of Venice*." In Barnet, 81–90.

——. "The Realization of Shylock: A Theatrical Criticism." In Wheeler, 263–291.

Bruford, W.H. *Theatre, Drama, and Audience in Goethe's Germany.* (London: Routledge and Kegan Paul, Ltd., 1950).

Cardozo, Jacob Lopes. *The Contemporary Jew in the Elizabethan Drama.* (Amsterdam: 1925).

Cassirer, Ernst. *The Philosophy of the Enlightenment.* (Princeton: Princeton University Press, 1951).

Coghill, Nevill. "The Theme of *The Merchant of Venice*." In Barnet, 108–113.

Cohen, Jeremy. "Medieval Jews on Christianity: Polemical Strategies and Theological Defense." In Fisher, 77–89.

Cohen, Tova. "Hatekhnika halamdanit—tsofen shel sifrut hahaskala." *Mekhkerei yerushalayim besifrut ivrit* 13 (1992), 137–169.

——. "Bein-tekstualiut besifrut hahaskala: mekomo shel hatekst habilti katuv." *Bikoret ufarshanut* 31 (1995), 37–52.

——. "The Maskil as Lamdan: The Influence of Jewish Education on Haskalah Writing Techniques." In Abramson and Parfitt, 61–74.

Conte, Gian Biagio. *The Rhetoric of Imitation: Genre and Poetic Memory in Virgil and Other Latin Poets.* (Ithaca: Cornell University Press, 1986).

Dahlstrom, Daniel O. "Introduction." In Mendelssohn *Philosophical Writings* ix–xxxix.

Dan, Joseph. *Hasipur hakhasidi.* (Jerusalem: Keter Publishing House, 1975).

——. *Iyunim besifrut khasidei ashkenaz.* (Ramat Gan: Masada, 1975).

——. "Preface." In Nachman of Bratslav *Tales* xiii–xix.

——. *Gershom Scholem and the Mystical Dimension of Jewish History.* (New York: New York University Press, 1988).

Dan, Joseph, and Frank Talmadge, eds. *Studies in Jewish Mysticism*. (Cambridge, MA: Association of Jewish Studies, 1978).

Danson, Lawrence. *The Harmonies of The Merchant of Venice*. (New Haven: Yale University Press, 1978).

Dauber, Jeremy. "Some Notes on Hebraisms in the Yiddish 'Megale Temirin'," *Zutot* 1:1 (Fall 2001), 180–185.

——. "New Thoughts on 'Night Thoughts': Mendelssohn and Translation," *Modern Jewish Studies* 2:2 (2003), 132–147.

——. "The City, Sacred and Profane: Between Hebrew and Yiddish in the Fiction of the Early Jewish Enlightenment," in *Urban Diaspora: The City in Jewish History*, forthcoming.

Deleuze, Gilles, and Félix Guattari. *Kafka: Toward a Minor Literature*. Trans. Dana Polan. (Minneapolis: University of Minnesota, 1986).

Dreyfus, Theodor. "Yakhaso shel Moshe Mendelson el R' Yaakov Emden." In Khalamish and Schwartz, 99–112.

Dubin, Lois C. "The Social and Cultural Context: Eighteenth-Century Enlightenment." In Frank and Leaman, 636–659.

Dubnow, Simon. "Der ershter kamf fun haskole kegn khsides." *YIVO-Bleter* 1 (1930), 4–8.

Eisen, Arnold. "Divine Legislation as 'Ceremonial Script': Mendelssohn on the Commandments." *AJSReview* 15:2 (1990), 239–267.

Eisenstein-Barzilay, Isaac. "The Treatment of the Jewish Religion in the Literature of the Berlin Haskalah." *Proceedings of the American Academy for Jewish Research* 24 (1955), 39–68.

——. "The Ideology of the Berlin Haskalah." *Proceedings of the American Academy for Jewish Research* 25 (1956), 1–37.

——. "National and Anti-National Trends in the Berlin Haskalah." *Jewish Social Studies* 21:3 (1959), 165–192.

——. "The Italian and Berlin Haskalah." *Proceedings of the American Academy for Jewish Research* 29 (1960), 17–54.

——. "Smolenskin's Polemic Against Mendelssohn in Historical Perspective." *Proceedings of the American Academy for Jewish Research* 53 (1986), 11–48.

——. "Early Responses to the Emancipation in Hebrew Haskalah Literature." *Judaism* 38:4 (1989), 517–526.

Elbaum, Yaakov. *Petikhut vehistagrut: hayetsira harukhanit-hasifrutit bePolin ubeartsot Ashkenaz beshilhei hamea hashesh-esre*. (Jerusalem: Magnes Press, 1990).

Elior, Rachel. "Between *Yesh* and *Ayin*: The Doctrine of the Zaddik in the Works of Jacob Isaac, the Seer of Lublin." In Rapoport-Albert and Zipperstein, 393–455.

Elshteyn, Yoav. *Haekstaza vehasipur hakhasidi*. (Ramat Gan: Bar-Ilan, 1998).

Elzet, Yehuda. "Shmuesn vegn hebreyish-yidish un yidish-hebreyish." In Mark *Yofe-bukh* 236–256.

Encyclopaedia Judaica. (Jerusalem: Keter Publishing House, Ltd., 1971).

Erik, Max. *Di komedyes fun der berliner oyfklerung*. (Melukhe-Farlag: Kiev, 1933).

Ernst, Sh. "Tekstn un kveln tsu der geshikhte fun teyatr, farveylungn un masker- adn bay yidn." In Shatsky *Arkhiv-geshikhte* 5–37.

Etkes, Immanuel. "Hasidism as a Movement—The First Stage." In Safran, 1–26.

——, ed. *Hadat vehakhayim: tnuat hahaskala hayehudit bemizrakh eyropa*. (Jeru- salem: Zalman Shazar, 1993).

——. "The Zaddik: The Interrelationship Between Religious Doctrine and Social Organization." In Rapoport-Albert *Hasidism Reappraised* 159–167.

Euchel, Isaac. *Toldot rabeinu hakhakham moshe ben menakhem*. (Berlin: 1788).

Fackenheim, Emil L. and Raphael Jospe, eds. *Jewish Philosophy and the Academy*. (Teaneck, NJ: Farleigh Dickinson Unversity Press, 1996).

Faierstein, Morris M. "Hasidism—the Last Decade in Research." *Modern Judaism* 11 (1991), 111–124.

Fedye, Khaviva. "Lehitpatkhuto shel hadegem hakhevrati-dati-kalkali bakhasidut: hapidyon, hakhavura, vehaaliya laregel." In Ben-Sasson, 311–374.

Feiner, Shmuel. "Yitzkhak Aykhl—ha'yazam' shel tenuat hahaskala begermania." *Zion* 52 (1987), 427–469.

——. "Mendelson ve'talmidei Mendelson': bekhina mekhadash." *Kongres olami lemakhshevet yisrael* 11B2 (1994), 1–8.

——. *Haskala vehistoria: toldoteha shel hakarat-avar yehudit modernit*. (Jerusalem: Zalman Shazar, 1995).

——. "Mendelssohn and 'Mendelssohn's Disciples': A Re-examination." *Leo Baeck Institute Yearbook* 40 (1995), 133–167.

——. "Sefarad Dans Les Representations Historiques de la Haskala—Entre Mod- ernisme et Conservatisme." In Benbassa, 239–250.

——. *Haskala and History: The Emergence of a Modern Jewish Historical Consciousness*. (Oxford: Littman Library of Jewish Civilization, 2002).

Feingold, Ben-Ami. "Hasefer vehasifrut kenose besiporet hamaskilit." *Teuda* 5 (1986), 85–100.

——. "Makhazaei hahaskala vehamikra." *Teuda* 7 (1991), 429–449.

Fischer, Barbara. "Residues of Otherness: On Jewish Emancipation during the Age of German Enlightenment." In Lorenz and Weinberger, 30–38.

Fish, Stanley. *Self-Consuming Artifacts: The Experience of Seventeenth Century Liter- ature*. (Berkeley, CA: University of California Press, 1972).

——. *Is There a Text in This Class?* (Cambridge, MA: Harvard University Press, 1980).

Fishbane, Michael, ed. *The Midrashic Imagination: Jewish Exegesis, Thought, and History*. (Albany, NY: State University of New York Press, 1993).

Fisher, Eugene J., ed. *Interwoven Destinies: Jews and Christians Through the Ages*. (New York: Paulist Press, 1993).

Fishman, David E. "A Polish Rabbi Meets the Berlin Haskalah: The Case of R. Barukh Schick." *AJSReview* 12:1 (1987), 95–121.

Fishman, Joshua A., ed. *Readings in the Sociology of Jewish Languages.* (Leiden: E.J. Brill, 1985).

——. *Language and Ethnicity in Minority Sociolinguistic Perspective.* (Philadelphia: Multilingual Matters Ltd., 1989).

Fleischer, Ezra. "The Gerona School of Hebrew Poetry." In Twersky *Nachmanides* 35–49.

Frank, Daniel H. and Oliver Leaman, eds. *History of Jewish Philosophy.* (London: Routledge Press, 1997).

Frankel, Jonathan, and Steven J. Zipperstein, eds. *Assimilation and Community: The Jews in Nineteenth Century Europe.* (Cambridge: Cambridge University Press, 1992).

——. "Assimilation and the Jews in Nineteenth Century Europe: Towards a New Historiography?" In Frankel and Zipperstein, 1–37.

Frei, Hans W. *The Eclipse of Biblical Narrative: A Study in Eighteenth and Nineteenth Century Hermeneutics.* (New Haven: Yale University Press, 1974).

Freimark, Peter. "Language Behaviour and Assimilation: The Situation of the Jews in Modern Germany in the First Half of the Nineteenth Century." *Leo Baeck Institute Year Book* 24 (1979), 157–177.

Friedlander, Yehuda. "Mekomo shel hahalakha besifrut hahaskala—hayakhas leRambam keposek." *Mekhkerei yerushalayim bemaskhshevet yisrael* 5 (1986), 349–392.

——. "HaRambam veElisha ben Avuya kearkhetipusim besifrut haivrit hakhadasha." In Nash, 271–282.

Friedman, Philip. "Yoysef Perl vi a bildungs-tuer un zayn shul in Tarnopol." *YIVO-Bleter* 21–22 (1948), 131–190.

Funkenstein, Amos. *Tadmit vetodaa historit.* (Tel Aviv: Am Oved, 1991).

——. *Perceptions of Jewish History.* (Berkeley: University of California Press, 1993).

Gelber, Mark H., ed. *Identity and Ethos: A Festschrift for Sol Liptzin on the Occasion of His 85th Birthday.* (New York: Peter Lang, 1986).

Gelber, N.H. "Mendl-Lefin Satanover vehatzaotav letikun orakh khayim shel yehudei polin bifnei haseym hagadol (1788–1792)." In Lander, 271–306.

The *Geneva Bible.* Facsimile of 1560 Edition. (Madison, WI: University of Wisconsin Press, 1969).

Gerhard, Anselm, ed. *Musik und Ästhetik im Berlin Moses Mendelssohns.* (Tübingen: Niemeyer, 1999).

Gilboa, Menakhem. "Shlomo Maimon: sefer khaiei Shlomo Maimon—katuv bidei atsmo." In Nash, 75–99.

Gilboa, Menukha. "'Avtalyon'—Rei letfisa hahistoriografit shel hahaskala hakitsonit." *Mahut* 8–9 (1991–1992), 214–218.

——. "Merkezei hasifrut haivrit hekhadasha ad mea haesrim." In Shamir and Holz-man, 113–123.

Gilman, Sander L. *Jewish Self-Hatred*. (Baltimore: Johns Hopkins University Press, 1986).

Gilon, Meir. *Kohelet musar leMendelson al reka tkufato*. (Jerusalem: Publications of the Israel Academy of the Sciences and Humanities, 1979).

——. "Hasatira haivrit bitkufat hahaskala begermania—anatomia shel mekhkar." *Zion* 52 (1987), 211–250.

Girard, René. "'To Entrap the Wisest': A Reading of *The Merchant of Venice*." In Said, 100–119.

Glinert, Lewis, ed. *Hebrew in Ashkenaz: A Language in Exile*. (Oxford: Oxford University Press, 1993).

Goetschel, Roland. "L'hostilité du monde hassidique à la révolution française." In Hadas-Lebel and Oliel-Grausz, 267–283.

Golomb, Tsvi Nison. *Milim bilshoyni: hebreyish-yidishes verter-bukh*. (Vilna: Yavor-ski, 1910).

Gordon, Nathan. "Joseph Perl's Megalleh Temirin." *Hebrew Union College Annual* (1904), 235–242.

Granville-Barker, Harley. "The Merchant of Venice." In Barnet, 55–80.

Green, Arthur. *Tormented Master: A Life of Rabbi Nachman of Bratslav*. (University, Alabama: University of Alabama Press, 1979).

Green, Kenneth Hart. "Moses Mendelssohn's Opposition to the Herem: The First Step Towards Denominationalism?" *Modern Judaism* 12:1 (1992), 39–60.

Greenblatt, Stephen. "Resonance and Wonder." In Ryan, 55–60.

Gries, Zeev. "The Hasidic Managing Editor as an Agent of Culture." In Rapoport-Albert *Hasidism Reappraised* 141–155.

Gross, John. *Shylock: Four Hundred Years in the Life of a Legend*. (London: Chatto & Windus, 1992).

Grossman, Jeffrey A. *The Discourse on Yiddish in Germany: From the Enlightenment to the Second Empire*. (Rochester, NY: Camden House, 2000).

Grözinger, Karl Erich. "The Source Value of the Basic Rescensions of *Shivhei HaBesht*." In Rapoport-Albert *Hasidism Reappraised* 354–363.

Gruenwald, Ithamar. "Midrash & The 'Midrashic Condition': Preliminary Con-siderations." In Fishbane, 6–22.

Gründer, Karlfried. "Johann David Michaelis und Moses Mendelssohn." In Katz and Rengstorf, 25–50.

Haas, Peter J., ed. *Recovering the Role of Women: Power and Authority in Rabbinic Jewish Society*. (Atlanta, GA: Scholars Press, 1992).

Haberman, A.M. *Kvutsei yakhad*. (Jerusalem: Rubin Mass, 1980).

——. "Haim katav Yosef Perl khiburim beyidish." In Haberman, 143–149.

Hadas-Lebel, Mireille, and Evelyn Oliel-Grausz, eds. *Les juifs et la Révolution française: Histoire et mentalités*. (Paris: E. Peeters, 1992).

Haftorot mikol hashana im targum ashkenazi vebeiur. (Berlin: 1790).

Halbertal, Moshe. *People of the Book: Canon, Meaning, and Authority.* (Cambridge, MA: Harvard University Press, 1997).

Halivni, David Weiss. *Peshat and Derash: Plain and Applied Meaning in Rabbinic Exegesis.* (New York: Oxford University Press, 1991).

Halkin, Simon. *Modern Hebrew Literature: Trends and Values.* (New York: Schocken Books, 1950).

Hameasef. (Königsberg and Berlin, 1784–1797).

Handelman, Susan. "'Everything Is In It': Rabbinic Interpretation and Modern Literary Theory." *Judaism* 35:4 (1986), 429–40.

Harris, Jay. *Nachman Krochmal: Guiding the Perplexed of the Modern Age.* (New York: New York University Press, 1991).

Harshav, Benjamin. *The Meaning of Yiddish.* (Berkeley: University of California Press, 1990).

——. *Language in Time of Revolution.* (Berkeley: University of California Press, 1993).

Heinemann, Joseph, and Shmuel Werses, eds. *Studies in Hebrew Narrative Art Throughout the Ages.* (Jerusalem: Hebrew University, 1978).

Hellerstein, Kathryn. "Gender Studies and Yiddish Literature." In Lerner, Norich, and Sokoloff, 249–255.

Hertz, Deborah. *Jewish High Society in Old Regime Berlin.* (New Haven: Yale University Press, 1988).

Hildesheimer, Meir. "Moses Mendelssohn in Nineteenth Century Rabbinical Literature." *Proceedings of the American Academy for Jewish Research* 55 (1989), 79–133.

——. "The Attitude of the Hatam Sofer Toward Moses Mendelssohn." *Proceedings of the American Academy for Jewish Research* 60 (1994), 141–187.

Holland, Eva Engel. "The World of Moses Mendelssohn." *Leo Baeck Institute Year Book* 36 (1991), 27–43.

Hundert, Gershon David, ed. *Essential Papers on Hasidism.* (New York University Press: New York, 1991).

——. "The Conditions in Jewish Society in the Polish-Lithuanian Commonwealth in the Middle Decades of the Eighteenth Century." In Rapaport-Albert *Hasidism Reappraised* 45–50.

Hyman, Paula E. "Traditionalism and Village Jews in 19th Century Western and Central Europe: Local Persistence and Urban Nostalgia." In Wertheimer, 191–201.

Idel, Moshe. *Hasidism: Between Ecstasy and Magic.* (Albany: State University of New York Press, 1995).

Iram, Yaacov. "L'éducation juive moderne de l'époque de la Haskala à la fondation de l'État d'Israël." *La société juive a travers l'histoire* II (1992), 351–381.

Iser, Wolfgang. *The Range of Interpretation.* (New York: Columbia University Press, 2000).

Israel, Jonathan I. *European Jewry in the Age of Mercantilism, 1550–1750.* (Oxford: Clarendon Press, 1989).

Jacobs, Louis. "Hasidism and the Dogma of the Decline of the Generations." In Rapoport-Albert *Hasidism Reappraised* 208–213.

Jospe, Raphael. "Biblical Exegesis as a Philosophic Literary Genre: Abraham Ibn Ezra and Moses Mendelssohn." In Fackenheim and Jospe, 48–92.

Kalmanovitsh, Zelig. "Yoysef Perl's yidishe ksovim: literarisher un shprokhiker analiz." In Perl *Yidishe ksovim* lxxi–cvii.

Kaplan, Lawrence. "Supplementary Notes on the Medieval Jewish Sources of Mendelssohn's *Jerusalem.*" *Jewish Quarterly Review* 87:3–4 (1997), 339–342.

Katan, Moshe. "Dmut hamahapekha beshira haivrit shel yehudei tsarfat beshilhei hamea hayud khet uvereishit hamea hayud tet." *Mahut* 19 (1987), 37–45.

Katz, Dovid. "Hebrew, Aramaic, and the Rise of Yiddish." In Fishman *Readings* 85–103.

——. "On Yiddish, in Yiddish, and for Yiddish: 500 Years of Yiddish Scholarship." In Gelber *Identity* 23–36.

——. "Notions of Yiddish." In Abramson and Parfitt, 75–92.

Katz, Jacob. "Lemi ana Mendelson bi'Yerushalayim' shelo?" *Zion* 29 (1964), 112–132; 36 (1971), 116–117.

——. *Emancipation and Assimilation: Studies in Modern Jewish History.* (Westmead: Gregg International Publishers, 1972).

——. "Freemasons and Jews." In Katz *Emancipation* 147–158.

——. "The German-Jewish Utopia of Social Emancipation." In Katz *Emancipation* 90–110.

——. "Judaism and Christianity Against the Background of Modern Secularism." In Katz *Emancipation* 111–127.

——. "A State Within a State: The History of an Anti-Semitic Slogan." In Katz *Emancipation* 47–76.

——. "The Term 'Jewish Emancipation': Its Origin and Historical Impact." In Katz *Emancipation* 21–45.

——. *Out of the Ghetto: The Social Background of Jewish Emancipation 1770–1870.* (New York: Schocken Books, 1978).

——. "Rabbinical Authority and Authorization in the Middle Ages." In Twersky *Studies* 41–56.

——. "R' Raphael Cohen, yerivo shel Moshe Mendelson." *Tarbiz* 56:2 (1987), 243–264.

——, ed. *Toward Modernity: The European Jewish Model.* (New York: Leo Baeck Institute, 1987).

——. "The Unique Fascination of German-Jewish History." *Modern Judaism* 9:2 (1989), 141–150.

——. *Tradition and Crisis: Jewish Society at the End of the Middle Ages.* (New York: Schocken Books, 1993).

——. "Frühantisemitismus in Deutschland." In Katz and Rengstorf, 79–89.

Katz, Jacob, and Rengstorf, Karl Heinrich, eds. *Begegnung von Deutschen und Juden in der Geistgeschichte des 18. Jahrhunderts.* (Tübingen: Max Niemayer Verlag, 1994).

Katz, Simkha. "Hosafot lireshimat dfusei Tarnopol." *Kiryat Sefer* 15 (1938), 515–516.

——. "Naye materyaln fun dem Perl-arkhiv: Yoysef Perl's hakdome tsu zayn 'Megale Tmirin' in yidish." *YIVO-Bleter* 13 (1938), 557–576.

——. "Targumei tanakh meet Menakhem Mendel Lefin misatanov." *Kiryat Sefer* 16 (1939–1940), 114–133.

——. "Igrot maskilim bignutam shel khasidim." *Mosnayim* 10:2–3 (1940), 266–276.

Kerler, Dov-Ber. "The Eighteenth Century Origins of Modern Literary Yiddish." (D.Phil. thesis, University of Oxford, 1988).

Khalamish, Moshe, and Moshe Schwartz, eds. *Hitgalut, Emuna, Tevuna: Kovets Hartsaot.* (Ramat Gan: Bar-Ilan University, 1996).

Kittel, Harald, ed. *Di literarische Übersetzung: Stand und Perspektiven ihrer Erforschung.* (Berlin: Erich Schmidt Verlag, 1988).

Klausner, Joseph. *A History of Modern Hebrew Literature (1785–1930).* (London: M.L. Cailingold, 1932).

——. *Historia shel hasifrut haivrit hakhadasha.* (Jerusalem: Hebrew University Press, 1937).

——. *Hanovela besifrut haivrit.* (Tel Aviv: J. Chachik, 1947).

——. *Kitvei Prof. Yosef Klausner: Beaiot shel sifrut umada.* (Tel Aviv: Masada 1956).

——. "Hishtalsheluto shel signon-hamishna besifrut haivrit hakhadasha." In Klausner *Kitvei* 118–146.

Knowles, James. "Reader-response criticism." In Bradford, 559–567.

Kochan, Lionel E. "La fin de la kehila: Forces sociales dans la société juive d'Europe centrale et orientale aux xviie et xviiie siècles." *Le société juive a travers l'histoire* I (1992), 531–563.

——. "Moses Mendelssohn as Political Educator." In Abramson and Parfitt, 299–306.

Kohler, Max J. "Educational Reforms in Europe in Their Relation to Jewish Emancipation—1778–1919." *Publications of the American Jewish Historical Society* 28 (1922), 83–132.

Kronfeld, Chana. "Beyond Deleuze and Guattari: Hebrew and Yiddish Modernism in the Age of Privileged Difference." In Boyarin and Boyarin, 257–278.

Kurzweil, Baruch. *Sifruteinu hakhadasha: hemshekh o mahapekha?* (Jerusalem: Schocken, 1960).

——. *Bemaavak al erkhei hayahadut.* (Schocken: Jerusalem, 1969).

——. "Al hasatira shel Yosef Perl." In Kurzweil *Bemaavak* 55–85.

Lachover, Fishel. *Toldot hasifrut haivrit hakhadasha.* (Tel Aviv: Dvir, 1947).

Lander, Bernard, ed. *The Abraham Weiss Jubilee Volume.* (New York: Shulsinger Bros., 1964).

Lerner, Anne Lapidus, Anita Norich, and Naomi B. Sokoloff, eds. *Gender and Text in Modern Hebrew and Yiddish Literature.* (New York: Jewish Theological Seminary, distrib. Harvard University Press, 1992).

Lesley, Arthur M. "Proverbs, Figures, and Riddles: The *Dialogues of Love* as a Hebrew Humanist Composition." In Fishbane, 204–225.

Lewalski, Barbara K. "Biblical Allusion and Allegory in *The Merchant of Venice*." In Barnet, 33–54.

Liberman, Khayim. *Ohel Rokhl.* (Empire Press: New York, 1980).

——. "Legende un emes vegn khsidishe drukerayen." In Liberman *Ohel Rokhl* 2:17–160.

——. "R[eb] Nakhman Bratslaver un di umaner maskilim." In Liberman *Ohel Rokhl* 2:161–197.

——. "Tsu der frage vegn der batsiyung fun khsides tsu yidish." In Liberman *Ohel Rokhl* 2:1–11.

Loebl, Israel. *Sefer Vikuakh.* (Warsaw: 1798).

Lorenz, Dagmar C. G., and Gabriele Weinberger, eds. *Insiders and Outsiders: Jewish and Gentile Culture in Germany and Austria.* (Detroit: Wayne State University Press, 1994).

Löwenbrück, Anna-Ruth. "Johann David Michaelis und Moses Mendelssohn: Judenfeindschaft im Zeitalter der Aufklärung." In Albrecht, Engel, and Hinske, 316–332.

Lowenstein, Steven M. "Jewish Upper Crust and Berlin Jewish Enlightenment: The Family of Daniel Itzig." In Malino and Sorkin, 182–201.

——. "Two Silent Minorities: Orthodox Jews and Poor Jews in Berlin 1770–1823." *Leo Baeck Institute Yearbook* 36 (1991), 3–25.

——. *The Mechanics of Change: Essays in the Social History of German Jewry.* (Atlanta: Scholars Press, 1992).

——. "The Readership of Mendelssohn's Bible Translation." In Lowenstein *Mechanics* 29–64.

——. "The Yiddish Written Word in Nineteenth Century Germany." In Lowenstein *Mechanics* 183–199.

——. "The Social Dynamics of Jewish Responses to Moses Mendelssohn (with Special Emphasis on the Mendelssohn Bible Translation and on the Berlin Jewish Community)." In Albrecht, Engel, and Hinske, 333–348.

——. *The Berlin Jewish Community: Enlightenment, Family, and Crisis, 1770–1830.* (Oxford: Oxford University Press, 1994).

Lyon, John. "Beginning in the Middle." In Wheeler, 217–240.

Magnus, Shulamit S. "German Jewish History." *Modern Judaism* 11 (1991), 125–146.

Magocsi, Paul Robert. *Galicia: A Historical Survey and Bibliographic Guide.* (Toronto: University of Toronto Press, 1983).

Mahler, Raphael. *Hasidism and the Jewish Enlightenment: Their Confrontation in Galicia and Poland in the First Half of the Nineteenth Century.* (Philadelphia: Jewish Publication Society, 1985).

——. "Milkhamto shel Yosef Perl bekhasidut leor mismakhim." In Etkes *Hadat* 64–88.

Maimon, Solomon. "On a Secret Society, and Therefore a Long Chapter." In Hundert *Essential Papers* 11–24.

——. "Recollections of Mendelssohn." In Robertson, 46–53.

Maimonides, Moses. *Yad Hakhazaka.* (Amsterdam: 1702).

Malino, Frances, and David Sorkin, eds. *From East and West: Jews in a Changing Europe, 1750–1870.* (London: Basil Blackwell, 1990).

Manuel, Frank E. *The Broken Staff: Judaism Through Christian Eyes.* (Cambridge, MA: Harvard University Press, 1992).

Mark, Yudl, ed. *Yuda A. Yofe-bukh.* (New York: Bibliotek fun YIVO, 1958).

——. "Vos iz a vort fun der yidisher shprakh?" In Mark *Yofe-bukh* 287–298.

——. "Tsu der geshikhte fun der yidisher literatur-shprakh." In Shtarkman, 121–143.

Marten, Wolfgang. "Zur Figur eines edlen Juden im Aufklärungsroman vor Lessing." In Katz and Rengstorf, 65–77.

Mazor, Yair. "The Poetics of Composition of the Hebrew Short Story in the Haskalah Period." *AJS Review* 10:1 (1985), 89–110.

Mendelssohn, Moses. *Megilat shir hashirim meturgemet ashkenazit al yedei harav rabeinu moshe ben menakhem zs'l venilve eilav beiur hamilot meet aharon benvolf umar'ehu yoel bril.* (Berlin: 1788).

——. *Phaedon, or the Death of Socrates.* Trans. Charles Cullen. (London: J. Cooper, 1789).

——. *Gesammelte Schriften.* Ed. G.B. Mendelssohn. (Leipzig: 1843–1845).

——. *Gesammelte Schriften: Jubiläumausgabe* (Stuttgart-Bad Connstatt: F. Fromam, 1971–).

——. *Kohelet Musar.* In Gilon *Kohelet Musar* 157–180.

——. *Jerusalem.* Trans. and ed. Allan Arkush. (Hanover, NH: University Press of New England, 1983).

——. *Philosophical Writings.* Ed. Daniel O. Dahlstrom. (Cambridge: Cambridge University Press, 1997).

Mendes-Flohr, Paul. "Mendelssohn and Rosensweig." *Journal of Jewish Studies* 38:2 (1987), 203–11.

Mendes-Flohr, Paul, and Jehuda Reinharz, eds. *The Jew in the Modern World.* (New York: Oxford University Press, 1995).

Meyer, Michael A. *The Origins of the Modern Jew: Jewish Identity and European Culture in Germany, 1749–1824.* (Detroit: Wayne State University Press, 1967).

——. "Modernity as a Crisis for the Jews." *Modern Judaism* 9:2 (1989), 151–164.

——, ed. *German Jewish History in Modern Times: Volume 1: Tradition and Enlightenment, 1600–1780.* (New York: Columbia University Press, 1996).

——, ed. *German Jewish History in Modern Times: Volume 2: Emancipation and Acculturation, 1780–1871.* (New York: Columbia University Press, 1997).

Michael, Reuven. "Hahaskala bitkufat hamahapekha hatsarfatit—hakets le'haskalat berlin'?" *Zion* 56:3 (1991), 275–298.

——. *Haketiva hahistorit hayehudit: meharenesans ad haet hakhadasha.* (Jerusalem: Mosad Bialik, 1993).

Mintz, Alan. *"Banished from Their Father's Table": Loss of Faith and Hebrew Autobiography.* (Bloomington: Indiana University Press, 1989).

Miron, Dan. "Al aharon volfson vemakhazehu 'kalut dat utseviut' (r' henokh verav yosefkhe)." In Wolfssohn *Kalut Dat* 5–55.

——. "Rediscovering Haskalah Poetry." *Prooftexts* 1 (1981), 292–305.

——. *A Traveler Disguised.* (Syracuse, NY: University of Syracuse Press, 1996, 2nd ed.).

Morgan, Michael L. "Mendelssohn's Defense of Reason in Judaism." *Judaism* 38:4 (1989), 449–459.

——. *Dilemmas in Modern Jewish Thought: The Dialectics of Revelation and History.* (Bloomington: University of Indiana Press, 1992).

——. "Mendelssohn." In Frank and Leaman, 660–681.

Murray, John Middleton. "Shakespeare's Method: *The Merchant of Venice.*" In Wheeler, 37–57.

Nachman of Bratslav. *Likutei Moharan.* (Mohilev: 1809).

——. *Kitsur Likutei Moharan.* (Mohilev: 1811).

——. *Likutei Moharan Tanina.* (Mohilev: 1809).

——. *Sikhot Haran.* (Jerusalem: Kedem, 1944).

——. *The Tales.* Ed. and trans. Arnold J. Band. (New York: Paulist Press, 1978).

——. *Sipurei Maasiyot.* (Jerusalem: 1985).

Nash, Shlomo, ed. *Bein historia lesifrut.* (Jerusalem: Keren Yitchak Kiyov, 1997).

Nigal, Gedaliah. *Hasiporet hakhasidit: toldoteha venos'eha.* (Jerusalem: Marcus Press, 1981).

——. *Magic, Mysticism, and Hasidism.* (London: Jason Aronson Inc., 1994).

——. "New Light on the Hasidic Tale and Its Sources." In Rapoport-Albert *Hasidism Reappraised* 345–353.

Niger, Shmuel. *Dertseylers un romanistn.* (New York: CYCO Bikher Farlag, 1946).

——. *Bleter-geshikhte fun der yidisher literatur.* (New York: Alveltlekhn yidishn kultur-kongres, 1959).

——. "R[eb] Nakhman Bratslaver un zayne sipurey-mayses." In Niger *Bleter-geshikhte* 111–177.

——. "Di yidishe literatur un di lezerin." In Niger *Bleter-geshikhte* 37–107.

Noble, Richmond. *Shakespeare's Biblical Knowledge.* (New York: Octagon Books, 1970).

Noble, Shlomo. *Khumesh-taytch.* (New York: YIVO, 1943).

Norich, Anita. "Yiddish Literary Studies." *Modern Judaism* 10:3 (1990), 297–309.

Overton, Bill. "The Problem of Shylock." In Wheeler, 293–313.

Pagis, Dan. *Hebrew Poetry of the Middle Ages and the Renaissance.* (Berkeley: University of California Press, 1991).

Parush, Iris. "Mabat akher al 'khayei haivrit hameta'." *Alpayim* 13 (1987), 65–106.

——. "Readers in Cameo: Women Readers in Jewish Society of Nineteenth Century Eastern Europe." *Prooftexts* 14 (1994), 1–23.

——. "The Politics of Literacy: Women and Foreign Languages in Jewish Society of 19th Century Eastern Europe." *Modern Judaism* 15:2 (1995), 183–206.

Pasco, Allan H. *Allusion: A Literary Graft*. (Toronto: University of Toronto Press, 1994).

Patterson, David. "Moses Mendelssohn's Concept of Tolerance." In Altmann *Between East and West* 149–163.

Patterson, Lee. "Historical Criticism and the Claims of Humanism." In Ryan, 92–102.

Pelli, Moshe. *Moshe Mendelson: bekhavlei masoret*. (Israel: Hotzaat sefarim aleph, 1972).

——. *The Age of Haskalah: Studies in Hebrew Literature of the Enlightenment in Germany*. (Leiden: E.J. Brill, 1979).

——. "The Beginning of the Epistolary Genre in Hebrew Enlightenment Literature in Germany: The Alleged Affinity Between Lettres Persanes and 'Igrot Meshulam'." *Leo Baeck Institute Year Book* 24 (1979), 83–103.

——. *Bemaavakei tmura: iyunim behaskala haivrit begermania beshilhei hamea hayud khet*. (Tel Aviv: Mifalim universitiyim, 1988).

——. "Moshe Mendelson kidmut hayehudi hekhadash bemoral biografi shel Yitzkhak Aykhl." *Bitsaron* 45–48 (1990–91), 118–127.

——. "The Literary Genre of the Travelogue in Hebrew Haskalah Literature: Shmuel Romanelli's Masa Ba'arav." *Modern Judaism* 11:2 (1991), 241–260.

——. "Tfisat hamelitsa bereshit sifrut hahaskala haivrit." *Lashon veivrit* 8 (1991), 31–48.

——. "On the Role of *Melitzah* in the Literature of the Hebrew Enlightenment." In Glinert, 99–110.

——. "Hasuga shel hamashal besifrut hahaskala haivrit begermania: giluyei hamashal beHameasef." *Kongres olami lemakhshevet yisrael* 11C3 (1994), 45–52.

——. "'Ktav Yosher' leShaul Berlin: lereshita shel hasatira behaskala haivrit begermania." *Hebrew Union College Annual* 64 (1994), 1–25, Hebrew section.

——. "Leshimusha shel hamelitsa besifrut hahaskala—piknik leshoni im Romaneli, Aykhl veakherim." *Bikoret ufarshanut* 31 (1995), 53–65.

——. "Habiografia kezhanr behaskala: dmuto shel Yitzkhak Abravanel kemaskil hamegasher bein shtei tarbuyot." *Mekhkerei Yerushalayim Besifrut Ivrit* 17 (1997), 75–88.

——. "Likviat reshita shel sifrut hahaskala haivrit uvkhinat hamodernism." In Nash, 235–269.

——. *Sugot vesugyot basifrut hahaskala*. (Tel Aviv: Hakibbutz Hameukhad, 1999).

——. *Dor hameasfim beshakhar hahaskala: terumatam hasifrutit shel khalutsei "Hameasef", ktav-haet haivri harishon, lehaskala haivrit bereshita*. (Tel Aviv: Hakibbutz Hameukhad, 2001).

Perferkovitsh, N. *Hebreyismen in yidish.* (Riga: 1931).

Perl, Joseph. *Megale Temirin.* (Vienna: Anton Strauss, 1819).

——. *Yoysef Perls yidishe ksovim.* Ed. Zelig Kalmanovitch. (Vilna: Bibliotek fun YIVO, 1937).

——. *Bokhen Tsaddik.* (Prague: M.J. Landau, 1838).

——. *Maasiyot veigrot mitsadikim umeanshei shlomeinu.* Ed. Khone Shmeruk and Shmuel Werses. (Jerusalem: Publication of the Israel Academy of Sciences and Humanities, 1969).

——. *Über das Wesen der Sekte Chassidim.* Ed. A. Rubinstein. (Jerusalem: Israel Academy of Sciences and Humanities, 1977).

——. *Joseph Perl's Revealer of Secrets: The First Hebrew Novel.* Ed. and trans. Dov Taylor. (Boulder, CO: Westview Press, 1997).

Perri, Carmela. "On Alluding." *Poetics* 7 (1978), 289–307.

Piekarz, Mendel. *Khasidut bratslav: prakim bekhayei mekhollela uviketaveha.* (Jerusalem: Mossad Bialik, 1995).

Price, Lawrence Marsdale. *English Literature in Germany.* (Berkeley: University of California Press, 1953).

Pucci, Joseph. *The Full-Knowing Reader: Allusion and the Power of the Reader in the Western Literary Tradition.* (New Haven: Yale University Press, 1998).

Rafel, Dov. "Al sifrut haigronut." *Mekhkerei yerushalayim besifrut ivrit* 13 (1992), 119–135.

——. *Bibliografia shel sifrei limud yehudiim (1488–1918).* (Tel Aviv: Tel Aviv University, 1995).

——, ed. *Mekhkarim bamikra uvekhinukh mugashim leprofesor Moshe Arend.* (Jerusalem: Touro College, 1996).

——. "Khanut hasfarim kemosad khinukhi lemaskil yehudi." In Rafel *Mekhkarim* 336–344.

Rathaus, Ariel. "Hashira hapastoralit haivrit beitalia bemeot hayud zayin vehayud khet." *Italia Judaica* 3 (1989), 111–120.

Rapoport-Albert, Ada. "Hagiography with Footnotes: Edifying Tales and the Writing of History in Hasidism." *History and Theory* 27 (1987), 119–159.

——. "On Women in Hasidism, S. A. Horodecky, and the Maid of Ludmir Tradition." In Rapoport-Albert and Zipperstein, 495–525.

——, ed. *Hasidism Reappraised.* (London: Littman Library of Jewish Civilization, 1996).

——. "Hasidism After 1772: Structural Continuity and Change." In Rapoport-Albert *Hasidism Reappraised* 76–140.

——, and Steven J. Zipperstein, eds., *Jewish History: Essays in Honour of Chimen Abramsky* (London: Peter Halban, 1988).

Reinharz, Jehuda, and Walter Schatzberg, eds. *The Jewish Response to German Culture: From the Enlightenment to the Second World War.* (London: University Press of New England, 1985).

Reyzen, Zalmen. *Fun Mendelson biz Mendele.* (Warsaw: Farlag Kultur-Lige, 1923).

Robertson, Ritchie, ed. *The German-Jewish Dialogue: An Anthology of Literary Texts, 1749–1993.* (Oxford: Oxford University Press, 1999).

Rosenbloom, Noah. *Haeifus hamikrai meieidan hahaskala vehaparshanut.* (Rubin Mass: Jerusalem, 1983).

Roskies, David G. "The Emancipation of Yiddish." *Prooftexts* 1 (1981), 28–42.

——. *Against the Apocalypse: Responses to Catastrophe in Modern Jewish Culture.* (Cambridge, MA: Harvard University Press, 1984).

——. *A Bridge of Longing: The Lost Art of Yiddish Storytelling.* (Cambridge, MA: Harvard University Press, 1995).

Rosman, Moshe. "Letoldotav shel makor histori." *Zion* 58 (1993), 175–214.

——. *Founder of Hasidism: A Quest for the Historical Ba'al Shem Tov.* (Berkeley: University of Calfornia Press, 1996).

——. "Social Conflicts in Miedzyboz." In Rapoport-Albert *Hasidism Reappraised* 51–62.

Rubinstein, Avraham. "Al mahut kat khasidim." *Kiryat Sefer* 38 (1964), 263–272, 415–424; 39 (1965), 117–136.

——. "Hahaskala vehakhasidut: peiluto shel Yosef Perl." *Bar Ilan Annual* (1974), 166–178.

——. "Midrash hashemot shel Yosef Perl." *Tarbiz* 43 (1974), 205–216.

Ruderman, David. *Jewish Thought and Scientific Discovery in Early Modern Europe.* (New Haven: Yale University Press, 1995).

——. "Haim hayta 'haskala' beanglia—iyun mekhadash." *Zion* 62:2 (1997), 109–131.

——. *Jewish Enlightenment in an English Key: Anglo-Jewry's Construction of Modern Jewish Thought.* (Princeton, NJ: Princeton University Press, 2000).

Ryan, Kiernan, ed. *New Historicism and Cultural Materialism: A Reader.* (London: Arnold, 1996).

Sadan, Dov. *A vort bashteyt.* (Tel Aviv: Y.L. Peretz Farlag, 1975).

Safran, Bezalel, ed. *Hasidism: Continuity or Innovation?* (Cambridge, MA: distrib. Harvard University Press, 1988).

Said, Edward, ed. *Literature and Society.* (Baltimore: Johns Hopkins University Press, 1980).

Sandler, Peretz. *Habiur letora shel Moshe Mendelson vesiato: hithavahuto vehashpaato.* (Jerusalem: Rubin Mass, 1984).

Schatz-Uffenheimer, Rivka. *Hasidism as Mysticism: Quietistic Elements in Eighteenth Century Hasidic Thought.* (Princeton: Princeton University Press, 1993).

Schmelzer, Menachem. "Hebrew Printing and Publishing in Germany 1650–1750—On Jewish Book Culture and the Emergence of Modern Jewry." *Leo Baeck Institute Year Book* 33 (1988), 369–383.

Scholem, Gershom. *The Messianic Idea in Judaism and Other Essays in Jewish Spirituality.* (New York: Schocken Books, 1971).

——. "Redemption Through Sin." In Scholem *Messianic Idea* 78–141.

——. *Sabbatai Sevi: The Mystical Messiah*. (Princeton, NJ: Princeton University Press, 1973).

——. *Major Trends in Jewish Mysticism*. (New York: Schocken, 1974).

Schorch, Ismar. "The Myth of Sephardic Supremacy." *Leo Baeck Institute Year Book* 34 (1989), 47–66.

Schwartz, Dov. "Hahitpatkhut shel hamin haenoshi bemishnato shel Mendelson—perek betoldotav shel haraayon hameshikhi." *Daat* 22 (1989), 109–121.

Schweid, Eliezer. "The Impact of Enlightenment on Religion." *Judaism* 38:4 (1989), 389–398.

Sefer Khakhmei Yisrael Besht: *Kitvei kodesh mikol raboteinu hakedoshim khokhmei yisrael*. (New York: Ner Tamid Press, 1924).

Segal, Eliezer. "Midrash and Literature: Some Medieval Views." *Prooftexts* 11 (1991), 57–65.

Seidman, Naomi. *A Marriage Made in Heaven: The Sexual Politics of Hebrew and Yiddish*. (Berkeley: University of California Press, 1997).

Septimus, Bernard. "'Open Rebuke and Concealed Love': Nahmanides and the Andalusian Tradition." In Twersky *Nachmanides* 11–34.

Shaanan, Avraham. *Iyunim besifrut hahaskala*. (Merkhavia: Sifriyat Poalim, 1952).

Shaheen, Naseeb. *Biblical References in Shakespeare's Comedies*. (Newark: University of Delaware Press, 1993).

Shamir, Ziva, and Avner Holzman, eds. *Nekudot mifne besifrut haivrit vezikatan lemagaim im sifruyot akherim*. (Tel Aviv: Tel Aviv University, 1993).

Shapiro, James. *Shakespeare and the Jews*. (New York: Columbia University Press, 1996).

Shatsky, Yaakov, ed. *Arkhiv-geshikhte fun yidishn teatr un drame*. (New York: YIVO, 1933).

——. "Vegn Arn Hale-Volfsons pyesn (naye materyaln)." In Shatsky *Arkhiv-geshikhte* 147–150.

——. "Der kamf kegn purim-shpiln in praysn." *YIVO-Bleter* 15 (1940), 30–38.

Shavit, Uzi. *Bepetakh hashira haivrit hakhadasha: masat mavo*. (Tel Aviv: Tel Aviv University, 1986).

——. *Shira veidiologia*. (Tel Aviv: Hakibbutz Hameukhad: 1987).

——. "Lemaamada shel hashira bitnuat hahaskala haivrit." In Shavit *Shira* 99–113.

——. *Baalot hashakhar: shirat hahaskala: mifgash im hamoderniut*. (Tel Aviv: Hakibbutz Hameukhad: 1996).

——. "Hahaskala mahi—leveirur musag hahaskala besifrut haivrit." In Shavit *Baalot* 12–36.

——. "Intertekstualiut keeven-bokhan lemaavar bein tkufa letkufa: Yalag ke'historiyon khadash'." In Shavit *Baalot* 85–96.

——. "Model hahashpaa hakfula: leyikhuda shel situatsia sifrutit-historit ulehashlikuteha hamekhkariut-parshaniut." In Shavit *Baalot* 37–75.

——. "Shira vehaskala: kesher simbiotit." In Shavit *Baalot* 7–12.

Shavit, Yaacov. "A Duty Too Heavy to Bear: Hebrew in the Berlin Haskalah, 1783–1819: Between Classic, Modern, and Romantic." In Glinert, 111–128.

Sheffer, Anne. "Beyond Heder, Haskalah, and Honeybees: Genius and Gender in the Education of Seventeenth and Eighteenth Century Judeo German Women." In Haas, 85–112.

Shiper, Yitzkhak. *Geshikhte fun yidisher teater-kunst un drame fun di eltste tsaytn biz 1750*. (Warsaw: Kultur-Lige, 1923–28). 3 vols.

Shivkhei HaBesht. (Kopust: 1814; critical edition Jerusalem: Reuven Mass, 1991, ed. Avraham Rubinstein). Hebrew version.

Shivkhey HaBesht. (Korets: 1816, reprinted Jerusalem: 1965). Yiddish version.

Shmeruk, Khone. "Dvarim kehavayatam udvarim shebadimyon be'Megale Temir-in' shel Yosef Perl." *Zion* 21 (1956), 92–99.

——. "Hashem hamashmauti Mordekhai Markus—gilgulo hasifruti shel ideal khevrati." *Tarbiz* 29 (1959–1960), 76–98.

——. "Vegn etlekhe printsipn fun mendl lefins mishley-iberzetzung." *Di yidishe shprakh* 24 (1964), 33–52.

——. *Sifrut yidish: prakim letoldoteha*. (Tel Aviv: Porter Institute, Tel-Aviv University, 1978).

——. "Nusakh bilti yadua shel hakomediya haanonimit 'Di Genarte Velt'." *Kiryat Sefer* 54 (1979), 802–816.

——, ed. *Makhazot mikraiim beyidish, 1697–1750*. (Jerusalem: Israel Academy of Sciences and Humanities, 1979).

——. *Sifrut yidish bepolin: mekhkarim veiyunim historiim*. (Magnes Press, Jerusalem: 1981).

——. "Al ekronot akhadim shel targum Mishlei leMendel Lefin." In Shmeruk *Sifrut* 165–183.

——. "Hasipurim shel Reb Adam Baal Shem vegilguleihem benuskhaot sefer *Shivkhei HaBesht*." In Shmeruk *Sifrut* 119–146.

——. *Prokim fun der yidisher literatur-geshikhte*. (Farlag Y.L.Peretz: Tel Aviv, 1988).

——, and Werses, Shmuel. "Introduction." In Perl *Maasiyot veigrot* 1–88.

Shmueli, Efraim. "Khavlei tarbut—khavlei lashon: Moshe Mendelson ubeayat ribui haleshonot besifrut yisrael." *Kivunim* 33 (1987), 129–152.

Shoham, Chayim. *Betsel haskalat berlin*. (Tel Aviv: Publication of the Porter Institute for Poetics and Semiotics, 1996).

Shohat, Azriel. *Im khilufei tekufot: reishit hahaskala beyahadut germania*. (Jerusalem: Mossad Bialik, 1960).

Shtarkman, Moyshe, ed. *Shloyme Bikel yoyvel-bukh*. (New York: Farlag "Matones," 1967).

Shteynberg, Yisroel. *Hebreyismen in der yidisher shprakh*. (Warsaw: "Nidershleyze", 1949).

Silberschlag, Eisig. *From Renaissance to Renaissance: Hebrew Literature from 1492–1970*. (New York: Ktav Publishing House, Inc., 1973).

Sinfield, Alan. "Cultural Materialism, *Othello*, and the Politics of Plausibility." In Ryan, 61–82.

Sinkoff, Nancy Beth. "Tradition and Transition: Mendel Lefin of Satanów and the Beginnings of the Jewish Enlightenment in Europe, 1749–1826." Ph.D. dissertation, Columbia University, 1996.

——. *Out of the Shtetl: Making Jews Modern in the Polish Borderlands* (Providence: Brown Judaic Studies, 2004).

Slouchz, Nachum. *The Renascence of Hebrew Literature.* (Philadelphia: Jewish Publication Society, 1909).

Sokoloff, Naomi. "Gender Studies and Modern Hebrew Literature." In Lerner, Lapidus, Norich, and Sokoloff, 257–263.

Sorkin, David. *The Transformation of German Jewry, 1780–1840.* (Oxford: Oxford University Press, 1987).

——. "Preacher, Teacher, Publicist: Joseph Wolf and the Ideology of Emancipation." In Malino and Sorkin, 107–125.

——. "Jews, the Enlightenment, and Religious Toleration—Some Reflections." *Leo Baeck Institute Year Book* 37 (1992), 3–16.

——. "Juden und Aufklärung: Religiöse Quellen der Toleranz." In Beck, 50–66.

——. "The Case for Comparison: Moses Mendelssohn and the Religious Enlightenment." *Modern Judaism* 14:2 (1994), 121–138.

——. *Moses Mendelssohn and the Religious Enlightenment.* (London: Peter Halban, 1996).

——. "The Mendelssohn Myth and Its Method." *New German Critique* 77 (Spring-Summer 1999), 7–28.

——. *The Berlin Haskalah and German Religious Thought: Orphans of Knowledge.* (Portland, OR: Valentine Mitchell, 2000).

Spivak, Khaim, and [Bloomgarden, Shloyme] Yehoyesh. *Yidish veterbukh.* (New York: Yehoyash, 1911).

Stampfer, Shaul. "Heder Study, Knowledge of Torah, and the Maintenance of Social Stratification in East European Jewish Society." *Studies in Jewish Education* 3 (1988), 271–289.

——. "Gender Differentiation and Education of the Jewish Woman in Nineteenth-Century Eastern Europe." *Polin* 7 (1992), 63–87.

——. "What Did 'Knowing Hebrew' Mean in Eastern Europe?" In Glinert, 129–140.

Stein, Siegfried, and Raphael Loewe, eds. *Studies in Jewish Religious and Intellectual History.* (University, Alabama: University of Alabama Press, 1979).

Stern, Selma. *The Court Jew.* (Philadelphia: Jewish Publication Society, 1950).

——. *Di preusiche Staat und die Juden.* (Tübingen: J.C.B. Mohr, 1962–1975). 4 vols.

Sternhartz, Natan. *Khayei Moharan.* (Jerusalem: 1976).

Stock, Brian. *Listening for the Text: On the Uses of the Past.* (Baltimore: Johns Hopkins University Press, 1990).

Stoll, E. E. "Shylock." In Wheeler, 247–262.

Strauss, Janine. "Yakhasam hashlili shel hamaskilim lemahapekha hatsarfatit." *Kongres olami lemakhshevet yisrael* 10B1 (1990), 225–230.

Strauss, Jutta. "Aaron Halle-Wolfssohn: A Trilingual Life." D.Phil. thesis, University of Oxford, 1994.

——. "Aaron Halle-Wolfssohn: ein Leben in drei Sprachen." In Gerhard, 57–75.

Tamar, David. "Kat hakhasidim beeinei Yosef Perl." *Haaretz*, 18 November 1977.

Taylor, Dov. "Introduction." In Perl *Revealer of Secrets* xix–lxxv.

Tewarson, Heidi Thomann. *Rahel Levin Varnhagen: The Life and Work of a German Jewish Intellectual.* (Lincoln, NE: University of Nebraska Press, 1998).

Theodor, J., ed. *Bereschit Rabba mit kritischem Apparat und Kommentar.* (Berlin: 1912).

Toury, Gideon. "Translating English Literature Via German—and Vice Versa: A Symptomatic Reversal in the History of Modern Hebrew Literature." In Kittel, 139–157.

——. "Shimush muskal bemashal maskili: Kristin Firkhtgut Gelert besifrut haivrit." In Shamir and Holzman, 75–86.

Tsamriyon, Tsemach. *Moshe Mendelson vehaidiologia shel hahaskala.* (Tel Aviv: University Publishing Press, 1984).

——. *Hameasef: ktav haet hamoderni harishon beivrit.* (Tel Aviv: University Publishing Press, 1988).

Turnianski, Chava. "Nusakh hamaskili shel 'Tsena ureena'." *Hasifrut* 2 (1971), 835–841.

Twersky, Isidore, ed. *Studies in Medieval Jewish History and Literature.* (Cambridge, MA: Harvard University Press, 1979).

——, ed. *Rabbi Moses Nachmanides (Ramban): Explorations in His Religious and Literary Virtuosity.* (Cambridge, MA: distrib. Harvard University Press, 1983).

Tsvik, Yehudit. "Reshit tsmichato shel ha'sipur' behaskala hagermanit: hatakhbula hadialogit." *Kongres olami lemakhshevet yisrael* 11C3 (1994), 53–60.

Unger, Menashe. "Khaykl Horovitses yikhes-briv." *Filologishe shriftn* 3 (1929), 83–88, 605–606.

Vaynlez, Yisroel. "Fun Yoysef Perls arkhiv." *Historishe shriftn* 1 (1929), 809–814.

——. "Mendl-Lefin Satanover (biografishe shtudiye afn smakh fun hantshriftlikhe materyaln)." *YIVO-Bleter* 2 (1931), 334–357.

——. "Yoysef Perl, zayn lebn un shafn." In Perl *Yidishe ksovim* vii–lxx.

Veeser, H. Aram, ed. *The New Historicism Reader.* (New York: Routledge, 1994).

——. "The New Historicism." In Veeser, 1–32.

Viner, Meyer. *Tsu der geshikhte fun der yidisher literatur in 19tn yorhundert.* (New York: YKUF Farlag, 1945).

Volkov, Shulamit. "Juden und Judentum, im Zeitalter der Emanzipation: Einheit und Vielfalt." In Beck, 86–108.

Weinberg, Werner. "Language Questions Relating to Moses Mendelssohn's Pentateuch Translation." *Hebrew Union College Annual* 55 (1984), 197–242.

Weinreich, Max. *Geshikhte fun der yidisher shprakh.* (New York: Bibliotek fun YIVO, 1973).

Weinryb, Bernard. "An Unknown Hebrew Play of the German Haskalah." *Proceedings of the American Academy for Jewish Research* 24 (1955), 165–170.

——. "Aaron Wolfssohn's Dramatic Writings in Their Historical Setting." *Jewish Quarterly Review* 48 (1957–1958), 35–50.

Weissler, Chava. "The Religion of Traditional Ashkenazic Women: Some Methodological Issues." *AJS Review* 12:1 (1987), 73–94.

Werses, Shmuel. "Iyunim bemivne shel 'Megale Temirin' ve'Bokhen Tsaddik'." *Tarbiz* 31 (1962), 377–411.

——. "Khibur satiri lo noda shel Yosef Perl." *Hasifrut* 1 (1968), 206–217.

——. *Sipur veshorsho.* (Ramat Gan: Masada, 1971).

——. "Shitot hasatira shel Yosef Perl." In Werses *Sipur* 9–45.

——. "Tsvishn dray shprakhn: Vegn yoysef perls yidishe ksovim in likht fun naye materyaln." *Di Goldene Keyt* 89 (1976), 150–177.

——. "On the History of the Hebrew Novella in the Early Nineteenth Century: Studies in Zahlen's 'Salmah mul Eder'." In Heinemann and Werses, 107–124.

——. "Hazikot bein hasifrut hayafa levein khokhmat yisrael." *Tarbiz* 55:4 (1986), 567–602.

——. *Haskala veshabtaut: toldotav shel maavak.* (Jerusalem: Zalman Shazar, 1988).

——. "Hamahapekha hatsarfatit beaspaklaria shel hasifrut haivrit." *Tarbiz* 58:3–4 (1989), 483–521.

——. *Megamot vetsurot besifrut hahaskala.* (Jerusalem: Magnes Press, 1990).

——. "Al mekhkar sifrut hahaskala beyameinu." In Werses *Megamot* 356–412.

——. "Beikvotav shel hakhibur 'Makhkimat Peti' heavud." In Werses *Megamot* 319–337.

——. "Bein shnei olamot: Yaakov Shmuel Bik bein haskala lekhasidut—iyun mekhudash." In Werses *Megamot* 110–159.

——. "Hakhasidut beeinei sifrut hahaskala." In Werses *Megamot* 91–108.

——. "Hanusakh hamekori habilti yadua shel igeret Yaakov Shmuel Bik el Tuvia Feder." In Werses *Megamot* 338–355.

——. "Orkhot veshvilim bekheker sifrut hahaskala." *Mekhkerei yerushalayim besifrut ivrit* 13 (1992), 7–28.

——. "Hameshorer R' Yehuda Halevi beolama shel hasifrut haivrit hakhadasha." *Peamim* 53 (1993), 18–45.

——. "Geirush sfarad beaspaklaria shel hahaskala." *Peamim* 57 (1994), 48–81.

——. "Igrot vikuakh genuzot al mahut hakhasidut." *Mekhkerei yerushalayim bemakhshevet yisrael* 13 (1996), 447–493.

——. "Mekhkarim khadashim vegam yeshanim besifrut hahaskala utekufata." *Madaei hayahadut* 36 (1996), 43–72.

——. "Milashon el lashon: semamanei hanusakh beyidish shel 'Megale Temirin' shel Yosef Perl." *Khulyot* 3 (1996), 59–108.

——. *Milashon el lashon: yetsirot vegilguleihen besifruteinu.* (Jerusalem: Magnes Press, 1996).

——. "Yosef Perl kemetargem leyidish shel 'Tom Dzhons' leFilding." In Werses *Milashon* 383–405.

——. "Yad yamin dokhe yad smol mkarevet: al yakhasam shel sofrei hahaskala lelashon yidish." *Khulyot* 5 (1998), 9–49.

Wertheim, Aaron. "Traditions and Customs in Hasidism." In Hundert *Essential Papers* 363–398.

Wertheimer, Jack, ed. *The Uses of Tradition: Jewish Continuity in the Modern Era.* (New York: Jewish Theological Seminary, distributed by Harvard University Press, 1992).

Wheeler, Thomas, ed. *The Merchant of Venice: Critical Essays.* (New York: Garland Publishing, 1991).

Wiesemann, Falk. "Jewish Burials in Germany—Between Tradition, Enlightenment, and the Authorities." *Leo Baeck Institute Year Book* 37 (1992), 17–31.

Wilhelmy-Dollinger, Petra. "Emanzipation durch Geselligkeit: Die Salons jüdischer Frauen in Berlin zwischen 1780 und 1830." In Awerbuch and Jersch-Wenzel, 121–138.

Williams, Raymond. "Base and Superstructure in Marxist Cultural Theory." In Ryan, 22–28.

Wisse, Ruth. *The Modern Jewish Canon: A Journey Through Language and Culture.* (New York: The Free Press, 2000).

Wolfson, Elliot R. "Beautiful Maiden Without Eyes: *Peshat* and *Sod* in Zoharic Hermenuetics." In Fishbane, 155–203.

Wolfssohn, Aaron Halle. *Megilat eikha im targum ashkenazi vebeiur.* (Berlin: 1789).

——. *Megilat ester im targum ashkenazi vebeiur.* (Berlin: 1789).

——. *Megilat rut im targum ashkenazi vebeiur.* (Berlin: 1789).

——. *Laykhtzin un Fremelay.* (Breslau: 1796).

——. *Jeschurun.* (Breslau: 1804).

——. *Avtalyon.* (Vienna: Anton Schmid, 1814).

——. *Kalut daat utseviut.* (Israel: Sman Keriah, 1977).

Yaffe, Martin D. *Shylock and the Jewish Question.* (Baltimore: Johns Hopkins University Press, 1997).

Yitzchaki, Yedidia. "Sifrut khaya bilshon meta." *Bikoret ufarshanut* 25 (1989), 89–100.

Yitzchaki, Yosef. "Deoteihem shel sofrei hahaskala al lashon haivrit vedarkheihem beharkhavata vekhidusha." *Leshonenu* 34:4 (1963), 287–305; 35:1 (1964), 39–59; 35:2, 140–159.

Zinberg, Israel. *Di geshikhte fun literatur ba yidn.* (Buenos Aires: Altveltlekher yidisher kultur-kongres, 1969).

Index